Henry Nettleship, John Conington

The Satires of A. Persius Flaccus

Third Edition

Henry Nettleship, John Conington

The Satires of A. Persius Flaccus
Third Edition

ISBN/EAN: 9783337292799

Printed in Europe, USA, Canada, Australia, Japan

Cover: Foto ©Thomas Meinert / pixelio.de

More available books at **www.hansebooks.com**

Clarendon Press Series

PERSIUS

HENRY FROWDE, M.A.
PUBLISHER TO THE UNIVERSITY OF OXFORD

LONDON, EDINBURGH, AND NEW YORK

THE SATIRES

OF

A. PERSIUS FLACCUS

WITH A TRANSLATION AND COMMENTARY

BY

JOHN CONINGTON, M.A.

LATE CORPUS PROFESSOR OF LATIN IN THE UNIVERSITY OF OXFORD

TO WHICH IS PREFIXED

A LECTURE ON THE LIFE AND WRITINGS OF PERSIUS

DELIVERED AT OXFORD BY THE SAME AUTHOR, *JANUARY* 1855

EDITED BY

H. NETTLESHIP, M.A.

CORPUS PROFESSOR OF LATIN IN THE UNIVERSITY OF OXFORD

THIRD EDITION, REVISED

Oxford
AT THE CLARENDON PRESS
1893

Oxford
PRINTED AT THE CLARENDON PRESS
BY HORACE HART, PRINTER TO THE UNIVERSITY

PREFACE TO THE THIRD EDITION
BY THE EDITOR

For the third edition of this volume the text and commentary have been revised. In place of the notes from the Gale manuscript, formerly printed at the foot of the page, I have inserted the *apparatus criticus* of Jahn's edition (1868) as revised and reprinted by Bücheler in 1886. In explanation of the *apparatus* I have added a few words on the text of Persius (pp. xxxvii and xxxviii).

I have carefully studied the ancient *scholia*, and especially the selection from them printed by Bücheler at the foot of his text (1886). In the general study of Persius' age and surroundings, I have derived invaluable assistance from Professor J. E. B. Mayor's recent edition of Juvenal, as well as from Friedländer's editions of Martial and Petronius' *Cena Trimalchionis*. I wish also to express my obligation to Professor Gildersleeve's edition (New York, Harper, 1875), and also to three short treatises dealing especially with Persius. These are, (1) by Dr. J. Bieger, *De Auli Persii Codice Pithoeano C recte aestimando*, Berlin, 1890; (2) by Dr. J. van Wageningen, *Persiana*, Groningen, 1891; (3) by Dr. J. H. Ovink, *Adversaria ad Persii Prologum et Satiram Primam*, Leyden, 1886. The

Prologue, or rather Epilogue, I have now printed at the end of the Satires, in deference to the authority of the best MS.

Plautus and Terence are quoted not by act and scene, but by single lines, as numbered in the edition of Plautus by Goetz and Schöll, and in that of Terence by Umpfenbach. Propertius is cited according to Baehrens; Pliny according to the small sections in Jan and Detlefsen; the Latin grammarians according to Keil; the Latin-Greek and other glossaries according to Goetz and Gundermann.

All additions of my own are indicated by square brackets [ ].

HENRY NETTLESHIP.

OXFORD, *July* 27, 1892.

PREFACE TO THE SECOND EDITION

BY THE EDITOR

Most of the late Mr. Conington's friends and pupils will remember his lectures on Persius, which were perhaps the most generally popular of all that he gave during his tenure of the chair of Latin at Oxford, owing to the sympathetic humour with which he caught the peculiar force and flavour of his author's manner, as well as to the nerve and spirit of his translation. The lecture prefixed to the commentary and translation now published was among the first-fruits of his professorial labours. I have no means of knowing how far he considered it a final exposition of his views on Persius; but its interest and merit are such that I need not, I am sure, apologize for having it printed exactly as it was delivered. The commentary and translation were written for delivery as lectures. For this purpose they were left pretty nearly complete; but some references had to be filled in, and many, I found as I went on with the revision of the notes, required correction. I verified and corrected a great many for the first edition, and for the second edition I have examined a considerable number more which I had previously taken on trust. A fresh revision of the commentary has convinced me that Mr. Conington would not have considered it complete as a written work, nor is it always possible to know how he would have finally decided in doubtful cases of reading or of interpretation, or in what form he would have put the last touch to the less finished portions. I have, in several instances, added to the notes a reference to works now recognized as of standard authority, which had not appeared at the time when the commentary was written. Some parallel passages and illustrations I added for the first edition, and have increased their number for the second, enclosing all additions in square brackets [ ]. The references to Lucilius, Lucretius, Catullus, and Propertius have been altered (where necessary) to suit Lucian Müller's, Munro's, Ellis', and Paley's editions respectively.

The text adopted by Mr. Conington as a basis for his notes was Otto Jahn's of 1843. In 1868, however, Jahn published a new text, which differs in many places from his earlier one. I do not know how far, if at all, Mr. Conington would have followed him in his alterations, and have therefore been guided by the translation in fixing the reading to be adopted where doubt would have arisen. It will thus be found that the present text approximates, on the whole, more nearly to Jahn's of 1843 than to that of 1868.

Mr. Conington collated, or had collated for him, seven MSS. of Persius, two of which are in the Gale collection in the library of Trinity College, Cambridge. One of these is known as Bentley's Codex Galeanus, and is lettered γ by Jahn in his edition of 1843. 'It is,' says Mr. Conington in his description of it, 'a small vellum MS. of the 8vo or 12mo size. It contains *Horatii Opera, Persii Satirae, Theoduli Eclogae, Cato de Moribus,* and *Aviani Fabulae.* Collations of the Avianus, the Persius, and the Cato, were published in the *Classical Journal,* vol. 4, the former at pp. 120 foll., the two latter at pp. 353 foll., by M. D. B. The Persius collation is very scanty and not always accurate: but it appears to be the only one known to Jahn. Mr. Bradshaw refers the MS. to the twelfth or thirteenth century, almost certainly the former.' The other MS. in the Gale collection is referred by Mr. Bradshaw to the ninth or tenth century, and is the most valuable of the seven MSS. collated. It consists of one hundred and ten folios in quires of eight, beginning on the second folio of the first quire, and contains *Juvenalis Satirae* 1, *Annotatio Cornuti* 93, *Persii Satirarum Proemium* 94 verso, *Persii Satirae* 95. 'It appears' (I quote from Mr. Conington) 'to be written throughout in the same hand, the glosses being written in a much smaller character. The only doubt is about certain glosses on the margin of the first four pages of the Persius (fol. 94 *verso* to fol. 96), where the letters are tall and thin, not, as generally, broad and flat. The characters, however, appear to be the same. There are other glosses, apparently written at the same time as the text and in the same hand, some between the lines, some towards the margin, evidently earlier than those just spoken of, which in one place leave a space in the middle of a line for an intrusive word of the earlier gloss written out of the straight line. These earlier glosses are much less copious than the later: they extend, however, somewhat further, to folio 98, the end of Sat. 1, after which they almost disappear, scarcely averaging one in a page[1].' The chief peculiarity of the writing of this MS. (which I have myself collated with Jahn's text of 1868) is the shape of *r*, which is so formed as to be easily confused with *n*. *I* initial is often written tall, so that in Sat. 4. 35 it is not at

---

[1] A full account of this and of the Bodleian MS., and of their relations to each other, is given by Mr. G. R. Scott in the *Classical Review*, 1890, pp. 17–19, 241–248.

first sight easy to decide whether the reading is *in mores* or *hi mores*. As regards orthography, this MS. is much freer from mistakes than the MS. of Juvenal bound in the same cover and apparently written by the same hand, in the tenth satire of which I found such misspellings as *gretia* for *Graecia*, *canicies* for *canities, contentus* for *concentus, sotio* for *socio*, and *thomatula* for *tomacula*. This confusion between *c* and *t* is almost unknown to the MS. of Persius: *patritiae* (Sat. 6. 73) being perhaps the only instance of it. In Sat. 1. 116, however, it is difficult to make out whether the scribe has written *muti* or *muci*. The chief confusions of consonants which this MS. exhibits are between *b* and *p* (*obtare* for *optare, rapiosa* for *rabiosa*): between *g* and *gu* (*pingue* for *pinge, longuos* for *longos*): between *s* and *ss* (*ammisus, asigna : cassiam, recusso* for *casiam, recuso*, etc.): between *m* and *mm, p* and *pp, c* and *cc* (*imitere* for *immittere, ammomis* for *amomis, suppellex* for *supellex, quipe* for *quippe, peccori* for *pecori*, etc.). Among the vowels, *a* and *o* are occasionally confused, as *centurianum, Salones* for *centurionum, Solones*: so with *o* and *u* (*fumusa, furtunare* for *fumosa, fortunare; sopinus, conditor* for *supinus, conditur*): to say nothing of the interchange, common in such MSS., of *ae* and *e, y* and *i*. The monosyllabic prepositions are almost invariably joined with their nouns (*etumulo, inluxum*, etc.) and sometimes even assimilated. The same is often the case with monosyllabic conjunctions (*cumscribo, noncocta, sivocet*, etc.). In words compounded with *in*, the preposition is sometimes assimilated, sometimes not; thus we find *inprimit, inprobe, conpossitum* by the side of *implerunt, impulit, compossitus*. *Ad*, on the other hand, is generally assimilated : *arrodens, afferre, assit*, etc.

'It is doubtful,' says Mr. Conington, 'whether this MS. was

PREFACE.

known until lately, as it was generally classed simply as a MS. of Juvenal.' I have therefore thought it worth while to give a fuller account of it than is required by the others, and have had its various readings printed in italics under the text, though they add little or nothing to the materials collected in Jahn's elaborate *apparatus criticus* of 1843 [1].

The other MSS. are—

(1) In the Library of the British Museum (Royal MSS. 15, B. xix. f. 111), assigned to the earlier part of the tenth century. It is lettered ρ by Jahn, who apparently only knew it through a collation made by Bentley, and published in the *Classical Journal*, xviii. p. 62 foll. (Jahn, Prolegomena to edition of 1843, p. ccxiii). A much fuller collation of it was made for Mr. Conington by Mr. Richard Sims, of the MS. Department of the British Museum. The orthography of this MS. is not so good as that of the one last mentioned.

(2) In the Library of the British Museum (Add. MSS. 15601). Assigned to the end of the tenth or beginning of the eleventh century. Collated by Mr. Sims.

(3) In the Bodleian Library (799 Arch. F. 58). Assigned by Mr. Coxe to the early twelfth century. Collated by Mr. Conington.

(4) In the Library of the British Museum (Add. MSS. 11672). Assigned to the thirteenth century. Collated by Mr. Sims to the fifty-sixth line of Sat. 2.

(5) In the Library of Corpus Christi College, Oxford. This MS. contains *Juvenalis, Persius cum notis, Dionysii Periegesis ex versione Prisciani, Anonymus de Tropis et Figuris, Ciceronis Orationes in Catilinam cum commentario.* The Persius was collated by Hauthal (who finally assigned the MS. to the end

---

[1] In the third edition these readings are omitted.

of the fourteenth century) in 1831, and subsequently by Mr. Conington. Hauthal communicated the results of all his collations to Jahn (Jahn, Prolegomena, p. ccxiv).

My thanks are due to Mr. Evelyn Abbott of Balliol College for his kindness in assisting me to revise the proof-sheets of the second edition.

H. NETTLESHIP.

OXFORD, *April* 24, 1874.

CONTENTS

	PAGE
LECTURE ON THE LIFE AND WRITINGS OF PERSIUS	xv
[ON THE TEXT OF PERSIUS]	xxxvii
SATIRE I	2
" II	34
" III	50
" IV	74
" V	86
" VI	122
EPILOGUE	138
INDEX	143

LECTURE

ON THE

LIFE AND WRITINGS OF PERSIUS

Delivered at Oxford, January 24, 1855.

It is my intention for the present to deliver general lectures from time to time on the characteristics of some of the authors whom I may select as subjects for my terminal courses. To those who propose to attend my classes they will serve as prolegomena, grouping together various matters which will meet us afterwards as they lie scattered up and down the course of our expository readings, and giving the point of view from which they are to be regarded: to others I trust they may not be without their use as Sketches Historical and Literary, complete in themselves, in which an attempt will be made to bring out the various features and circumstances of each author into a broad general light, and exhibit the interest which they possess when considered independently of critical minutiae.

The writer of whom I am to speak to-day is one who, as it seems to me, supplies ample materials both for detailed study and for a more transient survey. It is a very superficial criticism which would pretend that the reputation of Persius is owing simply to the labour which has been spent upon him: still, where the excellence of an author is undoubted, the difficulties of his thought or his language are only so many additional reasons why the patient and prolonged study of him is sure to be profitable. The difficulties of Persius, too, have the advantage of being definite and unmistakable—like those of Aeschylus, not like those of Sophocles—difficulties which do not elude the grasp, but close with it fairly, and even if they should be still unvanquished, are at any rate palpably felt and appreciated. At the same time he presents many salient points to the general student of literature; his individual characteristics as a writer are sufficiently prominent to strike the most careless eye; his philosophical creed, ardently embraced and realized with more or less distinctness, is that which proved itself most congenial to the best parts of the Roman mind, the Stoicism of the empire; while his profession of authorship, as avowed by himself, associates him not only with Horace, but with the less known name of Lucilius, and the original conception of Roman satire.

The information which we possess concerning the personal history of Persius is more copious than might have been expected in the case of one whose life was so short and so uneventful. His writings, indeed, cannot be compared with the 'votive tablets' on which his two great predecessors delighted to inscribe their own memoirs: on the contrary, except in one famous passage, the autobiographical element is scarcely brought forward at all. We see his character written legibly enough in every line, and there are various minute traces of experience with which the facts of his life, when ascertained, are perceived to accord; but no one could have attempted to construct his biography from his Satires without passing even those extended limits within which modern criticism is pleased to expatiate. But there is a memoir[1], much more full than most of the biographical notices of that period, and apparently quite authentic, the authorship of which, after being variously assigned to his instructor and literary executor Cornutus, and to Suetonius, is now generally fixed, agreeably to the testimony of the best MSS., on Valerius Probus, the celebrated contemporary grammarian, from whose commentary, doubtless an exposition of the Satires, it is stated to have been extracted. Something has still been left to the ingenuity or research of later times to supply, in the way of conjectural correction or illustration, and in this work no one has been more diligent than Otto Jahn, to whom Persius is probably more indebted than to any other editor, with the single exception of Casaubon. I have, myself, found his commentary quite invaluable while preparing my own notes, and I shall have to draw frequently upon his Prolegomena in the course of the present lecture.

Aulus Persius Flaccus was born on the 4th of December, A.D. 34, little more than two years before the death of Tiberius, at Volaterrae in Etruria, a country where antiquity of descent was most carefully cherished, and which had recently produced two men well known in

---

[1] [The memoir is printed in Bücheler's edition of Jahn's Persius (Berlin, 1886), pp. 54-56.]

the annals of the empire, Maecenas and Sejanus. His father was of
equestrian rank, and his relatives included some of the first men of his
time. The connection of the family with his birth-place is substantiated
by two inscriptions which have been discovered there [1], as its memory
was long preserved by a tradition professing to point out his residence,
and by the practice of a noble house which was in the habit of using
his name. That name was already not unfamiliar at Rome, having
been borne by a contemporary of Lucilius, whose critical judgment
the old poet dreaded as that of the most learned man of the age, as
well as by a successful officer in the time of the Second Punic War.
Persius' early life was passed in his native town, a time to which he
seems to allude when he speaks of himself in his third satire as
evading the lessons in which he was expected to distinguish himself
by his admiring father, and ambitious only of eminence among his
playmates. When he was six years old his father died, and his
mother, Fulvia Sisennia, a genuine Etruscan name, found a second
husband, also of equestrian rank, called Fusius, who within a few
years left her a second time a widow. At twelve years of age Persius
was removed to Rome, where he studied under Remmius Palaemon
the grammarian, and Verginius Flavus the rhetorician. Of the latter,
we only know that he had the honour of being banished by Nero—
on account, so Tacitus says, of the splendour of his reputation—in
the burst of jealous fury which followed the conspiracy of Piso; that
he wrote the treatise on rhetoric, to which Quintilian so repeatedly
refers with respect [2], and that he made a joke on a tedious rival,
asking him how many miles long his speech had been. Of the
former an odious character is given by Suetonius, who says that his
extraordinary memory and facility of expression made him the most
popular teacher in Rome, but represents him as a man of inordinate
vanity and arrogance, and so infamous for his vices that both Tiberius
and Claudius openly declared him to be the last man who ought to be
trusted with the instruction of youth. The silence with which Persius
passes over this part of his experience may perhaps be regarded as
significant when we contrast it with the language in which he speaks
of the next stage in his education. It was, he tells us, when he first
laid aside the emblems of boyhood and assumed the toga—just at the
time when the sense of freedom begins, and life is seen to diverge
into different paths—that he placed himself under another guide.

---

[1] [In Gori's collection. Quoted by Jahn (1843), Prolegg. p. iv. A T. Persius is mentioned in an inscription found at Turin, C. I. L. 5. 7101.]

[2] [Institutio Oratoria 3. 1. 21, 3. 6. 45, 7. 4. 24, 11. 3. 126.]

This was Annaeus Cornutus, a Stoic philosopher of great name, who was himself afterwards banished by Nero for an uncourtly speech,— a man who, like Probus, has become a sort of mythical critic, to whom mistake or forgery has ascribed writings really belonging to a much later period. The connection thus formed was never afterwards broken, and from that time Persius seems to have declared himself a disciple of Stoicism. The creed was one to which his antecedents naturally pointed, as he was related to Arria, daughter of that 'true wife' who taught her husband how to die, and herself married to Thrasea, the biographer and imitator of the younger Cato. His literary profession was made soon after his education had been completed. He had previously written several juvenile works—a tragedy, the name of which has probably been lost by a corruption in the MS. account of his life; a poem on Travelling (perhaps a record of one of his tours with Thrasea, whose favourite and frequent companion he was) in imitation of Horace's journey to Brundisium, and of a similar poem by Lucilius; and a few verses commemorative of the elder Arria. Afterwards, when he was fresh from his studies, the reading of the tenth book of Lucilius diverted his poetical ambition into a new channel, and he applied himself eagerly to the composition of satires after the model of that which had impressed him so strongly. The later Scholiasts[1], a class of men who are rather apt to evolve facts, as well as their causes, partly from the text itself which they have to illustrate, partly from their general knowledge of human nature, tell us that this ardour did not preclude considerable vacillation: he deliberated whether to write or not, began and left off, and then began again. One of these accounts says that he hesitated for some time between a poetical and a military life—a strange but perhaps not incredible story, which would lead us to regard the frequent attacks on the army in his Satires not merely as expressions of moral or constitutional antipathy, but as protests against a former taste of his own, which may possibly have still continued to assert itself in spite of the precepts of philosophy. He wrote slowly, and at rare intervals, so that we may easily imagine the six Satires which we possess—an imperfect work, we are told—to represent the whole of his career as a professed author. The remaining notices of his life chiefly respect the friends with whom his philosophical or literary sympathies led him to associate. The earliest of these were Caesius Bassus, to whom his sixth Satire is addressed—himself a poet of some celebrity,

---

[1] [The Scholia to Persius have been edited, after the Berne MSS., by Dr. E. Kurz, in three programmes, dated 1875, 1888, and 1889.]

being the only one of his generation whom Quintilian could think of including with Horace in the class of Roman lyrists—and Calpurnius Statura, whose very name is a matter of uncertainty. He was also intimate with Servilius Nonianus, who would seem from an incidental notice to have been at one time his preceptor—a man of consular dignity, distinguished, as Tacitus informs us, not merely by high reputation as an orator and an historian, but by the polished elegance of his life. His connection with Cornutus, who was probably a freedman of the Annaean family, introduced him to Lucan; and dissimilar as their temperaments were, the young Spaniard did ample justice to the genius of his friend, scarcely restraining himself from clamorous expressions of rapture when he heard him recite his verses. At a later period Persius made the acquaintance of Seneca, but did not admire him. Two other persons, who had been fellow-students with him under Cornutus, are mentioned as men of great learning and unblemished life, and zealous in the pursuit of philosophy—Claudius Agathemerus of Lacedaemon, known as a physician of some name, and Petronius Aristocrates of Magnesia. Such were his occupations, and such the men with whom he lived. The sixth satire gives us some information about his habits of life, though not more than we might have been entitled to infer from our knowledge of his worldly circumstances and of the custom of the Romans of his day. We see him there retired from Rome for the winter to a retreat on the bay of Luna, where his mother seems to have lived since her second marriage, and indulging in recollections of Ennius' formal announcement of the beauties of the scene, while realizing in his own person the lessons of content and tranquillity, which he had learned from the Epicureanism of Horace no less than from the Stoicism of his philosophical teachers. This may probably have been his last work—written, as some have thought from internal evidence, under the consciousness that he had not long to live, though we must not press the language about his heir, in the face of what we are told of his actual testamentary dispositions. The details of his death state that it took place on the 24th of November, A.D. 62, towards the end of his twenty-eighth year, of a disease of the stomach, on an estate of his own eight miles from Rome, on the Appian road. His whole fortune, amounting to two million sesterces, he left to his mother and sister, with a request that a sum, variously stated at a hundred thousand sesterces, and twenty pounds weight of silver, might be given to his old preceptor, together with his library, seven hundred volumes, chiefly, it would seem, works of Chrysippus, who was a most voluminous writer. Cornutus showed himself worthy of his pupil's liberality by relinquishing the money and accepting the books only. He also undertook the office of reviewing his works, recommending that the juvenile productions should be destroyed, and preparing the Satires for publication by a few slight corrections and the omission of some lines at the end, which seemed to leave the work imperfect—perhaps, as Jahn supposes, the fragment of a new satire. They were ultimately edited by Caesius Bassus, at his own request, and acquired instantaneous popularity. The memoir goes on to tell us that Persius was beautiful in person, gentle in manners, a man of maidenly modesty, an excellent son, brother, and nephew, of frugal and moderate habits. This is all that we know of his life—enough to give the personal interest which a reader of his writings will naturally require, and enough, too, to furnish a bright page to a history where bright pages are few. Persius was a Roman, but the only Rome that he knew by experience was the Rome of Tiberius, Caligula, Claudius, and Nero—the Rome which Tacitus and Suetonius have pourtrayed, and which pointed St. Paul's denunciation of the moral state of the heathen world. Stoicism was not regnant but militant—it produced not heroes or statesmen, but confessors and martyrs; and the early death which cut short the promise of its Marcellus could not in such an age be called unseasonable.

It was about two hundred years since a Stoic first appeared in Rome as a member of the philosophic embassy which Athens despatched to propitiate the conquering city. Like his companions, he was bidden to go back to his school and lecture there, leaving the youth of Rome to receive their education, as heretofore, from the magistrates and the laws; but though the rigidity of the elder Cato triumphed for a time, it was not sufficient effectually to exorcise the new spirit. Panaetius, under whose influence the soul of Stoicism became more humane and its form more graceful, gained the friendship of Laelius, and through him of Scipio Aemilianus, whom he accompanied on the mission which the conqueror of Carthage undertook to the kings of Egypt and Asia in alliance with the republic. The foreign philosophy was next admitted to mould the most characteristic of all the productions of the Roman mind—its jurisprudence, being embraced by a long line of illustrious legists; and the relative duties of civil life were defined and limited by conceptions borrowed from Stoic morality. It was indeed a doctrine which, as soon as the national prejudice against imported novelties and a systematic cultivation had been surmounted, was sure to prove itself congenial to the strictness and practicality of the old Roman character; and when in the last struggles of the commonwealth the younger Cato endeavoured to take up the position of his great ancestor as a reformer of manners, his rule of life was derived not only from the traditions of undegenerate antiquity, but from the precepts of Antipater and Athenodorus. The lesson was one not to be soon lost. At the extinction of the republic, Stoicism lived on at Rome under the imperial shadow, and the government of Augustus is said to have been rendered milder by the counsels of one of its professors; but when the pressure of an undisguised despotism began to call out the old republican feeling, the elective affinity was seen to assert itself again. This was the complexion of things which Persius found, and which he left. That sect, as the accuser of Thrasea reminded the emperor, had produced bad citizens even under the former *régime*: its present adherents were men whose very deportment was an implied rebuke to the habits of the imperial court; its chief representative had abdicated his official duties and retired into an unpatriotic and insulting privacy; and the public records of the administration of affairs at home and abroad were only so many registers of his sins of omission. There was, in truth, no encouragement to pursue a different course. Seneca's attempt to seat philosophy on the throne by influencing the mind of Nero, had issued only in his own moral degradation as the lying apologist of matricide, and the receiver of a bounty which in one of its aspects was plunder, in another corruption; and though his retirement, and still more his death, may have sufficed to rescue his memory from obloquy, they could only prove that he had learned too late what the more consistent members of the fraternity knew from the beginning. From such a government the only notice that a Stoic could expect or desire was the sentence which hurried him to execution or drove him into banishment. Even under the rule of Vespasian the antagonism was still unabated. At the moment of his accession, Euphrates the Tyrian, who was in his train, protested against the ambition which sought to aggrandize itself when it might have restored the republic. Helvidius Priscus, following, and perhaps deforming, the footsteps of his father-in-law Thrasea, ignored the political existence of the emperor in his edicts as praetor, and asserted his own equality repeatedly by a freedom of speech amounting to personal insult, till at last he succeeded in exhausting the forbearance of Vespasian, who put him to death and banished the philosophers from Italy. A similar expulsion took place under Domitian, who did not require much persuasion to induce him to adopt a policy recommended by the instinct of self-preservation no less than by Nero's example. Meantime the spirit of Stoicism was gradually undergoing a change. The theoretic parts of the system, its physics and its dialectics, had found comparatively little favour with the Roman mind, and had passed into the shade in consequence: but it was still a foreign product, a matter of learning, the subject of a voluminous literature, and as such a discipline to which only the few could submit. It was still the old conception of the wise man as an ideal rather than a reality, a being necessarily perfect, and therefore necessarily superhuman. Now, however, the ancient exclusiveness was to be relaxed, and the invitation to humanity made more general. 'Strange and shocking would it be,' said Musonius Rufus, the one philosopher exempted from Vespasian's sentence, 'if the tillers of the ground were incapacitated from philosophy, which is really a business of few words, not of many theories, and far better learnt in a practical country life than in the schools of the city.' In short, it was to be no longer a philosophy but a religion. Epictetus, the poor crippled slave, as his epitaph proclaims him, whom the gods loved, turned Theism from a speculative dogma into an operative principle, bidding his disciples follow the divine service, imitate the divine life, implore the divine aid, and rest on the divine providence. Dependence on the Deity was taught as a correlative to independence of external circumstances, and the ancient pride of the Porch exchanged for a humility so genuine that men have endeavoured to trace it home to a Christian congregation. A Stoic thus schooled was not likely to become a political propagandist, even if the memory of the republic had been fresh, and the imperial power had continued to be synonymous with tyranny—much less after the assassination of Domitian had inaugurated an epoch of which Tacitus could speak as the fulfilment of the brightest dreams of the truest lovers of freedom. Fifty years rolled away, and government became continually better, and the pursuit of wisdom more and more honourable, till at last the ideal of Zeno himself was realized, and a Stoic ascended the throne of the Caesars, and the philosophy of political despair seemed to have become the creed of political hope. The character of Marcus Aurelius is one that is ever good to dwell on, and our sympathies cling round the man that could be rigorously severe to himself while tenderly indulgent to his people, whose love broke out in their fond addresses to him as their father and their brother: yet the peace of his reign was blasted by natural calamities, torn by civil discord, and tainted by the corruption of his own house, and at his death the fair promise of the commonwealth and of philosophy expired together. Commodus ruled the Roman world, and Stoicism, the noblest of the latter systems, fell the first before the struggles of the enfeebled yet resisting rivals, and the victorious advances of a new and living faith.

It is not often that a poet has been so completely identified with a system of philosophy as Persius. Greece had produced poets who were philosophers, and philosophers who were writers of poetry; yet our first thought of Aeschylus is not as of a Pythagorean, or of Euripides as of a follower of the Sophists; nor should we classify Xenophanes or Empedocles primarily as poets of whose writings only fragments remain. In Lucretius and Persius, on the other hand, we see men who hold a prominent place among the poets of their country, yet whose poetry is devoted to the enforcement of their peculiar philosophical views. The fact is a significant one, and symptomatic of that condition of Roman culture which I have noticed on a former occasion. It points to an age and nation where philosophy is a permanent, not a progressive study—an imported commodity, not an indigenous growth,—where the impulse that gives rise to poetry is not so much a desire to give musical voice to the native thought and feeling of the poet and his fellow-men, as a recognition of the want of a national literature and a wish to contribute towards its supply. At first sight there may seem something extravagant in pretending that Persius can be called the poet of Stoicism in the sense in which Lucretius is the poet of Epicureanism, as if there were equal scope for the exposition of a philosophy in a few scholastic exercises and in an elaborate didactic poem. On the other hand, it should be recollected that under the iron grasp of the Roman mind, Stoicism, as was just now remarked, was being reduced more and more to a simply practical system, bearing but a faint impress of those abstruse cosmological speculations which had so great a charm for the intellect of Greece even in its most sober moments, and exhibiting in place of them an applicability to civil life the want of which had been noted as a defect in the conceptions of Zeno and Chrysippus[1]. The library and the lecture-room still were more familiar to it than the forum or the senate; but the transition had begun: and though Persius may have looked to his seven hundred volumes for his principles of action, as he did to Horace for information about the ways of the world, the only theory which he strove to inculcate was the knowledge which the founders of his sect, in common with Socrates, believed to be the sole groundwork of correct practice. Using the very words of Virgil, he calls upon a benighted race to acquaint itself with the causes of things:

[1] Cic. Legg. 3. 6.

but the invitation is not to that study of the stars in their courses, of eclipses, and earthquakes and inundations, of the laws governing the length of days and nights, which enabled Lucretius to triumph over the fear of death, but to an inquiry into the purpose of man's being, the art of skilful driving in the chariot-race of life, the limits to a desire of wealth and to its expenditure on unselfish objects, and the ordained position of each individual in the social system. Such an apprehension of his subject would naturally lead him not to the treatise, but to the sermon—not to the didactic poem, but to the satire or moral epistle. But though the form of the composition is desultory, the spirit is in the main definite and consistent. Even in the first satire, in which he seems to drop the philosopher and assume the critic, we recognize the same belief in the connection between intellectual knowledge and practice, and consequently between a corrupt taste and a relaxed morality, which shines out so clearly afterwards when he tells the enfranchised slave that he cannot move a finger without committing a blunder, and that it is as portentous for a man to take part in life without study as it would be for a ploughman to attempt to bring a ship into port. | It is true that he follows Horace closely, not only in his illustrations and descriptions of manners, but in his lessons of morality—a strange deference to the man who ridiculed Crispinus and Damasippus, and did not even spare the great Stertinius; but the evil and folly of avarice, the wisdom of contentment and self-control, and the duty of sincerity towards man and God, were doctrines at least as congenial to a Stoic as to an Epicurean, and the ambition with which the pupil is continually seeking to improve upon his master's felicity of expression shows itself more successfully in endeavours to give greater stringency to his rule of life and conduct. In one respect, certainly, we may wonder that he has failed to represent the views of that section of the Stoics with which he is reported to have lived on terms of familiar intercourse. There is no trace of that political feeling which might have been expected to appear in the writings of a youth who was brought into frequent contact with the revolutionary enthusiasm of Lucan, and may probably have been present at one of the banquets with which Thrasea and Helvidius used to celebrate the birthdays of the first and the last of the great republican worthies. The supposed allusions to the poetical character of Nero in the first satire shrink almost to nothing in the light of a searching criticism, while the tradition that in the original draught the emperor was directly satirized as Midas receives no countenance, to say the least, from the poem itself, the very point of which, so far as we can apprehend it, depends on the truth of the reading given in the MSS. The fourth satire does undoubtedly touch on statesmanship: but the tone throughout is that of a student, who in his eagerness to imitate Plato has apparently forgotten that he is himself living not under a popular but under an imperial government, and the moral intended to be conveyed is simply that the adviser of the public ought to possess some better qualification than those which were found in Alcibiades—a topic about as appropriate to the actual state of Rome as the schoolboy's exhortation to Sulla to lay down his power. Thus his language, where he does speak, enables us to interpret his silence as the silence not of acquiescence or even of timidity, though such times as his might well justify caution, but rather of unworldly innocence, satisfied with its own aspirations after moral perfection, and dreaming of Athenian licence under the very shade of despotism. On the other hand, it is perfectly intelligible that he should have seen little to admire in Seneca, many as are the coincidences which their common philosophy has produced in their respective writings. There could, indeed, have been but little sympathy between his simple earnestness and that rhetorical facility—that Spanish taste for inappropriate and meretricious ornament—that tolerant and compromising temper, able to live in a court while unable to live in exile, which, however compatible with real wisdom and virtue, must have seemed to a Stoic of a severer type only so many qualifications for effectually betraying the good cause. So, again, he does not seem to exhibit any anticipation of the distinctly human and religious development which, as we have seen, was the final phase of Stoicism. His piety is simply the rational piety which would approve itself to any Roman moralist—the piety recommended by Horace, and afterwards by Juvenal—pronouncing purity of intent to be more acceptable in the sight of Heaven than costly sacrifice, and bidding men ask of the gods such things only as divine beings would wish to grant. In like manner his humanity, though genial in its practical aspect, is still narrowed on the speculative side by the old sectarian exclusiveness which barred the path of life to every one not entering through the gate of philosophy. In short, he is a disciple of the earlier Stoicism of the empire—a Roman in his predilection for the ethical part of his creed, yet conforming in other respects to the primitive traditions of Greece—neither a patriot nor a courtier, but a recluse student, an ardent teacher of the truths which he had himself learnt, without the development which might have been generated by more mature thought, or the abatement which might have been forced upon him by a longer experience.

We have already observed that the character of Persius' opinions determined his choice of a poetical vehicle for expressing them. With his views it would have been as unnatural for him to have composed a didactic treatise, like Lucretius, or a republican epic, like Lucan, as to have rested satisfied with multiplying the productions of his own boyhood, tragedies and pilgrimages in verse. And now, what was the nature and what the historical antecedents of that form of composition which he adopted as most congenial to him?

The exploded derivation of satire from the Greek satyric drama is one of those infrequent instances where a false etymology has preserved a significant truth. There seems every reason to believe that the first beginnings of satire among the Romans are parallel to the rudimental type from which dramatic entertainments were developed in Greece. 'When I am reading on these two subjects,' says Dryden, in his admirable essay on Satire, 'methinks I hear the same story told twice over with very little alteration.' The primitive Dionysiac festivals of the Greek rustic populations seem to have answered with sufficient exactness to the harvest-home rejoicings of agricultural Italy described by Horace, when the country wits encountered each other in Fescennine verses. Nor did the resemblance cease at this its earliest stage. Improvised repartee was succeeded by pantomimic representation and dancing to music, and in process of time the two elements, combined yet discriminated from each other, assumed the form of a regular play, with its alternate dialogues and *cantica*. Previous to this later development there had been an intermediate kind of entertainment called the *satura* or medley, either from the miscellaneous character of its matter, which appears to have made no pretence to a plot or story, or from the variety of measures of which it was composed—a more professional and artistic exhibition than the Fescennine bantering-matches, but far removed from the organized completeness of even the earlier drama. It was on this narrow ground that the independence of the Roman genius was destined to assert itself. Whether from a wish to take advantage of the name, or to preserve a thing, once popular, from altogether dying out in the process of improvement, a feeling which we know to have operated in the case of the *exodia* or interludes introduced into the representation of the Atellane plays, Ennius was led to produce certain compositions which he called satires, seemingly as various both in character and in versification as the old dramatic medley, but intended not for acting but for reciting or reading—in other words, not plays but poems. All that we know of these is comprised in a few titles and a very few fragments, none of which tell us much, coupled with the fact that in one of them Life and Death were introduced contending with each other as two allegorical personages, like Fame in Virgil, as Quintilian remarks, or Virtue and Pleasure in the moral tale of Prodicus. Little as this is, it is more than is known of the satires of Pacuvius, of which we only hear that they resembled those of Ennius. What was the precise relation borne by either to the later Roman satire with which we are so familiar can but be conjectured. Horace, who is followed as usual by Persius, ignores them both as satirists, and claims the paternity of satire for Lucilius, who, as he says, imitated the old Attic comedy, changing merely the measure; nor does Quintilian mention them in the brief but celebrated passage in which he asserts the merit of the invention of satire to belong wholly to Rome. This silence may be taken as showing that neither Ennius nor Pacuvius gave any exclusive or decided prominence to that element of satire which in modern times has become its distinguishing characteristic—criticism on the men, manners, and things of the day; but it can scarcely impeach their credit as the first founders of a new and original school of composition. That which constitutes the vaunted originality of Roman satire is not so much its substance as its form: the one had already existed in perfection at Athens, the elaboration of the other was reserved for the poetic art of Italy. It is certainly not a little remarkable that the countrymen of Aristophanes and Menander should not have risen to the full conception of familiar compositions in verse in which the poet pours out desultory thoughts on contemporary subjects in his own person, relieved from the trammels which necessarily bind every dramatic production, however free and unbridled its spirit. That such a thing might easily have arisen among them is evident from the traditional fame of the Homeric Margites, itself apparently combining one of the actual requisites of the Roman medley, the mixture of metres, with the biting invective of the later satire—a work which, when fixed at its latest date, must have been one of the concomitants, if not, as Aristotle thinks, the veritable parent, of the earlier comedy of Greece. In later times we find parallels to Roman satire in some of the idylls of Theocritus, not only in those light dialogues noticed by the critics, of which the Adoniazusae is the best instance, but in the poem entitled the Charites, where the poet complains of the general neglect into which his art has fallen in a strain of mingled pathos and sarcasm which may remind us of Juvenal's appeal in behalf of men of letters, the unfortunate fraternity of authors. But Greece was not ordained to excel in everything; and Rome had the opportunity of cultivating a virtually unbroken field of labour which was suited to her direct practical genius, and to her mastery over the arts of social life. There can be no question but that the conception of seizing the spirit of comedy—of the new comedy no less than the old—the comedy of manners as well as the comedy of scurrilous burlesque—and investing it with an easy undress clothing, the texture of which might be varied as the inward feeling changed, was a great advance in the progress of letters. It would seem to be a test of the lawful development of a new form of composition from an old, that the latter should be capable of including the earlier, as the larger includes the smaller. So in the development of the Shaksperian drama from the Greek, the chorus is not lost either as a lyrical or as an ethical element, but is diffused over the play, no longer seen indeed, but felt in the art which heightens the tone of poetry, and brings out the moral relations of the characters into more prominent relief. So in that great development which transcends as it embraces all others, the development of prose from poetry, the superiority of the new form to the old as a general vehicle of expression is shown in the expansive flexibility which can find measured and rhythmic utterance for the raptures of passion or imagination, yet give no undue elevation to the statement of the plainest matters of fact. And so it is in the generation of satire from comedy: the unwieldy framework of the drama is gone, but the dramatic power remains, and may be summoned up at any time at the pleasure of the poet, not only in the impalpable shape of remarks on human character, but in the flesh-and-blood fulness of actual dialogue such as engrosses several of the satires of Horace, and enters as a more or less important ingredient into every one of those of Persius. Or, if we choose to regard satire, as we are fully warranted in doing, in its relation not only to the stage but to other kinds of poetry, we shall have equal reason to admire it for its elasticity, as being capable of rising without any ungraceful effort from light ridicule to heightened earnestness—passing at once with Horace from a ludicrous description of a poet as a marked man, to an emphatic recognition of his essential greatness; or with Juvenal from a sneer at the contemptible offerings with which the gods were commonly propitiated, to a sublime recital of the blessings which may lawfully be made objects of prayer. This plastic comprehensiveness was realized by the earlier writers, as we have seen, by means of the variety of their metres, while the latter were enabled to compass it more artistically by that skilful management of the hexameter which could not be brought to perfection in a day. But the conception appears to have been radically the same throughout; and the very name *satura* already contains a prophecy of the distinctive value of Roman satire as a point in the history of letters.

If, however, the praise of having originated satire cannot be refused to Ennius, it must be confessed as freely that the influence exercised over it by Lucilius entitles him to be called its second father. It belongs to one by the ties of birth—to the other by those of adoption and education. Unlike Ennius, the glories of whose invention may well have paled before his fame as the Roman Homer and the Roman Euripides, Lucilius seems to have devoted himself wholly to fostering the growth and forming the mind of the satiric muse. He is thought to have so far departed from the form of the old medley as to enforce a uniformity of metre in each separate satire, though even this is not certainly made out; but he preserved the external variety by writing sometimes in hexameter, sometimes in iambics or trochaics, and also by a practice, seemingly peculiar to himself, of mixing Latin copiously with Greek, the language corresponding to French in the polite circles of Rome. It is evident, too, both from his numerous fragments and from the notices of the early grammarians, that he encouraged to a large extent the satiric tendency to diversity of subject—at one moment soaring on the wing of epic poetry and describing a council of the gods in language which Virgil has copied, the next satirizing the fashion of giving fine Greek names to articles of domestic furniture,—comprehending in the same satire a description of a journey from Rome to Capua, and a series of strictures on his predecessors in poetry, whom he seems to have corrected like so many school-boys;—now laying down the law about the niceties of grammar, showing how the second conjugation is to be discriminated from the third, and the genitive singular from the nominative plural; and now talking, possibly within a few lines, of seizing an antagonist by the nose, dashing his fist in his face, and knocking out every tooth in his head. But his great achievement, as attested by the impression left on the minds of his Roman readers, was that of making satire henceforward synonymous with free speaking and personality—he comes before us as the reviver of the Fescennine licence, the imitator of Cratinus and Eupolis and Aristophanes. There seems to have been about him a reckless animal pugnacity, an exhilarating consciousness of his powers as a good hater, which in its rude simplicity may remind us of Archilochus, and certainly is but faintly represented in the arch pleasantry of Horace, the concentrated intellectual scorn of Persius, or of the declamatory indignation of Juvenal. Living in a period of political excitement, he plunged eagerly into party quarrels. The companion of the younger

Scipio and Laelius, though a mere boy, and himself of equestrian rank, he attacked great consular personages who had opposed his friends: as Horace phrases it, he tore away the veil from private life and arraigned high and low alike—showing no favour but to virtue and the virtuous—words generally found to bear a tolerably precise meaning in the vocabulary of politics. It was the satire of the republic, or rather of the old oligarchy, and it was impossible that it could live on unchanged into the times of the Empire. But the memory of its day of freedom was not forgotten: the ancient right of impeachment was claimed formally by men who intended no more than a common criminal information; and each succeeding satirist sheltered himself ostentatiously under an example of which he knew better than to attempt to avail himself in practice.

It was to Lucilius, as we have already seen, that Persius, if reliance is to be placed on the statement of his biographer, owed the impulse that made him a writer of satire. Of the actual work which is related to have produced so remarkable an effect on its young reader, the tenth book, scarcely anything has been preserved; while the remains of the fourth, which is said to have been the model of Persius' third satire, comparatively copious and interesting as they are, contain nothing which would enable us to judge for ourselves of the degree of resemblance. Hardly a single parallel from Lucilius is quoted by the Scholia on any part of Persius: but when we consider that the aggregate of their citations from Horace, though much larger, is utterly inadequate to express the obligations which are everywhere obvious to the eye of a modern scholar, we cannot take their omissions as even a presumptive proof that what is not apparent does not exist. On the other hand, the Prologue[1] to the Satires, in scazon iambics, is supposed, on the authority of an obscure passage in Petronius, to have had its prototype in a similar composition by Lucilius; and it is also a plausible conjecture that the first line of the first satire is taken bodily from the old poet—two distinct proclamations of adhesion at the very outset, in the ears of those who could not fail to understand them. There is reason, also, for believing that the imitation may have extended further, and that Persius' strictures on the poets of his day, and in particular on those who affected a taste for archaisms, and professed to read the old Roman drama with delight, may have been studied after those irreverent criticisms of the fathers of poetry, some of which, as the Scholiasts on Horace inform us, occurred in this very tenth book of

---

[1] [Rather, the Epilogue: see Preface to the Third Edition, p. v.]

Lucilius. On the ethical side we should have been hardly prepared to expect much similarity: there is, however, a curious fragment of Lucilius, the longest of all that have come down to us, containing a simple recital of the various constituents of virtue, the knowledge of duty no less than its practice, in itself sufficiently resembling the enumeration of the elements of morality which Persius makes on more than one occasion, and showing a turn for doctrinal exposition which was sure to be appreciated by a pupil of the Stoics. So there are not wanting indications that the bold metaphors and grotesque yet forcible imagery which stamp the character of Persius' style so markedly may have been encouraged if not suggested by hints in Lucilius, who was fond of tentative experiments in language, such as belong to the early stages of poetry, when the national taste is in a state of fusion. The admitted contrast between the two men, unlike in all but their equestrian descent,—between the premature man of the world and the young philosopher, the improvisatore who could throw off two hundred verses in an hour, and the student who wrote seldom and slowly,—may warrant us in doubting the success of the imitation, but does not discredit the fact. Our point is, that Persius attempted to wear the toga of his predecessor, not that it fitted him.

The influence of Horace upon Persius is a topic which has, in part, been anticipated already[1]. It is a patent fact which may be safely assumed, and I have naturally been led to assume it as a help towards estimating other things which are not so easily ascertainable. Casaubon was, I believe, the first to bring it forward prominently into light in an appendix to his memorable edition of Persius; and though one of the later commentators has endeavoured to call it in question, cautioning us against mistaking slight coincidences for palpable imitations, I am confident that a careful and minute study of Persius, such as I have lately been engaged in, will be found only to produce a more complete conviction of its truth: nor can I doubt that an equally careful perusal of Horace, line by line and word by word, would enable us to add still further to the amount of proof. Yet it is curious and instructive to observe that it is a point which, while established by a superabundance of the best possible evidence, that of ocular demonstration, is yet singularly deficient in those minor elements of probability to which we

---

[1] [Perhaps owing to this fact, or perhaps because of the identity of their *cognomen* Flaccus, Horace and Persius were sometimes confused by the grammarians. Persius is called simply Flaccus by Diomedes, p. 327 Keil. He is quoted as Horace by Charisius, according to the Neapolitan MS., p. 202, and by Consentius, p. 348; conversely, Horace is quoted as Persius by Servius on Georgic 3. 363.]

are constantly accustomed to look in the absence of anything more directly conclusive. The memoir of Persius mentions Lucilius, but says not a word of Horace: the quotations from Horace in the commentary of the pseudo-Cornutus are, as I have said, far from numerous: while the difference of the poets themselves, their personal history, their philosophical profession, their taste and temperament, the nature and power of their genius, is greater even than in the case of Persius and Lucilius, and is only more clearly brought out by the clearer knowledge we possess of each, in the possession of the whole of their respective works. The fact, however, is only too palpable—so much so that it puzzles us, as it were, by its very plainness: we could understand a less degree of imitation, but the correspondence which we actually see makes us, so to speak, half incredulous, and compels us to seek some account of it. It is not merely that we find the same topics in each, the same class of allusions and illustrations, or even the same thoughts and the same images, but the resemblance or identity extends to things which every poet, in virtue of his own peculiarities and those of his time, would naturally be expected to provide for himself. With him, as with Horace, a miser is a man who drinks vinegar for wine, and stints himself in the oil which he pours on his vegetables; while a contented man is one who acquiesces in the prosperity of people whose start in life is worse than his own. The prayer of the farmer is still that he may turn up a pot of money some day while he is ploughing: the poet's hope is still that his verses may be embalmed with cedar oil, his worst fear still that they may furnish wrapping for spices. Nay, where he mentions names they are apt to be the names of Horatian personages: his great physician is Craterus, his grasping rich man Nerius, his crabbed censor Bestius, his low reprobate Natta. Something is doubtless due to the existence of what, to adopt a term applied by Colonel Mure to the Greek epic writers, we may call satirical commonplace, just as Horace himself is thought to have taken the name Nomentanus from Lucilius; or as, among our own satirists, Bishop Hall talks of Labeo, and Pope of Gorgonius. So Persius may have intended not so much to copy Horace as to quote him—advertising his readers, as it were, from time to time that he was using the language of satire. But the utmost that can be proved is, that he followed prodigally an example which had been set sparingly, not knowing or not remembering that satire is a kind of composition which of all others is kept alive not by antiquarian associations, but by contemporary interest—not by generalized conventionalities, but by direct individual portraiture. We can hardly doubt that a wider

LIFE AND WRITINGS OF PERSIUS. xxxiii

worldly knowledge would have led him to correct his error of judgment, though the history of English authors show us, in at least one instance, that of Ben Jonson, that a man, not only of true comic genius but of large experiences of life, may be so enslaved by acquired learning as to satirize vice and folly as he reads of them in his books, rather than as he sees them in society.

But time warns me that I must leave the yet unfinished list of the influences which worked or may have worked upon Persius, and say a few words upon his actual merits as a writer. The tendency of what has been advanced hitherto has been to make us think of him as more passive than active—as a candidate more for our interest and our sympathy than for our admiration. But we must not forget that it is his own excellence that has made him a classic—that the great and true glory which, as Quintilian says, he gained by a single volume, has been due to that volume alone. If we would justify the award of his contemporaries and of posterity, we may be prepared to account for it. It was not, as we have seen, that he was an originating power in philosophy, or a many-sided observer of men and manners. He was a satirist, but he shows no knowledge of many of the ingredients which, as Juvenal rightly perceived, go to make up the satiric medley. He was what in modern parlance would be called a plagiarist—a charge which, later if not sooner, must have told fatally on an otherwise unsupported reputation. I might add that he is frequently perplexed in arrangement and habitually obscure in meaning, were it not that some judges have professed to discover in this the secret of his fame. A truer appreciation will, I believe, be more likely to find it in the distinct and individual character of his writings, the power of mind and depth of feeling visible throughout, the austere purity of his moral tone, relieved by frequent outbreaks of genial humour, and the condensed vigour and graphic freshness of a style where elaborate art seems to be only nature triumphing over obstacles. Probably no writer ever borrowed so much and yet left on the mind so decided an impression of originality. His description of the wilful invalid and his medical friend in the third satire owes much of its colouring to Horace, yet the whole presentation is felt to be his own—true, pointed, and sufficient. Even when the picture is entirely Horatian, like that of the over-covetous man at his prayers, in the second satire, the effect is original still, though the very varieties which discriminate it may be referred to hints in other parts of Horace's own works. We may wish that he had painted from his own observation and knowledge, but we cannot deny that he has shown a painter's power. And where he draws the

c

life that he must have known, not from the descriptions of a past age but from his own experience, his portraits have an imaginative truth, minutely accurate yet highly ideal, which would entitle them to a distinguished place in any poetical gallery. There is nothing in Horace or Juvenal more striking than the early part of the third satire, where the youthful idler is at first represented by a series of light touches, snoring in broad noon while the harvest is baking in the fields and the cattle reposing in the shade, then starting up and calling for his books only to quarrel with them—and afterwards as we go further the scene darkens, and we see the figure of the lost profligate blotting the background, and catch an intimation of yet more fearful punishments in store for those who will not be warned in time—punishments dire as any that the oppressors of mankind have suffered or devised—the beholding of virtue in her beauty when too late, and the consciousness of a corroding secret which no other heart can share. Nor would it be easy to parallel the effect of the sketches in the first satire, rapidly succeeding each other,—the holiday poet with his white dress and his onyx ring tuning his voice for recitation; a grey and bloated old man, giving himself up to cater for the itching ears of others; the jaded, worn company at the table, languidly rousing themselves in the hope of some new excitement; the inferior guests at the bottom of the hall ready to applaud when they have got the cue from their betters—all flung into a startling and ghastly light by the recollection carefully presented to us that these men call themselves the sons of the old Romans, and recognise poetry as a divine thing, and acknowledge the object of criticism to be truth. Again we see the same pictorial skill and reality, though in a very different style, toned down and sobered, in those most sweet and touching lines describing the poet's residence with his beloved teacher, when they used to study together through long summer suns and seize on the first and best hours of the night for the social meal, each working while the other worked and resting while the other rested, and both looking forward to the modest enjoyment of the evening as the crown of a well-spent day. Persius' language has been censured for its harshness and exaggeration: but here, at any rate, he is as simple and unaffected as an admirer of Horace or Virgil could desire. The contrast is instructive, and may perhaps suggest a more favourable view of those peculiarities of expression which are generally condemned. The style which his taste leads him to drop when he is not writing satire, is the style which his taste leads him to assume for satiric purposes. He feels that a clear, straightforward, everyday manner of speech would not suit a subject over which the gods themselves might hesitate whether to laugh or to weep. He has to write the tragi-comedy of his day, and he writes it in a dialect where grandiose epic diction and philosophical terminology are strangely blended with the talk of the forum, the gymnasia, and the barber's shop. I suggest this consideration with the more confidence, as I find it represented to me, and, as it were, forced on me by the example of a writer of our own country, perhaps the most remarkable of the present time, who, though differing as widely from Persius in all his circumstances as a world-wearied and desponding man of the nineteenth century can differ from an enthusiastic and inexperienced youth of the first, still appears to me to bear a singular resemblance to him in the whole character of his genius—I mean Mr. Carlyle. If Persius can take the benefit of this parallel, he may safely plead guilty to the charge of not having escaped the vice of his age, the passion for refining still further on Augustan refinements of expression, and locking up the meaning of a sentence in epigrammatic allusions, which in its measure lies at the door even of Tacitus.

I have exhausted my time and, I fear, your patience also, when my subject is still far from exhausted. I am glad, however, to think that in closing I am not really bringing it to an end, but that some of my hearers to-day will accompany me to-morrow and on future days in the special study of one who, like all great authors, will surrender the full knowledge of his beauties only to those who ask it of him in detail.

THE TEXT OF PERSIUS[1]

[To judge from the praise bestowed upon him by Quintilian and Martial[2], and from the numerous quotations made from him by the grammarians, Persius must have had a considerable number of readers in the first four centuries after Christ. The palimpsest of Bobbio[3] (now No. 5750 in the Vatican Library), a fragment of which still exists, must have belonged to this early period.

In A.D. 402 Flavius Julius Tryfonianus Sabinus, a young man of high rank, attempted, as he tells us in a *subscriptio* now preserved at the end of the two best manuscripts, to correct the text of Persius: 'Flavius Julius Tryfonianus Sabinus, v.c., protector domesticus, temptavi emendare sine antigrapho meum et adnotavi Barcellone, coss. dd. nn. Arcadio et Honorio V.' It is important to observe that in the Latin of this period, 'emendare' implies not conjectural emendation as we understand it, but bare correction of such obvious errors as abounded in most manuscripts, even the oldest, at that time. 'Adnotatio' probably means the insertion of critical and explanatory notes. The corrector generally made use of another copy ('antigraphon') with which to compare his own; but Sabinus is careful to tell us that his work was performed without one.

At the time of the Carolingian revival, and during the succeeding centuries, many copies of Persius were made, and many still exist. From these Jahn, who gave the readings of a great number in 1843, selected three as the basis of his text of 1868. The three are, (1) No. 212 in the Library of the Medical School at Montpellier (A), collated for Jahn by Adolf Michaelis in 1857; (2) No. 36 H in the Vatican Library (B), first carefully collated by Dr. J. H. Wheeler in 1879. (A)

---

[1] For the main facts here mentioned I am indebted to Jahn and Bücheler.

[2] Quintilian 10. 1. 94 'multum et verae gloriae quamvis uno libro Persius meruit.' Martial 4. 29. 7 'Saepius in libro numeratur Persius uno | Quam levis in tota Marsus Amazonide.'

[3] Recently edited by Goetz: *Juvenalis et Persii fragmenta Bobiensia edita a Georgio Goetz*, Jena, 1884.

and (B) are assigned to the tenth and the ninth centuries respectively. (3) No. 125 in the Library of the Medical School at Montpellier (C). This manuscript, which is assigned to the ninth century, once belonged to Pierre Pithou, and contains also the celebrated *Pithoeanus* of Juvenal. It was again collated by Rudolf Beer in 1885. The two first MSS., (A) and (B), are evidently copied directly from one lost original (*a*), while (C) represents a different recension. Jahn and Bücheler give, I think rightly, a general preference to (*a*); but their decision has been recently impugned in some points by Dr. J. Bieger, whose essay I have mentioned in the Preface to the Third Edition.

Each of these three manuscripts has been corrected by a second hand, which is indicated by the letters (a), (b), and (c) respectively. The other manuscripts are indicated by the letter *r*.

The variants of the Bobbio palimpsest, the fragment of which contains only vv. 53–104 of the first satire, I have given with all possible minuteness. I have also added a few references to the grammarians which are not to be found in Bücheler's edition.

A glance at the *apparatus criticus* will show how seriously the text of Persius had been corrupted before it was copied anew in the Carolingian era. H. N.]

[EXPLANATION OF THE LETTERS USED IN THE
APPARATUS CRITICUS.

Fragm. Bob.	=	fragmentum palimpsesti Bobbiensis (nunc Vaticanus 5750).
a	=	consentiens lectio codicum A et B.
A	=	codex Montepessulanus 212.
B	=	codex Vaticanus 36 H.
C	=	codex Montepessulanus 125.
a	=	manus altera codicis A.
b	=	„ „ „ B.
c	=	„ „ „ C.
ς	=	codices alii.]

A. PERSII FLACCI

SATURARUM

LIBER

SATURA I.

'O CURAS hominum! O quantum est in rebus inane!
Quis leget haec?
      'Min tu istud ais? Nemo hercule.'
                  Nemo?
'Vel duo, vel nemo.'
     Turpe et miserabile!
              'Quare?
ne mihi Polydamas et Troiades Labeonem

An attack on the corruptions of literature, as symptomatic of corruption in morals, intended as introductory to the Satires, as would seem from the latter part. He is disgusted with the taste of his day, and would have his reader's mind formed on the old models.

The form is that of a dialogue, more or less regularly sustained, between Persius and a friend, who lectures him very much as Trebatius does Horace. Nothing can be decided about the time of the composition of this Satire from its subject. The mention of Pedius, if it proves anything, only proves that passage to have been written late. 'The connection between intellectual and moral vigour would naturally be suggested by the Stoic doctrine (Sat. 5), that virtue consists in correct knowledge. With the whole Satire comp. Sen. Ep. 114.

1–12. P. 'Vanity of vanities!' F. You will get no readers if you write like that. P. 'I want none—every one at Rome, princes and people, is—may I say what?' F. Certainly not. P. 'But I must have my laugh somehow.'

1. [The Scholia say that this line is from the first book of Lucilius.] But **in rebus inane** is found in Lucr. 1. 330, 382, 511, 569, 655, 660, 742, 843; 5. 365 (most of them quoted by Jahn), with reference to the Epicurean theory; and it is at least as likely that Persius was alluding to this. 'How great a vacuum (human) nature admits!'

2. The friend says, **Quis leget haec?** as Hor. 1 S. 4. 22 complains of finding no readers. Persius says, **Min tu istud ais?** apparently expressing surprise at the address. **Nemo hercule.**' 'Readers? I want none.' (Jahn. Others give 'Nemo hercule' to the friend, 'Nemo' to P.)

SATIRE I.

Persius. 'O THE vanity of human cares! O what a huge vacuum man's nature admits!'
Friend. Whom do you expect to read you?
P. 'Was your question meant for me? Nobody, I assure you.'
F. Nobody?
P. 'Well—one or two at most.'
F. A most ignominious and pitiable catastrophe.
P. 'Why? are you afraid that Polydamas and the Trojan ladies will be setting their own dear Labeo above me? Stuff! If that

3. Persius repeats his disclaimer, 'One or two, which is as good as none.' Casaubon refers to the Greek phrases, ἢ ὀλίγοι ἢ οὐδείς and ἤ τις ἢ οὐδείς. 'A most lame and impotent conclusion to it all,' returns the friend. 'Why?' asks P.

4. ne connects the sentence not with 'turpe et miserabile,' but with something similar implied by 'Quare.' 'For fear that Polydamas,' etc. 'Nae,' which Heinr. prefers, with some of the old commentators, would destroy the sense, the ironical assertion showing that he doubted the fact, and 'ne praetulerint,' 'suppose they were not to prefer,' would be equally inappropriate here, though idiomatic. For 'Polydamas,' two MSS. have 'Pulydamas,' representing Homer's Πουλυδάμας. The reference is to Il. 22. 100, 105, the former of which is quoted by Aristot. Eth. 3. 8, and both of them more than once by Cicero (Ep. Att. 2. 5. 1; 7. 1. 4; 8. 16. 2), who applies the name Polydamas to Cato, and also to Atticus himself. Here the expression is particularly pointed; 'Polydamas and the Trojan ladies' of course stand for the bugbears of respectability, the influential classes of Rome: the pride of the Romans as 'Troiugenae' is glanced at (Juv. 1. 100; 8. 181; 11. 95), while the women are dwelt on rather than the men, Ἀχαιΐδες, οὐκέτ' Ἀχαιοί [comp. (with Mr. Pretor on Cic. ad Att. 1. 12) Cicero's Τεῦκρις, in all probability a nickname for C. Antonius.] To crown all, there is an allusion to Attius Labeo [see Teuffel, Geschichte der Römischen Literatur, § 307. 6, fifth edition, Warr's translation] as the author of a translation of the Iliad, of which the Schol. has preserved one line, 'Crudum manduces Priamum Priamique pisinnos' (Il. 4. 35), as if he had said, 'Lest Labeo's interest with Polydamas and the Trojan ladies should get them to prefer him to me.' The story perhaps only rests on a statement by Fulgentius (see Jahn), but the internal evidence is very strong, and it is much more probable than the supposition that 'Labeo' is merely used as a Horatian synonym for a madman (Hor. 1 S. 3. 82), to which Jahn inclines, Prolegomena, pp. 72, 73.

praetulerint? nugae. non, si quid turbida Roma
elevet, accedas examenque improbum in illa
castiges trutina, nec te quaesiveris extra.
nam Romae quis non—? a, si fas dicere—sed fas
tum, cum ad canitiem et nostrum istud vivere triste
aspexi ac nucibus facimus quaecumque relictis,
cum sapimus patruos. Tunc, tunc ignoscite.'

Nolo.

'Quid faciam? sed sum petulanti splene cachinno.

[5. *praetulerunt* B.   6. *examenue* C.   7. *quaesiverit* a.   8. *romae est* a C. *ac* a C. *at* vel *ah* ς.]

5. nugae. 'Nugas' is used similarly as an exclamation in Plaut. Most. 1088, Pers. 718. [Non si elevet accedas is of the same stamp as 'non, si me satis audias, Speres,' Hor. 1 Od. 13. 13; 'non si solvas invenias,' ib. 1 S. 4. 60: 'nec si certes concedat,' Virg. E. 2. 57. Mr. Yonge, in the Journal of Philology for 1873. Add Ov. 1 Pont. 7. (6.) 24, 'non agites, si qua coire velis.']
turbida, 'muddled,' like Aeschylus' ὄμμα ᾠνωμένον (Supp. 394), in keeping with the metaphor which follows from weighing in a balance.
6. elevet, 'makes light of,' suggesting the metaphor of a balance.
improbum, 'unfair,' 'not telling truth.' Not unlike is 'merces improbae,' Plaut. Rud. 374. [The trutina was a pair of scales for weighing large objects, 'aequa ponderum lances ... facta propter talenta et centenaria appendenda': Isid. Orig. 16. 25. 4. 'Ad ea probanda quae non aurificis statera, sed *populari* quadam *trutina* examinantur,' Cic. de Or. 2. 38. 'Examen' is the string which held the beam: 'filum medium quo trutinae statera regitur et lances aequantur,' Isid. 16. 25. 5: so the Scholia here: Serv. on Aen. 12. 725, Paulus, p. 80, Müller.]
7. The construction is 'Non accedas castigesque, nec quaesiveris extra te,' 'Nor ask any opinion but your own.'
8. Most MSS. insert 'est' before 'quis non,' the transcribers not seeing that Persius here breaks off what he afterwards completes in v. 121. The stolidity of Rome is treated as a secret, like the ass's ears of Midas, and kept till the end of the Satire, when it breaks out.

a, si fas, four MSS. and two others from a correction, most of the others 'ac,' a few 'at' or 'et,' none of which would be equally appropriate. 'If I might only say it—but I feel I *may*, when—.'
9. canitiem. The reproach of old age runs through the Satire, vv. 22, 26, 56; an unhonoured old age, produced partly by luxury (v. 56), partly by useless sedentary pursuits (here and v. 26), and instead of teaching wisdom, employing itself with corrupting the taste of youth (v. 79), and aping youthful sentimentalism. [Comp. perhaps Lucilius 15. 4 '*senium* atque insulse sophista.']
nostrum istud vivere triste. The austerity of affected morality, such as is lashed by Juvenal (S. 2), dreary fretting over study, and genuine peevishness. Persius is very fond of the use of the inf. as a regular subst. 'scire tuum' v. 27; 'ridere meum' v. 122; 'pappare minutum' 3. 17; 'mammae lallare' ib. 18; 'velle suum' 5. 53; 'sapere nostrum' 6. 38. [Wölfflin, in the Archiv für Lateinische Lexicographie, vol. iii. p. 70 foll., has a paper on the subject of the substantival infinitive, the results of which may be summed up as follows. There are no instances of the construction in Cicero's speeches, in Caesar, or in Livy, a fact which stamps it as colloquial; but (1) the infinitive is used as an accusative after prepositions in Cic. Fin. 2. c. 13 'inter optime valere et gravissime aegrotare': Hor. 2 S. 5. 69, 'praeter plorare': Ov. Her. 7. 164 'praeter amasse.' (2) The infinitive is used as a neuter substantive with a pronoun or an adjective in the colloquial Latin of the classical period, and gen-

muddle-headed Rome *does* make light of a thing, don't you be walking up and correcting the lying tongue in that balance of theirs, or asking any opinion but your own—for who is there at Rome that has not—if I *might* only say it! But surely I may, when I look at these gray hairs of ours, and this dreary way of living; and, in short, all our actions from the time of flinging our toys aside, when we take the tone of uncles and guardians. Yes, you must excuse me, *then*.'

F. No, I won't.

P. 'What am I to do? but I am constitutionally a great laugher, with a saucy spleen of my own.

---

erally in post-Augustan Latin, e.g. Plaut. Curc. 28 'tuom amare': Bacch. 158 'hic vereri perdidit': Cic. Att. 13. 21. 3 '*inhibere* illud tuum': 13. 28. 2 'cum vivere ipsum turpe sit nobis': Fam. 15. 15. 2 'ut ipsum vinci contemnerent': Brut. 37 'ipsum Latine loqui': De Or. 2. 6 'hoc ipsum nihil agere': Hor. 1 Ep. 7. 28 'reddes dulce loqui, reddes ridere decorum': Petronius 52 'meum enim intellegere nulla pecunia vendo': Pliny 7. 187 'ipsum cremare': Quint. 1. 1. 28 'scribere ipsum.' In Cicero's philosophical dialogues it is safer to assume that the construction is a conscious imitation of the Greek τό with inf. Fin. 1. 1 'totum hoc displicet philosophari': Tusc. 4. 20 'ipsum illud aemulari': *ib.* 5. 11 'totum hoc beate vivere': Parad. Stoicorum 3. 1. (20) 'ipsum illud peccare': Fin. 2. 27 'beate vivere vos in voluptate ponitis': 2. 6 'hoc non dolere': 3. 13 'sapere solum ipsum.' This passage of Persius and 'hoc ridere meum' v. 122 below are noticed as peculiar by Quint. 9. 3. 9, and Julius Rufinianus, p. 58. 10 (Halm). (3) The infinitive as a substantive with a genitive case is found in Val. Max. 7. 3. 7 'cuius non dimicare vincere fuit': Sen. Ep. 101. 13 'quid autem huius vivere est': Cons. ad Polyb. 16. 2 'hoc fuit eius lugere'; and in later Latin.]

10. aspicere ad, an archaism, used by Pacuvius and Plautus (Freund).

nucibus . . . relictis = Horace's 'abiectis nugis' (2 Ep. 2. 141). Catull. 61. 131 'Da nuces pueris, iners Concubine: satis diu Lusisti nucibus.' Hor. 2 S. 3. 171 'talos nucesque.' Suet. Aug. 83: talis aut ocellatis nucibusque ludebat cum pueris minutis.' Comp. the poem 'de Nuce,' also 3. 50. ['Tristis nucibus puer relictis' Martial 5. 84 1. See generally Servius on Virg. Ecl. 8. 30.]

11. cum, referring to 'nucibus relictis,' not in apposition to 'cum' preceding.

sapimus may have a double sense. The Romans probably acknowledged no such sharp distinction between the different meanings of the same word as we do, being less conscious and critical. 'Sapere' with acc. of the flavour or of the thing about which one is wise is common enough, and here 'patruos,' though a person, is equivalent to a thing, so that we may compare such expressions as 'Cyclopa moveri.' [Sorn, Der Sprachgebrauch des Satiriker Aulus Persius (Laibach, 1890), notices the following uses of intransitive verbs with cognate acc. in Persius: 'demorsos sapit ungues' 1. 106: 'oscitat hesternum' 3. 59: 'sonat vitium' 3. 21: 'plorabit verum' 1. 91: 'spirare surdum' 6. 35: 'dicenda tacendaque calles' 4. 5: 'solidum crepare' 5. 25: 'crassum ridere' 5. 190: 'mendosum tinnire' 5. 106: 'acre despuere' 4. 34: 'quid victuri sumus' 3. 67.]

patruos, 'patruae verbera linguae' Hor. 3 Od. 12. 3, 'ne sis patruus mihi' 2 S. 3. 88.

nolo is said by the friend, 'I won't admit the excuse,' 'tunc tunc ignoscite' being only another way of saying 'fas est tunc.'

12. quid faciam, etc., imitated from Hor. 2 S. 1. 24, who asks the same question, and appeals similarly to his temperament and tastes. Laughter was attributed to the spleen by the ancient

Scribimus inclusi, numeros ille, hic pede liber,
grande aliquid, quod pulmo animae praelargus anhelet.
scilicet haec populo pexusque togaque recenti   15
et natalicia tandem cum sardonyche albus
sede leges celsa, liquido cum plasmate guttur
mobile collueris, patranti fractus ocello.
hic neque more probo videas nec voce serena

[14. *quo a.*   15. *pexus (que* om.) *a.*   17. *legens a* C, Porphyr. Hor. 2 S. 2. 21.
               18. *fraetus a.*]

physiologists. Pliny 11. 205 'Sunt qui putent adimi simul risum homini, intemperantiamque eius constare lienis magnitudine.' Serenus Sammonicus 426 [Baehrens] ' Splen tumidus nocet, et risum tamen addit ineptum.'
12. '**petulantes** et petulci appellantur qui protervo impetu et crebro petunt laedendi alterius gratia' Fest. p. 206 Müll. [' Secundum physicos dicit, qui dicunt homines splene ridere, felle irasci, iecore amare, corde sapere.' Schol. = Isid. Orig. 11. 1. 127.]
cachinno, according to the Schol. a noun, like 'gluto' 5. 112, 'palpo' *ib.* 176. Lucilius appears to have been fond of words of this kind, no doubt as being in use among the common people, as 'lurco,' 'comedo,' 5. 29: 'conbibo' 26. 53, 'mando' Inc. 128, 'catillo' 28. 31. ['Comedo' also in Varro Modius fr. 13 Bücheler, 16 in Riese's ed. of the Saturarum Menippearum Reliquiae.] Hermann, following Heindorf, makes 'cachinno' a verb, taking ' ignoscite . . splene' as a parenthesis—'Excuse me, I am sorry to do it, but I cannot help my spleen;' but this would be awkward: and though 'cachinno,' as a noun, is found nowhere else, the evidence of the Schol. is enough to show that its existence was not thought impossible at the time when Latin was still a living language.
13–23. The attack begins. *P.* 'A composition is produced with intense labour. It is then recited in public by the author, dressed in holiday attire, with the most effeminate intonation; and the descendants of Romulus are tickled, and feel their passions excited. Shame that an old man like that should so disgrace himself!'
13. The form of the verse was possibly suggested by Hor. 2 Ep. 1. 117 ' Scribimus indocti,' etc.
inclusi points the satire—'a man shuts himself up for days and days, and this is the upshot.' Jahn compares Ov. Trist. 1. 1. 41 ' Carmina secessum scribentis et otia quaerunt.' Juv. 7. 28 ' Qui facis in parva sublimia carmina cella.' Markland ingeniously but needlessly conjectures ' inclusus numeris ille.'
pede liber opposed to 'numeros,' apparently = 'soluta oratio,' as no kind of verse could be well contrasted with ' numeri,' even Pindar's dithyrambics being considered ' numeri lege soluti.' The stress, however, is laid throughout the Satire on poetical recitations, as in Juv. S. 1 and 7; and rhetoric is merely introduced (v. 87) with reference to the courts of law. ' Pede liber '=' pede libero.'
14. **grande aliquid**, in apposition to ' numeros' and to the notion contained in 'pede liber.' ' Res grandes' v. 68, 'grande locuturi' 5. 7. ' Grandis' seems to have been a cant term at Rome in Persius' time. [Sen. Ep. 48. 11 ' Quid descenditis ab ingentibus promissis, et *grandia* locuti effecturos vos,' etc. ' *Grande aliquid* et par prioribus ' *ib.* 79. 7. ' *Aliquid grande* temptanti' *ib.* 114. 11.] Comp. 5. 10 ' Tu neque anhelanti, coquitur dum massa camino, Folle premis ventos.' Heinr. quotes Cic. de Or. 3. 11 ' Nolo verba exiliter animata exire, nolo inflata et *anhelata* gravius.'
quod pulmo, etc. 'for the purpose of mouthing it.' [Jahn, in his text of 1868, adopts ' quo' from *a*, and so Bücheler, 1886.]
praelargus, a rare word. ' Largus animae' occurs Stat. Theb. 3. 603 for prodigal of *life*, perhaps from Hor. 1

'We shut ourselves up and write, one verse, and another prose, all in the grand style to be panted forth by the lungs with a vast expenditure of breath. Yes—you hope to read this out some day, got up sprucely with a new toga, all in white with your birthday ring on at last, perched up on a high seat, after gargling your supple throat by a liquid process of tuning, with a languishing roll of your wanton eye. At this you may see great brawny sons

Od. 12. 37 'animaeque magnae prodigum.'
15. haec, emphatic. '*This* is what is to be delivered with pompous accompaniments and with effeminate articulation.' Compare 2. 15 '*haec* sancte ut poscas.'
populo, 'a public recitation.' 'Ventosae *plebis* suffragia' Hor. 1 Ep. 19. 37 'laetam cum fecit Statius *urbem* . . . tantaque libidine *vulgi* Auditur' Juv. 7. 83. 5. Horace elsewhere has '*populi* suffragia' (2 Ep. 2. 103).
pexus. 'Ille pexus pinguisque doctor' Quint. 1. 5. 14, or perhaps = 'pexis vestibus.' Hor. 1 Ep. 1. 95 'pexae tunicae.' [Sen. Ep. 115. 2 connects overcare in dress with an effeminate style in writing.]
16. The Schol. doubts whether the ring is called natalicia as a birthday present, or as worn on birthdays. Casaubon, who remarks, 'utro modo accipias pili non interest unius,' quotes Plaut. Curc. 656 'Hic est [anulus] quem ego tibi misi natali die;' Hor. 2 S. 2. 60 'Ille repotia, *natales*, aliosve dierum Festos *albatus* celebret,' which Persius seems to have had in view, supports the latter. Compare Juv. 1. 28 'aestivum aurum,' 7. 89 'semestri auro.' Rings were worn on occasions of public display. Juv. 7. 140 foll.
tandem, 'at last, when the "expectata dies" has come.'
sardonyche. 'Primus autem Romanorum sardonyche usus est Africanus prior . . et inde Romanis gemmae huius auctoritas' Plin. H. N. 37. 85, quoted by Mayor on Juv. 7. 144.
albus, 'obviously' = 'albatus,' Hor. l. c. The notion of paleness [suggested by the Schol. and Porphyrion on Hor. 2 S. 2. 21 and] adopted by Heinr., is here quite out of place.
17. leges . . collueris is probably the true reading, though all MSS. but two, one of the 11th century, have 'legens,' and a considerable majority 'colluerit.' Jahn remarks that the 2nd and 3rd persons are frequently interchanged in the MSS. of Persius. If 'legens' and 'colluerit' be adopted, a comma must be put after 'ocello.'
sede celsa, 'ex cathedra,' like a lecturer. Heinr. refers to Wyttenbach on Plut. 1, p. 375, for a similar description of the Greek rhetoricians.
liquido . . plasmate, 'modulation.' Gr. πλάττειν φωνήν. 'Sit autem imprimis lectio virilis . . . non in canticum dissoluta, nec *plasmate, ut nunc a plerisque fit, effeminata*' Quint. 1. 8. 2, quoted by Jahn, who compares 'liquido' with 'eliquat,' v. 35. Otherwise we might have followed the Scholiast's interpretation of a 'gargle,' as such a custom was undoubtedly in use on these occasions.
18. collueris explained by 'liquido,' the modulation having, as it were, the effect of rinsing the throat.
fractus = 'dissolutus.' Here 'fractus ocello' seems to be a translation of κλαδαρόμματος. The Greeks also talked of κεκλασμένη φωνή. ['Ρυθμὸς κεκλασμένος λόγῳ καὶ σεσοβημένος Longinus 41. 1. 'Illum (animum) non esse sincerum et habere aliquid *fracti*' Sen. Ep. 115. 2.] Compare too θρύπτεσθαι. 'Fragilis' is similarly used of effeminacy, Hor. 1. S. 8. 39. The meaning of patranti is doubted, but we shall probably be right in rendering it 'wanton.' ['*Patratio* est rei veneriae consummatio' Schol.]
19. hic is probably 'hereupon,' as in v. 32, where see note, though König explains it 'illo loco ubi recitatur.'
probus = 'pudicus,' with which it was constantly coupled. 'Saltare elegantius quam necesse est *probae*' Sall. Cat. 25.
serena = 'composita.'

8   PERSII

ingentis trepidare Titos, cum carmina lumbum   20
intrant, et tremulo scalpuntur ubi intima versu.
tun, vetule, auriculis alienis colligis escas,
auriculis, quibus et dicas cute perditus *ohe*?'
   Quo didicisse, nisi hoc fermentum et quae semel intus
innata est rupto iecore exierit caprificus?   25
   'En pallor seniumque! O mores! usque adeone
scire tuum nihil est, nisi te scire hoc sciat alter?'
   At pulchrum est digito monstrari et dicier *hic est!*
ten cirratorum centum dictata fuisse

[22. *tunc* C.   23. *perditosoai* a.   24. *qď* B *c.*   27. *sicire* a.   28. *sed bonum est* Priscian 1. p. 226, 342 Keil.]

20. **ingentis** . . Titos, like 'celsi Rhamnes' Hor. A. P. 342, only that 'ingentis' refers to the *physical* size of these sons of old Rome (like 'ingens Pulfennius' 5. 190, 'torosa iuventus' 3. 86, 'caloni alto' 5. 95), to show the monstrousness of the effeminacy to which they are surrendering themselves. [The Schol. say that 'titus' meant a wild pigeon. Bücheler, in the Archiv für Lateinische Lexicographie, compares the Sardinian word *tidu, tidone*, or *tudone*, = *columbaccio, palombo*, and Photius, Lex. p. 592 Porson, τιτίς, βραχὺ ὀρνίθιον.]
   trepidare like 'exsultat,' v. 82, 'they cannot keep their posture.' Virgil's 'stare loco nescit.'
   21. **tremulo** seems to express the movement of the line.
   22. **vetule**, note on v. 9. 'Do you lend yourself to pampering the ears of others?' Casaubon compares the Greek phrases εὐωχίαι and ἑστιάσεις ἀκοῶν.
   23. 'When, after all, you are sure to be tired before they are satisfied.' [Madvig, in the second volume of his Adversaria, conj. *articulis.*]
   cute perditus = 'cute perdita,' like 'pede liber' = 'pede libero.' It is variously explained. The early commentators seem divided between [three interpretations, 'emaciated by midnight study,' 'pale with old age,' 'so diseased as to show it even externally'], several of them quoting Juvenal's 'deformem pro cute pellem.' Casaubon, followed by Jahn, understands it as = dropsical, though he thinks it may denote cutaneous disease. König accepts neither view, but supposes the point intended to be inability to blush, however produced. Heinr. thinks it refers to the parched skin of high fever. May it mean, 'You will at least have to cry Hold when you burst'? [In support of the third explanation we may perhaps compare the language of Seneca, Ep. 122. 4, about people who feast all night and sleep all day: 'quippe suspectior illis quam morbo pallentibus color est: languidi evanidi albent, *et in vivis caro morticina est.*']
   ohe. Hor. 1 S. 5. 12; 2. 5. 96, in which latter passage the first syllable is short. [Ovink quotes Mart. 4. 89. 1, 'Ohe, iam satis est, ohe, libelle.']
   24–27. *F.* What is the good of study, unless a man brings out what he has in him? *P.* 'Hear the student! as if knowledge did no good to the possessor unless he were known to possess it!'
   24. **Quo** is read by a few MSS. Most of the others have 'quid,' which seems to make no sense. 'Quo tibi, Tilli, Sumere depositum clavum fierique tribuno?' Hor. 1 S. 6. 24.
   25. **iecore** seems to mean little more than the breast (like 'fibra,' v. 47; 5. 29). In 5. 129 it probably denotes the liver as the seat of passion, as in Hor. 1 Od. 13. 4.
   caprificus. 'Ad quae Discutienda valent sterilis mala robora fici' Juv. 10. 145. The harshness of the expression is probably Persius' own, not an attempt to ridicule the style he condemns.

of Rome all in a quiver, losing all decency of gesture and command of voice, as the strains glide into their very bones, and the marrow within is tickled by the ripple of the measure. What! an old man like you to become caterer for other men's ears—ears to which you will be fain to cry *Enough* at last when bursting yourself?'

F. What is the good of past study, unless this leaven—unless the wild fig-tree which has once struck its root into the breast break through and come out?

P. 'So much for pale looks and austerity! Alas for our national character! Is this knowing of yours so utterly of no account, unless some one else know that you are knowing?'

F. But it is a fine thing for men to point one out and say,

26. **pallor**, of study, v. 124; 3. 85; 5. 62.

senium. Hor. 1 Ep. 18. 47 'inhumanae senium depone Camenae.' Whether it refers here to actual old age or to moroseness may be doubted. Comp. note on v. 9. The latter is Horace's sense. 'Here is the true student character for you!' [Jahn (1868) gives 'En pallor seniumque' to the friend, and so Bücheler.]

O mores! Cicero's famous exclamation (Cat. 1. 1. 2; Verr. 4. 25. 56).

usque adeone. 'Usque adeone mori miserum est?' Virg. Aen. 12. 644. 'Usque adeo nihil est' Juv. 3. 84.

27. The Schol. quotes from Lucilius, 'Ut me scire volo dici mihi conscius si sum, Ne damnum faciam. Nescit, nisi alios id scire scierit;' ['"Moechum scire volo." "Dicemus, consciu' sum mi: at Ne damnum faciam, scire hoc sibi nesciat is me"' L. Müller, Lucilius, p. 141. Calvus, quoted by Quint. 6. 1. 12, 'factum ambitum scitis omnes, et hoc vos scire omnes sciunt.'] Suet. Ner. 20 says that Nero was fond of using a Greek proverb (Τῆς λανθανούσης μουσικῆς οὐδεὶς λόγος Gell. 13. 30. 3), 'occultae musicae nullum esse respectum,' as a reason for exhibiting his musical talents in public. [Δεῖ δὲ πᾶν οὕτω βλέπειν καὶ πράσσειν, ὥστε........ τὸ ἐκ τῆς περὶ ἑκάστων ἐπιστήμης αὐθαδὲς σώζεσθαι λανθάνον, οὐχὶ κρυπτόμενον M. Aurelius 10. 9.]

28–43. *F*. But the reputation! You may be 'canonized as a classic' by the aristocracy. *P.* 'To be sure: they talk poetry after dinner; an exquisite gets up and drawls out a poem: the illustrious audience applauds, and there is posthumous fame for you.' *F.* Snarl as you will, there *is* something in writing a poem that the world will not let die.

28. 'Quod monstror digito praetereuntium' Hor. 4 Od. 3. 22. So δακτυλοδεικτεῖν.

dicier, an archaism, like 'fallier' 3. 50.

hic est refers to the story of Demosthenes' elation at hearing a poor woman say Οὗτος ἐκεῖνος. Juv. 1. 161 imitates Persius. [Mart. 5. 13. 3 'sed toto legor orbe frequens, et dicitur *Hic est*.']

29. Hor. 1 Ep. 20. 17 gives the contemptuous side of the picture, 'Hoc quoque te manet ut pueros elementa docentem Occupet extremis in vicis balba senectus.' (Comp. Juv. 7. 226.) Persius takes not only higher schools but higher lessons, 'dictata' being passages from the poets read out by the master (for want of books) and repeated by the boys. 'Sic iterat voces, et verba cadentia tollit, Ut puerum saevo credas dictata magistro Reddere' Hor. 1 Ep. 18. 12. In 1 S. 10. 74, Horace asks 'An tua demens Vilibus in ludis dictari carmina malis?' as if such popularity were an actual evil, and proved that the poet had not sought to please the few. Statius thinks differently, saying triumphantly of his Thebaid (Theb. 12. 815)

pro nihilo pendas?

      'Ecce inter pocula quaerunt   30
Romulidae saturi, quid dia poemata narrent.
hic aliquis, cui circa umeros hyacinthia laena est,
rancidulum quiddam balba de nare locutus,
Phyllidas Hypsipylas, vatum et plorabile si quid,
eliquat ac tenero supplantat verba palato.   35
adsensere viri: nunc non cinis ille poetae
felix? non levior cippus nunc inprimit ossa?
laudant convivae: nunc non e manibus illis,
nunc non e tumulo fortunataque favilla
nascentur violae?'

[30. *pendes* C. 31. *satuli* a. *quis*...*narret* a. 32. *circum* C. 34. *vanum* C.
 aut pro *et* Eutyches p. 480 Keil. *prorabile* a. *quis* C. 36. *illi* a.
  37. *cipus* B. 38. *de* B. 39. *et* a.]

'Itala iam studio discit memoratque iuventus.'

29. **cirratorum** apparently denotes no more than 'puerorum.' Jahn cites Mart. 9. 30. 7 'Matutini *cirrata* caterva magistri,' and mentions that in the representation of a school at Pompeii the boys wear their hair long. [So they are called 'capillati' Mart. 10. 62. 2.] But the descriptive epithet naturally points to boys of the better classes.

30. **Ecce** introduces a narrative in the heroic style.

inter pocula. 'Inter vina' 3. 100, 'inter scyphos' Cic. Fam. 7. 22, 'media inter pocula' Juv. 8. 217; 'in poculis' is used similarly Cic. Sen. 14: 'during drinking,' 'over the wine,' rather than 'in the intervals of drinking.' Persius probably mistakes Hor. 2 S. 2. 4 'Discite, non *inter* lances mensasque nitentes,' as the thing satirized is the wretched dilettante conception of literature as an accompaniment to a dining-table; and so in the next line, 'saturi' is strongly contrasted with Horace's '*impransi* disquirite.'

31. **Romulidae**, like 'Titi,' v. 20.

quid .. narrent, a phrase, 'What is the news?' Plaut. Pers. 498 'quid istaec (tabellae) narrant?' referring probably to the subject-matter of the poems—'What are they about?' 'What have they to tell us?' Nebrissensis rightly explains 'quid dicant et contineant.' The rest of the commentators and the Schol. apparently take 'dia poemata' as the acc. after 'narrent' = 'recitent.' ['Dius' a rare and in this context an affected word.]

32. **hic**, 'hereupon,' 'extremely seldom,' says Freund, referring to Ter. And. 389, Virg. Aen. 1. 728; but in Virgil, at any rate, it is not unfrequent: see Aen. 2. 122, 533; 3. 369, etc. 'Hic aliquis' occurs again, 3. 77. The use of the 'laena' for the 'toga' was a mark of luxury. 'Coccina laena' Juv. 3. 283. Jahn. So of Aeneas, Virg. Aen. 4. 262 'Tyrio ardebat murice laena Demissa ex umeris.' Robes of the colour of the 'suave rubens hyacinthus' are mentioned by Athenaeus 12, p. 525 D. Jahn.

33. **rancidulum.** 'Rancide ficta verba' Gell. 18. 11. 2, like 'putidus,' 'mawkish.' The diminution, of course, heightens the contempt. [Diminutives are common in colloquial Latin. Van Wageningen notices the following in Persius: (1) adjectives: 'horridulus' 1. 54; 'beatulus' 3. 103; 'rubellus' 5. 147; 'vetulus' 1. 22. (2) substantives: 'ocellus' 1. 18; 'auricula' 1. 22; 'aqualiculus' 1. 57; 'popellus' 4. 15; 'elegidia' 1. 51; 'canicula' 3. 49; 'pellicula' 5. 116; 'plebecula' 4. 6; 'cuticula' 4. 18; 'seriola' 4. 29; 'tesserula' 5. 74.]

balba de nare, 'lisping and snuf-

'There he goes!' Do you mean to say that you don't care to become the dictation-lesson of one hundred curly-headed urchins?

'Listen. The sons of Rome are sitting after a full meal and enquiring in their cups, What news from the divine world of poesy? Hereupon a personage with a hyacinth-coloured mantle over his shoulders brings out some mawkish trash or other with a snuffle and a lisp, something about Phyllises or Hypsipyles, or any of the many heroines over whom poets have snivelled, filtering out his tones, and tripping up the words against the roof of his delicate mouth. The heroes have expressed approval—now is not the poet happy in his grave? Now does not the stone press on his bones more lightly? The humbler guests follow with their applause—now will not a crop of violets spring up from those remains of his—from the sod of his tomb, and from the ashes so highly blest?'

fling.' The former at least implies an affectation of tenderness. 'Cum balba feris annoso verba palato' Hor. 2 S. 3. 274, which Persius had in view, as appears from v. 35.

34. **Phyllidas**, plural indicative of contempt. Χρυσηΐδων μείλιγμα τῶν ὑπ' Ἰλίῳ Aesch. Ag. 1439. Sentimental subjects from mythology, such as those celebrated by Ovid in his Heroides.

vatum et plorabile si quid. Casaubon and Jahn compare Claud. Eutrop. 1. 261 'verbisque sonat plorabile quiddam Ultra nequitiam fractis.' These accusatives are constructed with 'locutus,' not with 'eliquat.'

35. **eliquat**, 'strains' or 'filters.' A natural extension of the metaphor which calls a voice 'liquid.' Comp. 'collueris' v. 18. Heinr. and Jahn compare Apul. Flor. 15. 54 'Canticum videtur ore tereti semihiantibus in conatu labellis *eliquare*.'

supplantat. A word from wrestling or running, translated from Greek ὑποσκελίζω, as would seem from Non. 36. 4 '*Supplantare* dictum est pedem supponere:' Lucilius, 'supplantare aiunt Graeci,' so that Persius must have had Lucilius in his view. 'Trips up his words,' i. e. minces them. Comp. Horace, referred to on v. 33. ['Immutatis accentibus curtat' Schol.]

36. **adsensere viri** is in the heroic strain, like Juvenal, 'consedere duces' 7. 115. Jahn compares Virg. Aen. 2.

130 'adsensere omnes' Ov. M. 9. 259; 14. 592 'adsensere dei.' For the effect of praise after death on the bones of the deceased, comp. Virg. E. 10. 33 'O mihi tum quam molliter ossa quiescant, Vestra meos olim si fistula dicat amores!' (quoted also by Casaubon). ['Veteres dixerunt praegravari corpora eorum qui corpori tantum studentes nihil memorabile reliquerunt' Schol.]

37. **cippus**, 'a pillar.' Hor. 1 S. 8. 12. The formula S. T. T. L. ('sit tibi terra levis') was frequently engraved on the pillar.

38. **convivae**, as in Hor. 1 S. 10. 80, 1 Ep. 13. 15; Juv. 7. 74; 9. 10, most of which Jahn compares; the inferior guests as distinguished from 'viri,' the great men who sit with the giver of the feast. We must suppose a large entertainment, at which there is a recitation, not of the patron's verses, but of those of some deceased poet whom he admires. **laudant** may be meant to be stronger than 'adsensere,' as the humbler sort would be less measured in their approbation.

manibus. Jahn compares Prop. 2. 13. 31 'Deinde ubi suppositus *cinerem* me fecerit ardor, Accipiat *manes* parvula testa meos,' and the use of 'cineribus' in inscriptions as synonymous with 'Dis manibus.' So also Virg. Aen. 4. 34 'Id cinerem aut manes credis curare sepultos?'

39. **fortunata favilla** = 'felix cinis.'

Rides, ait, et nimis uncis 40
naribus indulges. an erit qui velle recuset
os populi meruisse et cedro digna locutus .
linquere nec scombros metuentia carmina nec tus?
'Quisquis es, o, modo quem ex adverso dicere feci,
non ego cum scribo, si forte quid aptius exit, 45
quando hoc rara avis est, si quid tamen aptius exit,
laudari metuam, neque enim mihi cornea fibra est;
sed recti finemque extremumque esse recuso
euge tuum et belle. nam belle hoc excute totum:
quid non intus habet? non hic est Ilias Atti 50
ebria veratro? non si qua elegidia crudi .

[40. *ast a.* 42. *hos a.* 44. *dicere fas est a.* 45. *conscribo a.* vv. 46, 47 invert. a. 46. *haec* ς. 47. *mihi* om. a. 51. *sique legidia a.*]

40. König refers to a Greek inscription [fragm. adesp. 705, in Jacobs' Anthologia Graeca] ἀλλ' ἴα καὶ σάμψυχα καὶ ὑδατίνη νάρκισσος, Οὐείβιε, καὶ περὶ σοῦ πάντα γένοιτο ῥόδα. The friend interrupts, telling Persius that this is mere buffoonery, which leaves the reason of the case untouched. [Van Wageningen quotes the expression 'dies violaris,' the day when violets were offered at tombs, from Fabretti Inscr. 443, 724.]
Rides, ait is from Hor. 1 Ep. 19. 43.
nimis with 'indulges.' Uncis naribus is Horace's 'naso adunco,' 'naribus' being probably used to give an additional notion of fastidiousness, like 'acutis naribus' Hor. 1 S. 3. 29, where Bentley suspects 'aduncis,' though 'acutis' is evidently opposed to another expression of Horace, 'naris obesae.' 'Naribus uti' Hor. 1 Ep. 19. 45.
41. velle recuset. 'Recusem minui senio' 6. 15. Jahn. 'Will you find any man to disclaim the desire of deservedly becoming a household name?'
42. 'In ore esse' or 'in ora venire,' 'abire,' etc. was a phrase: comp. 'volito vivus per ora virum' Enn. ap. Cic. Tusc. 1. 15. 34, imitated by Virg. G. 3. 9. 'Romana brevi venturus in ora' Hor. 1 E. 3. 9. For the use of the perf. inf. Jahn comp. vv. 91, 132; 2. 66; 4. 7, 17; 5. 33; 6. 3, 17, 77.
cedro, 'cedar oil.' 'Linenda cedro' Hor. A. P. 332. Persius probably imitated Virg. Aen. 6. 662 'Phoebo digna locuti.'
43. scombros, 'mackerel,' is an image borrowed from Catull. 95. 7 'Volusi annales Paduam morientur ad ipsam, Et laxas *scombris* saepe dabunt tunicas,' as tus is from Hor. 2 Ep. 1. 269 'Deferar in vicum vendentem tus et odores Et piper et quicquid chartis amicitur ineptis.' [Bieger comp. Mart. 3. 50. 9, 4. 86. 3 'quod si non scombris scelerata poemata donas': 'nec scombris tunicas dabis molestas.' Add *ib.* 3. 2. 5 'vel turis piperisve sis cucullus.']
44-62. *Persius.* 'I quite admit the value of honest praise well deserved. I should not be human if I did not feel it; but I protest against measuring excellence by this fashionable standard of yours—a standard which accommodates itself to trash like Labeo's and all the mawkish stuff which great folks write when they ought to be digesting their dinners. The praise given in your circles is not disinterested—it is simply payment for patronage received. You are not blessed with the eyes of Janus—so you will need pains to discriminate between what is said to your face and what is said behind your back.'
44. Persius is disputing not with any definite antagonist, but with the spirit of the age, as Passow and Jahn remark.
modo, 'just now,' referring especially to v. 40, and generally to the whole preceding part.

F. Ah, you are laughing (says he) and letting your nostrils curl more than they should. Will you ever find a bard who will disown the wish to earn a place in the mouths of men, to deliver utterances worthy of cedar oil, and leave behind him poems which need not fear the contact of mackerel or spices?

P. 'Whoever you are, my imaginary opponent, I am not the man if in writing I chance to hatch anything good—for that is a phoenix indeed—but if I *do* hatch anything good, I am not the man to shrink from praise—no—my heartstrings are not of horn. But I utterly deny that the be-all and end-all of excellence is your Bravo and Exquisite—for just sift this Exquisite to the bottom, and what do you not find there? Is there not Attius' Iliad dead-drunk with hellebore? Are there not all the sweet little love poems ever dictated by persons of quality after their meals—in a word,

---

45. [Cic. Planc. 14 'et quia, ut fit in multis, *exit* aliquando aliquid si non perfacetum, attamen fortasse non rusticum': Quint. 12. 10. 26 'et si quid numeris *exierit* aptius (fortasse non possit, sed tamen si quid exierit' . . .)] **exit** probably has a double reference—to a vessel turned out by the potter, as Hor. A. P. 22 'urceus exit,' and to a bird hatched from an egg, Plin. 10. 38 'exire de ovo a cauda,' as 'rara avis' seems to show.

46. **quando** used as 'since' only in poetry and post-Aug. prose. Freund. [But Madvig on Cic. Fin. 5. 8. 21, 23. 67 allows it in Cicero.]

rara avis, seemingly a proverbial expression, imitated by Juv. 6. 165. Jerome adv. Jovin. t. 1. 4. 2, p. 190 Ben. (Jahn). 'A black swan' Juv. l. c.; 'a white crow' ib. 7. 200.

47. **cornea** is applied by Pliny (31. 102) as an epithet to the bodies of fishermen; [comp. also his observation 7. 81, 'quibus natura concreta sunt ossa, qui sunt rari admodum, *cornei* vocantur.'] Heinr. and Jahn refer to Sidon. Apoll. Epp. 4. 1; 8. 11. The Stoics, as Casaubon shows, did not altogether exclude fame from consideration, but regarded it as one of the ἀδιάφορα which were προηγμένα: they however differed among themselves as to whether it was desirable for its own sake or for any advantage which it might bring, Chrysippus taking the latter view.

fibra, 5. 29.

48. **finemque extremumque**, 'the standard and limit.' Jahn comp. Cic. Fin. 2. 2. 5 'Nam hunc ipsum sive *finem*, sive *extremum*, sive ultimum definiebas id esse quo omnia, quae recte fierent, referrentur.'

recusare, with an object-clause not common. 'Maxime vero quaestum esse manipretio vitae recusabant' Plin. 29. 16.

49. **euge tuum et belle**. Like 'suum χαῖρε' Prol. 8. Hor. A. P. 428, a passage which Persius had in view, makes the 'derisor' exclaim 'Pulchre, bene, recte.' [Cic. de Or. 3. 26 'quae *bene* et *praeclare* nobis saepe dicatur; *belle* et *festive* nimium saepe nolo.' Mart. 2. 7. 1 'Declamas belle, causas agis, Attice, belle . . . . Nil bene cum facias, facias tamen omnia belle, Vis dicam quid sis?' So that even 'belle' is a doubtful compliment.]

excute, 5. 22 'Excutienda damus praecordia.' Met. from shaking out the folds of a robe. 'Excutedum pallium' Plaut. Aul. 646. ['Nemo nostrum quid veri esset *excussit*' Sen. Ep. 110. 5.]

50. 'What rubbish does it not contain?' 'What is there not room for in it?' **Atti** 'Labeonis,' v. 4 note.

51. **veratrum** was the Latin name for hellebore. 'Nobis veratrum est acre venenum' Lucr. 4. 640. Hellebore was taken, according to Pliny (25. 51), not only to cure madness, but to clear the heads of students. Thus it will satirize the artificial helps used for study, as well as the madness which requires deep and intoxicating draughts of hellebore to cure it.

dictarunt proceres? non quidquid denique lectis
scribitur in citreis? calidum scis ponere sumen,
scis comitem horridulum trita donare lacerna,
et 'verum' inquis 'amo: verum mihi dicite de me.' 55
qui pote? vis dicam? nugaris, cum tibi, calve,
pinguis aqualiculus protenso sesquipede extet.
o Iane, a tergo quem nulla ciconia pinsit,
nec manus auriculas imitari mobilis albas,
nec linguae, quantum sitiat canis Apula, tantum! 60
vos, o patricius sanguis, quos vivere fas est
occipiti caeco, posticae occurrite sannae!

[53. *cereis* a.   54. *trito* a.   *laconna* a.   56. *nugares* fragm. Bob.   57. *protenso* fragm. Bob. a. Hieron. adv. Jovin. 2. t. 4. 2, p. 214 Ben. *propenso* C. *protento* Priscian 1 p. 251 Keil.   *exitet* fragm. Bob.   58. *pincsit* a. 'Est apud Persium ambiguum *a tergo ciconia pisat* an *pinsit* legendum sit' Diomedes p. 373 Keil. 59. *imitata est* a.   60. *linquae* fragm. Bob. *tantae* fragm. Bob. a C.   61. *bivere* fragm. Bob.   *ius est* C.]

51. **elegidia**, a contemptuous diminutive; [see note on v. 33.] 'Exiguos elegos' Hor. A. P. 77. Comp. Juv. 1. 4.

crudi. 'Crudi tumidique lavemur' Hor. 1 Ep. 6. 61.

52. Jahn comp. Hor. 2 Ep. 1. 109 'pueri patresque severi Fronde comas vincti cenant et carmina dictant.'

53. For writing in a recumbent posture, comp. Prop. 3. 6. 14 'Scriniaque ad lecti clausa iacere pedes.' Augustus retired after supper to his 'lecticula lucubratoria' Suet. Aug. 78. The rich man in Juvenal (3. 241) reads or writes in his litter.

citreis. Citron wood, used for couches here, as for tables Cic. Verr. 4. 37.

ponere. [Varro Res Rust. 3. 6. 6 'primus pavones Q. Hortensius . . . posuisse dicitur.'] 3. 111 'positum est algente catino Durum holus,' 6. 23 'rhombos libertis ponere lautus.' Imitated from Hor. A.. P. 422 'unctum recte qui ponere possit' the thought in the two passages being the same.

sumen. 'Vulva nil pulchrius ampla' Hor. 1 E. 15. 41. ['Altilia et sumina leporemque' Petronius 36. According to Pliny 8. 209, it was Publilius Syrus who first used the word 'sumen' in this sense.] Comp. Juv. 11. 138. For the custom of entertaining clients that they might applaud their host's poetry, comp. Hor. 1 Ep. 19. 37 'Non ego ventosae plebis suffragia venor *Impensis cenarum et tritae munere vestis.*'

54. Hor. l. c. Juvenal (1. 93) imitates this passage 'horrenti tunicam non reddere servo,' though with a different meaning, as he is thinking of a master's duty to clothe his slaves.

comitem, as in Juv. 1. 46. 119, etc.

horridulum, dimin. expressing inferiority; [see on v. 33.]

55. Casaubon comp. Plaut. Most. 181, where a girl questions her waitingmaid about her beauty, saying, 'Ego verum amo, verum volo dici mihi, mendacem odi.' Jahn comp. Mart. 8. 76 'Dic verum mihi, Marce, dic amabo: Nil est quod magis audiam libenter . . . Vero verius ergo, quid sit, audi: Verum, Gallice, non libenter audis.'

dicite, Jahn, from the majority of MSS., instead of 'dicito.' The host seems to be addressing his dependants *en masse.*

56. **qui pote**, supply probably 'sunt verum dicere.' 'Pote' seems rather an abbreviated form of 'potis,' which is itself of all genders and both numbers, than a neuter, as is shown by such passages as Prop. 4. 7. 9 'Et mater non iusta piae dare debita terrae, Nec *pote* cognatos inter humare rogos.' 's' is elided before a consonant, and 'i' con-

all the verse that is produced on couches of citron? You know how to serve up a sow's paunch smoking hot—you know how to present a poor shivering dependant with a cast-off cloak—and you say, 'Truth is my idol—pray tell me Truth about myself.' Truth—how can you expect to hear it? Well, will you have it, then? You're a twaddler, you old baldpate, with your bloated stomach projecting a good half yard before you. O lucky Janus, never to have a stork's bill pecking at you behind—or a hand that can imitate by its motion a donkey's white ears, or a length of tongue protruded like an Apulian dog's in the dog-days! But you, my aristocratic friends, whom Nature has ordained to live with no eyes behind you, turn round and face this back-stairs gibing.

sequently becomes 'e,' as the final 'i' in Latin would not be short. So 'magis' and 'mage.'

nugari is used elsewhere, as in Hor. 2 Ep. 1. 93, for graceful trifling in art and literature; here it has the force of the bitterest contempt—'You are a wretched dilettante.'

calve, note on v. 9.

57. aqualiculus is used by Sen. Ep. 90. 22 for the ventricle or ulterior stomach—'Cibus cum pervenit in ventrem, aqualiculi fervore coquitur.' The transference to the exterior stomach or paunch is probably Persius' own. The Schol. and Isidorus (Orig. 11. 1. 136) say that it is properly a pig's stomach. ['*Aqualiculum* ventriculum,' Gloss. Vat. p. 19. 35 G.]

The sentiment, as the Scholia say, is the same as that of the Greek proverb, quoted by Galen 5. p. 878 K, παχεῖα γαστὴρ λεπτὸν οὐ τίκτει νόον, probably with the additional notion that the would-be poet is a bloated debauchee, 'pinguis vitiis albusque' (Hor. 2 S. 2. 21).

58. These three ways of making game of a person behind his back appear to be mentioned nowhere else, except in an imitation by Jerome, though the second, the imitation of an ass's ear, is still common in Italy.

ciconia. The fingers seem, according to the Schol., to have been tapped against the lower part of the hand, so as to imitate the appearance and the sound of a stork's bill. Jerome, however (E. 4. t. 4, 2. p. 776 Ben.) has 'ciconiarum deprehendes post te colla curvari.'

pinsit is explained by the Schol., (who makes it the perf. of a supposed 'pindo,') 'assidue percussit.' Whether it denotes simply the effect of the mockery, like 'vellicare,' or anything in the manner of it, is not clear. Plaut. Merc. 416 has 'pinsere flagro.'

59. imitari mobilis, like 'artifex sequi' Prol. 11.

albas distinguishes the ears as belonging to an ass. Ov. Met. 11. 174 says of the transformation of Midas, 'Delius aures . . . villisque *albentibus* implet Instabilesque imo (*al.* illas) facit, et dat posse moveri,' which Persius may have thought of, comp. v. 121 (Nebr.), and the choice of the epithet is quite in the manner of Persius, so that we need not embrace the reading of one MS. 'altas.'

60. sitiat, where a prose writer would have said 'sitiens protendat.' Britannicus says, 'deest *cum*, ut sit *cum sitiet*.'

The drought of Apulia is a familiar image from Hor. Epod. 3. 16 'siticulosae Apuliae.'

Jahn reads tantae with the best MSS.; but 'tantum,' which is supported by most copies, is much neater, and 'tantae' may have been introduced, carelessly or intentionally, in order to agree with 'linguae.'

61. Hor. A. P. 291 'Vos, O Pompilius sanguis.' 'Whom Providence has ordained to live.'

62. Sall. Jug. 107 calls the back 'nudum et caecum corpus.'

posticus generally used of a building.

occurrite, 'turn round and face.'

sanna, 5. 91. Gr. μῶκος or μυκτηρισμός. 'Sannio' is a character in Terence, 'a buffoon.' The general sense

'Quis populi sermo est?' quis enim, nisi carmina molli
nunc demum numero fluere, ut per leve severos
ecfundat iunctura unguis? scit tendere versum 65
non secus ac si oculo rubricam derigat uno;
sive opus in mores, in luxum, in prandia regum
dicere, res grandis nostro dat Musa poetae...
'Ecce modo heroas sensus adferre videmus
nugari solitos graece, nec ponere lucum 70
artifices nec rus saturum laudare, ubi corbes
et focus et porci et fumosa Palilia faeno,

[64. *lebe* fragm. Bob. *severo* fragm. Bob. 65. *et fundat* fragm. Bob. *vaesis* fragm. Bob. 66. *dirigat* fragm. Bob. 69. *heroos* ϛ. *docemus* fragm. Bob. *docemus* vel *videmus* C. 70. *Graeci* fragm. Bob. 72. *fumusa* fragm. Bob.]

is equivalent to Hor. A. P. 436 'si carmina condes, Nunquam te fallant animi sub vulpe latentes.'

63–68. Persius resumes his description —'What is the opinion of the public?' asks the patron. 'Oh! they say, we *have* got a poet at last, able to write smoothly, and equal to any kind of composition.'

63. The rich man addresses his dependants, as in v. 55.

populi, note on v. 15.

enim, used in an answer to a question. Plaut. Poen. 854 'Quomodo? Ut enim, ubi mihi vapulandum est, tu corium sufferas.' 'What? Why, what should it be, but.'

64. nunc demum, 'now at last, the coming poet *has* come.'

numero, sing., 'like in numerum'. Lucr. 2. 630. 'Arma *gravi numero* violentaque bella parabam Edere' Ov. 1 Am. 1. 1.

per leve, imitated from Hor. 2 S. 7. 86 'teres atque rotundus, Externi ne quid valeat *per leve* morari.' The image is that of a polished surface which the nail could run along without being stopped. Whether the image is the same in Horace's 'factus ad unguem' (1 S. 5. 32), 'castigavit ad unguem' (A. P. 294), is not clear. Jahn in the latter passage would derive it from a workman moulding images in wax or clay (comp. Juv. 7. 237, Pers. 5. 39), quoting from Plut. Symp. Qu. 2. p. 636 ὅταν ἐν ὄνυχι ὁ πηλὸς γένηται. Orelli on Hor. 1 S. 5, 32 quotes Columella 11. 2, 13 'materiam dolare ad unguem.' We need not think of any 'iunctura' as actually existing in the thing to which the verses are compared. Persius merely says that the verses are turned out so smooth, that there is no break or sense of transition from one foot to another.

65. ecfundat, stronger than 'sinat perlabi.' ['*Ecfundi* verba. non *figi*' of a flowing style, Sen. Ep. 100. 1. The spelling 'ecfundat' is from the reading of fragm. Bob. 'et fundat.']

tendere refers to the length and completeness of the verse. 'He can make his verses as straight as a mason's line.'

66. The mason shuts one eye to make sure of getting the line straight. König comp. Lucian. Icaromenipp. 14 ἐπεὶ καὶ τοὺς τέκτονας πολλάκις ἑωράκεναι μοι δοκῶ θατέρῳ τῶν ὀφθαλμῶν ἄμεινον πρὸς τοὺς κανόνας ἀπευθύνοντας τὰ ξύλα. The 'rubrica' or ruddled cord was stretched along the wood or stone, jerked in the middle, and let go.

67. 'He is equally great too in satire.'

sive in the sense of 'vel si' without 'si' preceding. See Freund in v. [Van Wageningen would read 'etsi.'] In with the 'acc.' may mean simply 'upon;' but the expressions 'in mores,' 'in luxum' seem to show it means 'against.' To describe the rich poet as a satirist himself gives the finishing touch to the picture.

mores, v. 26.

prandia regum, then will be 'the feasts of the great,' 'reges' having a peculiar signification in the mouth of

'What does the town say?' What *should* it say—but that now at last we have verses which flow in smooth measure, so that the critical nail runs glibly along even where the parts join. He can make a long straight line, just as if he were ruling it with a ruddle cord, with one eye shut. Whatever the subject—the character of the age, its luxurious habits, the banquets of the great, the Muse is sure to inspire our poet with the grand style.

'Yes—lo and behold! we now see heroic sentiments heralded forth by men who used merely to dabble in Greek, not artists enough to describe a grove or to eulogise the plenty of a country life, with all its details, baskets, and a turf-fire, and pigs, and the smoking hay on dependants, as in Hor. 1 Ep. 7. 33; 17. 43; A. P. 434; Juv. 1. 136; 5. 161; 8. 161 (Hor. 2 S. 2. 45 'epulis regum.') 'Public entertainments given by the great' were common at Rome, and called 'prandia,' Suet. Jul. 38; Tib. 20, and possibly these may be referred to as a further stroke of irony.

68. res grandis = 'grandia.' 'Bene mirae eritis res' v. 111. 'grandis' expresses the literary quality, which is the great object of ambition: see on v. 14.

69-82. Persius drops his irony, and talks in his own person. 'Every kind of composition! Yes, we now see heroics written by men who cannot compose a simple rural piece without introducing some heterogeneous jumble. Then there is the mania for archaisms—the affectation of studying the old poets—as if anything but corrupt taste and relaxed morality would be the result!'

69. modo, apparently referring to time *just* past, and so nearly = 'nunc.' 'Modo dolores (mea tu) occipiunt' Ter. Ad. 289, where Donatus says, 'Evidenter hic *modo* temporis praesentis adverbium est.'

heroas, used as an adjective. 'Heroas manus' Prop. 2. 1. 18 (Jahn).

sensus, 'thoughts' or 'sentiments.' 'Communes sensus' is used by Tac. Or. 31 for 'common places.' ['Inconditi sensus' *ib.* 21 : 'sensus audaces et fidem egressi' Sen. Ep. 114. 1. The usage is also common in Quintilian.] An antithesis is intended between 'heroas sensus' and 'nugari.'

adferre probably in the sense of 'bringing news.' 'Attulerunt quieta omnia apud Gallos esse' Livy 6. 31. Comp. 'narrent' v. 31. For 'videmus' Casaubon and Heinr. adopt 'docemus' [see critical note], supposing that Persius is speaking of the compositions of boys at school; but there seems no reason to believe that education is referred to before v. 79.

70. nugari, v. 56 note. 'Who used to confine themselves to dilettante efforts in Greek.' Hor. 1 S. 10. 31 tells us how he once tried composing in Greek.

ponere artifices, like 'artifex sequi' Prol. 11.

ponere. Prop. 2. 3. 42 'Hic dominam exemplo *ponat in arte* meam,' and Paley's note. 'Sollers nunc hominem *ponere*, nunc deum' Hor. 4 Od. 8. 8, which perhaps Persius imitated. ['*Pone* Tigellinum' Juv. 1. 155, where Mayor quotes Ov. A. A. 3. 401 'si Venerem Cous nunquam *posuisset* Apelles.']

lucum is one of the commonplaces instanced by Hor. A. P. 16, who evidently intends a description of scenery, not, as Juv. 1. 7, a mythological picture.

71. saturum, 'fertile.' '*Saturi* petito longinqua Tarenti' Virg. G. 2. 197.

laudare, 'to eulogize.' Hor. 1 Od. 7. 1 'Laudabunt alii claram Rhodon aut Mitylenen.'

corbes, part of the farm furniture—baskets for gathering fruits. Cato R. R. 136. Varro R. R. 1. 50. 1 (Freund). Since Wordsworth, there would be nothing incongruous in introducing these details (except perhaps the pigs) into a poem of country life; but though he may have done service in breaking down the rule of conventional description, it does not follow that poets in Persius' time were justified in offending against the taste of their day, as in them it probably argued a want of perception of any kind of propriety in writing, whether great or small.

72. focus. Casaubon refers to Virg.

unde Remus, sulcoque terens dentalia, Quinti,
quem trepida ante boves dictatorem induit uxor
et tua aratra domum lictor tulit—euge poeta! 75
'Est nunc Brisaei quem venosus liber Atti,
sunt quos Pacuviusque et verrucosa moretur
Antiope, aerumnis cor luctificabile fulta.

[73. *sulcosque* fragm. Bob. *dentialia* C, *dentilia* c. 74. *quem* ... *dictatorem* fragm. Bob. α C : *cum* aut *cui* ς. *dictaturam* C. 'Quintius Cincinnatus *cum* suum agrum araret et sereret, *dictatura* ei a populo Romano delata est' Schol. unde lectiones *cum* et *dictaturam* ortae videntur.   76. *Acci* fragm. Bob.   77. *Pacuius* fragm. Bob.   78. *Antiope* fragm. Bob., *Antiopa* a C.]

E. 5. 69, 7. 49, to which add G. 2. 528. We may observe that, in E. 7. 49, the only place where sitting round the fire is *dwelt* on, Virgil implicitly condemns the choice of the subject by putting it into the mouth of Thyrsis, in contrast to Corydon's description of summer and out-door life.

72. **fumosa Palilia faeno**. Compare Prop. 4. 4. 73–78 'Urbi festus erat : dixere Palilia patres : Hic primus coepit moenibus esse dies : Annua pastorum convivia, lusus in urbe, Cum pagana madent fercula deliciis, Cumque *super raros faeni flammantis acervos Traicit immundos ebria turba pedes.*' ['Varro sic ait: *Palilia tam privata quam publica sunt, et est genus hilaritatis et lusus apud rusticos, ut congestis cum faeno stipulis ignem magnum transiliant, quod Pali faciunt eam se expiare credentes.*' Schol.]

73. The poet appears to have introduced a reference to the rural glories of Roman history. Remus is introduced partly on account of the 'Palilia,' which were on the anniversary of the foundation of Rome (Prop. l. c.), partly as having himself led a country life, 'Hanc olim veteres vitam coluere Sabini, Hanc *Remus* et frater' Virg. G. 2. 533. This seems better than to understand 'unde' 'after these antecedents he comes to write of Remus.'

sulcoque terens dentalia. Perhaps imitated from Virg. Aen. 6. 844, 'vel te sulco, Serrane, serentem.' Compare also G. 1. 46 '*sulco attritus* splendescere vomer.'

dentalia, 'share-beams.' G. 1. 172 note.

For the story of L. Quinctius Cincinnatus, see Livy 3. 26. For the change from the third person to the second, comp. Virg. Aen. 7. 684 'quos dives Anagnia pascit, Quos, Amasene pater.'

74. [Conington read 'cum,' but the best MSS. decidedly support 'quem': see critical note.] Casaubon remarks that 'cum' is better than 'quem,' as fixing the time of the investiture, in connexion with 'terens.'

75. The contrast is heightened by making the lictor act as a farm-servant. Persius hurries over the particulars, so as to increase the impression of incongruity, and winds up with the 'euge' which the poet expected.

76. [Like Lucilius, Persius dislikes the antique harshness of Pacuvius and Attius. 'Tristis contorto aliquo ex Pacuviano exordio' Lucilius 29. 63.] **Est quem . . . sunt quos**: compare Hor. 2 Ep. 2. 182 '*Sunt qui* non habeant, *est qui* non curat habere.' Attius, not Labeo, but the old tragedian (coupled with Pacuvius by Hor. 2 Ep. 1. 55 'aufert Pacuvius docti famam senis, Attius alti,' and by Mart. 11. 90. 5 'Attonitusque legis *terraï frugiferaï*, Attius et quicquid Pacuviusque vomunt') is called 'Brisaeus' from 'Briseus,' a name of Bacchus, Macrob. Sat. 1. 18, probably with reference to the Dionysiac beginnings of tragedy, so that the notion intended would be 'antiquated,' and also perhaps to remind us of Horace's theory (1 Ep. 19) that all the old poets were wine-drinkers.

'Briseis,' a conjecture of Scoppa, approved by Casaubon, is found in one MS., but though 'Briseis' would go well

Pales' holiday—out of all which comes Remus, and thou, Quintius, wearing thy ploughshare bright in the furrow, when in hot haste thy wife clothed thee dictator in presence of the oxen, and the lictor had to drive the plough home—Bravo, poet!

'I know a man who hangs over that shrivelled volume of the old Bacchanal Attius. Nay, I know more than one who cannot tear themselves from Pacuvius and his Antiope, the lady with the warts, whose dolorific heart is stayed on tribulation. When these

with 'Antiope,' there is no reason for supposing that the former was ever a subject of tragedy, whether Greek or Roman.

venosus again implies old age; the flesh shrunk, and the veins consequently standing out. Heinr. and Jahn compare Tac. Or. 21 (speaking of Asinius Pollio) 'Pacuvium certe et Attium non solum tragoediis, sed etiam orationibus expressit: adeo durus et siccus est. Oratio autem, sicut corpus hominis, ea demum pulchra est, in qua non eminent venae, nec ossa numerantur, sed temperatus ac bonus sanguis implet membra et exsurgit toris, ipsosque nervos rubor tegit et decor commendat.' [Perhaps the same thing is intended by Fronto (ad Verum 1, p. 114 Naber) when he says that Attius is 'inaequalis.' Velleius 2. 9. 2 goes in the opposite direction, praising Attius as having 'plus sanguinis' than the Greeks.]

liber, of a play. Quint. 1. 10. 18 'Aristophanes quoque non uno *libro* demonstrat.' Prop. 3. 21. 28 '*Librorumque* tuos, docte Menandre, sales.' Jahn.

77. **verrucosa**, warty,' opposed to a smooth clear skin, and hence rugged; the epithet being accommodated to the heroine, who was confined in a loathsome dungeon, as 'venosus' was to the author. 'Verrucosus' was a nickname of Q. Fabius Maximus Cunctator. Freund.

moretur. Hor. A. P. 321 'Fabula ... Valdius oblectat populum meliusque *moratur*.'

78. **Antiope**, imitated from a lost play of Euripides (Ribbeck, Fr. Lat. Tr. pp. 278 foll.). Cic. Fin. 1. 2 asks, 'Quis Ennii Medeam et Pacuvii Antiopam contemnet et reiciat?' In Pacuv. Fr. 5 (9), ed. Ribbeck, she is described as 'perdita inluvie atque insomnia. Compare also Prop. 3. 15. 12 foll., where the sufferings of Antiope are related at some length. [Comp. perhaps Plaut. Psend. 772 'parvis magnisque miseriis praefulcior,' where Acidalius alters 'miseriis' into 'ministeriis.']

Words seemingly taken or adapted from the tragedy itself. ['Aerumna' is found in the fragments of Pacuvius and Attius, as well as in Plautus, and the fragments of Ennius and Caecilius; it is also put into Caesar's mouth by Sallust (Cat. 51) and used by Lucretius (3. 50).] Cicero uses it several times in order to designate by one word the many modifications and shadings of the condition of mental suffering. Freund. '*Maeror* est aegritudo flebilis : *aerumna* aegritudo laboriosa: *dolor* aegritudo crucians' Cic. Tusc. 4. 8. 18. ['Maiores nostri labores non fugiendos tristissimo tamen verbo *aerumnas* etiam in deo nominaverunt,' says Cic. Fin. 2. 35.] It was, however, obsolete in the time of Quintilian, who explains it by 'labor.' [Quintil. 8. 3. 23 : but the reading is doubtful.]

luctificabile is another archaism, like 'monstrificabile' in Lucil. 26. 42.

fulta, pressed on all sides, and so apparently supported. Compare Prop. 1. 8. 7 'Tu pedibus teneris positas *fulcire* pruinas?' where nothing more than treading on is meant; and the use of ἐρείδω, as in Aesch. Ag. 64 γόνατος κονίαισιν ἐρειδομένου, which Statius seems to have translated (Theb. 3. 326) 'stant fulti pulvere crines.' [Lucilius, 26. 31, has two lines, 'Squalitate summa ac scabie summa in aerumna obrutam, Neque inimicis invidiosam neque amico exoptabilem,' which L. Müller thinks may refer to Antiope.]

hos pueris monitus patres infundere lippos
cum videas, quaerisne, unde haec sartago loquendi 80
venerit in linguas, unde istuc dedecus, in quo
trossulus exsultat tibi per subsellia levis?
'Nilne pudet capiti non posse pericula cano
pellere, quin tepidum hoc optes audire *decenter?*
"Fur es" ait Pedio. Pedius quid? crimina rasis 85
librat in antithetis : doctas posuisse figuras
laudatur "bellum hoc!" hoc bellum? an, Romule, ceves?

[81. *istut* C. 84. *tepidum os hoc* fragm. Bob. 85. *at is Pedio* fragm. Bob. *qui* fragm. Bob. *rosis* a. 86. *potuisse* fragm. Bob. 87. *laudatis* a, *laudatus* fragm. Bob. C. *bellum hoc hoc bellum* fragm. Bob., *bellum hoc bellum* a, *bellum hoc bellum est* ϛ. *cebes* fragm. Bob., *cevis* Plotius Sacerdos p. 487, 489 K: *ceves* ut futurum citat Probus p. 37 Keil.]

79. 'When you see purblind fathers recommend these as models of style to their children.' Hos monitus apparently for 'monitus de his.' 'Nec dubiis *ea* signa dedit Tritonia monstris' Virg. Aen. 2. 171, '*Hic* nostri nuntius esto' 4. 237.

infundere is the same metaphor as Hor. 1 Ep. 2. 67 'Nunc *adbibe* puro Pectore verba puer.'

lippos, as in 2. 72, expressing probably partly physical blindness brought on by excess, partly mental blindness. Hor. 1 S. 1. 120 'Crispini scrinia *lippi*,' also *ib.* 3. 25.

80. sartago, a kettle or frying-pan. Juv. 10. 64 and Mayor's note : called so from the hissing of its contents, according to Isidor. 20. 8. Jahn, who compares Eubul. ap. Athen. 7. p. 229 A λοπὰς παφλάζει βαρβάρῳ λαλήματι. Not very dissimilar is Horace's (1 S. 10. 20 foll.) ridicule of the practice of interlarding Latin with Greek.

81. venerit in linguas instead of 'in mentem.' Compare 'in buccam venire.'

dedecus conveys the notion of a scandal both to taste and morals. Hier. in Jov. 1. t. 4. 2. p. 145 Ben. 'Rogo, quae sunt haec portenta verborum, quod *dedecus* descriptionis?' Jahn.

in quo may either mean 'at which (over, about which),' like 'laborantes in uno Penelopen vitreamque Circen' Hor. 1 Od. 17. 20, or 'during which.'

82. trossulus, an old name of the Roman knights, originally a title of honour, afterwards a nickname, as in Varro, compared by Casaubon, 'Sesquiulixes' (ap. Non. s. v. 'trossuli,' 'Nunc emunt *trossuli* nardo nitidi vulgo Attico talento ecum.') Sen. Ep. 87. 9 'O quam cuperem illi [Catoni] nunc occurrere aliquem ex his *trossulis* in via divitibus.' ['*Trossuli* et iuvenes' *ib.* 76. 2.] Persius probably has both references in view. [Pliny 32. 35, quoting Junius Gracchanus, says that the name 'trossulus' remained in use till after the time of C. Gracchus. From the words of Junius Gracchanus it would seem that some slur attached to the expression.]

exsultat, like 'trepidare,' v. 20. Jahn compares Quint. 2. 2. 9 'At nunc proni atque succincti ad omnem clausulam non exsurgunt modo verum etiam excurrunt, et cum indecora *exsultatione* conclamant,' as Casaubon had already compared Plut. de Aud. 5 τὰς κραυγὰς καὶ τοὺς θορύβους καὶ τὰ πηδήματα τῶν παρόντων. Compare also ἀναπηδᾶν τῶν ὀρχηστῶν μᾶλλον. Dion. Chrys. p. 378 (680) (πρὸς Ἀλεξανδρεῖς) quoted by Sewell, Plato p. 336.

subsellia, benches occupied during a recitation. Juv. 7. 45, 86 ; not, as Jahn thinks, the seats in court, as nothing is said about a trial till the next paragraph, though such a hybrid style may very likely have crept into oratory. Compare Tac. Or. 21 above cited.

levis = 'levigatus'—opposed to the

are the lessons which you see purblind papas pouring into their children's ears, can you ask how men come to get this hubble-bubble of language into their mouths? What is the source of the scandal, which puts your effeminate grandees, along the benches, into such ecstasies of motion?

'Are you not ashamed not to be able to plead against perils threatening your gray hairs, but you must needs be ambitious of hearing mawkish compliments to your " good taste"? The accuser tells Pedius point blank, You are a thief. What does Pedius do? Oh, he balances the charges in polished antitheses—he is deservedly praised for the artfulness of his tropes. Monstrous fine that! That monstrous fine? What, old Romulus, you turning

'hispida membra' of the old Romans: so that 'trossulus levis' may be a kind or oxymoron.

83-91. Persius continues, 'This miserable affectation of fine writing besets even our criminal courts—even trials for life and death. The defendant studies the requirements of rhetoric, and lays traps for applause—which he gets. We shall have starving beggars turning rhetoricians next.'

83. [With this criticism of the style prevalent in the law-courts comp. Tac. de Or. 26.] 3. 31 'Non pudet?'

capiti more probably the dative, whether explained as an ethical dative, or as originally convertible with the abl., than a rare form of the abl., for which Jahn compares Catull. 68. 123, Tibull. 1. 1. 72. [See Neue, Formenlehre d. Lat. Sprache, 1. § 57.] Jahn cites Virg. E. 7. 47 'Solstitium *pecori* defendite.' 'Caput canum' are frequently found together. See Freund.

cano, v. 9 note.

84. tepidum nearly = 'frigidum.' Gr. ψυχρόν. 'Ceteros eiusdem lentitudinis ac teporis libros' Tac. Or. 21.

decenter, like 'euge and belle.' 'What admirable taste!'

85. Fur es is put as plainly as possible, to contrast with the elaboration of the reply.

Pedius seems to be a mixture of the advocate named by Hor. 1 S. 10. 28, seemingly in connexion with the trial of Petillius for 'furtum' and 'Pedius Blaesus,' who was tried and condemned under Nero for extortion from the Cyrenians two years before Persius' death. Persius probably refers to the passage in Horace, the gist of which is an appeal to the apes of Lucilius, who interlarded their poetry with Greek. 'Would you do so if you had to plead in a criminal trial for a great criminal, with the famous Pedius against you, putting out all the powers of his mother tongue?' So here Persius may mean, 'Even the eloquence of the bar, to which Horace would point as a genuine unaffected thing, has caught the taint—even our Pediuses talk like schoolboys or pedants.'

crimina ... librat, not that he balances the charges against each other, but that he makes each the subject of balanced antitheses.

rasis = 'teretibus.'

86. antithetis. 'Semper haec, quae Graeci ἀντίθετα nominant, cum contrariis opponuntur contraria, numerum oratorium necessitate ipsa faciunt, et eum sine industria' Cic. Orator. 50.

'doctus,' which Scaliger proposed for doctas, is adopted by Plaut., Nebriss., and Heinr., the latter of whom puts a full stop after ' figuras.'

posuisse ... laudatur = 'laudatur quod posuit,' the inf. being really the cognate acc. expressing the praise received. See Madvig, § 400, though he does not mention this instance, which is more remarkable than any there given.

figura, Gr. σχῆμα, [an artificial expression whether grammatical or literary] Cic. de Or. 3. 53, Or. 39, Quint. 9. 1. Freund.

87. Romule, like 'Titi,' 'Romulidae,' ' Trossulus.'

ceves, like ' trepidare,' ' exsultare,

men moveat quippe, et, cantet si naufragus, assem
protulerim? Cantas, cum fracta te in trabe pictum
ex umero portes? verum, nec nocte paratum 90
plorabit, qui me volet incurvasse querella.'
  Sed numeris decor est et iunctura addita crudis.
claudere sic versum didicit *Berecyntius Attis*
et *qui caeruleum dirimebat Nerea delphin*
sic *costam longo subduximus Appennino.* 95

[88. *moneat* a. *mobeat* fragm. Bob.   90. *portes* vel *portas* C.   91. *querellas* fragm. Bob.   92. *cruris* a.   93. *cludere* a, *claudere* fragm. Bob. C.   *si* a. *dedicit* a, *didici* C.   94. *quae* fragm. Bob.   *delphi* a.   95. *si* a C.]

but with a further notion of moral debasement.
  88. 'men moveat cimex Pantilius?' Hor. 1 S. 10. 78. The sentiment is the same as Hor. A. P. 202 'Si vis me flere, dolendum est Primum ipsi tibi,' compared by Lubin. Compare also Hor. 1 S. 10. 25 'Cum versus facias, te ipsum percontor, an et cum Dura tibi peragenda rei sit causa Petilli?' which forms part of the context of the passage referred to on v. 85, as being in Persius' mind. The subject of 'moveat' here is 'naufragus.' From this we may infer that the custom of beggars singing ballads was not unknown at Rome.
  89. Draws out the image of the shipwrecked sailor. 'Si fractis enatat exspes Navibus aere dato qui pingitur' Hor. A. P. 20. Compare 6. 32 'ne pictus oberret Caerulea in tabula,' and Juv. 14. 302.
  pictum in trabe and 'pictum in tabula' are very different, the one expressing the manner of the painting ('in trabe' constructed closely with 'te'), the other the material on which the painting is made. The question may be raised whether 'fracta in trabe' is for 'in naufragio' (compare 'trabe rupta' 6. 27, 'fractis trabibus' Juv. 14. 296, 'fractis navibus' Hor. l. c.), or 'on a broken plank'? Jahn thinks from Martial 12. 57. 12 'fasciato naufragus loquax trunco,' that the painting may be actually *on* the plank.
  90. **verum ... paratum** are neuters, but the construction is that of a cognate acc.

  nocte paratum may be illustrated by a beautiful passage in Lucr. 1. 140 'Sed tua me virtus tamen, et sperata voluptas Suavis amicitiae, quemvis sufferre laborem Suadet, et *inducit noctes vigilare serenas*.' So Juv. 7. 27 '*vigilata*que proelia dele.' Compare the use of 'lucubro.' Persius taunts the pleaders with their labour, while, in v. 106, he taunts the poets with their want of labour, choosing the sneer which seems most appropriate in each case, probably without much regard to absolute consistency.
  91. **plorabit ... volet** in the sense of 'ploret ... velit.' '*Ibit* eo quo vis, qui zonam perdidit' Hor. 2 Ep. 2. 40.
  incurvare is used in this metaphorical sense more than once in Seneca, e. g. Ep. 71 'hoc, ut opinor, succidere mentem, et *incurvari*, et succumbere.' So Hor. 3 Od. 10. 16 'Nec tinctus viola pallor amantium ... *Curvat*;' A. P. 110 'Aut *ad humum* maerore gravi *deducit* et angit.'
  92-106. The distribution of these lines is difficult. Casaubon's plan, which is really that of the early editors, and has been followed by most of the later, gives v. 92 to the objector, vv. 93-5 to Persius, who takes him up, 'as for instance in these specimens;' v. 94 to the objector, who defends the despised lines by the example of Virgil; v. 95 to Persius, who shows that Virgil supplies no parallel; v. 96 to the objector, who opens another line of defence, and the rest to Persius, who retorts as before by quoting specimens, on which he in-

spaniel? Am I to be touched forsooth and pull out a penny, if a shipwrecked man begins singing me a song? You sing, when you have actually got yourself painted in a wreck to carry on your shoulders? No—a man's tears must come from his heart at the moment, not from his brains overnight, if he would have me bowed down beneath his piteous tale.'

F. But they have given grace and smoothness to our unpolished Roman numbers. Thus it is a point gained to round a verse with *Berecynthian Attis* and the *dolphin that was cutting through sea-green Nereus,* or *We have fetched off a rib from the long sides of Appenninus.*

dignantly comments. Jahn, however, seems right in giving vv. 92-95 to the objector, as nothing is there said *ipso facto* disparaging to the poets, and in giving vv. 96, 97 to Persius; but he would have done better by assigning v. 98 not to the objector but to Persius, who asks for a fresh specimen.

F. Well, they have at any rate succeeded in giving polish to our poetry, as, for instance, ... *P.* 'Shade of Virgil! what frothy, fungous trash! Oblige me by another specimen of the tenderer sort.' *F.* gives one. *P.* ' And this is *manly* poetry—mere drivelling, poured out involuntarily from an idiot's lips, not wrung with toil from an artist's brain.'

92. iunctura, as in v. 64, is the welding of the different parts of a verse together so that there may be no roughness. This roughness is expressed by crudis, though through a different metaphor. With ' crudis' compare 5. 5 ' quantas robusti carminis offas Ingeris.'

93. claudere ... versum ('concludere versum' Hor. 1 S. 4. 40), as Jahn remarks, is not merely to *conclude* a verse, but to *compose* it, or to express it in metrical compass. Hor. 2 S. 1. 28 ' me pedibus delectat claudere verba.'

Berecyntius Attis would seem to be the nom. to 'didicit,' as Heinr. takes it. 'So Berecyntian Attis is taught to round the measure.' The point of ridicule appears to be the rhythm, which the poet doubtless thought excellent, a long sweeping word like 'Berecyntius' being a great point gained. Thus there is no occasion to read 'Attin' with three MSS., so as to produce a jingle with ' delphin.' For Attis, see Catullus' poem. Dio says of Nero ἐπιθαρρύδησέ τε Ἄττιν τινὰ ἢ Βάκχας (61. 20).

94. qui ... delphin is another nom. to ' didicit.' Perhaps the expression is meant to be ridiculed as well as the rhythm, as the image of the dolphin cleaving Nereus is nearly as grotesque as Furius' of Jupiter spitting snow on the Alps (Hor. 2 S. 5. 41), or as Alpinus' of the muddy head of the Rhine (*ib.* 1 S. 10. 37). Valerius Flaccus, however (1. 450, quoted by Jahn), has ' remo Nerea versat.' The dolphin in question may be Arion's, as the Schol. say. Stat. Theb. 5. 482 has 'Spumea porrecti dirimentes terga profundi.'

95. Both expression and rhythm seem to be ridiculed here. The rhythmical trick evidently is the spondaic ending with the jingle in the middle, like Virgil's (Aen. 3. 549, quoted by the Schol.) 'Cornua velatarum obvertimus antennarum.' The sense is extremely obscure. We can see the absurdity of the image of ' fetching off a rib of the Apennine,' as if by the process of carving (compare Juv. 11. 142 ' Nec frustum capreae subducere nec latus Afrae Novit avis noster'), but it is not easy to understand what was the original reference of the line. The Schol. see in it a metaphor [referring to the two previous lines; ' thus have we emasculated the Latin language by an intermixture of Greek terms']. Ascensius and Plautius understand it of Hannibal: Nebrissensis of the convulsion which separated Sicily from Italy. Gifford seems to have no authority for asserting that 'subducere' is a military term, meaning to occupy a position by forced marches, as κλέπτειν is not parallel. The construction appears to be 'Sic

'Arma virum! nonne hoc spumosum et cortice pingui,
ut ramale vetus vegrandi subere coctum?
quidnam igitur tenerum et laxa cervice legendum?'
 *Torva mimalloneis inplerunt cornua bombis,
et raptum vitulo caput ablatura superbo* 100
*Bassaris et lyncem Maenas flexura corymbis
euhion ingeminat, reparabilis adsonat echo.*
'Haec fierent, si testiculi vena ulla paterni
viveret in nobis? summa delumbe saliva

[97. *praegrandi* fragm. Bob., a C: *vegrandi* Servius Aen. 11. 553, Porphyrion Hor. 1 S. 2. 129.   99. *Torbam mallonis* fragm. Bob., a.   *Torva mimalloniis inflatur tibia bombis* Diomedes p. 499 K.   100. *ratum* fragm. Bob.   *aplatura* fragm. Bob. *corimpis* a.   101. *lycem* fragm. Bob., *licet* a.   103. *venulla* fragm. Bob.   104. *summe* a.]

costam . . . Appennino [' claudere versum didicit '].

96. **Arma virum**, rightly understood by Meister as an ejaculation. Persius compares Virgil with these poetasters, as Hor. A. P. 141 contrasts the opening of the Odyssey with 'Fortunam Priami cantabo.' Persius does not say 'bellum hoc' (v. 87), but 'nonne hoc spumosum.'

spumosum. Compare 5. 19 'bullatis ut mihi nugis Pagina turgescat.'

cortice pingui. 'Aridus' and 'siccus' are terms of reproach in style, and Persius carries out the metaphor by comparing these verses to a dried-up branch with a large puffy bark. [φλοιώ-δης = *puffy*, of style, Longinus 3. 2. See Wyttenbach on Plutarch, p. 81 B.]

97. **ramale**, 5. 59. Jahn refers to Theophr. Hist. Plant. 4. 18, 3. 16, Pliny 17. 234, to show that the swelling of the bark withers the bough of the cork tree, which has occasionally to be stripped of its outer bark to preserve its vitality.

vegrandis is well explained by Jahn, after Festus and Nonius, as 'male grandis,' so as to include the two senses attributed to it by Gell. 5. 12, 16. 5, of *small* and *too large*, the former of which is the more common, the latter being only found in this passage and Cic. Agr. 2. 34. 93 'hominem vegrandi macie torridum.' Compare 'vepallida' Hor. 1 S. 2. 129, where the meaning is plainly *very* pale.

suber points specifically to the cork tree, which has two barks, an outer and an inner.

coctum. Compare Prop. 4. 5. 61 'Vidi ego odorati victura rosaria Paesti Sub matutino *cocta* iacere Noto.'

98. **igitur** is common in interrogations, as we use 'then.' 'If these are your specimens of finished versification, give us something peculiarly languishing.'

tenerum. 'Aut nimium *teneris* iuventur versibus unquam' Hor. A. P. 246.

laxa cervice. Jahn refers to Meineke, Fr. Com. Gr. 4. p. 612, and to Quint. 9. 4. 31, who says that, in speaking, the neck should not be bent in either direction. 'Tereti cervice reposta' Lucr. 1. 35.

99. These lines are commonly supposed to be Nero's, on the authority of the Schol., which, however, say elsewhere that they are represented by others as Persius' own. From Dio, quoted on v. 93, it appears that Nero sang a poem on the Bacchae to his harp. The line seems imitated from Catull. 64. 263 'Multis raucisonos efflabant cornua bombos.' Lucr. 4. 544 'Et revocat raucum retro cita ("regio cita " Lachm.) barbara bombum.' ['Bombus,' of a deep or bass sound, Plin. 11. 20, 26; Apuleius Florida 1. 3. 12, ' acuto tinnitu et gravi *bombo* concentum musicum miscuit.']

Torva, transferred from aspect to sound, as by Virg. Aen. 7. 399 'torvumque repente Clamat,' which the author may have had in view, as Virgil is describing Bacchanalian ravings. [Lucr. 6. 131 uses 'torvus' of the sound of an explosion. 'Voce hominis tuba rudore torvior,' Apul. Florid. 17. 79.]

SAT. I.

P. 'Arms and the Man! Can one call *this* anything but frothy and fluffy, like an old dried-up branch with a huge overgrown bark upon it? Well, what should you instance as soft and adapted for being recited with a gentle bend of the neck?'

F. Their grim horns they filled with Mimallonean boomings—the Bassarid, ready to tear the scornful calf's head from his shoulders, and the Maenad, ready to rein in the lynx with ivy branches, shout Evios again and again, and the redeeming power of Echo chimes in.

P. 'Would such things be produced if we had one spark of our fathers' manhood alive in us? Nerveless stuff—it floats in the mouth on the top of the spittle, and comes drivelling out

---

'mimallonis' occurs Ov. A. A. 1. 541 for a Bacchante, and 'mimallones' Stat. Theb. 4. 660.

inplerunt, sc. the Bacchanals.

100. vitulo... superbo is from Eur. Bacch. 743 ταῦροι δ' ὑβρισταὶ κεὶς κέρας θυμούμενοι Τὸ πρόσθεν κ.τ.λ. The Bacchanals overcome powerful bulls and tear them to pieces.

ablatura... flexura. See Madvig. §§ 424. 5, 425 a, b, 428. 3. The participle originally denoted only future time; then it came to be used to express an intention, like the fut. part. in Greek; then to express a conditional proposition, where the Greeks would have used ἄν, so that it is sometimes found in the abl. absol., a construction unknown to the older writers. Here it appears to be used attributively, and almost as an adj., the future being probably intended to express *habit*, as in 2. 5 'tacita libabit acerra.'

101. Bassaris. Jahn compares Anth. Pal. 6. 74 [Agathias 27. 1, Jacobs, vol. 4. p. 13] Βασσαρὶς Εὐρυνόμη σκοπελοδρόμος, ἥ ποτε ταύρων Πολλὰ τανυκραίρων στέρνα χαραξαμένη, Ἡ μέγα καγχάζουσα λεοντοφόνοις ἐπὶ νίκαις, Παίγνιον ἀτλήτου θηρὸς ἔχουσα κάρη. 'Non ego te, candide Bassareu, Invitum quatiam' Hor. 1 Od. 18. 11. The lynx was sacred to Bacchus, as the conqueror of India. 'Victa racemifero lynces dedit India Baccho' Ov. M. 15. 413. 'Quid lynces Bacchi variae?' Virg. G. 3. 264. Elsewhere he is drawn by tigers, as in Hor. 3 Od. 3. 13. Virg. Aen. 6. 804 'Nec qui *pampineis* victor iuga *flectit habenis* Liber, *agens* celso Nysae de vertice tigres,' where 'pampineis habenis' explains 'corymbis.'

102. euhion. Εὔιος is an epithet of Bacchus, as invoked with the cry εὐοῖ, εὐά. Soph. Oed. R. 201 (quoted by Jahn) οἰνῶπα Βάκχον εὔιον μαινάδων ὁμόστολον. So that 'Euhion' is probably intended here as a Greek acc.

reparabilis, actively, restoring the lost sound. Ov. M. 1. 11 of the moon, 'reparat nova cornua.'

adsonat. 'Plangentibus *adsonat* Echo' Ov. M. 3. 505.

103. [Petronius 44 'si nos coleos haberemus, non tantum sibi placeret.' Spartianus, Pescennius 3. 9, quotes Severus as saying 'si ulla vena paternae disciplinae viveret.' 'Hoc' (an effeminate and artificial style) 'a magno animi malo oritur: ... illo sano ac valente oratio quoque robusta, fortis, virilis est: si ille procubuit, et cetera ruinam sequuntur' Sen. Ep. 114. 22.]

104. summa... saliva, a stronger version of 'summis labris,' which Seneca uses (Ep. 10. 3) 'Non *a summis labris* ista venerunt: habent hae voces fundamentum,' apparently from the Greek ἀπὸ χειλέων, which Plut. Cato Maj. 12 opposes to ἀπὸ καρδίας. Jahn, who also compares Gell. 1. 15 'qui nullo rerum pondere innixi *verbis umidis et lapsantibus diffluunt*, eorum orationem bene existimatum est *in ore nasci*, non in pectore;' and Quint. 10. 3. 2 'sine conscientia profectus *non a summo* petiti, ipsa illa ex tempore dicendi facultas inanem modo loquacitatem dabit, et *verba in labris nascentia*.' Compare v. 81 above, 'venerit in

26   PERSII

hoc natat in labris, et in udo est, Maenas et Attis,   105
nec pluteum caedit, nec demorsos sapit unguis.'
 Sed quid opus teneras mordaci radere vero
auriculas? vide sis, ne maiorum tibi forte
limina frigescant: sonat hic de nare canina
littera.
 'Per me equidem sint omnia protinus alba;   110
nil moror. euge! omnes, omnes bene mirae eritis res.
hoc iuvat? "hic" inquis "veto quisquam faxit oletum."
pinge duos anguis: pueri, sacer est locus, extra
meite! discedo. secuit Lucilius urbem,
te Lupe, te Muci, et genuinum fregit in illis.   115

[105. *aitis* a. 107. *verbo* C. 108. *sis* om. a. 109. *camaena* a.
110. *abba* a. 111. *murore* a. *euge omnes bene* a C. 113. *pinguedo sanguis* a.
exita a. 114. *mei cedis (mercedis* B) *sevit cedo lucilius* a.]

linguas.' [Cornificius ad Herennium 4. 11 'eius generis quod appellamus *fluctuans et dissolutum*, eo quod sine nervis et articulis fluctuat huc et illuc, nec potest confirmate neque viriliter sese expedire.']
 104. **delumbis**, a rare word. Cic. Or. 69 has 'concidat *delumbetque* sententias.' Tac. Or. 18 'Ciceronem male audisse a Bruto, ut ipsius verbis utar, tanquam fractum atque elumbem.'
 delumbe . . . **hoc**, like ' bellum hoc.'
 105. With **natat** Heinr. compares Quint. 10. 7. 28 '*innatans* illa verborum facilitas.' Heinr. puts a semicolon after 'natat.' Jahn (1843), with the rest, after 'labris.' Perhaps it might be better to make 'hoc' the nom. to both 'natat' and 'est,' and put 'Maenas et Attis' in apposition to it.
 in udo est. Jahn compares ἐν ὑγρῷ ἐστιν ἡ γλῶττα Theoph. ch. 8, of a talkative man.
 106. The Schol. seem right in explaining **pluteum** here of the backboard of the 'lecticula lucubratoria' (v. 53 note). 'Sponda est exterior pars lecti, *pluteus* interior.' Suetonius Cal. 26 'cenanti modo ad *pluteum*, modo ad pedes stare.' Prop. 4. 8. 68 'Lygdamus ad plutei fulcra sinistra latens.' The man lies on his couch after his meal,
listlessly drivelling out his verses, without any physical exertion or even movement of impatience.
 caedit, like 'caedere ostium' Lucil. 29. 35. Heinr. Greek κόπτειν. 'Caedit' rhetorical for 'caedere facit.' Compare 2. 64 'Haec sibi corrupto casiam dissolvit olivo: Haec Calabrum coxit vitiato murice vellus.'
 demorsos sapit unguis. Imitated from Hor. 1 S. 10. 70, speaking of what Lucilius failed to do, 'in versu faciendo saepe caput scaberet, *vivos et roderet ungues.*'
 107-123. F. Even if this be truth, why tell it? You will only offend those whom it is your interest not to offend. P. 'Very well, then—have it your own way—put up a board against nuisances, and I will leave you. But Lucilius indulged his humour, and Horace his, though in a quicker way—is there no place where I may bury my secret?' F. None. P. 'Well, I will confide it to my book: listen—*All the world are asses.* There, that is worth all your Iliads.'
 107. **teneras... auriculas,** 'molles auriculae' Hor. 2 S. 5. 32.
 teneras...radere. 3. 113 '*ten* latet ulcus in ore Putre, quod haud deceat plebeia *radere* beta.'
 mordaci. 5. 86 'aurem *mordaci* lotus aceto.' 'Mordax verum,' like

involuntarily. Maenad and Attis—it involves no battery of the writing-chair, and has no smack of nails bitten down to the quick.'

F. But where is the occasion to let rough truths grate on tender ears? Do take care that you are not frozen some day on a great man's doorstep. Notice—human snarlers kept on the premises.

P. 'Ah, well—paint everything white from this day forward for me—I won't spoil your game. Bravo, you shall be wonders of the world, every one of you. Is that what you would like? No nuisances, say you, to be committed here. Draw a couple of snakes; young gentlemen, the ground is sacred: retire outside. I'm off. Lucilius, though, bit deep into the town of his day, its Lupuses

'generosum honestum' 2. 74, 'opimum pingue' 3. 32.
108. 'Vide sis signi quid siet' Plaut. Am. 787. vidĕ shortened like 'cavĕ' Hor. 1 Ep. 13. 19.
maiorum, imitated from Hor. 2 S. 1. 60 'O puer, ut sis Vitalis metuo, et *maiorum* ne quis amicus *Frigore* te feriat.'
109. The coldness of the master is transferred to the threshold, because the door shut leaves the applicant in the cold. Prop. 1. 16. 22 'Tristis et in tepido limine somnus erit.' 2. 17. 15 'Nec licet in triviis sicca requiescere. luna.' Hor. 3 Od. 10. 19 'Non hoc semper erit liminis aut aquae Caelestis patiens latus.'
canina littera. R. 'Inritata canes quod homo quam planiu' dicit' Lucil. 1. 27. So dogs were said 'hirrire.' The snarl is that of the great man—'ira cadat naso' 5. 91, but the image suggested is that of the dog at the door. 'Cave canem.'
110. Per me. 'Per me vel stertas licet' Cic. Acad. 2. 29.
equidem, used, though the verb is not in the 1st person, as in 5. 45 'non equidem dubites.' Here it is as if he had said 'equidem concedo.'
protinus, 'from this day forward.'
alba, 'mark them with white (Hor. 2 S. 3. 246) and I will not blacken them.' The sense is the same as Hor. A. P. 442 'Si defendere delictum quam vertere malles, Nullum ultra verbum aut operam insumebat inanem Quin sine rivali teque et tua solus amares.'
111. nil moror. Not 'I don't care'

(Jahn), but 'I don't object' = 'per me nulla mora est.'
euge, v. 49. 'You shall all of you be the marvels of creation.' ['Omnes bene! mirae' etc. Bücheler.]
With mirae res [evidently a colloquialism] we may compare such expressions as 'dulcissime *rerum*' Hor. 1 S. 9. 4, if they are to be explained as partitive. ['Omnes etenim' Jahn (1843), 'omnes, omnes,' from some of his later copies, Jahn (1868).]
112. hoc iuvat, interrogatively, as in Hor. 1 S. 1. 78. Jahn. The decree is couched in legal phrase.
113. anguis, as the genii of the place. Virg. Aen. 5. 95. There are some remains of a similar painting and inscription on a wall at Rome which once formed part of Nero's golden palace, where Titus' baths were afterwards built. (A. de Romanis, 'Le antiche Camere Esquiline,' Rome, 1822. Osann. Syll. p. 494. 45, referred to by Jahn.)
114. discedo implies that Persius takes the warning to himself.
secuit is applied to any kind of wound. 'Ambo (postes) ab infumo tarmes *secat*' Plaut. Most. 825, 'gnaws.' Here we might take it for 'secuit flagello' but for 'genuinum.' Hor. 1 S. 10. 3 says of Lucilius, 'sale multo Urbem defricuit.' [Ovink quotes Tibullus 1. 9. 22 'corpus et intorto verbere terga seca.']
115. Lupus and Mucius were enemies of Scipio, Lucilius' patron.
Lupus is said by the Schol. on Hor. 2 S. 1. 68 'Famosisve *Lupo* cooperto versibus' to have been P.

omne vafer vitium ridenti Flaccus amico
tangit et admissus circum praecordia ludit,
callidus excusso populum suspendere naso:
me muttire nefas? nec clam, nec cum scrobe?'

                                                        Nusquam.

'Hic tamen infodiam. vidi, vidi ipse, libelle: 120
auriculas asini quis non habet? hoc ego opertum,
hoc, ridere, meum, tam nil, nulla tibi vendo
Iliade. Audaci quicumque adflate Cratino

[118. *collidus a.*   119. *me a* C, *men c* ſ.   *scribe a.*   121. *auricula a.*
123. *afflante cradina a.*]

Rutilius Lupus, who was consul a. u. c. 664 with L. Julius Caesar, but as Lucilius had then been dead thirteen years, it seems more likely to have been L. Lentulus Lupus, who was consul with C. Marcius Figulus a.u.c. 597, which is the opinion of Tarentius in loc. Hor.

115. **Mucius.** P. Mucius Scaevola, consul 621. 'Quid refert dictis ignoscat *Mucius* an non?' Juv. 1. 154.

genuinum fregit, perhaps with reference to the story of the viper and the file, alluded to by Hor. 2 S. 1. 77, though the image here is meant to be to the honour of Lucilius, who fastened on his enemies without caring for the consequences. 'Animasque in vulnere ponunt' Virg. G. 4. 238. Contrast the different ways in which Hor. ll. cc. and Juv. 1. 165 characterize Lucilius with the present passage.

116. **omne ... vitium.** Compare such passages as Hor. 2 Ep. 2. 205 'Non es avarus: abi. Quid? *cetera* iam simul isto Cum vitio fugere?' The remark is more true of Horace's later than of his earlier works, though the word **ridenti** expresses a principle laid down more than once in the Satires, e.g. 1 S. 1. 24, 10. 14.

vafer seems to answer to our 'rogue.' 'Alfenus *vafer*' Hor. 1. S. 3. 130. 'Surrentina *vafer* qui miscet faece Falerna' 2 S. 4. 55. Horace is so called because he takes his friend in.

amico is opp. to 'populum.' Horace takes his friends playfully to task for their weaknesses, but is more contemptuous in speaking of men in general, and mentions obnoxious individuals even with bitterness. Possibly 'amico' may refer more particularly to the Epistles.

117. **admissus**, 'into the bosom.'

praecordia is emphatic—he plays, but it is with the innermost and most sensitive feelings.

118. **callidus ... suspendere**, Prol. 11.

excusso. 'Nares inflare et movere ... et pulso subito spiritu *excutere*' Quint. 11. 3. 80, si lectio certa. 'Sursum iactato,' Heinr., who compares '*excussa* bracchia' Ov. M. 5. 596. [It is more probable that Persius is thinking of Horace's 'emunctae naris,' applied (1 S. 4. 8) to Lucilius, and explained by Porphyrion 'tersus, atque eleganter dicens et ridens.' The Scholia here explain 'excusso' as='emuncto,' adding 'ut e contrario qui stulti sunt *mucosi* dicuntur.']

populum. See note on v. 116, and compare such passages as Hor. 1 Ep. 1. 70 'Quod si me populus Romanus forte roget,' etc.

suspendere naso, v. 40 note.

119. **muttire.** Colloquial word, used by Plautus and Terence. See Freund.

muttire ... clam, opp. to 'muttire palam' Enn. Fr. Teleph. apud Fest. (p. 145 Müll.), who says that 'muttire' there='loqui:' but the passage will bear the ordinary sense.

nec (fas).

cum scrobe, because the hole in the ground is the supposed *partner* of the secret. The allusion, of course, is to the story of Midas. ['Nec clam nec cum scrobe, nusquam?' Jahn, 1868.]

120. **infodiam**, as Madan remarks,

and Muciuses, and broke his jaw-tooth on them. Horace, the rogue, manages to probe every fault while making his friend laugh; he gains his entrance, and plays about the innermost feelings, with a sly talent for tossing up his nose and catching the public on it. And is it sacrilege for me to mutter a word? May it not be done in confidence between myself and a ditch?'

F. In no place or circumstance whatever.

P. 'Well, I will dig a hole and bury it here. I have seen it, my dear book, I have seen it with my own eyes. *Who is there that has not the ears of an ass?* This dead and buried secret, this joke of mine, trumpery as it seems, I am not going to sell you for any of your Iliads.

'To all who draw their inspiration from the bold blasts of Cra-

is more applicable to the ancient than to the modern manner of writing.

vidi was the form of giving evidence. Juv. 7. 13, 16. 30.

libelle. 'I, puer, atque meo citus haec subscribe *libello*' Hor. 1 S. 10. 92. Persius chooses his book as his confidant, as Horace, of whom he was thinking, says Lucilius did (2 S. 1. 30), 'Ille velut fidis arcana sodalibus olim Credebat libris.'

121. Casaubon changed **quis non habet** into 'Mida rex habet,' on the authority of the Life of Persius, which says that Persius left 'Mida rex,' but Cornutus, in revising the work for posthumous publication, thought it better to suppress so obvious a reflection on Nero, and altered it into 'quis non.' 'Quis non,' however, is clearly required by the satire as we now have it, the fact that *everybody* has ass's ears being the secret with which Persius has been labouring ever since v. 8; and the whole tone of the preceding part of the poem makes it much more likely that the sarcasm, as intended, should be universal than particular.

'*Operta* recludit' Hor. 1 Ep. 5. 16.

122. **hoc ridere meum,** v. 9 note.

tam nil. 'Usque *adeo nihil* est?' Juv. 3. 84.

vendo is not only 'I sell,' but 'I offer for sale,' (venum do) 'quoniam *vendat*, velle quem optime vendere' Cic. 3 Off. 12.

123. **Iliade,** v. 50, note on v. 4.

123-134. Persius concludes. 'Let *my* readers be the few that can relish the old comedy of Greece, not the idle loungers and senseless buffoons of the day—*they* may kill time in a more congenial manner.'

123. An answer to 'Quis leget haec,' v. 2. He has already disclaimed the reading public which his friend values; and now, after repeating that he values his own joke, slight as it is, infinitely higher than Labeo's Homer, which he foresaw from the first would be his rival, he sketches the reader whom he really wishes to attract. Thus the end of the poem corresponds to the beginning. It is evidently modelled on the latter part of Hor. 1 S. 10. Horace intends his words to apply to the whole book of which they form a conclusion: whether Persius means his to apply merely to this Satire, or to the whole book, is not clear: probably the latter, if we suppose the Satire to be introductory—designed to clear the ground by sweeping away the popular trash of the time before he asks attention for his own more manly strains. The appeal to the old comedians as his masters is from Hor. 1 S. 4. 1 foll.

audaci, 'bold-spoken.' Jahn refers to Platon. de Com. p. 27 οὐ γὰρ ὥσπερ ὁ Ἀριστοφάνης ἐπιτρέχειν τὴν χάριν τοῖς σκώμμασι ποιεῖ ... ἀλλ' ἁπλῶς καὶ κατὰ τὴν παροιμίαν γυμνῇ κεφαλῇ τίθησι τὰς βλασφημίας κατὰ τῶν ἁμαρτανόντων, and to Anon. de Com. p. 29 γέγονε δὲ ποιητικώτατος κατασκευάζων εἰς τὸν Αἰσχύλου χαρακτῆρα.

adflate, like 'adflata numine' Virg. Aen. 6. 50. Jahn. Possibly also

iratum Eupolidem praegrandi cum sene palles,
aspice et haec, si forte aliquid decoctius audis. 125
inde vaporata lector mihi ferveat aure :
non hic, qui in crepidas Graiorum ludere gestit
sordidus, et lusco qui possit dicere 'lusce,'
sese aliquem credens, Italo quod honore supinus
fregerit eminas Arreti aedilis iniquas; 130
nec qui abaco numeros et secto in pulvere metas
scit risisse vafer, multum gaudere paratus,
si cynico barbam petulans nonaria vellat.

[127. *cratorum laudere* A, *oratorum audere* B. 128. *es* A, *possis* a.
129. *seque* C. 131. *qui in abato* a. *secto pulvere* a.]

with a reference to the Epigram on Cratinus, Ταῦτ' ἔλεγεν, Διόνυσε, καὶ ἔπνεεν, οὐχ ἑνὸς ἀσκοῦ Κρατῖνος, ἀλλὰ παντὸς ὠδωδὼς πίθου Anthol. Pal. 2. p. 543. [Nicaenetus 4. 3, Jacobs 1. p. 206.] 'Adflate' voc. for nom. like 'millesime, trabeate' 3. 28, 9. 'Quibus Hector ab oris *Expectate* venis?' Virg. Aen. 2. 282.

124. **iratum.** Jahn quotes Anon. de Com. l. c. ζηλῶν Κρατῖνον πολύ γε λοίδορον ἐπιφαίνει. Persius expressly wishes to imitate the old poets in their licence of invective.

praegrandi cum sene, as Jahn remarks, must refer to Aristophanes, who is called 'praegrandis' in respect of his genius, as Cic. Brut. 83. 287 calls Thucydides 'grandis,' 'senex' in respect of his antiquity as one of the *ancients*, as Horace calls Lucilius, who died at forty-four, 'senex' (2 S. 1. 34). Heinr. (who thinks Lucilius himself is meant) compares Hor. 2 Ep. 1. 55 'Aufert Pacuvius docti famam *senis*, Attius alti.'

palles. The paleness which Persius attacks (v. 26) is that of debauchery and dilettante study; but he is ready to sympathize with the paleness of the genuine student, 3. 85, 5. 62. Possibly some connexion may be intended here, as in v. 26, between 'pallor' and 'senium'—the student poring so long over the ancients that he catches their colour. At any rate 'Eupolidem pallere' is to be explained as a cogn. acc., like 'sapimus patruos' (v. 11) = 'pallere pallorem Eupolideum.' 'Multos pallere colores' Prop. 1. 15. 39. 'Sabbata palles' (5. 184) is a different construction.

125. 'Hanc etiam, Maecenas, *aspice* partem' Virg. G. 4. 2. 'Tamen *aspice*, si quid Et nos, quod cures proprium fecisse, loquamur' Hor. 1 Ep. 17. 4.

decoctius opp. to 'spumosus' v. 96. Virg. G. 1. 295 'Aut dulcis musti Vulcano decoquit umorem, Et foliis undam trepidi *despumat* aëni.'

126. Possibly **vaporata . . . aure** may be intended as a continuation of the metaphor.

ferveat opp. to 'tepidus,' v. 84, frigid dilettantism. Ears were cleansed by steaming as well as by washing with vinegar. Jahn.

127. 'Not the low wit that laughs at national peculiarities and personal infirmities.' Compare the English footman in Dr. Moore's Zeluco, quoted by Macaulay in his Essay on Johnson. Jealousy was felt of the Greek dress, the 'pallium' and 'crepidae,' as likely to encroach on the Roman, the 'toga' and 'calcei;' and one of the things which tended to bring Tiberius into contempt during his early residence at Rhodes was his adoption of this costume (Suet. Tib. 13, referred to by König). It would be unpopular too as associated with the professors of philosophy.

ludere in, a very rare construction. 'Who loves to have his joke at.' Heinr. remarks of this and the follow-

SAT. I.   31

tinus, and owe their paleness to the indignant Eupolis and the third of those ancient giants, I say, Cast a look here too, if you have an ear for something which has lost its first froth. Let my reader come with the glow of their strains still in his ears. I don't want the gentleman who loves to have his low fling at the slippers of the Greeks, and is equal to calling a one-eyed man Old One-eye, thinking himself somebody forsooth, because once, stuck up with provincial dignity, he has broken short half-pint measures officially at Arretium; nor the man who has the wit to laugh at the figures on the slab and the cones drawn in sand, ready to go off in ecstasies if a woman pulls a Cynic by the beard. To

ing lines, 'Schilderung der damaligen römischen Philisterwelt.'

128. **sordidus.** Frequently in Cicero applied to a person in the sense of base or mean—opposed to generosity or liberality of mind. Jahn makes the opposition between the refinement of the elegant Greek and the vulgarity of the low Roman—the eternal feud between good clothes and bad.

possit after 'gestit,' like 'deceat' (3. 71) in the middle of a number of indicatives. Here the force may be, 'Who would be able on occasion,' etc. 'He knows that the man has only one eye, and can tell him so.' Jerome (c. Jovin. 2. t. 4. 2. p. 214) says, 'Quid prodest *luscum vocare luscum?*' Schrevelius quotes Arist. Eth. 3. 5 τοῖς διὰ φύσιν αἰσχροῖς οὐδεὶς ἐπιτιμᾷ.

129. **aliquem,** an expression common in Greek and Latin. Theocr. 11. 79 (Jahn), Acts 5. 36, Juv. 1. 74, Cic. ad Att. 13. 15. 8, opposed to οὐδείς or 'nullus.'

Italo, provincial, opposed not to *Greek*, but to *Roman*, to the magistracies ('honores') of the metropolis.

supinus here = 'superbus,' only more graphic, 'head in air.' Haec et talia dum refert *supinus*' Mart. 5. 8. 10.

130. Imitated by Juv. 10. 101 'Quam de mensura ius dicere, vasa minora Frangere pannosus vacuis aedilis Ulubris,' where see Mayor's notes. The same duty devolved on the aediles at Rome. In the 'municipia' the aediles ranked among the chief magistrates, 'sufficiunt tunicae *summis aedilibus* albae' Juv. 3. 179. Horace (1 S. 5. 34 foll.) laughs at the provincial importance of the praetor of Fundi.

emina, half a sextarius, both dry and liquid measure.

131. 'Nor the man who laughs at philosophy simply because he cannot understand it.' The 'abacus' was a slab of marble or some other material used by mathematicians, and covered with sand for the purpose of drawing figures and making calculations. Jahn. Heinr. quotes Apul. Apol. 16. 426 'si non modo campo et glaebis, verum etiam abaco et pulvisculo te dedisses.' Others, like Casaubon, separate the 'abacus' from the 'pulvis,' making the former an arithmetical counting-board—the latter the sand on the ground on which geometers described their diagrams, as Archimedes, called by Cic. Tusc. 5. 23 'homunculus a pulvere et radio' (König), was doing at the time of his murder. Cicero (N. D. 2. 18) speaks of '*eruditus* pulvis.' Casaubon. The original meaning of 'meta' is 'a cone.' See Freund. 'Gallicum genus buxi in metas emittitur' Plin. 16. 70.

132. **scit risisse,** v. 53, 'has the discernment to laugh.'

vafer, v. 116. 'Laudare paratus' Juv. 3. 106, who is fond of the construction, 'he has learnt his lesson and is primed and ready to go off.'

133. *Vellunt tibi barbam* Lascivi pueri' Hor. 1 S. 3. 133, speaking to a Stoic.

nonaria, seemingly only found here, so called because not allowed to appear in public before the ninth hour, the time of dining (Hor. 1 Ep. 7. 71).

his mane edictum, post prandia Calliroën do.'

[134. *parandia* a. *Calliroën do* om. a.]

134. Persius probably thought of Horace's edict (1 Ep. 19. 8) 'Forum putealque Libonis Mandabo siccis, adimam cantare severis,' as Casaubon observes.

edictum seems best taken as the 'play-bill,' as in Sen. Ep. 117. 30 (quoted by Marcilius) 'Nemo qui obstetricem parturienti filiae sollicitus arcessit, *edictum et ludorum ordinem*

these I allow the play-bill for their morning's reading and after luncheon Calliroe.'

perlegit.' The 'edictum' of the praetor would be less interesting to this class of idlers, and besides cannot have been a *daily* object of curiosity.

Calliroē, a poem of the Phyllis and Hypsipyle stamp (v. 34), which would be recited after dinner. The Schol. says that one Asinius Celer wrote a puerile comedy (?) on the subject. The context seems to require some *literary* trash, as a set off against Persius' own productions. The spelling 'Calliroën' is adopted by Jahn from the MSS. There is no such form as 'Callirhoe,' the choice being between Καλλιρρόη and Καλλιρόη.

SATURA II.

HUNC, Macrine, diem numera meliore lapillo,
qui tibi labentis apponit candidus annos.
funde merum genio. non tu prece poscis emaci,
quae nisi seductis nequeas committere divis ;
at bona pars procerum tacita libabit acerra.   5

[*Ad Macrinum de vitae honestate* a.   *Ad Plotium Macrinum de bona mente* C.
2. *quid* a.   *apponet* C.   3. *murum* C.   5. *ad* C.   *libavit* C.]

On right and wrong prayers to the gods. A birthday poem to Macrinus.

Comp. generally Plato's Second Alcibiades, Juv. Sat. 10. The subject was one commonly discussed in the schools of the philosophers. Jahn.

1-16. 'Enjoy your birthday freely, my friend, and propitiate the power that governs your happiness. *Your* prayers are sure to be acceptable, unlike those of most of our great men, who dare not express their wishes openly. They pray selfishly for money, and for the death of those who stand between them and their enjoyment—aye, and think they shall be heard, as they have gone through all the ritual forms.'

1. Plotius Macrinus, the Schol. say, was a learned man who loved Persius as his son, having studied in the house of the same preceptor, Servilius. He had sold some property to Persius at a reduced price. Birthday gifts were common at Rome. Authors used to send their works as presents 'natalicii titulo.' Censorinus de Die Nat. 1. 5, referred to by Casaubon.

meliore lapillo. [Martial 9. 52. 5 'diesque nobis Signandi *melioribus lapillis.*'] 'O lucem *candidiore nota*' Catull. 107. 6. 'Quem *lapide* illa diem *candidiore* notat' *ib.* 68. 148. 'Cressa ne careat pulchra dies nota' Hor. 1 Od. 36. 10, commonly explained by a story of Pliny's (H. N. 7. 131) that the Thracians used to lay aside a white or black stone for every day of their lives, accordingly as it was lucky or unlucky, like the pebbles used in voting on criminal trials ; and so doubtless it was understood by Pliny the younger (Ep. 6. 11. 3) and Martial (12. 34. 5 foll.), who use the word 'calculus.' [Mart. 8. 45. 2 speaks in this connection of 'lactea gemma ;' and so 11. 36. 2 : in 10. 38. 5 of 'caris litoris Indici lapillis.'] But it may be doubted (comp. Hor. l. c. with 2 Sat. 3. 246) whether 'lapis candidior' in Catull. means anything more than *chalk*, and whether Persius has not copied him, using 'numero' as equivalent to 'noto.' With the general sentiment comp. Hor. 2 Ep. 2. 210 'Natales grate numeras?'

2. labentis apponit. The years, as they glide away unobserved (Hor. 2 Od. 14. 2), are kept in check by the birthday, which adds each to the account. 'Apponit' contains the notion of gain ('lucro appone' Hor. 1 Od. 9. 15), each year being looked upon as so much more pleasure realized. Comp. Hor. 2 Od. 5. 13 'Currit enim ferox Aetas, et illi quos tibi demserit *Apponet* annos,'

SATIRE II.

This day, Macrinus, mark with a stone of more auspicious hue, the white day, which adds to your account each year as it glides away. Pour the wine to your Genius. You are not the man to make higgling prayers, asking the gods for things which you can only confide to them when you have got them in a corner. Meantime, the mass of our upper classes will go on making libations from a censer that tells no tales. It is not every one who is

though there the thought turns on the gradual diminution of the disparity of years between an old man and a young woman.

candidus. Jahn comp. Tib. 1. 7. 63 'At tu, *Natalis*, multos celebrande per annos, *Candidior* semper *candidiorque veni.*'

3. 'Scit Genius, natale comes qui temperat astrum, Naturae deus humanae, mortalis in unum Quodque caput, vultu mutabilis, albus et ater' Hor. 2 Ep. 2. 187. The Genius was the deification of the happier or impulsive part of man, so that an offering to it implied that the day was to be spent in real enjoyment. 'Cras *genium* mero Placabis, et porco bimestri' Hor. 3 Od. 17. 10; 'vinoque diurno Placari genius festis impune diebus' A. P. 209; 'piabant Floribus et vino *genium*, memorem brevis aevi' 2 Ep. 1. 144, where the last words may be compared with the city mouse's exhortation to the country mouse, 2 S. 6. 96 'Dum licet, in rebus iucundis vive beatus, Vive memor quam sis aevi brevis.' By connecting **funde merum genio** with what follows, Persius seems to say that Macrinus may indulge his inclinations safely, and be sure that the gods will grant them. Censorinus [2.

2] tells us, on the authority of Varro, that the Romans offered only wine to the Genius on their birthday, 'ne die qua ipsi lucem accepissent, aliis demerent:' but Jahn refers to Hertzberg de Dis Rom. Patriis, p. 24, to show that this was not an invariable rule.

emaci, 'fond of bargaining,' 'higgling.' v. 29 'qua tu mercede deorum *Eméris* auriculas?' Casaubon comp. Hor. 3 Od. 29. 59 'ad miseras preces Decurrere, et *votis pacisci.*' Jahn comp. Plato Euthyph. p. 14 E ἐμπορικὴ ἄρα τις ἂν εἴη τέχνη ἡ ὁσιότης θεοῖς καὶ ἀνθρώποις παρ' ἀλλήλων.

4. **seductis.** 6. 42 'paullum a turba *seductior* audi.' Casaubon refers to Sen. Ep. 41 for the statement that worshippers used to get the templekeeper to allow them access to the *ears* of the statues, that they might be able to be heard better. 'Facis rem optimam et tibi salutarem, si, ut scribis, perseveras ire ad bonam mentem, quam stultum est optare, cum possis a te impetrare. Non sunt ad caelum elevandae manus, nec exorandus aedituus ut nos ad aures simulacri, quasi magis exaudiri possimus, admittat.'

5. 'At bona pars hominum' Hor. 1 S. 1. 61.

libabit, is used to do, and therefore

haut cuivis promptum est murmurque humilisque susurros
tollere de templis et aperto vivere voto.
'Mens bona, fama, fides' haec clare et ut audiat hospes;
illa sibi introrsum et sub lingua murmurat 'o si
ebulliat patruus, praeclarum funus!' et 'o si   10
sub rastro crepet argenti mihi seria dextro
Hercule! pupillumve utinam, quem proximus heres
inpello, expungam! namque est scabiosus et acri
bile tumet. Nerio iam tertia ducitur uxor.'

[6. *aut* α. *murmur humilisque* α; *murmur, susurros* om. C.   7. *aperte* α,
a perito C.   10. *ebullit patrui* α : *ebullet* ς : *patru* ... C. apud Servium
Aen. 6. 187 varie praebent codices *ebulliat, ebullit, ebullat*.   11. *crepat* α.
12. *quam* α.   13. *expungas* α.   *nam et est* α, *nam est* C, *namque est* ς.
14. *conditur* αC, *ducitur* ς, Serv. Georg. 4. 256.]

will do, will be found to do. Jahn
comp. Juv. 8. 182 'quae Turpia cerdoni,
Volesos Brutumque *decebunt*.' 'Farre
pio et plena supplex veneratur acerra'
Virg. Aen. 5. 745.
6. '*Non cuivis* homini contingit'
Hor. 1 Ep. 17. 36. 'Formam optat
modico pueris, maiore puellis murmure'
Juv. 10. 289. Clem. Alex. Strom. 4. 26.
§ 173 is referred to by Casaubon as
giving the Pythagorean rule μετὰ φωνῆς
εὔχεσθαι.
7. 'Nec voto vivitur uno' 5. 53. *vivere* refers to daily prayers for daily
blessings.
8. Imitated from Hor. 1 Ep. 16. 57
foll. The *secret* prayer in Persius is
more 'bona fide,' and consequently
more disguised than in Horace, who
apparently merely means that while
the worshipper asks the gods for one
thing his heart is set on another.
Possibly **Mens bona, fama, fides**
are not things prayed for, but *persons*,
like Janus and Apollo, Hor. l. c. Casaubon refers to Prop. 3. 24. 19 'Mens
Bona, si qua dea es, tua me in sacraria
dono,' [and inscriptions 'Menti Bonae'
are given in the Berlin Corpus Inscriptionum,' i. nos. 1167, 1168, 1237. See
Preller's Römische Mythologie, p. 628,
note 2. 'Quod rarissimum est, amas
bonam mentem,' Petronius 3. The
opposite is 'mala mens;' Catull. 40. 1,
15. 14: Tibull. 2. 5. 104.] Against
this may be urged that no gods are
particularised in the secret prayer, like
Laverna Hor. l. c., with the incidental
exception of Hercules. What 'mens
bona' is is explained by Sen. (quoted
by the Delphin editor and Jahn) Ep.
10 'Roga *bonam mentem*, bonam valetudinem animi, deinde tunc corporis'
(nearly Juvenal's 'mens sana in corpore
sano' 10. 356), Ep. 16 'Perseverandum
est et assiduo studio robur addendum,
donec *bona mens* sit, quod bona voluntas est,'—'health of mind.' [With the
whole comp. Sen. Ep. 10. 5 'Nunc
enim quanta dementia est hominum:
turpissima vota dis insusurrant : si quis
admoverit aurem, conticescunt. Et quod
scire hominem nolunt, deo narrant.'
Ben. 2. 1. 4 'vota homines parcius
facerent, si palam facienda essent;
adeo etiam deos, quibus honestissime
supplicamus, tacite malumus et intra
nosmetipsos precari.' Petronius 88 'ac
ne bonam quidem mentem aut bonam
valetudinem petunt, sed statim, ante
quam limen Capitolii tangant, alius
donum promittit si propinquum divitem
extulerit, alius si thesaurum effoderit,
alius si ad trecentiens sestertium salvus
pervenerit.' Mart. 1. 39. 6 'nihil arcano
qui roget ore deos.']
hospes, 'a stranger,' 'so that any
one may hear.'
9. **sub lingua** is compared by Casaubon to ὑπ' ὀδόντα.
10. **ebulliat** is restored by Jahn and
Heinr. for 'ebullit,' the reading of most

ready to do away with muttering and whispering from our temples, and live in the use of prayers to which all may listen. 'Sound mind, good report, credit'—so much is said aloud even in a stranger's hearing, the rest he mutters to himself under his breath. 'O that my uncle would go off in a splendid obituary. O that I could hear a crock of silver chinking under my harrow, by the blessing of Hercules—or that I might strike out my ward, on whose heels I tread as next in succession, so full of scrofula and acrid bile as he is already! There is Nerius actually marrying his third wife!' It is to make prayers like these piously, that

MSS., which used to be explained as a contraction of 'ebullierit.' [The synizesis is questioned by Lucian Müller, De Re Metrica, p. 256.] The full expression is 'ebullire (= efflare) animam' (Sen. Apocolocynt. 4, [Petronius 42, 62]).

patruus Orelli, Heinr., Jahn, from some MSS. The majority have 'patrui,' which seems to be a correction made by those who did not understand 'ebulliat.'

praeclarum funus is meant to bear the double sense 'a glorious (welcome) death' and 'a splendid funeral.' Jahn comp. Prop. 1. 17. 8 'Haeccine parva meum *funus* harena teget?' Virg. Aen. 9. 486, 7 'nec te *tua funera* mater Produxi.' Heinr. makes 'funus' cogn. acc. to 'ebulliat.' Comp. Juv. 6. 566, where the wife asks the astrologer 'quando sororem Efferat et *patruos*.'

11. 'O si urnam argenti fors quae mihi monstret . . . dives amico Hercule' Hor. 2 S. 6. 10. Casaubon makes a distinction between Hermes as the bestower of windfalls found on the way, and Hercules as the patron of treasures that are sought for. There was a custom at Rome [Preller, Römische Myth. p. 652] to consecrate a tenth part of gains to Hercules.

12. 'Non fraudem socio, puerove incogitat ullam *Pupillo*' Hor. 2 Ep. 1. 122. The man here does not compass his ward's death, but only prays for it. The Twelve Tables provided that where no guardian was appointed by will, the next of kin would be guardian, and he would of course be heir. 'Agnatus proximus tutelam nancitor.'

13. **inpello**, v. 29, 'unda inpellitur unda' Ov. M. 15. 181, equivalent to 'urgeo,' 'insto,' 'premo.' Jahn comp. Lucan 1. 149 'inpellens quidquid sibi summa petenti Obstaret.'

expungam from the tablets of the will. He wishes he may have the pleasure of striking the name out, as that of a person deceased.

acri bile. δριμεῖα χολή, Casaubon, referring to Chrysost. Hom. in Matth. 63. 'It is not much to grant, a great part has been done already; the gods in fact seem to have contemplated his death, and it would be such a release!' Casaubon quotes Juv. 6. 565 'Consulit ictericae lento de funere matris.'

14. **tumet.** 'turgescit vitrea bilis' 3. 8; 'mascula bilis Intumuit' 5. 145.

Nerius is the usurer mentioned by Hor. 2 S. 3. 69. Persius borrows not only his images but his names from Horace, e. g. Pedius 1. 85, Craterus 3. 65, [Natta 3. 31,] Bestius 6. 37; not unnatural in a young writer and probably a recluse, who must have formed his notions of life as much from books as from experience.

For **ducitur** the best MSS. give 'conditur,' perhaps, as Jahn thinks, from a confusion of this passage with Mart. 10. 43. Serv. on Virg. G. 4. 256 explains 'ducitur' 'is carried out to burial,' but 'ducitur uxor' can only have one meaning, and the words properly understood express the sense which Servius wishes, only with more skill. 'Nerius is just marrying a *third* time (has just buried his *second wife*).' ['Conditur' is adopted by Bücheler.]

haec sancte ut poscas, Tiberino in gurgite mergis 15
mane caput bis terque et noctem flumine purgas.
 Heus age, responde—minimum est quod scire laboro—
de Iove quid sentis? estne ut praeponere cures
hunc—'Cuinam?' cuinam? vis Staio? an scilicet haeres?
quis potior iudex, puerisve quis aptior orbis? 20
hoc igitur, quo tu Iovis aurem inpellere temptas,
dic agedum Staio, 'pro Iuppiter! o bone' clamet
'Iuppiter!' at sese non clamet Iuppiter ipse?
ignovisse putas, quia, cum tonat, ocius ilex
sulpure discutitur sacro quam tuque domusque? 25
an quia non fibris ovium Ergennaque iubente
triste iaces lucis evitandumque bidental,
idcirco stolidam praebet tibi vellere barbam

[15. *poscat* a. *mergit* a. 16. *nocte* a. *purgat* a. 18. *est ut* a. 19. *hunc cuinam vis* a C, *hunc cuiquam cuinam vis* ⸑. 23. *ad* a C. 26. *obvium* C.]

15. **haec**, emphatic. 'It is to ask for *this* with pure lips.'
 Tiberino foll. 'Illo Mane die quo tu indicis ieiunia, nudus In Tiberi stabit' Hor. 2 S. 3. 290. 'Ter matutino Tiberi mergetur, et ipsis Vorticibus timidum caput abluet' Juv. 6. 523.
 16. 'Ac primum pura somnum tibi discute lympha' Prop. 3. 10. 13. Comp. Virg. Aen. 8. 69, where Aeneas on rising dips his hands in the Tiber.
 noctem ... purgas, like 'totum semel expiet annum' Juv. 6. 521.
 17–30. [The Stoical doctrine of an all-seeing Deity, expounded frequently in Epictetus.] 'Let them only try the experiment of taking the least divine of their acquaintance and saying to him what they say to Jupiter, he would at once cry shame on them. The gods indeed do not take vengeance immediately, but that is no proof that such prayers are forgiven, unless we are to suppose that the sacrifice—what a sacrifice!—makes the difference, and acts as a bribe.'
 17. **scire laboro**, Hor. 1 Ep. 3. 2, 'nosse laboro' 2 S. 8. 19.
 18. **est ut** = 'perhaps.' 'Est ut viro vir latius ordinet Arbusta sulcis' Hor. 3 Od. 1. 9.

19. The inferior MSS. give 'cuiquam,' which was the reading of the old editions, and is recalled by Heinr., who points 'Hunc cuiquam?' 'Cuinam vis?' 'Staio.' The Schol. wrongly identify 'Staius' with Staienus, who was one of the judges in the trial of Oppianicus (Cic. pro Cluent.); the old commentators, taking the hint, confound him with Oppianicus himself. Jahn, who rejects the story, supposes Persius to have meant some respectable man of the day, but v. 20 looks very like a sarcasm not only on the worshipper, who is assumed to have qualms, but on Staius himself. [The name *Staius* is found several times in inscriptions of Northern Italy: see C. I. L. 5: at Nemi, C. I. L. 14. 4203 'Staia L. L. Quinta:' C. I. L. 2. 120 (Evora in Portugal): 2. 4975–60 (Madrid): 12. 5145 (Narbo).]
 scilicet. 'Do you mean to say that you have any hesitation?'
 20. The meaning may either be 'Who can be a better judge, or more suitable guardian?' or 'Who can be better or more suitable as a judge in a case between orphans and their guardian?' Plaut. amusingly explains **orbis** '*orbus* proprie dicitur qui lumen

you duck your head every morning twice and three times in the Tiber, and wash off the night in the running water.

Come, now, tell me, the question is the merest trifle: What is your view of Jupiter? May I assume that you would think of putting him above—'Above whom?' Whom? Oh, shall we say Staius? You hesitate? as if there could be a better judge or a more desirable guardian for orphan children? Well, then, just say to Staius the prayer which you wish to have an effect on the ear of Jupiter. 'Jupiter,' he would call out, 'gracious Jupiter!' And won't Jupiter call out his own name, think you? Do you suppose he has ignored all, because, when it thunders, the sacred bolt rives the oak rather than you and your house? or because you are not this moment lying in that forest, by order of Ergenna and the sheep's liver, a sad trophy of vengeance for men to turn

oculorum amisit, quasi amissis *orbibus* propter rotunditatem oculorum.'

21. inpellere = 'percutere.' 'Maternas *inpulit* auris Luctus Aristaei' Virg. G. 4. 349. 'Arrectasque *inpulit* aures Confusae sonus urbis' Aen. 12. 618. Jahn and König.

22. 'Agedum concede' Lucr. 3. 962. 'Agedum, sume hoc ptisanarium oryzae' Hor. 2 S. 3. 155.

dic ... clamet = 'si dices, clamabit' Heinr.

23. 'Maxime, quis non, Iuppiter, exclamat simul atque audivit?' Hor. 1. S. 2. 17. Persius may also have been thinking of 1 S. 1. 20 'Quid caussae est, merito quin illis Iuppiter ambas Iratus buccas inflet, neque se fore posthac Tam facilem dicat, votis ut praebeat aurem?'

24. The details intended to be presented appear to be these. The guilty worshipper is in a sacred grove during a thunderstorm; the lightning strikes not him, but one of the sacred trees; and he congratulates himself on his escape,—without reason, as Persius tells him. The circumstances are precisely those used by Lucretius to enforce his sceptical argument, 6. 390 'Cur quibus incautum scelus aversabile cumque est Non faciunt (sc. Divi) icti flammas ut fulguris halent Pectore perfixo, documen mortalibus acre?' *ib.* 416 'Postremo, cur sancta Deum delubra, suasque *Discutit* infesto praeclaras fulmine sedes?' [The text taken by Persius is fully treated by Plutarch 'De Sera Numinis Vindicta.']

25. 'Aetherioque nocens fumavit *sulpure* ferrum' Lucan 7. 160.

domus. The family of the criminal share his fate, Συμμάρψας ὀλέσει γενεήν, καὶ οἶκον ἅπαντα Oracle Hdt. 6. 86.

26. Prop. 4. 1. 104 'Aut sibi commissos *fibra* locuta Deos.'

Ergenna, an Etruscan name like Porsenna, Sisenna, Perpenna, Heinr. 'Prodigiosa fides et *Tuscis* digna *libellis*' Juv. 13. 62 (= 'digna procuratione') Mayor's note. König is wrong in saying that this line in construction follows 'evitandum.' Persius, to make the picture more vivid, fixes not on the moment of death, but on the time when the corpse is lying dead and the augur pronouncing on it. The corpse and the place where it fell, which was railed off and held sacred, are identified. 'Hominem ita exanimatum cremari fas non est, condi terra religio tradidit' Plin. 2. 145.

27. '*Triste bidental* Moverit incestus' Hor. A. P. 471.

lucis. 'Tu parum castis inimica mittes Fulmina *lucis*' Hor. 1 Od. 12. 60. See Freund v. 'bidental.'

28. vellere barbam, 1. 133. Comp. the story of the Gaul and Papirius. The images of the gods had beards, v. 58. There may also be an allusion to the mode of supplication by taking hold of the beard (Il. 10. 454).

Iuppiter? aut quidnam est, qua tu mercede deorum
emeris auriculas? pulmone et lactibus unctis? 30
 Ecce avia aut metuens divum matertera cunis
exemit puerum frontemque atque uda labella
infami digito et lustralibus ante salivis
expiat, urentis oculos inhibere perita ;
tunc manibus quatit et spem macram supplice voto 35
nunc Licini in campos, nunc Crassi mittit in aedis.
' hunc optet generum rex et regina! puellae
hunc rapiant! quidquid calcaverit hic, rosa fiat!'
ast ego nutrici non mando vota: negato,
Iuppiter, haec illi, quamvis te albata rogarit. 40

[29. *mercedeorum* a. 34. *expica* A, *exspica* B. 35. *quant* A, *quarit* B.
36. *lini* a. *hedis* a. 37. *optent* C. 40. *haec* om. a. *rogabit* a.]

29. Quidnam est ea merces, qua, etc. aut puts another case, like ' *aut ego fallor* '=' nisi fallor.'

30. Jahn explains **emere auriculas** on the analogy of ' praebere ' or ' dare aurem,' to which he might have added ' commodare' Hor. 1 Ep. 1. 40.

pulmone, etc. Comp. Juv. 10. 354 ' Ut tamen et poscas aliquid, voveasque sacellis *Exta et candiduli divina tomacula porci*,' 13. 115 ' Aut cur In carbone tuo charta pia tura soluta Ponimus, et *sectum vituli iecur albaque porci Omenta* ?' where the details are mentioned contemptuously as here.

lactibus. ' Ab hoc ventriculo *lactes* in homine et ove, per quas labitur cibus: in ceteris hillae' Plin. 11. 200.

31–40. ' No better are the silly prayers of old women for new-born children—that the darlings may be rich and marry princesses. They know not what they ask.'

31. **Ecce**, 1. 30.

metuens divum, a translation of δεισιδαίμων. ['Metuo' is a favourite word in this connection: Plaut. Pseud. 269 ' metuere deos :' Ter. Hec. 772 ' nec deos metuont istae:' Hor. 1 Od. 35. 13 ' te .... purpurei metuunt tyranni, Iniurioso ne pede proruas Stantem columnam:' Ov. Fast. 6. 259 ' quo non metuentius ullum Numinis ingenium terra Sabina tulit :' Met. 1. 323 ' aut illa metuentior ulla deorum :' C. I. L. 5. 1. 88 ' religionis Iudaicae metuenti :' Seneca Ben. 3. 17. 3 ' testes ingratorum animorum deos metuit.'] ' Mater delira . . . Quone malo mentem concussa ? timore deorum' Hor. 2 S. 3. 295.

matertera. ' Amita est patris soror ; *matertera* est matris soror' Paul. Dig. 38. 10. 10. 4.

33. **infami**=' medio.' ' Medinmque ostenderet unguem' Juv. 10. 53 Mayor's note. The ' infamis digitus ' was chosen as having more power against fascination on that very account. Jahn.

lustralibus. The eighth day, if the child were a girl, the ninth if a boy, was called ' dies lustralis ' or ' lustricus : ' the infant was then purified and named. Festus, p. 120 Müll. Comp. Suet. Nero 6.

salivis expiat. [Plin. 28. 35 ' simili modo' (i. e. usu salivae) ' fascinationes repercutimus.'] ' Mox turbatum sputo pulverem anus medio sustulit digito frontemque repugnantis signat' Petr. 131. Comp. the custom of spitting into the lap to avert fascination. Juv. 7. 111 Mayor's note.

34. ' Nescio quis teneros oculus mihi fascinat agnos' Virg. E. 3. 103. ' Non istic obliquo oculo mea commoda quisquam Limat' Hor. 1 Ep. 14. 37.

urentis is rightly explained by the

from, is that a reason why Jupiter is to give you his stupid beard to pull? or what is the price you pay for the ears of the gods? a dishful of lungs and greasy chitterlings?

Look here—a grandmother or a superstitious aunt has taken baby from his cradle, and is charming his forehead and his slavering lips against mischief by the joint action of her middle finger and her purifying spittle; for she knows right well how to check the evil eye. Then she dandles him in her arms and packs off the pinched little hope of the family, so far as wishing can do it, to the domains of Licinus or the palace of Crassus. 'May he be a catch for my lord and lady's daughter! May the pretty ladies scramble for him! May the ground he walks on turn to a rose-bed!' But *I* will never trust a nurse to pray for me or mine; good Jupiter, be sure to refuse her, though she may have put on white for the occasion.

Delph. ed. as 'withering' or 'blasting.' Jahn comp. Plut. Quaest. Sympos. 5. 1 γιγνώσκομεν γὰρ ἀνθρώπους τῷ καταβλέπειν τὰ παιδία μάλιστα βλάπτοντας, ὑγρότητι τῆς ἕξεως καὶ ἀσθενείᾳ τρεπομένης ὑπ' αὐτῶν καὶ κινουμένης ἐπὶ τὸ χεῖρον.

35. **manibus quatit.** Casaubon comp. Hom. Il. 6. 474 αὐτὰρ ὅγ' ὃν φίλον υἱὸν ἐπεὶ κύσε πῆλέ τε χερσίν, Εἶπεν ἐπευξάμενος Δί' τ' ἄλλοισίν τε θεοῖσι.

spem macram, etc. Comp. Juv. 14. 146 'Nocte boves *macri* lassoque famelica collo Iumenta ad virides huius *mittentur* aristas.' She speeds him thither by the force of her wish, and then turns him loose to fatten himself. The Delph. ed. comp. Virg. Aen. 11. 46 'Cum me complexus euntem Mitteret in magnum imperium.'

With voto .. mittit comp. Hor. 1 Ep. 14. 41 'Horum tu in numerum *voto ruis?*'

36. 'Quorum nomina cum Crasso Licinoque numerantur' Sen. Ep. 120. 20. Comp. Juv. 1. 109 Mayor's note, *ib.* 14. 305 foll., and see Dict. Biogr.

37. [Haupt, in *Hermes* vol. 7, p. 11, suggests that in this passage Persius was alluding to current popular fables about kings and queens, girls and roses.] 'Multi illum pueri, multae *optavere puellae*' Catull. 62. 42, referred to by König.

optet is restored by Jahn from the best MSS. instead of the vulg. 'optent,' which may be a correction, though it is perhaps as probable that the singular is a blunder.

rex et regina is explained by Jahn from 1. 67, where see note: but the words in the mouth of an old woman are more likely to be general, though there were no 'king and queen' at Rome.

38. **rapiant** seems to imply that the tables are to be turned, and that instead of his running off with them, they are to run off with him. Casaubon comp. the similar use of ἁρπάζειν and of 'diripere.' 'Editum librum continuo mirari homines et diripere coeperunt' Life of Persius.

quidquid, etc. Casaubon comp. Claud. 1 Seren. 89 'Quocunque per herbam Reptares, fluxere rosae.'

39. 'Quid voveat dulci nutricula maius alumno,' etc. Hor. 1 Ep. 4. 6 foll. Horace regards the prayers of a nurse more approvingly than Persius, having a higher opinion of her good sense. Seneca (Ep. 60, quoted by Casaubon) agrees with Persius, 'Etiamnum optas quod tibi optavit nutrix, aut paedagogus aut mater? Nondum intellegis quantum mali optaverint?' comp. *ib.* Ep. 32, Juv. 14. 208.

40. 'Though she ask it with every requisite form,' v. 15. **albata.** 'Casta placent superis: pura cum veste venite' Tibull. 2. 1. 13.

Poscis opem nervis corpusque fidele senectae.
esto; age; sed grandes patinae tuccetaque crassa
adnuere his superos vetuere Iovemque morantur.
Rem struere exoptas caeso bove Mercuriumque
arcessis fibra. 'Da fortunare Penatis, 45
da pecus et gregibus fetum!' quo, pessime, pacto,
tot tibi cum in flammas iunicum omenta liquescant?
et tamen hic extis et opimo vincere ferto
intendit 'iam crescit ager, iam crescit ovile,
iam dabitur, iam iam!' donec deceptus et exspes 50
nequiquam fundo suspiret nummus in imo.

[41. *poscit* a.   42. *pingens* et *grandes* C.   43. *mirantur* C.   45. *accessis* a, *accersis* Priscian. 1. p. 433 Keil.   *fibram* C.   *de* a.   48. *at tamen* a, *et tamen* C.   *festo* a.   49. *aser* a.]

41–51. 'One man prays for health and long life—a blessing doubtless—but one which *he* cannot have, being a glutton. Another actually ruins himself by the costliness of his sacrifices, while all the time his object is to obtain an increase to his possesions—and goes on spending and hoping to the last.'

41. **Poscis opem** is a common enough phrase, and **nervis** is added as the party for whom the blessing is sought.

senectae may either be constructed with 'poscis,' like 'nervis,' or with 'fidele,' which is Casaubon's view—'corpus cui suae vires permaneant ad senectam usque.'

42. '*Grandes* rhombi *patinaeque* Grande ferunt una cum damno dedecus,' Hor. 2 S. 2. 95. 'grandes' Jahn, from the best MSS., vulg. 'pingues.' ['Grandis' of plate, Plaut. Curc. 368, Cic. Verr. 2. 4. 21.]

tucceta. Arnobius 2. 42 talks of 'glacialia conditione tucceta,' and the word has been introduced conjecturally by some editors in 7. 24 of the same author. The Scholia make 'tuccetum' a Gaulish word, of the same origin with the proper name 'Tucca,' and describes it as beef steeped in a thick gravy, which enables it to keep a year. [The word occurs also in Apuleius Met. 2. 7., 7. 11. 'Tuccetum ζωμὸς παχύς,' Gloss. Lat. Graec. p. 202. 53.]

43. **adnuere** with the dative of the thing countenanced. 'Audacibus adnue coeptis' Virg. G. 1. 40.

vetuere implies that the restraining cause had anticipated the prayer, and prevented its taking effect. Diog. Laert. 6. 2. 28, quoted by Jahn, relates of Diogenes the cynic, ἐκίνει αὐτὸν τὸ θύειν τοῖς θεοῖς ὑπὲρ ὑγιείας, ἐν αὐτῇ δὲ τῇ θυσίᾳ κατὰ τῆς ὑγιείας δειπνεῖν.

44. **Rem struere** 'to increase your wealth,' 'acervo quem *struit*' Hor. 1 S. 1. 35.

Mercurium, note on v. 11., 6. 62.

45. **arcessis** stronger than 'vocas,' 'summon,' as implying a command, and one that will be obeyed, so that here it is used rhetorically, to express the confidence of the worshipper. The reference is to the *presence* of the gods, as Jahn remarks.

fibra (v. 26) is said in the same spirit as 'pulmone et lactibus unctis' v. 30.

fortunare is used absolutely, as in Afranius ap. Non. sub v., quoted by Jahn, 'Deos ego omnes ut *fortunassint* precor,' the subj. to 'fortunare' being 'penates.' 'Fortuno,' as Jahn remarks, is a 'vox sollemnis' in prayers, being invariably used of the gods. 'Tu quamcunque Deus tibi *fortunaverit* horam Grata sume manu' Hor. 1 Ep. 11. 22.

Penatis, as gods of the 'penus,'

You ask reinforcement for your physical strength, and a body to stand you in stead in old age. So far so good—go on; but your great dishes and thick gravies have laid an injunction on the gods not to grant it, and clog the gracious purposes of Jupiter.

You aim at increasing your wealth by sacrificing oxen, and serve a summons on Mercury in the shape of liver. 'Grant that my household gods may prosper me: grant me cattle and a teeming season for my flocks!' On what terms, pray, most wretched of creatures, when the fat of so many of your bullocks is melting into the fire? Yet the man strains every nerve to gain his end by entrails and rich puddings. 'Now my lands are getting broader; now my fold is widening; now I shall get it—now—now:' till at last, disappointed and despairing, the solitary coin sighs unavailingly at the bottom of the chest.

the domestic store. 'Cura *penum* struere et flammis adolere *penatis*' Virg. Aen. 1. 704.

46. 'Si *fetura gregem* suppleverit' Virg. E. 7. 36. 'Quo pacto, pessime' Hor. 2 S. 7. 22.

47. Imitated from Catull. 90. 6 'Omentum in flamma pingue liquefaciens.'

iunix ('iuvenix,' 'iuvencus') = 'iuvenca.' Plaut. Mil. 304.

48. ['At tamen' Bücheler.] 'He strains every nerve to win,' increasing his sacrifices as his means decrease. extis et .. ferto contemptuously, vv. 30, 45. Jahn explains 'fertum' from Festus sub v. and Cato R. R. 134, 141 as a kind of cake, which was frequently offered ('obmovebatur') in sacrifice, coupled with 'strues' in the tables of the Fratres Arvales 221, 222, 225, p. 135 Henzen. 'A ferendo' Schol.

49. Juv. 5. 166 'Ecce dabit iam Semesum leporem atque aliquid de clunibus apri: Ad nos *iam* veniet minor altilis.'

50. Jahn, following [one interpretation offered by the Scholia], ingeniously changes the punctuation, 'donec deceptus et exspes, *Nequiquam fundo*, suspiret, *nummus in imo* !' 'deceptus' being the man, and 'Nequiquam fundo nummus in imo!' (= 'nequiquam profudi opes meas') the words of his lament. But the old stopping is at once more obvious and more spirited, the last coin ('nummus' = 'sestertius') having been cheated into parting with its brethren by the promise that it should see them again and many more besides, and now sighing to find itself left quite alone without any more hope. Casaubon compares Hesiod's Works and Days 369 δειλὴ δ' ἐνὶ πύθμενι φειδώ (imitated by Sen. Ep. 1. 5 'Sera parsimonia in fundo est'): a parallel rather unfavourable to Jahn's punctuation, which calls attention more to the money expended than to the remainder. 'Nummi' are similarly personified 5. 149 'Quid petis? ut nummi, quos hic quincunce modesto Nutrieras, pergant avidos sudare deunces?'

51–75. 'To receive a present of gold or silver is the summit of human pleasure. Thence men conclude that the gods must value it too, and accordingly gild the statues of those whom they find most propitious—so that now gold supersedes everything else in our temples. Miserable blindness of earthly grovellers! as if pampered flesh were a measure of the desires of heaven! Luxury may be excused for her refinements, though they are so many sins against nature: at any rate she has the enjoyment of them: but will any priest tell me that the gods can care for such things? No, give me that which no wealth can buy,—an honest, pure, and generous heart, and the cheapest oblation will suffice.'

Si tibi creterras argenti incusaque pingui
auro dona feram, sudes et pectore laevo
excutiat guttas laetari praetrepidum cor.
hinc illud subiit, auro sacras quod ovato 55
perducis facies ; nam 'fratres inter aënos
somnia pituita qui purgatissima mittunt,
praecipui sunto sitque illis aurea barba.'
aurum vasa Numae Saturniaque inpulit aera

[52. *creterras* a, *crateras* C.   *incusasque* C.   53. *laeto* C.   54. *praetepidum* a.
creterram argenti sudabit praetrepidum cor Priscian. 1. p. 219 K.   55. *subit* a C.
56. *perducit* a.   57. *purgantissima* C.   58. *sit illis* a.   59. *auri* a.]

52. [Servius on Aen. 1. 724 says that the Latin form of κρατήρ is 'haec cratera:' but 'creterra' is attested by Paulus, p. 53 Müller, Nonius, p. 547, and Gloss. Vat. p. 33. 11 Goetz '*creterre* crateres.' In Cic. Fam. 7. 1. 2 the Medicean MS. has 'creterrarum ;' and so the old Blandinian MS. in Hor. 2 S. 4. 80. The form is also supported by Porphyrion, and by respectable MS. authority, in Hor. 3 Od. 18. 17.]

incusa is a translation of ἐμπαιστά (Casaubon), ἐμπαιστικὴ τέχνη being the art of embossing silver or some other material with golden ornaments ('crustae' or 'emblemata'). Hence 'creterras argenti incusaque dona' is probably a hendiadys.

pingui, opposed to 'levi' or 'tenui,' as the thickness of the gold would constitute its value. Can there be a reference to 'pingui munere' Hor. 2 Ep. 1. 267?

53. **dona feram**, Virg. G. 3. 22, Catull. 64. 34.

sudes. Casaubon refers to Aspasia ap. Athen. 5. 219 C κἀγὼ ὅπως ἤκουσα χαρᾶς ὑπὸ σῶμα λιπαίνω ἱδρῶτι.

pectore laevo, 'laeva parte mamillae Nil salit Arcadico iuveni' Jnv. 7. 159.

54. 'excutias' was preferred by Jahn in his edition of 1843, but he has since adopted **excutiat** which is supported by one of the oldest MSS. and by some others, and seems required by the relation between 'laevo pectore' and 'cor.'

guttas, 'tears' or 'sweat'? Heinr. says the latter, and it seems simpler. Juv. 1. 167 'tacita *sudant praecordia culpa.*'

laetari, construed with praetrepidum, 'overhasty to rejoice,' Hor. 2 Od. 4. 24 'Cuius octavum *trepidavit* aetas *Claudere* lustrum.' Catull. 46. 7 'Iam mens *praetrepidans* avet vagari.' Compare 'praelargus' 1. 14.

55. 'Hence it is that it has occurred to you to,' etc., 'subiit cari genitoris imago' Virg. Aen. 2. 560. 'animum (mentem)' or 'animo' sometimes expressed after 'subiit,' sometimes omitted. Compare 'succurrit' Aen. 2. 317.

illud subiit quod, otherwise expressed by the impersonal with an infinitive, 'misereri sortis humanae subit' Plin. 25. 23. Compare Ov. Trist. 3. 8. 38 'Quid sim quid fuerimque subit.' [The final syllable of the third person perf. sing. of the compounds of 'eo' ('abiit,' 'adiit,' etc.) is frequently lengthened by the poets, especially by Ovid.]

sacer, used of the gods themselves, not merely of things consecrated to them ; 'sacrae Vestae' Prop. 3. 4. 11, 'sacrae Cybelae' 3. 22. 3 [si l. c.].

auro ovato, like 'triumphatum aurum' Ov. ex Ponto 2. 1. 41. Jahn. The epithet may mark the unjust acquisition of the gold offered to heaven, as Madan thinks, Juv. 8. 100.

56. **perducis.** 'Quo totum nati corpus perduxit' Virg. G. 4. 416. For the custom of gilding statues compare Juv. 13. 151 'Radat *inaurati* femur Herculis, et *faciem ipsam* Neptuni, qui bratteolam de Castore ducat.' ['Hoc (aurum) suspiciunt, hoc suis optant, hoc dis velut rerum humanarum maximum, cum grati videri volunt, consecrant. Nihil illis (divitiis) melius nec dare videntur di

If I were to present you with cups of silver, chased with ornaments of thick gold, you would be all perspiration, and your heart in a flutter of joy would force out heart-drops from your left breast. This it is which has suggested it to you to give the faces of the gods a coating of triumphal gold. 'Among the brazen brethren, let those who send us dreams of nights most free from gross humours rank first in honour, and have a golden beard given them.' Yes, gold has driven out Numa's crockery and the brass

immortales posse nec habere' Sen. Ep. 115. 11, 12.]

fratres ... aënos is understood by Jahn of the gods generally, after Lubin and Famaly. The traditional explanation attributed by the Scholia to Acron, that the brethren are the sons of Aegyptus, statues of whom stood in the open air opposite to those of the Danaides in the portico of the Palatine Apollo, breaks down from want of evidence of the existence of any such statues (those of the Danaides being frequently mentioned, as by Prop. 2. 31. 4, who narrates the opening of the portico), as well as from the absence of any reason why they should preside over dreams. The Scholiast's other fancy, that Castor and Pollux are meant, is refuted by the words of the passage, which clearly points, as Casaubon observes, to more than two.

57. ' Dulcia se in bilem vertent, stomachoque tumultum Lenta feret *pituita*' Hor. 2 S. 2. 75. Persius doubtless means that those dreams which are freest from the gross humours of the body are likely to be truest—possibly he may also mean that those which are traceable to excess are *ipso facto* discredited as divine communications. Cicero however (De Div. 2. 58 foll.) and Lucretius (4. 907 foll.), in accounting for dreams naturally, make no use of this argument. Possibly there may be some point in 'pituita' in the mouth of a Stoic. Cicero l. c. says, ' *Stoici* autem tui negant quemquam nisi *sapientem* divinum esse posse,' and goes on to explain Chrysippus' views of the matter: while Horace reminds the Stoic (1 Ep. 1. 108) that phlegm is a drawback to the perfect sanity of the 'sapiens.' It does not appear that Persius refers particularly to the custom of sleeping in temples with a view to procure dreams. Jahn.

58. Cic. N. D. 3. 34 tells of Dionysius ' Aesculapii Epidaurii *barbam auream* demi iussit, neque enim convenire barbatum esse filium, cum in omnibus fanis pater imberbis esset.'

59. These **vasa Numae** were called ' capedines ' and ' simpuvia.' Cic. Parad. 1. 2 ' Quid? Numae Pompilii minusne gratas Dis immortalibus *capedines ac fictiles urnulas* fuisse quam filicatas aliorum pateras arbitramur?' Juv. 6. 343 ' *Simpuvium* ridere *Numae* nigrumque catinum, Et Vaticano fragiles de monte patellas.' They appear to have been bowls or dishes of some kind.

Saturnia ... aera. The Scholia, followed by Casaubon and Jahn, explains this of the use of brass coin, which was supposed to be connected with the early reign of Saturn in Italy; Janus, the first coiner, according to the legend, having stamped one side of the coin with his own head, the other with a ship, to commemorate the landing of Saturn (Macrob. Sat. 1): a connection further pointed to by the fact that the *aerarium* was in the temple of Saturn (Varro L. L. 5. 183). The 'vasa Numae,' however, would rather have led us to expect that the 'Saturnia aera' were temple furniture of some kind: and so the words are explained by the older commentators, who however are evidently merely guessing from the context. With the general sentiment compare Prop. 4. 1. 5 ' Fictilibus crevere deis haec aurea templa.' Juv. 11. 115 ' Hanc rebus Latiis curam praestare solebat *Fictilis et nullo violatus Iuppiter auro*.' [Euripides Philoctetes (fragm. 792 Nauck): (ὁρᾶς δὲ) ὡς κἀν θεοῖσι κερδαίνειν καλόν, Θαυμάζεται δ' ὁ πλεῖστον ἐν ναοῖς ἔχων Χρυσόν.]

inpulit, 'has pushed out,' v. 13, note.

46 PERSII

Vestalisque urnas et Tuscum fictile mutat. 60
o curvae in terris animae et caelestium inanis!
quid iuvat hoc, templis nostros inmittere mores
et bona dis ex hac scelerata ducere pulpa?
haec sibi corrupto casiam dissolvit olivo,
haec Calabrum coxit vitiato murice vellus, 65
haec bacam conchae rasisse et stringere venas
ferventis massae crudo de pulvere iussit.
peccat et haec, peccat; vitio tamen utitur; at vos
dicite, pontifices, in sancto quid facit aurum?

[60. *facile* B.   61. *terras* Lactantius I. D. 2. 2. 18.   62. *hoc* a C.   63. *ex* om. a.   65. *et calabrum* C.   66. *vacam* C.   67. *missae* a.   68. *peccaethaec* a.]

60. The Vestals used urns of pottery. König compares Ov. F. 3. 11 foll., Jahn, Val. Max. 4. 4. 11.

Tuscum fictile. 'An quia ex Etruriae figulinis Romam afferretur?... an eo respicit, quod pleraque ad religionem spectantia habuerunt Romani ab Etruscis?' (Casaubon). Why not both?

61. [For 'in terris,' which is the better attested reading, comp. perhaps Lucr. 3. 647 'in studio deditus;' 4. 815 'in rebus deditus;' Catull. 61. 101 'deditus in adultera;' Persius 4. 33 'figas in cute solem.'] Jahn compares Hor. 2 S. 2. 77 'Affigit humo divinae particulam aurae:' but the language rather suggests such passages as Ov. Met. 1. 84 'Pronaque cum spectant,' etc., which the old commentators compare.

inanis, with genitive. [Plaut. Stich. 526 'omnium me exilem atque inanem fecit aegritudinum;' Cic. Mur. 12 'inanissima prudentiae reperta sunt, fraudis autem et stultitiae plenissima;' De Or. 1. 9 'plena consiliorum, inania verborum.' Hor. 3 Od. 11. 26 'inane lymphae Dolium;' Ov. M. 2. 611 'corpus inane animae.'] The expression 'caelestium inanis' resembles 'Heu steriles veri' 5. 75. ['Ὁρᾶς ποῦ βλέπεις; ὅτι εἰς τὴν γῆν, ὅτι εἰς τὸ βάραθρον, ὅτι εἰς τοὺς ταλαιπώρους τούτους νόμους τῶν νεκρῶν; εἰς δὲ τοὺς τῶν θεῶν οὐ βλέπεις Epictetus 1. 13.]

62. **nostros... mores,** 'misce Ergo aliquid *nostris* de *moribus*' Juv. 14.

322. 'Mores,' as used by Roman authors, is a very characteristic, and, almost by consequence, untranslatable word, answering more or less to several distinct though connected notions in English: 'national character,' 'institutions,' 'traditions,' 'spirit of the age,' and the like. Here we may perhaps render it *views*.

templis... inmittere is the opp. to 'tollere de templis' v. 7.

63. **bona dis**, to be taken together. 'Campos militi Romano ad proelium bonos' Tac. Ann. 2. 14. Here it seems to stand for 'ea quae dis bona videntur.'

ducere, 'to deduce, infer;' ex quatuor temporum mutationibus omnium... initia caussaeque ducuntur' Cic. N. D. 2. 19.

pulpa is a remarkable word, coinciding as it does with the Christian language about the flesh, especially when coupled with the epithet 'scelerata;' 'caro mollis et enervis,' Jahn, who compares Auson. Epist. 4. 93 'Nec fas est mihi regio magistro *Plebeiam* numeris docere pulpam,' as if they were so much animal matter. [Epictetus 2. 8. 2 τίς οὖν οὐσία Θεοῦ; Σάρξ; Μὴ γένοιτο. This use of σάρξ is, according to Zeller (Philosophie d. Griechen 3. 1. p. 405), first due to Epicurus. In a letter of Epicurus quoted by Diogenes Laertius σάρξ occurs several times (137, 140, 144, 145,), being opposed in one passage to ψυχή, in another to διάνοια. The expression is quite common in Epictetus

of good old Saturn; it supersedes the Vestal urns and the Etruscan pottery. O ye souls that cleave to earth and have nothing heavenly in you! how can it answer to introduce the spirit of the age into the temple-service, and infer what the gods like from this sinful pampered flesh of ours? The flesh it is that has got to spoil wholesome oil by mixing casia with it—to steep Calabrian wool in purple that was made for no such use; that has made us tear the pearl from the oyster, and separate the veins of the glowing ore from their primitive slag. It sins—yes, it sins; but it takes something by its sinning; but you, reverend pontiffs, tell us what good gold can do in a holy place. Just as much or

1. 3. 5 τὰ δύστηνά μου σαρκίδια: i. 29. 6 (ἀπειλεῖς) ὅλῳ τῷ σαρκιδίῳ; *ib.* 1. 20. 17, 2. 23. 20; comp. M. Aurelius 10. 7. 24. 'Sed quidvis potius homo quam caruncula nostra' Varro Sat. Men. Rel. p. 102 Riese. Epicurus, according to Zeller, drew a distinction between σάρξ and σῶμα. Seneca is not so precise; 'nunquam me *caro* ista compellet ad metum ... nunquam in honorem huius *corpusculi* mentiar' Ep. 65. 22.]

64. 'Alba nec Assyrio fucatur lana veneno, Nec *casia* liquidi *corrumpitur* usus olivi' Virg. G. 2. 465.

sibi, to gratify itself—pointing the contrast with 'bona dis.'

65. Calabrum. Jahn quotes Columella 7. 2 'Generis eximii Milesias, *Calabras*, Apulasque (lanas) nostri existimabant, earumque optimas Tarentinas.'

vitiato, 'spoiled,' because changed from its proper use. The evil done is brought out more forcibly when it is asserted that *both* the natural products suffer from the violation of their natures. In Hom. Il. 4. 141, to which Jahn refers, μιαίνειν probably only means *to stain*, though Virgil in his imitation (Aen. 12. 67) has '*violaverit* ostro.' [Van Wageningen would read 'vitiatum.']

66. bacam, a common word for a pearl; 'diluit insignem *bacam*' Hor. 2 S. 3. 241, here used perhaps to indicate the relation of the pearl to the shell, as that of a berry to a tree. So crudo de pulvere implies an interference with the processes of nature for the sake of luxury. 'Aurum inrepertum et sic melius situm, Cum terra celat' Hor. 3 Od. 3. 49.

66. rasisse implies violence, such as was necessary to separate the pearl.

'Crassescunt etiam in senecta conchisque adhaerescunt, nec his avelli queunt nisi lima' Plin. 9. 109, quoted by Lubin.

stringere, 'to strip or tear,' like 'stringere folia, gladium,' etc., a stronger word here than 'solvere' would be. Jahn remarks that this use of 'stringere' has nothing to do with the 'strictura ferri' (στόμωσις) or hardening mentioned by Virg. Aen. 8. 421, Plin. 34. 143. 'Strigilis' occurs Plin. 33. 62, as a Spanish term for a small piece of native gold—whether with reference to either of these uses of 'stringo' does not appear.

67. massae, 5. 10, Virg. Aen. 8. 453, a lump of ore, containing both the 'vena' and the 'pulvis.'

crudus apparently expresses the natural state of the slag or scoria, as opposed to 'coquere,' the process of fusing the metal. Plin. 33. 98 'argenti vena in summo reperta *crudaria* appellatur.'

68. utitur, 'gets the benefit of,' nearly synonymous with 'fruitur,' with which it is often coupled. 'Utatur suis bonis oportet et *fruatur*, qui beatus futurus est' Cic. N. D. 1. 37. 103. So 'utar' 6. 22.

69. 'Recte *pontifices* compellat, penes quos omnium sacrorum cura, et a quibus sacerdotum omnium collegia pendebant.' Casaubon. Lampridius (A.D. 293) quotes the passage, Alex. Sev. 44 'in sanctis q. f. a.' 'Sacrum sacrove commendatum qui clepsit rapsitve parricida esto' Cic. Leg. 2. 9, where 'sacro' appears to mean a temple, like ἱερόν.

69. quid facit 'what is its business?' almost = 'quid prodest,' like 'plurimum facit' Quintil. 6. 4. 8. [Comp. a similar

nempe hoc quod Veneri donatae a virgine pupae.   70
quin damus id superis, de magna quod dare lance
non possit magni Messallae lippa propago :
conpositum ius fasque animo sanctosque recessus
mentis et incoctum generoso pectus honesto.
haec cedo ut admoveam templis et farre litabo.   75

[70. *a* om. α.   72. *messalae* C, *messala* α.   73. *animimo* B, *animos* C, *animi* ς, Lact. I. D. 2. 4. 11.   74. *honestum* α.   75. *admoneam* B, *admoveant* C.]

thought Sen. Prov. 5. 2 'Non sunt divitiae bonum; itaque habeat illas et Elius leno, ut homines pecuniam, cum in templis consecraverint, videant et in fornice.' Petronius 88 'ipse senatus, recti bonique praeceptor, mille pondo auri Capitolio promittere solet, et ne quis dubitet pecuniam concupiscere, Iovem quoque peculio exornat.']

70. 'Solebant enim virgines antequam nuberent quaedam virginitatis suae dona Veneri consecrare; hoc et Varro scribit' Scholia. Jahn compares 5. 31 'bullaque succinctis *Laribus donata* pependit,' König Hor. 1 S. 5. 66 'Donasset iamne catenam Exvoto Laribus.' So the sailor, Hor. 1 Od. 5. 16, hangs up the clothes, and the lover, 3 Od. 26. 3 foll., the harp, etc., with which he has now done.

71. 'Quin tu desinis' 4. 14.

de magna, etc. Jahn compares Ov. Ep. 4. 8. 39 'Nec quae de parva dis pauper libat acerra Tura minus *grandi* quam *data lance* valent.' '*Lancibus* et pandis fumantia reddimus exta' Virg. G. 2. 194, probably the kind of offering glanced at by Persius. With the ironical repetition 'magna—magni' compare Hor. 1 S. 6. 72 '*Magni* Quo pueri, *magnis* e centurionibus orti.' ['Porrectum *magno magnum* spectare catino Vellem' Hor. 2 S. 2. 39]

72. **Messallae lippa propago.** 'Cottam Messalinum dicit, qui tam vitiosos oculos in senectute habuit, ut palpebrae eius in exteriorem partem verterentur. Fuit enim et multis deditus vitiis' Scholia. L. Aurelius Cotta Messalinus was son of M. Valerius Messalla Corvinus (Hor. 1 S. 10. 85, A. P. 371), and was adopted by his maternal uncle, L. Aurelius Cotta. He is mentioned more than once by Tacitus, who calls him (Ann. 6. 7) 'nobilis quidem, sed egens

as little as the dolls which a young girl offers to Venus. Give *we* rather to the gods such an offering as great Messalla's bleareyed representative has no means of giving even out of his great dish—duty to God and man well blended in the mind, purity in the shrine of the heart, and a racy flavour of nobleness pervading the bosom. Let me have these to carry to the temple, and a handful of meal shall win me acceptance.

ob luxum, per flagitia infamis,' and is enumerated by Plin. 10. 52 among famous epicures, so that Persius doubtless gives him the epithet 'lippus' in order to note his excesses.

73. **conpositum** seems to mean harmonized or adjusted, so that each takes its proper place in the mind. 'Fas et iura sinunt' Virg. G. 1. 269, divine and human law.

sanctos, apparently a predicate, 'the recesses of the mind unstained.'

recessus mentis, φρενῶν μύχος, Theocr. 29. 3. Jahn. 'Ex adyto tanquam cordis responsa dedere' Lucr. 1. 737.

74. **incoctum** = 'imbutum.' 'Coxit' v. 65.

honestum is Cicero's translation of τὸ καλόν, defined by him, Fin. 2. 14, 'honestum id intellegimus, quod tale est ut, detracta omni utilitate, sine ullis praemiis fructibusve per se ipsum possit iure laudari,' here used with an epithet, as in Lucan 2. 389 'rigidi servator honesti' quoted by Jahn. [With the whole description comp. M. Aurelius 3. 4 'Ο γάρ τοι ἀνὴρ ὁ τοιοῦτος... ἱερεύς τις καὶ ὑπουργὸς θεῶν, χρώμενος καὶ τῷ ἔνδον ἱδρυμένῳ αὐτοῦ, ὃ παρέχεται τὸν ἄνθρωπον ἄχραντον ἡδονῶν ... δικαιοσύνῃ βεβαμμένον εἰς βάθος κ.τ.λ.]

75. **cedo**. 'Cedo ut bibam' Plaut. Most. 373, 'cedo ut inspiciam' *id*. Curc. 654.

admovere, a sacrificial word. 'Nec nos sacrilegos *templis admovimus* ignes' Tib. 3. 5. 11. '*Admovitque* pecus flagrantibus aris' Virg. Aen. 12. 171; Tac. Ann. 2. 69; Suet. Cal. 32; Lucan 1. 608, where see Cortius' note (Jahn), 7. 165. 'Obmovere' was also used in the same sense: '*obmoveto* pro admoveto dicebatur apud antiquos' Fest. p. 202, Müll.

farre litabo, after Hor. 3. Od. 22. 19 'Mollivit aversos Penates *Farre* pio et saliente mica,' i.e. with the 'mola salsa.' 'Mola tantum salsa litant qui non habent tura' Plin. praef. 11. (Freund.) ['Boni etiam farre ac fitilla religiosi sunt' Sen. Ben. 1. 6. 3.]

SATURA III.

'NEMPE haec adsidue? Iam clarum mane fenestras
intrat et angustas extendit lumine rimas:
stertimus indomitum quod despumare Falernum
sufficiat, quinta dum linea tangitur umbra.
en quid agis? siccas insana canicula messes   5
iam dudum coquit et patula pecus omne sub ulmo est.'
unus ait comitum. 'verumne? itane? ocius adsit
huc aliquis! nemon?' turgescit vitrea bilis:
'findor'—ut Arcadiae pecuaria rudere dicas.

[*Increpatio desidiae humanae* C.   1. *sepe* A, *seppe* B.   *haec a* C, Prisc. 2.
p. 85 K: *hoc* ⲋ.   7. *idanoocius a,. ita nec ocius* C.   8. *nemo* A.   *tigescit a.*
9. *oridas* C, *credas* ⲋ, Eutyches p. 471 K.]

An appeal to the young and well-to-do, against sloth and for earnestness—said by the Scholiast to be imitated from the 4th book of Lucilius.

1–9. 'Eleven o'clock, and still sleeping off last night's debauch, while everything is broiling out of doors!' 'Is it so late? I'll get up—here, somebody!' He gets into a passion because no one comes.

1. A young man of wealth is wakened by one of his companions—'comites,' a wide term, including tutors (Virg. Aen. 5. 545 '*Custodem* . . comitemque,' 9. 649; Suet. Tib. 12 'comitis et rectoris eius'), as well as associates of the same age (Virg. Aen. 10. 703 '*Aequalem* comitemque'): they seem, however, in both cases to have been selected by the youth's relatives, and to have been themselves of inferior rank. 'Comes' l. 54 is quite different.

clarum mane. 'Dum mane novum' Virg. G. 3. 325. 'Mane,' a substantive, more commonly used adverbially. 'Ad ipsum mane' Hor. 1 S. 3. 17. ['Proprium nobis et peculiare mane fiat,' Sen. Ep. 122. 9. With the whole comp. 'Turpis, qui alto sole semisomnus iacet, cuius vigilia medio die incipit .... Sunt qui officia lucis noctisque perverterint, nec ante diducant oculos hesterna graves crapula, quam adpetere nox coepit,' *ib.* 1, 2.]

2. rimas, 'the chinks' between the shutters, which are made longer or enlarged to the eye by the light coming through them.

3. stertimus, like 'scribimus' 1. 13, the speaker including himself when he really is only meaning others.

indomitum. Falernian was a very strong and heady wine, called 'ardens' Hor. 2 Od. 11. 19, 'severum' 1 Od. 27.

SATIRE III.

'Is this always the order of the day, then? Here is full morning coming through the window-shutters, and making the narrow crevices look larger with the light; yet we go on snoring, enough to carry off the fumes of that unmanageable Falernian, while the shadow is crossing the fifth line on the dial. What do you mean to do? The mad dog's star is already baking the crops dry, and the cattle have all got under cover of the elm.' The speaker is one of my lord's companions. 'Really? you don't mean it? Hallo there, somebody, quick? Nobody there?' The glass of his bile is expanding. 'I'm splitting'—till you would think all the herds in Arcadia were setting up a bray.

9, 'forte' 2 S. 4. 24, 'indomitum' again by Lucan 10. 163 '*Indomitum* Meroë cogens *spumare Falernum.*'
despumare = 'coquere,' 'to digest,' note on 1. 125.
4. quinta is made to agree with 'umbra,' though it more properly belongs to 'linea,' just as in Aesch. Ag. 504 δεκάτῳ σε φέγγει τῷδ' ἀφικόμην ἔτους, it is the tenth *year* that is really meant.
linea, of the sun-dial, 'Nec congruebant ad horas eius *lineae*' Plin. 7. 214. The fifth hour was the time of 'prandium.' 'Sosia, prandendum est: quartam iam totus in horam Sol calet: *ad quintam flectitur umbra notam*' Aus. Eph. L. O. C. 1 foll. quoted by Gifford.
5. 'En quid ago?' Virg. Aen. 4. 534.
siccas with 'coquit.'
insana canicula, with an allusion, of course, to the madness of the animal. 'Iam Procyon *furit*, Et stella *vesani* Leonis' Hor. 3 Od. 29. 18 '*rabiem Canis* et momenta Leonis, Cum semel accepit solem *furibundus* acutum' 1 Ep. 10. 16.
6. 'Iam pastor umbras cum grege languido Rivumque fessus quaerit' Hor. 3 Od. l. c. 'Nunc etiam pecudes umbras et frigora captant' Virg. E. 2. 8.
8. 'Nemon oleum feret ocius? ecquis Audit? cum magno blateras clamore furisque' Hor. 2 S. 7. 34, König. Jahn well remarks, 'qui ipse desidiosus tempus suum perdidit, excandescit cum non statim accurrit servus.'
vitrea bilis, a translation of ὑαλώδης χολή, the expression in the Greek medical writers (Casaubon), 'splendida bilis' Hor. 2 S. 3. 141. Casaubon quotes a Stoic definition, χόλος ἐστὶν ὀργὴ διοιδοῦσα.
9. findor ut was restored by Casaubon for 'finditur,' and is recalled by Jahn, though doubtfully, as he confesses its difficulty, and apparently inclines to Hauthal's conj. 'findimur.' 'Findor,' 'I am bursting,' is supported by Hor. 1

Iam liber et positis bicolor membrana capillis   10
inque manus chartae nodosaque venit harundo.
tunc querimur, crassus calamo quod pendeat umor,
nigra sed infusa vanescat sepia lympha;
dilutas querimur geminet quod fistula guttas.
o miser inque dies ultra miser, hucine rerum   15
venimus? a, cur non potius teneroque columbo
et similis regum pueris pappare minutum
poscis et iratus mammae lallare recusas?
'An tali studeam calamo?' Cui verba? quid istas
succinis ambages? tibi luditur, ecfluis amens,   20

[12, 14. *querimus* a.   13. *vanescit* C.   14. *quo* C.   15. *hunc ine* C.
16. *a cur a*, *aut cur* C, *at cur* ς.   *palumbo* a, *columbo* Servius Aen. 5. 213.
20. *et fluis* a C.]

S. 3. 135 '*Rumperis* et latras' (quoted by Heinr. who himself reads 'finditur'). The remainder of the verse is thrown in by the narrator abruptly, but not unnaturally, as we have only to supply 'clamat' or some such word.

9. **Arcadiae**; for the asses of Arcadia Casaubon refers to Varro R. R. 2. 1. 14, Brodaeus, on Juv. 7. 160, to Plaut. Asin. 333.

pecuaria, 'herds,' Virg. G. 3. 64.

rudo, long only here, and in the imitation by Auson. Epig. 5 (76) 3 (p. 313 Peiper), used particularly of the braying of asses. See Freund.

dicas most MSS., vulg. 'credas.'

10–18. 'He affects to set to work, but finds the ink won't mark. Wretched creature! better be a baby again at once!'

10. **bicolor**, variously explained: by the early commentators, Casaubon, and Heinr., of the two sides of the skin, one yellow, though cleared of hair, the other white—by Jahn of the custom of colouring the parchment artificially. 'Quod neque cum *cedro flavus* nec pumice levis' Ov. Trist. 3. 1. 13. The latter, however, seems to belong rather to copies of books than to parchment for ordinary writing—unless the touch is intended to show the luxury of the youth.

capillis = 'pilis.'

11. **chartae**, 'the papyrus.'

12. The ink is too thick at first—water is poured in—then he finds it too pale. [**querimur**, Jahn (1868)—by far the better attested reading.]

13. **nigra**, emphatic. '*Sepia* pro atramento a colore posuit, quamvis non ex ea, ut Afri, sed ex fuligine ceteri conficiant atramentum' Scholia. So Casaubon, who refers to Plin. 35. 41, and Dioscorides 5 ad fin. Jahn, however, on the authority of the present passage, and Auson. Epist. 14 (4) 76, p. 248 Peiper, 15 (7) 54, p. 252 Peiper, believes that the liquor of the cuttle-fish was actually used for ink at Rome. [So too Marquardt, Röm. Alt. 7 p. 801 notes.]

14. The ink when diluted runs from the pen in drops.

fistula, like 'calamus,' is a synonyme of 'harundo.'

15. **ultra** has the force of a comparative, and is consequently followed by 'quam.' 'Ultra quam satis est' Cic. Inv. 1. 49 (Freund), Hor. 1 Ep. 6. 16.

miser, vv. 66, 107.

hucine and words connected with it seemingly archaic—used later colloquially, as in Plautus and Terence, Cicero, and Horace's Satires. 'Sicine' is found in an impassioned passage of Catullus (64. 132, 134), and in Silius (9. 25), but not in Virgil or Horace.

16. **columbo** is explained by König and Jahn after the Scholia, as an epithet of endearment for children, so as to be synonymous with 'regum pueris:' but this is very harsh, and it seems better to

SAT. III.

Now he takes the book into his hand, and the parchment, which has had the hair taken off and shows two colours, and the paper, and the jointed reed. Next we begin to complain that the ink is thick and clots on the pen; and then, when water is poured in, that the blackness of the liquor is ruined, and that the implement makes two washy drops instead of one. Poor creature! poorer and poorer every day! is it come to this? Had you not better at once go on like pet pigeons and babies of quality, asking to have your food chewed for you, and pettishly refusing to let mammy sing you to sleep?

'Can I work with a pen like this?' Whom are you trying to take in? What do you mean by these whimpering evasions? It is *your* game that's playing, you are dribbling away like a simpleton

explain it with Casaubon of a pet dove, such as was commonly brought up in houses. ['Ut albulus columbus' Catull. 29. 8. Seneca Epist. 96. 3 uses 'turturilla' in the same way.] If we read 'palumbo,' which is found in most MSS., including some of the best, and approved by Bentley on Hor. 1 Od. 2. 10, we may explain it with the Delphin ed. of the wood-pigeon fed by its mother from her own crop.

17. **regum pueris** Hor. 2 Od. 18. 34, where it is contrasted with the 'sordidi nati' of the poor man. 'Reges' used generally for the great, see note on 1. 67.

pappare, a child's word for to eat. ' Novo liberto opus est quod *pappet*' Plaut. Epid. 727. 'Cum cibum ac potionem buas ac *pappas* docent (*vocent* Britann. *dicunt* Cas.) et matrem *mammam*, patrem tatam' Varro 'Cato vel de liberis educandis' fr. ap. Non. 81. 4. Persius here uses the infinitive as a noun (note on 1. 9) for the actual food, our 'pap.' [The spelling *pappare*, not *papare*, is preferred by Goetz in his preface to Plautus' Epidicus, p. xxiv. Gloss. Lat. Gr. p. 141. 53 *pappai μασᾶται*.]

minutum is explained by the Scholia '*commanducatos* cibos,' chewed apparently by the nurse (Lubin), but it may be only 'broken up.'

18. **mammae**, used for nurse, Inscr. ap. Visc. Mus. Pio-Clem. t. 2. p. 82, being in fact the child's name for any one performing a mother's offices.

lallare is interpreted by the Scholia as a verb formed from the nurse's cry *lalla*, which meant either ' go to sleep' or 'suck.' Auson. Epist. 12 (16) 90, p. 242 Peiper, ' Nutricis inter lemmata *Lalli*que somniferos modos,' as well as our *lullaby*, is in favour of the former. The construction is not ' iratus mammae,' as some of the old commentators, Casaubon and Heinr. have thought, but ' mammae lallare,' which is Plautius' interpretation. So it was understood by Jerome (Ep. 5 (1) T. 4. 2 p. 7 Ben. quoted by Jahn), ' Forsitan et laxis uberum pellibus mater, arata rugis fronte, *antiquum* referens *mammae lallare* congeminet.' lallare **recusas**, then, is like 'iussa recusat' Virg. Aen. 5. 749.

19-34. ' My pen won't write.' ' Nonsense—don't bring your excuses to *me*. You are going all wrong—just at the age, too, when you are most impressible. You have a nice property of your own—but *that* is not enough—no, nor your family either. Your life is virtually like Natta's, except that you can feel *your* state, while he cannot.'

19. ' Culpantur frustra calami ' Hor. 2 S. 3. 7.

studeam, absolutely, in our sense of study, post Aug., see Freund. Plin. Ep. 5. 5. 5 has ' compositus in habitum *studentis*,' as if the participle had come to be used as a noun.

cui verba (das), the verb omitted as in v. 30.

20. **succino**, ' to sing second,' Hor. 1 Ep. 17. 48. ' Agricultura succinit pastorali vitae, quod est inferior ' Varro R. R. 1. 2. 16; hence ' to sing small.'

ambages, 'beating about the bush,' opp. to direct narrative, Virg. G. 2. 46, Aen. 1. 342, hence any evasive ex-

contemnere : sonat vitium percussa, maligne
respondet viridi non cocta fidelia limo.
udum et molle lutum es, nunc nunc properandus et acri
fingendus sine fine rota. sed rure paterno
est tibi far modicum, purum et sine labe salinum—   25
quid metuas?—cultrixque foci secura patella.
hoc satis? an deceat pulmonem rumpere ventis,
stemmate quod Tusco ramum millesime ducis,
censoremve tuum vel quod trabeaté salutas?

[21. *cocyta* a.   22. *est* B.   24. *rupe* a.   26. *patella est* C.   29. *censoremve* C, Priscian. 2 p. 208, 211 K, Servius (Dan.) Aen. 3. 382 ; *censoremque* a.]

cuse which avoids the point. 'Quando pauperiem, *missis ambagibus*, horres' Hor. 2 S. 5. 9. Tiresias to Ulysses. [Thus in colloquial Latin it means 'nonsense:' Ter. Heaut. 313 'quas, malum, *ambages* mihi Narrare occepit?' Comp. Plin. 7. 188 'manium *ambages*:' 10. 137 'immensa vitae *ambage* circa auguria:' cf. 30. 7 'fabulam complexam *ambages* feminarum detrahentium lunam.']
20. tibi luditur, not 'te ipse illudis' Schol., Heinr., as if it were a direct answer to 'Cui verba?' (for then we should hardly have had the impersonal), but 'the game is *yours* (and no one's else)' '*you* are the player' (Madvig, § 250 a), metaphor from dice = 'tua res agitur.'
ecfluis, 'you are dribbling away.' 'Ecfluere' used not only of the liquor but of the jar which lets it escape, like 'mano.' Petr. 71 'amphoras gypsatas, ne *ecfluant* vinum,' quoted by Jahn.
21. contemnere, 'haec ab Horatio' (2 S. 3. 13), 'male translata intempestiva sunt : *Invidiam placare paras, virtute relicta. Contemnere miser*' Scholia. Perhaps we may say that Persius added 'contemnere,' the scorn of which is in itself sufficiently effective, without intending to continue the metaphor of 'ecfluis,' but afterwards changed his mind.
[The simile of a vessel seems to have come from Epicurus : Lucr. 6. 16 'intellegit' (Epicurus) 'ibi vitium vas efficere ipsum ... Partim quod fluxum pertusumque esse videbat,' &c. Hor. 1 Ep. 2. 54 'sincerum est nisi vas, quodcunque infundis acescit.' Usener, Epicurea, p. 263.]
sonat vitium, like 'nec vox *hominem sonat*' Virg. Aen. 1. 328, quoted by the Scholia. The same image from striking earthenware to judge of its soundness by its ring is repeated, with some variation, 5. 24 '*Pulsa*, dignoscere cautus Quid *solidum crepet*,' which is the opposite of 'sonat vitium' and 'maligne respondet;' so 5. 106, 'mendosum tinniat.' Jahn compares Lucr. 3. 873 'sincerum sonere.' Casaubon refers to Plato Theaet. 179 D, where σαθρὸν φθέγγεσθαι is opp. to ὑγιὲς φθέγγεσθαι.
maligne, 'grudgingly,' opp. to 'benigne;' 'laudare maligne' Hor. 2 Ep. 1. 209.
22. respondet. Stat. Ach. 2. 174 has '*respondentia* tympana.' Compare Hor. A. P. 348 'Nam neque chorda *sonum reddit* quem vult manus et mens, *Poscenti*que gravem persaepe *remittit* acutum.'
viridis = 'crudus,' opp. to 'coctus,' with a reference also to the natural colour of the clay, not browned by the baking.
23. Persius steps back, as it were, while pursuing the metaphor. 'In fact, you are really clay at this moment in the potter's hands,' imitating Hor. 2 Ep. 2. 8 'argilla quidvis imitaberis uda.' Possibly there may be some reference to the story of Prometheus as the maker of men. Hor. 1 Od. 16. 13, Juv. 14. 35.
properandus et ... fingendus = 'propere fingendus.' Casaubon, quoting Plaut. Aul. 270 'Vascula intus pure

SAT. III.

as you are. You will be held cheap—the jar rings flawed when one strikes it, and returns a doubtful sound, being made, in fact, of green ill-baked clay. Why, at this moment you are moist soft earth. You ought to be taken instantly, instantly, and fashioned without end by the rapid wheel. But you have a paternal estate with a fair crop of corn, a saltcellar of unsullied brightness (no fear of ruin surely!) and a snug dish for fireside service. Are you to be satisfied with this? or would it be decent to puff yourself and vapour because your branch is connected with a Tuscan stem and you are thousandth in the line, or because you wear purple on review days and salute your censor? Off with your

propera atque elue,' where 'pure' seems plainly to belong to 'elue,' so that 'propera atque' would seem to be thrown in, διὰ μέσου, as we might say in English. 'These are the things which I told him to *make haste and wash.*' [Wagner ad loc. however doubts the genuineness of the reading.] 'Properare' is used actively, as in Virg. G. 1.196.

24. **sed rure paterno.** Persius takes the words out of the youth's mouth, as the half-slighting words 'modicum' and 'patella' show. 'Rure paterno' is from Hor. 1 Ep. 18. 60 'interdum nugaris *rure paterno*.' 'Rus' for a *part* of the country, an estate. ' Laudato ingentia *rura*, Exiguum colito' Virg G. 2. 412. So Hor. 3 Od. 18. 2, 1 Ep. 15. 17.

25. **far,** a quantity of corn, 5. 74. The salinum was generally silver (Val. Max. 4. 4. 3, Plin. 33. 153, referred to by Jahn), whence Horace's 'paternum *splendet* in mensa tenui *salinum*' (2 Od. 16. 13), and perhaps **purum et sine labe** here, though these words also denote moral respectability. The purity of the salt, 'concha salis puri' Hor. 1 S. 3. 14, may also be intended. The 'salinum' and the 'patella' are mentioned as the two simplest articles of plate—the general sense being, 'You are the inheritor of a moderate and respectable property.' 'When the necessities of the state obliged the senate to call for a general sacrifice of the gold and silver of the people, the saltcellar and the paten were expressly exempted from the contribution.' Stocker, who refers generally to Laevinus' speech in Livy 26. 36.

26. **quid metuas** expresses the feeling of the youth as anticipated by Persius. The object of fear is poverty, which it would require strenuous exertion to avoid. Hor. 1 Ep. 1. 42 foll.

cultrix, possibly in a double sense, 'inhabitant' and 'worshipper,' as the 'patella' was used for offerings to the household gods. '*Patellae* vasula parva picata sacris faciendis apta' Fest. pp. 248, 9 Müll.

secura, both as an epithet of 'cultrix,' and as expressing the ease and comfort of the competency, with reference to 'quid metuas.'

27. **pulmonem rumpere ventis,** for 'inflatum esse,' Scholia; 'pulmo animae praelargus' 1. 14.

28. 'The *imagines* themselves, together with the *lineae* which connect them, constitute the *stemma* or pedigree' Becker Röm. Alt. 2. 1, p. 220 foll. referred to by Mayor on Juv. 8. 1.

stemma is properly the garland hung on the 'imagines' (Freund).

Tusco, like Maecenas, Hor. 3 Od. 29. 1, 1 S. 6. 1, Prop. 3. 9. 1, and like Persius himself.

ramus = 'linea,' Mayor.

millesime, voc. for nom. 1. 123, but with a rhetorical force. Jahn refers to Suet. Galba 2, who tells us that Galba had a 'stemma' in his 'atrium,' showing his descent from Jove by the father's side, from Pasiphaë by the mother's. There may be also a hint that this long descent tells against as well as for a man, as in Savage's 'No *tenth* transmitter of a foolish face.'

29. Niebuhr (Rhein. Mus. 1 p. 354 foll.), followed by Jahn, explains this line of the 'municipales equites.' 'Because you are a great man in your own provincial town;' compare 1. 129. In any case the allusion is to the annual

ad populum phaleras! ego te intus et in cute novi. 30
non pudet ad morem discincti vivere Nattae?
sed stupet hic vitio et fibris increvit opimum
pingue, caret culpā, nescit quid perdat, et alto
demersus summā rursum non bullit in unda.

Magne pater divum, saevos punire tyrannos 35
haud alia ratione velis, cum dira libido
moverit ingenium ferventi tincta veneno:
virtutem videant intabescantque relicta.
anne magis Siculi gemuerunt aera iuvenci,

[31. *districti a.* 34. *rursus a.* 37. *moverat a.*]

'transvectio' of the 'equites' before the censor, who used to review them ('recognoscere') as they defiled before him on horseback. Suet. Aug. 38 says that Augustus revived the practice, which had fallen into desuetude, but with certain modifications—abolishing the custom of making those objected to dismount on the spot, permitting the old and infirm to answer his summons on foot, and send their horses on, and allowing all above thirty-five years of age who chose to give up their horses. If **censorem** is understood of Rome, **tuum** will imply that the youth is related to the Emperor, like Juvenal's Rubellius Blandus 7. 41: otherwise it means, 'Your local censor.'

29. **ve ... vel** is apparently an unexampled tautology. Many MSS. have 'censoremque,' which does not help the sense, and is itself less likely. One has 'censoremne,' which Casaubon wished to read, explaining it 'vel eone tibi places, quod.' Heinr. conj. 'censorem fatuum,' which he thinks may stand for Claudius.

trabeate, because the 'equites' appeared in the 'trabea' on these occasions.

30. **phalerae**, contemptuously to an 'eques,' as the word is peculiarly used of a horse's trappings, while it means also a military ornament. 'Multo *phaleras* sudore receptas' Virg. Aen. 9. 458. 'Equites donati *phaleris*' Livy 39. 31.

ego te intus et in cute novi. 'I know what lies under those trappings.' Compare 4. 43 'ilia subter Caecum vulnus habes: sed lato balteus auro Praetegit.' Heinr. compares ἐν χρῷ.

31. **ad morem**, more commonly 'in morem,' 'ex more,' or 'more.'

discincti, '*discinctus* aut perdam *nepos*' Hor. Epod. 1. 34.

Natta is another character from Horace (1 S. 6. 124), where he appears not as a reprobate, but as a man of filthy habits. [In Tacitus Ann. 4. 34 Natta appears as a cognomen of the Pinarian *gens*. There may then be something in a view mentioned by the Scholia, 'Nattam fuisse quendam luxuriosum, qui ... *nobilitatem suam* male vivendo exturpaverit.']

32. **sed**, apparently used to show that the parallel does not now hold good, being rather in Natta's favour. Persius could not seriously think Natta's case better than that of the man whom 'a little grain of conscience makes sour,' any more than mortification is better than acute disease—indeed his description shows that he is fully alive to the horror of the state of moral death: but it is his object to enforce the stings of remorse, so, without drawing any direct comparison, he exhibits the former briefly, and then proceeds to dwell more at length on the latter.

stupet ... vitio, like 'stupere gaudio' Caelius in Quint. 9. 3. 58 (Freund). [Ἔτι τούτῳ διαλέγομαι; καὶ ποῖον αὐτῷ πῦρ, ἢ ποῖον αὐτῷ σίδηρον προσάγω, ἵν' αἴσθηται ὅτι νενέκρωται κ.τ.λ. Epictetus 1. 5. 7.]

fibris increvit, 'has overgrown his heart,' 1. 47; 5. 29. Madan compares Psalm 119. 70 'Their heart is as fat as brawn.' So S. Matth. 13. 15 ἐπαχύνθη γὰρ ἡ καρδία τοῦ λαοῦ τούτου.

trappings to the mob! I can look under them and see your skin. Are you not ashamed to live the loose life of Natta? But *he* is paralyzed by vice; his heart is overgrown with thick collops of fat; he feels no reproach; he knows nothing of his loss; he is sunk in the depth and makes no more bubbles on the surface.

Great Father of the Gods, be it thy pleasure to inflict no other punishment on the monsters of tyranny, after their nature has been stirred by fierce passion, that has the taint of fiery poison—let them look upon virtue and pine that they have lost her for ever! Were the groans from the brazen bull of Sicily more terrible, or

S. John 12. 40 πεπώρωκεν αὐτῶν τὴν καρδίαν.

opimus is a synonyme of ' pinguis.'

33. pingue is here used substantively, as Virg. G. 3. 124 ' Impendunt curas denso distendere *pingui.*' The application is analogous to that of ' pingue ingenium,' fat causing dullness of perception, though of course the sense here thought of is the moral sense.

caret culpa, a translation of ἀκόλαστός ἐστι? or implying that his deadness has virtually deprived him of responsibility? Such sentiments as Menander γνῶμ. μονόστ. 430, quoted by Casaubon and Jahn, ὁ μηδὲν εἰδὼς οὐδὲν ἐξαμαρτάνει, are scarcely in point, as the ἄγνοια here is ἄγνοια καθόλου or ἐν τῇ προαιρέσει (Arist. Eth. N. 3. 1).

34. bullit, not 'struggling, sends a bubble to the top,' as Gifford renders it, as it would be quite impossible that a body plunged in water should not do so, however unresisting, but 'rises, and makes bubbles at the surface by struggling,' as Casaubon, Jahn, and Heinr. understand it—and so perhaps the Scholia, though they confuse matters by supposing the image to be that of a man absorbed by a ' caenosa vorago.' Casaubon quotes Philo ὅτι τὸ χεῖρον κ.τ.λ. p. 142 D,—speaking of the flood of sensible objects that pours in on the mind—τότε γὰρ ἐγκαρπωθεὶς ὁ νοῦς τοσούτῳ κλύδωνι βύθιος εὑρίσκεται, μηδ᾽ ὅσον ἀνανήξασθαι καὶ ὑπερκύψαι δυνάμενος.

35–43. 'No torture that can be inflicted on the sinner can be worse than that in the moment of temptation he should see virtue as she is, and gnash his teeth that he cannot follow her. The bull of Phalaris, the sword of Damocles, are as nothing compared with the daily " sense of running darkly to ruin" from the effect of concealed sin.'

35. tyrannos, as inventors of tortures for others, and therefore deserving the worst tortures themselves, probably with reference to the historical allusions which follow, vv. 39–41. Persius doubtless thought of Hor. 1 Ep. 2. 58 'Invidia Siculi non invenere tyranni Maius tormentum,' ' intabescant' referring to ' invidia' (compare ' macrescit' v. 57). Juv. apparently imitates both (13. 196), ' Poena autem vehemens ac multo saevior illis Quas et Caedicius gravis invenit aut Rhadamanthus.'

36. libido moverit ingenium, ' ut *ingenium* est omnium Hominum ab labore proclive ad *libidinem*' Ter. Andr. 77.

37. ferventi . . veneno, ' Occultum inspires *ignem*, fallasque veneno' Virg. Aen. 1. 688, compare 7. 354-356, Lucan 9. 742.

38. [videant. Comp. Plato's language about φρόνησις, Phaedrus p. 251 D.]

intabescant seems taken from Ovid's description of envy (M. 2. 780), ' *intabescit*que videndo Successus hominum.'

relicta, abl. abs. Compare Virg. Aen. 4. 692 ' Quaesivit caelo lucem ingemuitque *reperta.*' Though ' relicta ' here stands not for ' postquam,' but for ' *quod* eam reliquerunt.' The line, as Jahn remarks, has more force, expressed as it is in the form of a prayer, than if it had been regularly connected with the preceding sentence, ' haud alia ratione quam ut.' The sentiment is Ovid's ' Video meliora,' etc.

39. gemuerunt, because the groans of the victims passed for the bellowings of the bull. ' Gemere' might possibly be used of the animal itself, as it is applied by Lucr. 3. 297 to the lion—but it is doubtless substituted here for ' mugire,' not only as adding to the poetry of the passage by combining the

et magis auratis pendens laquearibus ensis 40
purpureas subter cervices terruit, 'imus,
imus praecipites' quam si sibi dicat et intus
palleat infelix, quod proxima nesciat uxor?

Saepe oculos, memini, tangebam parvus olivo,
grandia si nollem morituri verba Catonis 45
discere, non sano multum laudanda magistro,
quae pater adductis sudans audiret amicis.
iure : etenim id summum, quid dexter senio ferret,
scire erat in voto; damnosa canicula quantum

[45, 46. *morituro verba Catoni Dicere* C; *morituri Catonis* a, Schol. *dicere* Schol. 'ne Catonis deliberativam orationem *recitarem.*' 46. *et insano* a, *non sano* C : utrumque agnoscunt Scholia. 48. *summo* a. *fervet* a.]

images of the bull and the victim, but for the sake of the comparison, which is to illustrate *human* suffering.

40. This reference to the story of Damocles is probably imitated from Hor. 3 Od. 1. 17 'Destrictus ensis cui super impia Cervice pendet, non Siculae dapes Dulcem elaborabunt saporem.'

41. purpureas .. cervices, a bolder expression than ' purpurei (= purpurati) tyranni' Hor. 1 Od. 35. 12, from which it is doubtless taken. The epithet so chosen suggests the notion not merely of splendour, but the splendour of a tyrant, so as to be virtually equivalent to Horace's '*impia* cervice.' ['Cervices' is usual for 'cervix.']

42. imus praecipites. 'Peccatis indulgens praecipitem amicum ferri sinit' Cic. de Amic. 24. The Delph. ed. and Jahn refer to the celebrated opening of Tiberius' letter to the Senate (Tac. Ann. 6. 6, Suet. Tib. 67) ' Quid scribam vobis, P. C., aut quomodo scribam, aut quid omnino non scribam hoc tempore, Di me Deaeque peius perdant *quam perire me quotidie sentio,* si scio:' but they omit Tacitus' comment, which is at least as much to the point : 'Neque frustra praestantissimus sapientiae firmare solitus est, si recludantur tyrannorum mentes, posse adspici laniatus et ictus: quando ut corpora verberibus, ita saevitia, libidine, malis consuetis, animus dilaceretur.'

[intus palleat, perhaps 'blenches at heart,' an outward physical effect being supposed to be produced within. Gildersleeve quotes Macbeth 2. 2, 'My hands are of your colour, but I shame To wear *a heart so white.*' Juvenal 1. 166 carries the idea still further, confusing his metaphors : ' rubet auditor, cui *frigida mens est Criminibus, tacita sudant praecordia culpa.*' The only other alternative seems to be to take ' intus ' as = ' at home :' the man has a skeleton in his cupboard. Comp. Cic. de Sen. 4 'nec vero ille in luce atque oculis civium magnus, sed *intus* domique.' Professor Housman conjectures ' ulcus ' for ' intus,' *Classical Review,* May 1889. For ' palleat' Van Wageningen would read ' calleat.']

43. palleat .. quod nesciat is the acc. of the object, as in 5. 184 ' recutitaque sabbata palles,' not the cogn., as in 1. 124 note.

proxima .. uxor, 'the wife of his bosom;' compare the use of 'propinquus.'

44-62. 'I remember my school days, which were unprofitable enough. I used to shirk recitation-lessons, because all my ambition was to excel in games of chance or skill—but you have had an insight into what wisdom is, and have learnt something of the excellence of virtue. Dropping off again—nodding and yawning? Have you really *no* object in life?'

44. tangebam, the reading of the best MSS. for 'tingebam,' is supported by Ov. A. A. 1. 661 'Si lacrimae .. Deficient, uda lumina *tunge* manu' (König, Jahn,) and by the Scholia 'Oculi oleo *tacti* perturbantur ad tempus.' The object of the application,

did the sword that hung from the gilded cornice strike more dread into the princely neck beneath it than the voice which whispers to the heart, 'We are going, going down the precipice,' and the ghastly inward paleness, which is a mystery, even to the wife of the bosom?

Often, I remember, as a small boy I used to give my eyes a touch with oil, if I did not want to learn Cato's grand dying speech, sure to be vehemently applauded by my wrong-headed master, that my father might hear me recite in a glow of perspiring ecstacy with a party of friends for the occasion. Reason good, for the summit of my scientific ambition was to know what that lucky sice would bring me, how much that ruinous ace would

however, as most of the old commentators, Heinr. and Jahn perceive, was not to produce irritation or anything which had the appearance of it, but to make believe that his eyes were weak by his use of the remedy. 'Cum tua pervideas *oculis mala lippus inunctis*' Hor. 1 S. 3. 25. 'Non tamen idcirco contemnas *lippus* inungi' 1 Ep. 1. 29.

parvus, 'when a child.' 'Memini quae plagosum *mihi parvo* Orbilium dictare' Hor. 2 Ep. 1. 70.

45. grandia; a dying speech made for Cato, like the oration to Sulla, Juv. 1. 16, and the 'suasoria' made for Hannibal, id. 7. 161 foll. See Tac. Or. 35. Here the speech seems not the boy's own composition, but that of some one else, perhaps the master, and learnt by the boy. [Bieger defends the reading of C, 'morituro verba Catoni Dicere,' 'to dictate a speech to Cato.' He compares the beginning of Annaeus Seneca's second *Suasoria*, where Alexander is told what to say. On the other hand comp. Petronius 5 'grandiaque indomiti Ciceronis verba minentur.']

46. non sano expresses Persius' scorn for the whole system of education—the choice of such subjects for boys, and the praise given to contemptible efforts— perhaps on account of the father's presence. There is much to the same effect in Tac. l. c.

laudanda = 'quae laudaret,' after the analogy of 'tradere, curare, etc., faciendum,' a use belonging to later Latin. Madvig, § 422.

47. The recitation was weekly, but the father does not seem to have attended so often. Juv. 7. 165, 6.

sudans, from pleasure and excitement. 2. 53. Jahn, who refers, after Casaubon, to Statius' words in his funeral poem on his father Silv. 5. 3. 215 foll. 'Qualis eras, Latios quotiens ego carmine patres Mulcerem, felixque tui spectator adesses Muneris! heu quali confusus gaudia fletu Vota piosque metus inter laetumque pudorem!'

48. iure: as a boy turning away from distasteful and injudicious teaching, fond of boyish amusements, and not able to appreciate the higher pursuits which would engage him afterwards. 'Iure' forming a sentence by itself: 'iure omnes' Hor. 1 S. 2. 46. So 'merito,' 1 S. 6. 22.

id summum . . . erat in voto. 'Esse in voto' or 'votis' means to be included in a person's prayers. 'Hoc erat in votis' Hor. 2 S. 6. 1. So 'venire in votum' 1 Ep. 11. 5. Compare Cic. N. D. 1. 14 'Deus qui nunquam nobis occurrit, neque in precibus, neque in optatis, neque *in votis*.'

senio, 'the sice' (compare 'ternio,' 'unio'), stands, as Jahn and Heinr. think, for three sices, τρὶς ἕξ, the highest throw with the 'tesserae' ('Venus,' or 'iactus Venereus'). The highest throw with the 'tali,' which were four in number, was when all four turned up differently (Lucian. Am. p. 415, Ov. A. A. 2. 204 foll., Tr. 2. 471 foll.). See Freund v. 'alea.'

quid . . . ferret = 'quem fructum ferret.' Boys played games of hazard as well as games of a more harmless sort. 'Puer . . . ludere doctior Seu Graeco iubeas trocho, Seu malis vetita legibus alea' Hor. 3 Od. 24. 55 foll.

49. 'Me quoque per talos Venerem

raderet ; angustae collo non fallier orcae ;   50
neu quis callidior buxum torquere flagello.
haud tibi inexpertum curvos deprendere mores,
quaeque docet sapiens bracatis inlita Medis
porticus, insomnis quibus et detonsa iuventus
invigilat, siliquis et grandi pasta polenta :   55
et tibi quae Samios diduxit littera ramos,
surgentem dextro monstravit limite callem.
stertis adhuc, laxumque caput conpage soluta

[51. *caliduor* a.   *torquaeret* a.   52. hic quartam saturam incipit C.   56. *deduxit* a C.   57. *collem* a C, *callem* ς, Schol., quae *limitem* interpretantur.]

quaerente secundos Semper *damnosi* subsiluere *canes*' Prop. 4. 8. 46, i. e. in the game with 'tali,' when all four fell alike, in the game with 'tesserae,' which is here meant, when all three were aces, τρεῖς κύβοι.

50. **raderet**, opp. to 'ferret.' Freund makes the 'orca' equivalent to the 'phimus' (Hor. 2 S. 7. 17) or box into which the dice were thrown, quoting Pompon. ap. Prisc. 1. p. 110 Keil, 'interim dum contemplor orcam taxillos (=talos) perdidi;' but it does not appear that throwing the dice with accuracy into the box constituted any part of the skill of the game, and the Schol. seem right in supposing Persius to allude, as Pomponius doubtless did, to the game with nuts ('nuces'), called in Greek τρόπα (Pollux 9. 7. 103), which was frequently performed with 'tali' (ἀστράγαλοι), the point being to throw them into a hole (βύθρος), or, as here, into a jar, so as not to count those which fell outside. The narrowness of the neck ('collo angustae orcae' = 'collo angusto orcae') would of course increase the difficulty.

51. 'Et (erat in voto) ne quis callidior (esset).'

buxum, 'the top,' as in Virg. Aen. 7. 382 'volubile buxum,' which Persius probably imitates, as no other instance is quoted where the word is so applied.

52. **curvos** = 'pravos,' apparently from Hor. 2 Ep. 2. 44 'Scilicet ut possem curvo dignoscere rectum,' which is used, as here, as a synonyme for higher education—a young man's as opposed to a boy's. Persius nearly repeats himself 4. 11 'rectum discernis ubi inter *Curva* subit, vel cum fallit pede regula varo' (referred to by Jahn). Comp. also 5. 38 'Adposita *intortos* extendit regula mores,' which Casaubon quotes.

53. We must either suppose a zeugma, borrowing 'cognoscere' or some such word from 'deprendere,' or make the construction,' neque inexperta sunt quae,' etc., just as 'scire' and 'neu quis' are two subjects connected with the same predicate 'summum erat in voto.'

sapiens... porticus, like 'sapientem barbam' Hor. 2 S. 3. 35, 'eruditus pulvis' Cic. N. D. 2. 18. The porch is personified as in Hor. 2 S. 3. 44 'porticus et grex Autumat.' The ποικίλη στοά, where Zeno and his followers used to resort, was adorned with paintings by Polygnotus, one of them representing the battle of Marathon. Laert. 7. 5; Paus. 1. 15, referred to by Casaubon. Whether the walls were themselves painted or merely hung with paintings is not clear, and not settled, as Jahn remarks, by the word 'inlita,' which cannot be pressed, as it is used improperly, and probably expresses some contempt.

bracatis. 'Tela fugacis equi, et *bracati* militis arcus' Prop. 3. 4. 17.

54. **et detonsa** was restored by Turnebus, whom Casaubon and later editors follow, from most MSS. for the old reading 'indetonsa.' The Stoics let their beard grow, but cut their hair close ('supercilio brevior coma' Juv. 2. 15, quoted by the Delph. ed. König

SAT. III. 61

sweep off—never to be balked by the narrow neck of the jar, or to let any one be cleverer at whipping the top. But you have had some practice in detecting deviations from the rule of right, and in the doctrines of the philosophic porch where the Medes are painted in their trowsers: doctrines which form the nightly study of close-shaven young men, dieted on pulse and vast messes of porridge: and the letter which spreads into Pythagorean ramifications has set your face towards the steep path which rises to the right. Snoring still? your head dropped, with the neck-joints all loose, yawning off yesterday, with your jaws starting

also refers to Luc. Vit. Auct. 20, Hermot. 18)—a practice, as Jahn remarks, common to them with athletes, mourners, and misers (Theophr. Char. 10), in opposition to the fashionable and luxurious habits of the κομῶντες.
55. **invigilat**, rather tautological after 'insomnis.' 'Nec capiat somnos invigiletque malis.' Ov. F. 4. 530.
siliquis, 'pulse.' Hor. 2 Ep. 1. 123, speaking of the poet, 'vivit *siliquis* et pane secundo.'
polenta, ἄλφιτα, 'pearl-barley,' a Greek, not a Roman, dish ('videtur tam puls ignota Graeciae fuisse, quam Italiae *polenta*' Pliny 18. 84), mentioned as a simple article of diet by Attalus, Seneca's preceptor (Sen. Ep. 110. 18, quoted by Jahn) 'Habemus aquam, habemus *polentam*: Iovi ipsi controversiam de felicitate faciamus:' called 'grandis.' as Virg. E. 5. 36 speaks of '*grandia* hordea'—perhaps, as Casaubon thinks, with a further reference to the abundance of the meal and its fattening effects. ['Grandis' was apparently applied specially to agricultural products; comp. the old 'carmen' quoted by Festus p. 93 (Müller) 'Hiberno pulvere, verno luto *grandia* farra, camille, metes:' so Cato, R. R. 108, has '*grandi* polenta,' and 141. 2 has 'virgulta.' Here it may perhaps mean 'coarsely ground,' 'ground into large fragments:' Pliny 18. 112 'ita fiunt alicae tria genera, maximum ac secundarium; *grandissimum* vero aphaerema appellant:' so too 115.]
56. The image of the two ways is as old as Hesiod, W. and D. 287-292 τὴν μέντοι κακότητα καὶ ἰλαδὸν ἔστιν ἑλέσθαι Ῥηϊδίως· λείη μὲν ὁδός, μάλα δ' ἐγγύθι ναίει· Τῆς δ' ἀρετῆς ἱδρῶτα θεοὶ προπάροιθεν ἔθηκαν Ἀθάνατοι· μακρὸς δὲ καὶ ὄρθιος οἶμος ἐς αὐτὴν Καὶ τρηχὺς τὸ πρῶτον, ἐπὴν δ' εἰς ἄκρον ἵκηται, Ῥηϊδίη δὴ ἔπειτα πέλει, χαλεπή περ ἐοῦσα. Pythagoras improved on it by choosing the letter Υ (the older form of Υ or Y), hence called *his* letter (Anth. Lat. 1076. 1 Meyer), as its symbol, the stem standing for the unconscious life of infancy and childhood, the diverging branches for the alternative offered to the youth, virtue or vice. Persius again refers to this 5. 34 'Cumque iter ambiguum est, et vitae nescius error diducit trepidas ramosa in compita mentes.'
Samius occurs Ov. F. 3. 153 as a synonym of Pythagoras.
'deduxit' most MSS., but diduxit is clearly right, as Jahn remarks. The two prefixes are constantly confounded, and the point is just one on which MSS. have no weight.
57. **surgentem**. Because the path of virtue was arduous, ὄρθιος οἶμος, and hence represented by the straight limb of the Υ (*dextro*).
monstravit perhaps conveys a similar notion, as if the letter itself by its form suggested the path to the right, that which went straight on. So **limes** would naturally mean a straight cut road, 'secto via limite quadret' Virg. G. 2. 278.
callis is properly a mountain path, as defined by Isid. Orig. 15. 16. 10 'callis est iter pecudum inter montes angustum et tritum.' Freund q. v. The general meaning of the two lines then is, 'You have arrived at the turning-point of life, and have been told which is the right way.' [Bücheler adopts 'collem:' see critical note.]
58. **stertis**, v. 3, the effect of the 'crapula.'
laxum, 1. 98.

oscitat hesternum, dissutis undique malis?
est aliquid quo tendis, et in quod derigis arcum? 60
an passim sequeris corvos testaque lutoque,
securus quo pes ferat, atque ex tempore vivis?
  Helleborum frustra, cum iam cutis aegra tumebit,
poscentis videas: venienti occurrite morbo,
et quid opus Cratero magnos promittere montis? 65
discite, o miseri, et causas cognoscite rerum:
quid sumus, et quidnam victuri gignimur; ordo

[60. *in quo* a. *dirigis* a C.   62. *bibis* a.   66. *disciteque o* Augustin. Civ. D. 2. 6: *disciteque o, discite et o miseri causas* ς: *discite o* a C, Schol. 67. *gignimus* a.]

58. **conpage**, 'conpages humana labat' Lucan 5. 119.
59. **oscitat hesternum**, like 'verum plorabit' 1. 90; 'corpus onustum *Hesternis* vitiis' Hor. 2 S. 2. 78.
undique, an intentional exaggeration for 'utraque parte.'
60. Casaubon compares Arist. Eth. N. 1. 1 ἆρ' οὖν καὶ πρὸς τὸν βίον ἡ γνῶσις τοῦ τέλους μεγάλην ἔχει ῥοπήν, καὶ καθάπερ τοξόται σκοπὸν ἔχοντες, μᾶλλον ἂν τυγχάνοιμεν τοῦ δέοντος; [Seneca de Brevitate Vitae 2. 2 'quibusdam nihil, quo cursum derigant, placet, sed marcentes oscitantesque fata deprendunt.']
  in quod is unquestionably the true reading, not 'in quo.' The change, as Jahn remarks, is one which might justifiably have been introduced even if totally unsupported, being demanded by the language, and really countenanced by the MSS., as 'd' has evidently dropped out before 'derigis.'
61. **passim**, 'volucres huc illuc passim vagantes' Cic. de Div. 2. 38, 'at random.' Comp. Aesch. Ag. 394 διώκει παῖς ποτανὸν ὄρνιν, and the Greek proverb τὰ πετόμενα διώκειν.
  testaque lutoque, 'the first missiles that come to hand,' opp. to 'arcus.' Casaubon. 'Sequi,' attempt to reach with: 'teloque sequi, quem prendere cursu Non poterat' Virg. Aen. 12. 775. Comp. 'pilo sequi' Tac. H. 4. 29, 'ferro sequi' Ov. M. 6. 665.
62. **securus** followed by a relative clause. 'Quid Tiridaten terreat, unice Securus' Hor. 1 Od. 26. 6: compare also 2 S. 4. 50, 2 Ep. 1. 176. See 6. 12 note.
  ex tempore, 'off-hand,' 'on the spur of the moment;' 'versus fundere *ex tempore*' Cic. de Or. 3. 50: so that 'ex tempore vivere' is 'to live by the rule of impulse;' not, as Heinr. thinks, equivalent to 'in diem vivere,' 'to live from hand to mouth.' [With the whole comp. Marcus Aurelius 2. 7 ληροῦσι γὰρ καὶ διὰ πράξεων οἱ κεκμηκότες ἐν τῷ βίῳ, καὶ μὴ ἔχοντες σκοπόν, ἐφ' ὃν πᾶσαν ὁρμὴν καὶ καθάπαξ φαντασίαν ἀπευθυνοῦσιν.]
  63-76. 'There is such a thing as trying to mend when it is too late. Be wise in time—learn your duty—where to bound your wishes—on what objects to spend money—what is your mission in life. Such knowledge will stand a lawyer in better stead than all the wealth his fees may be bringing him.'
63. **helleborum**. Black hellebore was given in dropsies, Plin. 25. 54, after Dioscorid. 4. 151, referred to by Jahn.
  cutis aegra tumebit, vv. 95, 98. Observe Persius' frequent reference to the dropsy, when he wishes to choose an instance of disease, 1. 23 (?) 55, 3. 63, 88 foll.; apparently because it is directly traceable to indulgence. In the present passage he may have thought of Horace, 1 Ep 2. 33 'Ut te ipsum serves, non expergisceris? atqui, Si noles sanus, curres hydropicus.'
64. 'Principiis obsta: sero medicina paratur, Cum mala per longas invaluere moras' Ov. R. A. 91 foll., quoted by Madan.
65. **et quid** is the reading of all the MSS. but one, which has 'ecquid,' as Orelli reads. Jahn (1843) seems right in connecting the present line closely

SAT. III.

asunder from all points of the compass? Have you any goal? any mark at which you aim? or are you on a vague wild-goose chase armed with broken pots and mud, not caring where you go, and living by the rule of the moment?

It is too late to ask for hellebore, as you see men doing, when the skin is just getting morbid and bloated. Meet the disease at its first stage, and what occasion is there to promise Craterus gold-mines for a cure? Be instructed, poor creatures, and acquaint yourselves with the causes of things,—what we are, what life we are sent into the world to lead, what is the rank assigned us at starting, where is the smooth turn round the goal and when to

with the preceding—'Meet the disease in its first stages, and what need will there be?' 'et' marking the consequence. 'Dic quibus in terris, et eris mihi magnus Apollo' Virg. E. 3. 104. [In his last edition Jahn puts a full-stop after 'morbo.']

Craterus, Hor. 2 S. 3. 161. See note on 2. 14.

magnos promittere montis, a proverbial phrase. Jahn compares Ter. Phorm. 68 'modo non montes auri pollicens,' Heinr., Sall. Cat. 23 'maria montesque polliceri coepit,' from which it appears that the expression was variously understood, some taking it of mountains of gold, others of actual mountains. [Comp. Plautus Stich. 25 'Persarum Montes qui esse aurei perhibentur:' 'argenti montes' *ib.* Mil. 1065: and Varro Sat. Menipp. p. 103 Riese.] 'You will not then be driven to the frantic offers which patients in desperation make to their physicians.'

66. **discite, o.** The hiatus is like that in Hor. 3 Od. 14. 11 'male ominatis Parcite verbis,' if the reading is correct. [Πότε δὲ (ἀπολαύσεις) τῆς ἐφ' ἑκάστου γνωρίσεως, τί τε ἐστὶ κατ' οὐσίαν, καὶ τίνα χώραν ἔχει ἐν τῷ κόσμῳ κ.τ.λ. M. Aurelius 10. 9; comp. *ib.* 2. 9. Persius' words contain a similar exhortation applied directly to practice.]

causas cognoscite rerum is doubtless from Virg. G. 2. 490; but Virgil means the physical causes of nature; Persius the final cause of human life, Juvenal's 'vivendi causas' (8. 84).

67. **sumus**, etc. The questions, though really dependent, are put in an independent form, except 'deceat' v. 71. Compare Prop. 3. 5. 25 foll. The questions here proposed are Stoic questions, and have been largely illustrated by Casaubon, though the whole passage is apparently modelled on Hor. 1 Ep. 18. 96 foll. 'Inter cuncta leges et percontabere doctos, Qua ratione queas traducere leniter aevum,' etc.

quid sumus. Cic. Fin. 4. 10, speaking of the points on which Stoics and Academics agree. 'Sequitur illud ut animadvertamus *qui simus ipsi* . . . Sumus igitur homines : ex animo constamus et corpore, quae sunt cuiusdam modi ;' from which he goes on to deduce the end of life, 'secundum naturam vivere,' so as to illustrate Persius' second inquiry. [Comp. Epictetus 2. 10. 1 σκέψαι τίς εἶ etc.; 1. 10. 10 παρὰ Χρυσίππου ἐπισκέψασθαι τίς ἐστιν ἡ τοῦ κόσμου διοίκησις, καὶ ποίαν τινὰ χώραν ἐν αὐτῷ ἔχει τὸ λογικὸν ζῷον· ἐπίσκεψαι δὲ καὶ τίς εἶ σύ. 1. 2. 6 Διὰ τοῦτο μάλιστα παιδείας δεόμεθα, ὥστε μαθεῖν τὴν τοῦ εὐλόγου καὶ ἀλόγου πρόληψιν ταῖς ἐπὶ μέρους οὐσίαις ἐφαρμόζειν συμφώνως τῇ φύσει. 2. 17. 31 εἰδέναι τί μοι πρὸς θεούς ἐστι καθῆκον, τί πρὸς γονεῖς, τί πρὸς ἀδελφούς, τί πρὸς πατρίδα, τί πρὸς ξένους.]

quidnam victuri gignimur. Casaubon also quotes Marc. Antonin. 8. 52 ὁ δὲ μὴ εἰδὼς πρὸς ὅ τι πέφυκεν, οὐκ οἶδεν ὅστις ἐστὶν οὐδὲ τί ἐστι κόσμος.

quidnam = 'quam vitam.'

victuri, not expressing time but purpose. See note on 1. 100.

ordo seems rightly explained by Heinr. and Jahn with reference to what follows, of the position for starting in the chariot race. Compare Soph. El. 710 στάντες δ' ἵν' αὐτοὺς οἱ τεταγμένοι βραβεῖς κλήροις ἔπηλαν καὶ κατέστησαν δίφρους. The word however is a Stoic one, τάξις and χώρα Epictet. 1. 9. 24; 3. 2 1. 18.

64   PERSII

quis datus, aut metae qua mollis flexus et unde;
quis modus argento, quid fas optare, quid asper
utile nummus habet, patriae carisque propinquis   70
quantum elargiri deceat, quem te deus esse
iussit, et humana qua parte locatus es in re.
disce, nec invideas, quod multa fidelia putet
in locuplete penu, defensis pinguibus Umbris,
et piper et pernae, Marsi monumenta clientis,   75
menaque quod prima nondum defecerit orca.
  Hic aliquis de gente hircosa centurionum

[68. *quam* C.   69. *argenti* Augustin. Civ. D. 2. 6.   71. *largiri* a,
Augustin. l. c.   74. *defensus* a.   75. om. a, in marg. add. *b luentis* C.]

68. Most MSS. read 'quam,' which Casaubon retains; but Orelli, Heinr., and Jahn rightly prefer qua. The difficulties of rounding the goal in a chariot race are well known. See Hom. Il. 23. 306 foll., Soph. El. 720, Hor. 1 Od. 1. 4.

metae ... flexus, like 'flectere metam' Stat. Theb. 6. 440. Jahn. 'In flectendis promuntoriis' Cic. Div. 2. 45.

mollis = 'facilis.' The turn must not be too sharp or abrupt. κλινθῆναι ... ἧκα Hom. l. c.

unde, whence to begin the turn. The choosing of places and the fixing of the goal are mentioned closely together. Hom. Il. 23. 358 ὅταν δὲ μεταστοιχεί· σήμηνε δὲ τέρματ' Ἀχιλλεύς, imitated by Virgil, Aen. 5. 129-132.

69. quis modus argento, probably imitated from Lucil. ap. Lact. I. D. 6. 5. 2 'Virtus, quaerendae finem rei scire modumque.'

quid fas optare carries us back to Sat. 2 'Quid sentire putas? quid credis, amice, precari?' Hor. 1 Ep. 18. 106, 'Nil ergo optabunt homines?' Juv. 10. 346.

asper ... nummus, Suet. Nero 44 for *new* coin, rough from the die. Possibly Persius may mean, 'What is the good of money hoarded up and not circulated' (*tritus*)? Compare Hor. 1 S. 1. 41 foll., 73 'Nescis quo valeat nummus? quem praebeat usum?'

70. Lucil. l. c. 'Commoda praeterea patriae sibi prima putare Deinde parentum, tertia iam postremaque nostra.' Persius however was thinking more of Hor. 2 S. 2. 104 'Cur, improbe, *carae* Non aliquid *patriae* tanto emetiris acervo?'

carisque propinquis is from Hor. 1 S. 1. 83. Compare also Hor. A. P. 312 'Qui didicit *patriae* quid debeat et quid *amicis*,' and Virg. G. 2. 514 'Hinc *patriam* parvosque penatis Sustinet.'

71. elargiri, a very rare word.

quem te deus esse iussit. 'Supra, *Discite quid sumus*: sed aliud est: nam ibi natura hominis proponebatur inquirenda, hic personae qualitas, ibi inquam φύσεως πέρι agebatur, hic περὶ σχέσεως.' Casaubon. The words appear to be explained by those which follow, 'humana qua parte locatus es in re,' and if so, not to differ materially from 'ordo quis datus.' Thus, quem ... esse = 'quas partes agere.'

72. humana ... res, apparently on the analogy of 'res Romana.' ['Sic etiam in magno quaedam res publica mundo est' Manilius 5. 737. The Stoical doctrine that the universe is a great πόλις of which all men are πολῖται is well known. Epictet. 2. 5. 26 τί γάρ ἐστιν ἄνθρωπος; Μέρος πόλεως πρῶτον μὲν τῆς ἐκ θεῶν καὶ ἀνθρώπων· μετὰ ταῦτα δὲ τῆς ὡς ἔγγιστα λεγομένης, ἥτις ἐστι μικρὸν τῆς ὅλης μίμημα.]

locatus seems to be another equivalent of τεταγμένος, implying the notion of a station or post which a man is bound not to desert. [Comp. Socrates' language in Plato's Apology, 17. 29.]

take it, what should be the limit to our fortune, what we may lawfully wish for, what is the good of coin fresh from the mint, how much ought to be spent on one's country and one's near and dear friends, what part God has ordained you to bear, and what is your position in the human commonwealth. Be instructed, and do not grudge the trouble on the strength of the jars of good things turning bad in your well-stored larder, your fees for defending your fat friends from Umbria, or the pepper and hams, the remembrancer of your Marsian client, or because you may not yet have come to the last sprat of the first barrel.

Here we may suppose a gentleman of the unsavoury profession of centurion to strike in, 'I know all I've any need to know.

'Locum virtutis deseruit' Hor. 1 Ep. 16. 67.

73. Persius changes from 'discite' to disce, as he had changed from 'gignimur' to 'locatus es.' It matters little whether we connect 'disce' with what goes before, or make it begin a new sentence.

invideas ('discere') as Jahn explains it. 'His te quoque *iungere*, Caesar, *Invideo*' Lucan 2. 550. μάνθανε, μηδὲ φθόνει. The lines which follow must refer to the man whom Persius is addressing, not to some other person, as there is no sort of specification. We must suppose then that Persius finally leaves the youth to whom he has been appealing at v. 62. He then delivers a more general admonition, at last singling out a person whom he chooses to describe as a rich lawyer. 'Do not grudge me your attention because your stores are full.'

multa fidelia putet. The details, and the word 'putet,' are meant to be contemptuous. 'Your stores are so full that you cannot eat the good things while they are fresh.' 'Quod hospes Tardius adveniens *vitiatum* commodius quam *Integrum edax dominus consumeret*' Hor. 2 S. 2. 90. There is a coarseness in fees paid in kind, as in Aristoph. Clouds 648, where Strepsiades offers to fill Socrates' trough with meal, though the notion here is that of rude plenty, not as in Juv. 7. 119, Mart. 4. 46, of a penurious truck-system.

74. 'Among your plenteous stores;' penus comprehending all the contents of the larder. 'Est enim omne quo vescuntur homines *penus*' Cic. N. D. 2. 27.

pinguibus, another touch of sarcasm. Men who have to borrow your wits and give you in return the sort of produce in which they are most abundant.

75. pernae. 'Siccus petasunculus et vas Pelamydum' form part of Juvenal's list (l. c. Mayor's note). For the simplicity of the Marsians, Jahn compares Juv. 3. 169, 14. 180.

76. 'You have not yet finished the first jar they sent you,' much less the others. The 'mena' was a common sort of sea fish. 'Qui enim voluptatem ipsam contemnunt, iis licet dicere, se acipenserem menae non anteponere' Cic. Fin. 2. 28.

orca. Hor. 2 S. 4. 66 'quam qua Byzantia *putuit orca*,' from which Persius probably got the word 'putet' v. 73.

77–87. '"Bah," says a soldier, "I know what's what well enough. I don't want to be one of your philosophers, standing dumbfoundered and puzzling how the world was made—a pretty reason for losing one's colour and going without one's dinner." A truly popular sentiment!'

77. The soldier is introduced after the lawyer. Compare Hor. 1 S. 1. 4 foll., where they are classed together. Persius hates the military cordially (compare 5. 181-191) as the most perfect specimens of developed animalism, and consequently most antipathetic to a philosopher. See Nisard, Études sur les Poètes Latins, 1. 236-239. Horace

dicat 'Quod satis est sapio mihi. non ego curo
esse quod Arcesilas aerumnosique Solones,
obstipo capite et figentes lumine terram, 80
murmura cum secum et rabiosa silentia rodunt
atque exporrecto trutinantur verba labello,
aegroti veteris meditantes somnia, *gigni
de nihilo nihilum, in nihilum nil posse reverti.*
hoc est, quod palles? cur quis non prandeat, hoc est?' 85
His populus ridet, multumque torosa iuventus
ingeminat tremulos naso crispante cachinnos.

[78. *dicta* a. *quod satis est sapio mihi* a. *quod sapio satis est mihi* C.
80. *fingentis* a.   84. *di* a. *in nihilo nil* a.]

merely glances at the education their sons received, as contrasted with that given to him by his father in spite of narrow means, 1 S. 6. 72. Juvenal has an entire satire on them (16), in which he complains of their growing power and exclusive privileges, but without any personal jealousy.

77. de gente, 'of the clan,' used contemptuously, to imply that the soldiers form a class by themselves.

hircosa, opp. to 'unguentatus' in a fragm. of Seneca ap. Gell. 12. 2. 11 'ut licet scripti sint inter *hircosos*, possint tamen inter *unguentatos* placere.' Compare Hor. 1 S. 2. 27. The Stoic simplicity is meant to be contrasted with the coarseness of the soldiery on the one hand, as with the effeminacy of the young aristocracy on the other—two different modes of pampering the body at the expense of the mind. Compare 'hirsuta capella' Juv. 5. 115, Mayor's note.

78. sapio mihi quod satis est = 'sapio mihi satis.' 'Quod satis est' an object clause. 'Sapimus patruos' 1. 11.

mihi, emphatic. 'I am wise for myself,' I know my own interest, like 'minui mihi' 6. 64. 'Dives *tibi*, pauper *amicis*' Juv. 5. 113.

79. Arcesilas, Dict. Biogr.
aerumnosi, like κακοδαίμων, Aristoph. Clouds (of Socrates) 105.

Solones, pl. contemptuously. See 1. 34 note. [Comp. perhaps Plaut. Asin. 598 'nunc enim Negotiosum interdius videlicet Solonem, Leges ut conscribat,' etc.]

80. obstipo capite, [Cicero Aratea 'obstipum caput'], Hor. 2 S. 5. 92. 'Bent forward' Freund.

figentes lumine terram, a stronger, and consequently more scornful, expression than 'figentes lumina in terra.' Jahn quotes a parallel from Stat. Silv. 5. 1. 140 'domum, torvo quam non haec lumine figat.' Casaubon compares Plato Alc. 2, p. 138 A φαίνει γέ τοι ἐσκυθρωπακέναι τε καὶ εἰς γῆν βλέπειν, ὥς τι ξυννοούμενος.

81. rabiosa silentia, 'a mad dog's silence' (Hor. 2 Ep. 2. 75), because mad dogs do not bark. ἄφωνοι τοὐπίπαν εἰσί ... χωρὶς ὑλαγμοῦ Paul. Aegin. 5. 3, cited by Jahn. Compare Hom. Il. 3. 217 foll., referred to by Jahn, στάσκεν, ὑπαὶ δὲ ἴδισκε κατὰ χθονὸς ὄμματα πήξας, Σκῆπτρον δ' οὔτ' ὀπίσω οὔτε προπρηνὲς ἐνώμα, 'Ἀλλ' ἀστεμφὲς ἔχεσκεν, ἀϊδρεϊ φωτὶ ἐοικώς· Φαίης κεν ζάκοτόν τινα ἔμμεναι ἀφρονά τ' αὔτως. Persius may have had the picture in his mind.

rodunt, 'biting the lips and grinding the teeth.' Whether 'murmura' and 'silentia' are acc. of the object or cognates is not clear.

82. exporrecto ... labello. Jahn compares Lucian Hermot. 1. 1 καὶ τὰ χείλη διεσάλευες ἠρέμα ὑποτονθορύζων. Casaubon compares Aristaenetus Ep. 2. 3 ἠρέμα τὼ χείλη κινεῖ καὶ ἄττα δήπου πρὸς ἑαυτὸν ψιθυρίζει.

trutinantur verba is copied no less than five times by Jerome (for the references see Jahn), who however mistakes the sense, as if Persius were speaking of inflated talk, not of slow balanced utterance.

I don't want to be like one of your Arcesilases or your poor louts of Solons, stooping their heads and nailing the ground with their eyes, as they stand grinding queer noises and mad-dog silence all to themselves, and putting out their lips like a pivot for balancing their words, lost in pondering over the dreams of some sick dotard or other. *Nothing can come out of nothing, nothing can go back to nothing.* Is this a thing to get pale on? is a man to go without his dinner for this?' Aye, and folks are amused at him, and the big brawny brotherhood send rippling waves of laughter again and again through their curled nostrils.

83. [Varro, Eumenides fragm. 15 Riese 'Postremo nemo *aegrotus* quicquam *somniat* Tam infandum, quod non aliquis dicat philosophus.'] 'Aegri somnia' Hor. A. P. 7. Jahn explains **aegroti veteris** like 'aegri veteris' Juv. 9. 16, one who has long been ill—a confirmed invalid; but it seems better to suppose that Persius means to combine the dotings of age with the wanderings of disease.

84. 'Nullam rem e nilo gigni divinitus unquam' is the first principle of the Epicurean philosophy, according to Lucr. 1. 150; but it was common to various schools. [See Munro ad loc.] Casaubon quotes Marc. Anton. 4. 4 οὐδὲν ἐκ τοῦ μηδενὸς ἔρχεται, ὥσπερ μηδ' εἰς τὸ οὐκ ὂν ἀπέρχεται.

in nilum, etc. 'Haud igitur possunt ad nilum quaeque reverti ... Haud igitur redit ad nilum res ulla: sed omnes Discidio redeunt in corpore materiaï' Lucr. 1. 248 foll. Here the repetition is meant to be ludicrous, as in 1. 27. Jahn.

85. Casaubon quotes Sen. Ep. 48, who exclaims seriously, 'O pueriles ineptias! in hoc supercilia subduximus? in hoc barbam demisimus? hoc est quod tristes docemus et pallidi?' which seems to show that 'quod palles' is to be explained here as a cogn. acc.

our quis non prandeat. '*Impransi* correptus voce *magistri*' Hor. 2 S. 3. 257. 'Prandium' was peculiarly a military meal, so it is mentioned here feelingly. 'Medo *prandente*' Juv. 10 178. See De Quincey, Casuistry of Roman Meals (Selections, vol. 3), who mistakes the present passage, doubtless quoting from memory, though right in his general view. With the whole line compare Juv. 7. 96 'tunc utile multis Pallere, et vinum toto nescire Decembri.

86. **his ... ridet.** Not a very common use of the dative. 'Dolis risit Cytherea repertis' Virg. Aen. 4. 128. Jahn compares Hor. 2 S. 8. 83.

multum, probably with 'torosa,' as Jahn takes it. ['Socer huius vir *multum bonus* est,' says Cicero, Leg. Agr. 3. 3, ironically: so that there may be a tinge of sarcasm in the idiom. Hor. 2 S. 3. 147 'medicus multum celer atque fidelis;' Fronto Epist. 3. 15 'multum necessarius.' Comp. 'bene mirae eritis res' S. 1. 111.]

torosa, an epithet of the necks of cattle, Ov. M. 7. 429.

torosa iuventus contrasts with 'insomnis et detonsa iuventus' v. 54, as being naturally the approving audience of the soldier's speech.

87. The description is not in the best taste, as the minuteness is not in itself pleasing, at the same time that it does not contribute to the contempt which the picture is meant to excite. The grandiloquence of expression rather recalls such sea pieces as Catull. 64. 273 'leni resonant plangore cachinni,' Val. Fl. 1. 311 'Alma novo *crispans* pelagus Titania Phoebo.'

tremulos seems intended to express the appearance of the sneering laugh as it runs down the nose, as well as its sound. Freund says the intransitive use of 'crispo' is confined to the pres. participle, of which he quotes two instances from Pliny. The line is altogether a strange one, suggesting the notion of affected and effeminate laughter, such as might be expected from a company like that mentioned 1. 19, not the 'crassum ridet' (5. 190) of a military auditory.

'Inspice; nescio quid trepidat mihi pectus et aegris
faucibus exsuperat gravis alitus; inspice, sodes!'
qui dicit medico, iussus requiescere, posquam   90
tertia conpositas vidit nox currere venas,
de maiore domo modice sitiente lagoena
lenia loturo sibi Surrentina rogavit.
'Heus, bone, tu palles!' 'Nihil est.' 'Videas tamen istuc,
quidquid id est: surgit tacite tibi lutea pellis.'   95
'At tu deterius palles; ne sis mihi tutor;
iam pridem hunc sepeli: tu restas.' 'Perge, tacebo.'
turgidus hic epulis atque albo ventre lavatur,
gutture sulpureas lente exalante mefites;
sed tremor inter vina subit calidumque trientem   100

[90. *posquam* A.   91. *videt* C.   92. *silente lagoaena* a.   93. *laturo* C.
locupo a.   *rogabis* a, *rogavit* C.   94. qu. *tu* om. a.   *pallens* C. *istud* a.   95. *hic
est* A.   97. *sepelii* a, *sepellitur istas* C, *tu restas* c.   99. *pulphereas* a.   *exilante* a.
100. *in terra subiit* a (i. e. *interea ?*) *trientem* a C, *triental* ς.]

88–107. 'A man feels ill—consults his physician, who recommends quiet and abstinence—obeys for three days—then, finding himself better, procures wine to drink after bathing. A friend cautions him on his way to the bath, but the advice is scorned—he bathes upon a full stomach—drinks—is seized with shivering—rejects his food—and in course of time makes the usual end, and is buried.'

88. A story of real disease—told to show what indulgence and want of self-command can do. 'Inspicere morbum,' of medical examination, Plaut. Pers. 316.

nescio quid, a cogn. acc. after 'trepidat.'

89. **faucibus**, 'from the throat.' '**Aegris**' and '**gravis**' are the emphatic words, as there is nothing strange in breath rising from the throat.

exsuperat neuter. '*Exsuperant* flammae' Virg. Aen. 2. 759.

90. **qui dicit** is introduced just in the same way, Hor. 1 Ep. 17. 46 foll. '"Indotata mihi soror est, paupercula mater, Et fundus neque vendibilis nec pascere firmus," Qui dicit, clamat '. Victum date."'

requiescere. Comp. Celsus 3. 2 [p. 76 Daremberg] 'omnium optima sunt quies et abstinentia.'

91. **tertia . . . nox**, a critical time in attacks of fever, though the danger was not over then, as the fever might be a quartan. Schol. Nebriss. referring to Celsus 3. 4 [p. 80 Daremberg.]

conpositas, predicate, taken with 'currere.'

currere, said of the veins, as containing blood. Jahn refers to Celsus 3. 6 [p. 89 Daremberg], who speaks of the veins as 'leniores' or 'celeriores.'

92. **de maiore domo**. 'Maiores' of the aristocracy, 1. 108 note. '*Maxima quaeque domus* servis est plena superbis' Juv. 5. 66. The rich used occasionally to make presents of small quantities of expensive wines to sick friends. 'Cardiaco numquam cyathum missurus amico' Juv. 5. 32, quoted by Casaubon.

93. **lenia**, 'mellowed by age,' opp. to 'aspera.' 'Ad mare cum veni, generosum et *lene* requiro' Hor. 1 Ep. 15. 18.

loturo. For the custom of drinking after bathing, Jahn compares Sen. Ep. 122. 6 'Atqui frequens hoc adulescentium vitium est, qui vires excolunt, ut in ipso paene balinei limine inter nudos bibant, immo potent.' Com-

'Examine me. I have a strange palpitation at heart. My throat is amiss, and foul breath is rising from it. Pray, examine me.' Suppose a patient to say this to his physician, and be told to keep quiet, and then when the third night has found the current of his veins steady, to have sent to a great house with a flagon of moderate swallow for some mellow Surrentine before bathing. 'My good sir, you look pale.' 'O, it's of no consequence.' 'You had better attend to it, though, of whatever consequence it may be; your skin is getting insensibly bloated and quite yellow.' 'I tell you you're paler than I am; don't come the guardian over me; I've buried *him* long ago, and now I've got you in my way.' 'Go on, I'm dumb.' So our hero goes to his bath, with his stomach distended with eating and looking white, and a vapour of sulphurous properties slowly oozing from his throat; but a shivering

pare also Juv. 8. 168 'thermarum calices,' and Mayor's note.

93. **Surrentina** (Hor. 2 S. 4. 55) was a thin light wine recommended for invalids when recovering. Plin. 14. 24, 23. 33. Jahn. Pliny tells us that Tiberius used to say the physicians had conspired to raise the credit of Surrentine, which was in fact only 'generous vinegar,' a name which Caligula improved upon by calling it 'nobilis vappa.'

94. A dialogue between the invalid and a friend who meets him on his way to the bath.

95. **surgit** and **lutea** emphatic, also **pellis**, which is used instead of 'cutis,' as in Hor. Epod. 17. 22, Juv. 10. 192, to express the abnormal condition of the skin, which looks as if it did not belong to the man. With 'lutea' Jahn compares Hor. Epod. 10. 16 'pallor *luteus*,' Tibull. 1. 8. 52 'Sed nimius *luto* corpore tingit amor.'

96. **ne sis mihi tutor.** Imitated from Hor. 2 S. 3. 88 'ne sis patruus mihi.' Britann.

97. Another imitation. Hor. 1 S. 9. 28 '"Omnis conposui." "Felices! nunc ego resto. Confice."' If we may trust Isid. Orig. 10. 5, quoted by Jahn, '*Tutor :* qui pupillum tuetur, hoc est, intuetur: de quo in consuetudine vulgari dicitur, *Quid me mones ? et tutorem et paedagogum olim obrui,*' Persius seems to be repeating a piece of Roman slang.

restas = ' superstes es,' 'you are above ground,' ' I have you to bury.'

98. '*Crudi tumidique* lavemur' Hor. 1 Ep. 6. 61. 'Poena tamen praesens, cum tu deponis amictus *Turgidus,* et *crudum* pavonem in balnea portas. Hinc subitae mortes, atque intestata senectus' Juv. 1. 142 foll.

albo ventre, not coupled with **epulis,** but answering to **turgidus.** 'Albo corpore' Hor. 2 Od. 2. 15, of the dropsy; 'pinguem vitiis albumque' 2 S. 2. 21. 'Vides ut *pallidus* omnis Cena desurgat dubia' *ib.* 76.

lavatur, middle.

99. See v. 89. **sulpureas** is the proper epithet of 'mefites.' 'Mefitis proprie est terrae putor qui de aquis nascitur sulpuratis' Serv. on Virg. Aen. 7. 84, where the 'saeva mefitis' spoken of is a vapour arising from the sulphureous spring Albunea, the source of the Albula, of which the modern name is la Solforata. Thus the whole line is rather grandiloquent, like v. 87.

100. **sed tremor.** Imitated from Hor. 1 Ep. 16. 22 foll. ' occultam febrem sub tempus edendi Dissimules, donec *manibus tremor incidat unctis.*' [Plin. 14. 142, of the effects of drunkenness, 'hinc pallor et genae pendulae, oculorum ulcera, tremulae manus effundentes plena vasa.']

inter vina, 1. 30 note.

calidum. The wine was heated, being drunk to promote perspiration. 'Sudorem quem moverunt potionibus

excutit e manibus, dentes crepuere retecti,
uncta cadunt laxis tunc pulmentaria labris.
hinc tuba, candelae, tandemque beatulus alto
conpositus lecto crassisque lutatus amomis
in portam rigidas calces extendit: at illum 105
hesterni capite induto subiere Quirites.

'Tange, miser, venas et pone in pectore dextram,
nil calet hic; summosque pedes attinge manusque,
non frigent.' Visa est si forte pecunia, sive
candida vicini subrisit molle puella, 110
cor tibi rite salit? positum est algente catino
durum holus et populi cribro decussa farina:

[101. *excidit* a.   105. *portas* a.   *cales* A.   106. *externi* a.   107. *dextra* C.
112. *cribo* A.   *decusa* C.]

crebris et *ferventibus*' Sen. Ep. 122. 6.
100. ['Trientem' is right, not 'triental,' which Jahn read, followed by Conington. Messala ap. Plin. 34. 137 'Serviliorum familia habet *trientem sacrum*' etc. Mart. 1. 106. 8, 10. 49. 1 'amethystini trientes.' 'Triental' is not found in good Latin.]
101. **excutit** (tremor). Compare v. 115.
crepuere, because of the 'tremor.'
retecti, because of the 'laxa labra.' Compare Prop. 4. 8. 53 foll. 'Pocula mi digitos inter cecidere remissos, Palluerant ipso labra soluta mero.'
102. His jaw drops, and he rejects the dainties he had lately gorged.
pulmentaria, properly ὄψον—anything eaten with bread as a relish: 'tu *pulmentaria* quaere sudando' Hor. 2 S. 2. 20. Hence *dainties*. 'Veniet qui *pulmentaria* condiat' Juv. 7. 185. 'Pulmentum' or 'pulpamentum' has the same meaning. 'Pulmento utor magis unctiusculo' Plaut. Pseud. 220, quoted by Casaubon.
103. **hinc**, 'hereupon.' Freund s. v. Persius hastens to the catastrophe, giving the funeral first, and then the death.
tuba. Hor. 1 S. 6. 42 foll. 'si plaustra ducenta, Concurrantque foro *tria funera*, magna sonabit *Cornua quod vincatque tubas*.' The Twelve Tables prescribed the number of trumpeters. 'Decem tibicines adhibeto, hoc plus ne facito.' Compare also Prop. 2. 7. 12, 4. 11. 9, to which König refers.
candelae, 'wax lights.' 'Totiens in vicinia mea conclamatum est, totiens praeter limen immaturas exequias fax cereusque praecepit' Sen. de Tranq. 11. 7. Some have supposed that 'funalia' were used at ordinary funerals: 'cerei' or 'candelae' where the death was an untimely one, and Jahn seems to agree; but Casaubon rejects the inference.
beatulus, μακαρίτης. Jahn compares Amm. Marc. 25. 3. 21 'quem cum *beatum* fuisse Sallustius respondisset praefectus, intellexit occisum.' The dimin. of course indicates contempt. 'The dear departed.'
alto, opp. 'humili,' to show his consequence. Virg. Aen. 2. 2, 6. 603.
104. **conpositus**. Hor. 1 S. 9. 28 above quoted.
crassis, 'contemptuously.' 'Crassum unguentum' Hor. A. P. 375: so lutatus.
amomis. '*Amomo* quantum vix reddent *duo funera*' Juv. 4. 108 foll.
105. **in portam**. A custom as old as Homer (Il. 19. 212) κεῖται ἀνὰ πρόθυρον τετραμμένος. Hesych. δι' ἐκ θυρῶν. τοὺς νεκροὺς οὕτω φασὶν ἑδράζεσθαι ἔξω τοὺς πόδας ἔχοντας πρὸς τὰς αὐλικοὺς θυράς.

SAT. III.

comes on over the wine, and makes him let fall his hot tumbler from his fingers; his teeth are exposed and chatter; the rich dainties come back again from his dropping jaws. The upshot is horn-blowing and tapers; and at last the deceased, laid out on a high bed and daubed with coarse ointment, turns up his heels stark and stiff towards the door; and citizens of twenty-four hours' standing in their caps of liberty carry him to the grave.

'Poor creature yourself, feel my pulse and put your hand on my chest, there's no heat there; touch my extremities, they're not cold.' Suppose you happen to catch sight of a bit of money, does your heart beat regularly then? Or say you have a tough vegetable mess served up on a cold dish, with meal sifted through the

106. **hesterni ... Quirites.** Slaves just manumitted by the deceased's will, or, as the Scholia and Heinr. think, just before his death. The sneer at the easy acquisition of citizenship is repeated and dwelt on 5. 75 'Quibus una Quiritem Vertigo facit.'

capite induto. Manumitted slaves used to shave their heads and assume the 'pilleus.' 'Faxit Iuppiter ut ego hic hodie, raso capite, calvus capiam pilleum!' Plaut. Amph. 462. [Petronius 42 'tam bene elatus est, vitali lecto, stragulis bonis. Planctus est optime; manu misit aliquot; etiamsi maligne illum ploravit uxor.']

subiere. [Virg. Aen. 4. 599 'subiisse umeris confectum aetate parentem.' Tac. Ann. 6. 28 'subire patrium corpus.'] 'Pars ingenti *subiere* feretro' Virg. Aen. 6. 222. Casaubon. ['Ipsum propere vix liberti semiatrati exsequiantur' Varro Bimarcus fr. 18 (p. 109, Reise).]

107–118. 'You tell me *you* have no disease—no fever—no chill. But does not the hope of gain or of pleasure quicken your pulse? Is not your throat too tender to relish a coarse meal? You are subject to shivering fits of fear and the high fever of rage, which makes you rave like a madman.'

107. The man addressed, some person not specified, 'quivis media electus turba,' retorts that *he* has no ailment, so that the moral against excess does not touch him, when he finds that the story is typical and intended to have a wider application.

miser, retorted, from v. 66. He goes through the symptoms of such an attack as has just been described.

venas, referring to v. 91.

pectore, to v. 88. 'Feel my pulse.' [Lucilius 26. 12 'nunquam priusquam venas hominis tetigit ac praecordia.'] Jahn quotes Sen. Ep. 22. 1 'non potest medicus per epistulas cibi aut balnei tempus eligere: *vena tangenda est.*' Casaubon refers to Julian. Misopogon (p. 88. ed. Mart. A.D. 1583), speaking of the story of Antiochus and Erasistratus the physician, who discovered his passion for his stepmother Stratonice. ταῦτα ὁρῶν ὁ ἰατρὸς προσάγει τῷ στέρνῳ τὴν χεῖρα, καὶ ἐπήδα δεινῶς ἡ καρδία καὶ ἔξω ἵετο. In Valerius Maximus' version (5. 7) it is said, '*bracchium* adulescentis dissimulanter apprehendendo, modo vegetiore, modo languidiore pulsu venarum comperit cuius morbi aeger esset.'

108. 'There is no undue heat or excitement.' König refers to Celsus 2. 4.

109. Compare 2. 52 foll., 4. 47.

110. **vicini.** Persius may have been thinking of Hor. 3 Od. 19. 24 '*vicina* seni non habilis Lyco,' so that **puella** probably = 'amica,' like 'mea puella' in Catullus.

111. **rite** = 'solito more.' 'Is there no unusual palpitation?' See the passage from Julian just quoted.

positum. '*Ponebant* igitur Tusco farrata *catino*' Juv. 11. 108.

algente. Jahn contrasts '*calidum sumen*' 1. 53.

112. **durum,** 'tough'—perhaps from insufficient boiling. 'Ne gallina malum responset dura palato' Hor. 2 S. 4. 18.

populi ... farina. Horace's 'panis

temptemus fauces : tenero latet ulcus in ore
putre, quod haud deceat plebeia radere beta.
alges, cum excussit membris timor albus aristas ; 115
nunc face supposita fervescit sanguis et ira
scintillant oculi, dicisque facisque, quod ipse
non sani esse hominis non sanus iuret Orestes.

[115. *alget* a.   116. *iram* C.   117. *discique* a.   118. *est* a.]

secundus' (2 Ep. 1. 123), otherwise called 'cibarius' (Cic. Tusc. 5. 34), as the allowance given to slaves 'Nigra farina' Mart. 9. 3. 4, opp. to 'siligineus,' Sen. Ep. 119. 3 'utrum hic panis sit *plebeius* an *siligineus* ad naturam nihil pertinet ;' 'sifted through the common sieve,' which was coarser.

112. populi, here = 'plebis.'

113. 'Let us see how your palate is. Ah! your mouth is tender from a concealed inflammation.'

tenero, emphatic, a sort of predicate.

latet ulcus, perhaps from Hor. 1 Ep. 16. 24 'Stultorum incurata pudor malus *ulcera celat*,' so as to remind us of the previous story, 'a sore which you have said nothing of to me, your medical adviser.' Persius has convicted his patient of palpitation—he now proves

that his mouth is inflamed—then shows that he is feverish—hot and cold alternately.

114. plebeia . . . beta, like ' panis plebeius,' quoted on v. 112. The irony is kept up by the word 'beta,' beet being proverbially tender. Suet. Aug. 87 quotes, as a peculiar expression, from Augustus' correspondence, '*betizare* pro *languere*, quod vulgo *lachanizare* dicitur.'

radere, like 'tergere palatum' Hor. 2 S. 2. 24, compared by the Scholia. Lucr. 4. 528, 532 '*Praeterea* radit vox *fauces* . . . ianua *raditur* oris.'

115. excussit, of raising suddenly, but without separation. See 1. 118 note.

aristas, proleptically : 'excussit pilos ita ut aristis similes essent.' Jahn compares Varro L. L. 6. 49 'tremor . . . cum etiam in corpore pili ut aristae in spica hordei horrent.' Stocker compares

common sieve: now let us examine your palate: ah, you have a concealed putrid ulcer, which makes your mouth tender, and it won't do to let that coarse vulgar beet rub against it. So you shiver, when pale fear sets up the bristles all over you, and then when a fire is lighted underneath your blood begins to boil, and your eyes sparkle with passion, and you say and do things which Orestes, the hero of madmen, would depose to be the words and actions of a madman.

with this and the following verses Lucr. 3. 288 foll. 'Est etiam calor ille animo quem sumit in ira, Cum fervescit, et ex oculis micat acribus ardor. Est et frigida multa comes formidinis aura, Qua ciet horrorem membris, et concitat artus:' a curious passage in itself, illustrating Lucretius' theory of the composition of the soul or mind from heat, wind (or cold), and atmospheric air (the medium temperature) by the different temperaments of different animals, and one too which Persius not improbably had in his mind. See next note.

116. **face supposita**; perhaps from Lucr. 3. 303 'Nec nimis *iraï fax* unquam *subdita* percit.' Persius' metaphor is from a boiling caldron: compare the simile in Virg. Aen. 7. 462 foll.; and this may be the meaning of Lucr. 1. c. 298 'Nec capere irarum fluctus in pectore possunt,' which answers exactly to Virgil's 'nec iam se capit unda.'

117. 'Ira furor brevis est' Hor. 1 Ep. 2. 62.

118. **non sanus**='insanus,' v. 46. The instance of Orestes is doubtless taken from Hor. 2 S. 3. 137 sq. 'Quin ex quo est habitus male tutae mentis Orestes, Nil sane fecit quod *tu* reprehendere possis,' where Damasippus argues that Orestes was mad when he killed his mother, not afterwards. But he was a favourite example of madness. Jahn refers to Plato, Alc. II. p. 143 D, and to Gell. 13. 4, who says that Varro wrote a work 'Orestes vel de Insania.' Comp. Plautus, Capt. 562 'Et quidem Alcumaeus, atque Orestes, et Lycurgus postea Una opera mihi sunt sodales, qua iste.'

SATURA IV.

"Rem populi tractas?" barbatum haec crede magistrum
dicere, sorbitio tollit quem dira cicutae
"quo fretus? dic hoc, magni pupille Pericli.
scilicet ingenium et rerum prudentia velox
ante pilos venit, dicenda tacendaque calles.　　　　　5
ergo ubi commota fervet plebecula bile,
fert animus calidae fecisse silentia turbae

[Hanc priori saturae continuat C.　*De his qui ambigunt honores* B.　2. *sorbiti tolli* a.　*dura* a.　3. *dic o* Ϛ.　*periclis* a, *pericli* C.　5. *tacendave* C.　*cales* a.]

On the want of self-command and self-knowledge in public men—a sort of continuation of the last Satire, being addressed to a supposed representative of the age, but complete in itself. The general notion and a few of the expressions are taken from Plato's (?) First Alcibiades, but the treatment is not particularly similar. The gist of the whole is contained in Alcibiades' speech in Plato Sympos. p. 216 A, quoted by König: ἀναγκάζει γάρ με ὁμολογεῖν, ὅτι πολλοῦ ἐνδεὴς ὢν αὐτὸς ἔτι ἐμαυτοῦ μὲν ἀμελῶ, τὰ δ' Ἀθηναίων πράττω. *Other philosophers appear to have written dialogues of the kind (Brandis Rhein. Mus. I. p.* 120 *foll.), so that the subject, as Jahn remarks, was probably a stock one in the schools. This would account for Persius choosing it, as it cannot have been particularly appropriate to the time, there being no field at Rome for the display of popular statesmanship, such as Persius represents in the early part of the Satire, vv.* 1-16. *Alcibiades is not Nero, as Brit. suggests, and Casaubon maintains at length, but one of the young nobility, such as those described in Sat.* 3—*only placed in circumstances which belong not to Rome but to Athens. Thus the general conception of the Satire is sufficiently weak; the working out, however, has all Persius' peculiar force.*

1-22. 'Alcibiades would be a statesman, would he? what are his qualifications? Ready wit and intuitive tact, impressive action, a power of logical statement, and a certain amount of philosophic training. But what is he in himself? he has no end beyond his own enjoyment. Why, the meanest old crone knows as much.'

1. **Rem populi** = 'rem publicam.' **Rem ... tractare**, as in Enn. in Cic. de Orat. 1. 45 'ut ne *res* temere *tractent* turbidas.'

barbatum ... magistrum is copied by Juv. 14. 12. Comp. Hor. 2 S. 3. 16, 35, where the beard is the especial mark of the Stoics.

2. **tollit** for 'sustulit.' So 'mutat' 2. 60. Comp. Hor. 1 S. 6. 13 'unde Superbus Tarquinius regno pulsus fugit,' id. 2 S. 3. 277 'Marius cum *praecipitat*

SATIRE IV.

"Do you charge yourself with the affairs of the nation?" Suppose this to be said by the bearded philosopher, whom the fatal draught of hemlock removes from the scene—"on the strength of what? tell me, ward of the great Pericles as you are. Oh yes, of course; ready wit and experience of business have been quick in coming, and arrived sooner than your beard: you know well what should be said and what not. And so when the lower orders are fermenting and the bile in their system beginning to work, the impulse within moves you to cause silence through the heated

se, Cerritus fuit?' [Cic. Fam. 5. 12. 5 'sibi avelli spiculum *iubet* Epaminondas;' see Conington on Aen. 8. 294.] The line is modelled on 2 S. 1. 56 'Sed mala *tollet* anum vitiato melle *cicuta*.'

3. **quo fretus**, from Plato, Alc. 1. p. 123 E τί οὖν ποτ' ἔστιν ὅτῳ πιστεύει τὸ μειράκιον;

magni pupille Pericli is emphatic, as Alcibiades' prestige depended very much on his connexion with Pericles, Plat. l. c. p. 104 B ξυμπάντων δὲ ὧν εἶπον μείζω οἴει σοι δύναμιν ὑπάρχειν Περικλέα τὸν Ξανθίππου ὃν ὁ πατὴρ ἐπίτροπον κατέλιπέ σοί τε καὶ τῷ ἀδελφῷ.

4. **scilicet** is here half ironical. The speaker does not mean to deny that Alcibiades has this ready wit and intuitive tact, but he affects to make more of it than it is worth.

ingenium et rerum prudentia are from Virg. G. 1. 416, 'talent and knowledge of life.'

velox with 'venit,' 'has come rapidly.' Comp. Ov. A. A. 1. 185 'Ingenium caeleste suis velocius annis surgit.'

5. **ante pilos**; 'sooner than your beard,' a contrast with 'barbatum magistrum.'

dicenda tacendaque calles is much the same as Aeschylus' σιγᾶν ὅπου δεῖ καὶ λέγειν τὰ καίρια (Cho. 582). The words are from Hor. 1 Ep. 7. 72 'dicenda tacenda locutus.' König quotes Quint. 2. 20. 5, who seems to have had the present passage in his view, 'Si consonare sibi in faciendis et non faciendis virtutis est, quae pars eius prudentia vocatur, eadem in dicendis et non dicendis erit.' There is a slight resemblance between this line and the preceding, and Plato, p. 110 C, quoted by Casaubon, ᾤου ἄρα ἐπίστασθαι καὶ παῖς ὤν, ὡς ἔοικε, τὰ δίκαια καὶ τὰ ἄδικα.

6. **commota fervet ... bile.** Hor. 1 Od. 13. 4 'fervens difficili bile.' Jahn.

plebecula. Hor. 2 Ep. 1. 186. The language is not unlike Virg. Aen. 1. 149 'saevitque animis ignobile vulgus.' Delph. ed.

7. **fert animus.** Ov. M. 1. 1. 'You have a mind to try the effect of your oratory on an excited mob.'

facere silentium, a phrase used either of the person who keeps silence, 'huic *facietis* fabulae *silentium*' Plaut. Amph. Prol. 15, or of the person who commands it, as here, and Tac. H. 3. 20 'ubi adspectu et auctoritate *silentium*

maiestate manus.   quid deinde loquere?   'Quirites,
hoc puta non iustum est, illud male, rectius illud.'
scis etenim iustum gemina suspendere lance   10
ancipitis librae, rectum discernis, ubi inter
curva subit, vel cum fallit pede regula varo,
et potis es nigrum vitio praefigere theta.
quin tu igitur, summa nequiquam pelle decorus,
ante diem blando caudam iactare popello   15
desinis, Anticyras melior sorbere meracas!
quae tibi summa boni est? uncta vixisse patella
semper et adsiduo curata cuticula sole?

[9. *illut* C.   10. *geminae* C.   11. *iter* A.   13. *est a* C.   14. *puelle a.*
16. *desinas a. merecas a.*]

fecerat.' The dative in the latter sense of the phrase has the same force as in *facere negotium alicui*, etc.

8. **maiestate manus.** Casaubon compares Lucan 1. 297 'tumultum Conposuit vultu, dextraque silentia iussit.' Heinr. compares Tac. Ann. 1. 25 'stabat Drusus, silentium manu poscens.' So Ov. M. 1. 205 'qui postquam voce manuque Murmura compressit, tenuere silentia cuncti.'

quid deinde loquere? may perhaps be meant, as Jahn thinks, to show that the orator had not thought beforehand of what he should say.

9. **puta.** Hor. 2 S. 5. 32.

non iustum est. So Alcibiades in Plato, p. 109, is made to admit that in deliberative oratory τὸ ὧδε ἢ ὧδε is equivalent to τὸ δικαίως ἢ ἀδίκως. Casaubon compares Hor. 1 S. 4. 134 'rectius hoc est: Hoc faciens vivam melius.'

10. 'You have studied philosophy.' Comp. 3. 52 foll. note, where the language is substantially the same.

iustum is what is put into each scale of the balance. 'You can weigh the justice of one course against that of another.'

gemina...lance = 'geminis lancibus,' like 'geminus pes' Ov. A. A. 2. 644.

11. 'You can distinguish right from the wrong on either side of it'—as there may be two opposite deviations from the perpendicular—a doctrine not unlike the Aristotelian theory of virtue as a mean, which Casaubon compares, 'where it (the right line) comes in between the curves.' Comp. 3. 52, 5. 38.

12. The meaning seems to be '*even* (vel) when the rule misleads you by its deviation,' i. e. as Casaubon explains it, when justice has to be corrected by equity.

pede, used apparently to suggest the notion of a foot measure. 'Metiri se quemque suo modulo ac *pede* verum est' Hor. 1 Ep. 7. 98.

varo possibly may denote that the rule branches into two parts. Comp. 6. 18 'Geminos, horoscope, *varo* Producis genio,' and note.

13. **potis es.** 1. 56, note.

theta; Θ, the initial of Θάνατος, was the mark of condemnation, apparently introduced from Greece in place of C ('Condemno'), which the judges used in Cicero's time. Isid. Orig. 1. 3. 8. Θ was also employed in epitaphs [Brambach's C. Insc. Rhen. 391] and by the quaestors in striking off dead soldiers' names from the roll, Mart. 7. 37. 2 [where see Friedländer's note]. The Scholiast and Isid. l. c. quote a line from an unknown writer [? Lucilius] 'O multum ante alias infelix littera *Theta*.'

14. The monitor suddenly turns round on the would-be statesman. 'Will you then be so good as to have done with that?'

igitur, as if it were the natural and expected consequence for all the admissions in his favour that have been made. The real reason is given afterwards, v. 17.

assemblage by the imposing action of your hand. Well, now that you have got it, what will you say? 'Citizens, this (say) is an injustice, that is ill-advised; of the three courses the third is nearer right.' Just so; you know how to weigh justice in the scales of the wavering balance. You can distinguish right where it comes in between the deviations on either side, even where the rule misleads you by its divarication, and you can obelize wrong with a staring black mark. Will you have the goodness, then, to stop, and not go on under the vain disguise of that goodly skin fawning so precociously on the mob that strokes you, when your better course would be to swallow the contents of all the Anticyras undiluted? What is your conception of the chief good? to live at a rich table every day and cultivate your dainty skin with constant sunning? Now

summa... pelle decorus, imitated from Hor. 1 Ep. 16. 45 'Introrsus turpem, *speciosum pelle decora.*' Comp. also 2 S. 1. 64, alluding to such fables as the ass in the lion's skin, etc., 5. 116.

nequiquam, because you cannot impose on me. Compare 3. 30.

15. **ante diem.** 'You may be led into it some day, but at any rate do not anticipate things.' So 4. 5.

'To be the people's pet.' The Scholia are quite right in saying that Persius is thinking of a pet animal that wags its tail, against Casaubon, who, on second thoughts, supposes the image to be that of a peacock, and Jahn, who suggests that it may be a horse. The action described is that of a dog, who fawns on those who caress him as in Hor. 2 Od. 19. 30 'leniter atterens Caudam;' but Persius probably meant to allude to the well-known comparison of Alcibiades to a lion's whelp, Aristoph. Frogs 1431 foll. Compare the description in Aesch. Ag. 725. **blando**; comp. Hor. 3 Od. 11. 15 'Cessit immanis tibi *blandienti* Ianitor aulae;' 'blandus' is applied to the animal itself, Lucr. 4. 998, Ov. M. 14. 258.

popello, contemptuously, 6. 50, Hor. 1 Ep. 7. 65.

16. **Anticyras,** freq. in Hor., 2 S. 3. 83, 166, A. P. 300. The plural is used because there were two towns of the name, both producing hellebore, one in Phocis, the other on the Maliac gulf—of course with an accompanying notion of exaggeration. This is further brought out by using the town as synonymous with its contents (comp. 'Anticyram *omnem*' Hor. 2 S. 3. 83).

melior sorbere = 'quem sorbere melius foret.' Jahn. Compare the Gr. expression δίκαιός εἰμι ποιεῖν τοῦτο.

meracas reminds us of another passage, Hor. 2 Ep. 2. 137 'Expulit helleboro morbum bilemque meraco.' Delph. ed.

17. **summa boni** = 'summum bonum,' just as 'summa rerum' and 'res summa' or 'summa res publica' are used convertibly.

vixisse, the inf. used as a noun and so coupled with a subst., as in 1. 9, 3. 53 foll. etc.

patella. 3. 26. Possibly the reference may be, as there, to a sacrificial dish. Comp. Jahn's suggestion quoted on 2. 42. For the general sense, comp. Hor. 1 Ep. 6. 56 foll. 'Si bene qui cenat bene vivit, lucet, eamus Quo ducit gula,' quoted by Delph. ed.

18. 'curare cutem' as in Hor. 1 Ep. 2. 29, 4. 15, from whom Persius and Juv. 2. 105 seem to have borrowed it.

cuticula, contemptuously, like '*pelliculam* curare' Hor. 2 S. 5. 38, where the dim. expresses luxury, as here, in substitution of 'pellis' for 'cutis,' old age, as in note on 3. 95. Juv. imitates the line (11. 203) 'Nostra bibat vernum contracta *cuticula solem.*'

sole, with reference to the custom of basking ('insolatio' or 'apricatio') after being anointed, see Mayor on Juv. l. c.

expecta, haud aliud respondeat haec anus. i nunc
'Dinomaches ego sum,' sufla 'sum candidus.' esto; 20
dum ne deterius sapiat pannucia Baucis,
cum bene discincto cantaverit ocima vernae."
Ut nemo in sese temptat descendere, nemo,
sed praecedenti spectatur mantica tergo!
quaesieris 'Nostin Vettidi praedia?' 'Cuius?' 25
'Dives arat Curibus quantum non miluus errat.'
'Hunc ais, hunc dis iratis genioque sinistro,

[19. *in hunc* AC. 21. *pannucea* a, Schol., *pannucia* C. 22. *ocyma* a C. 23. *nunc nemo* c. 25. *quesierit* a. *Victidi* A, *vectidi* B, *vettidis* C. 26. *miluus erat* a, *miluus oberrat* ς, Schol.]

19. **expecta**, 'listen.' The hearer waiting for the words of the speaker. '*Expecto* si quid dicas' Plaut. Trin. 98. Jahn compares Sen. de Benef. 5. 12. 1 'Dicis me abesse ab eo, qui operae pretium facit, imo totam operam bona fide perdere? Expecta: etiam hoc verius dicas.'

i nunc, ironically—'now then, after this proceed to do as you have done.' Hor. 1 Ep. 6. 17, 2 Ep. 2. 76.

20. **Dinomaches ego sum**. So Socrates in talking to Alcibiades calls him ὁ Δεινομάχης υἱός Plato, p. 123 C. The mother being mentioned in preference to the father, Cleinias, because it was through her that he was connected with the Alcmaeonidae. For the expression of the relationship by the gen. alone, see Madvig § 280, obs. 4. Here it is doubtless used as a Greek idiom.

sufla = 'dic suflatus'—to be connected closely with 'i nunc,' which in this form of expression is always followed by another imperative, sometimes with a copula, sometimes without.

candidus, of beauty, as in 3. 110. Madan compares Hor. 2 Ep. 2. 4 '*Candidus* et talos a vertice pulcher ad imos.' Alcibiades' beauty is admitted by Socrates (Plato, p. 104 A, quoted by Jahn) οἴει γὰρ δὴ εἶναι πρῶτον μὲν κάλλιστός τε καὶ μέγιστος, καὶ τοῦτο μὲν δὴ παντὶ δῆλον ἰδεῖν ὅτι οὐ ψεύδει.

21. 'Only do not set up to be wiser than the old lady there.'

pannucia, properly *ragged*, hence *shrivelled* (used as an epithet of apples, Plin. 15. 52), which is evidently its meaning here, to point the contrast with 'candidus.' [Petronius 14 '(vestis) pannucia.' The Schol. say that *pannucius* was the vulgar word for *pannosus*.]

Baucis (contrasted with 'Dinomaches'), a name chosen from the well-known story, Ov. M. 8. 640 foll., the point of which lies in the contrast between the grandeur of the gods and the meanness of the peasants who were deemed fit to entertain them—'a person not more below you than Baucis was below Jupiter.'

22. **bene** with **discincto**, like 'bene mirae' 1. 111. Jahn.

cantaverit ocima is explained Nebriss. and Casaubon as = 'dixerit opprobria,' on the strength of a passage in Pliny (19. 120) where it is said that 'ocimum,' or basil, ought to be sown with curses, that it may grow up more abundantly. But this superstition furnishes but a slender warrant for so strange an expression. It will be better then to follow the Scholia and the other commentators, ancient and modern, who make the old woman a herb-seller (λαχανόπωλις, like the mother of Euripides), crying basil ('cantaverit' with reference to her whining note) to a lazy liquorish slave. There is some doubt about the identity of 'ocimum' (otherwise written 'ozimum,' 'ocymum,' 'ocinum'), and Jahn thinks its real nature cannot be exactly ascertained: it appears however from Pliny, 20. 123, to have been a stimulant, and to have been considered injurious by some people. The sense then will be that the old woman, in trying to sell doubtful herbs to low customers, is acting on the same principle

listen: the old woman here will give the same answer to the same question. Go, then, mouth it out. 'My mother was a Dinomache. I inherit her beauty;' by all means, only remember that old shrivelled Baucis is just as good a philosopher as you, when she cries basil to a low creature of a slave."

How utter, utter is the dearth of men who venture down into their own breasts, and how universally they stare at the wallet on the man's back before them! Suppose you ask, 'Do you know Vettidius' property?' 'Whose?' 'That great proprietor who has estates at Cures which a kite cannot fly over.' 'Him, do you mean?

which Alcibiades has avowed. She would like to be idle and live well, and her labours are directed to that end—she pleases her public and you yours. 'Cantaverit' is probably meant to have a force, as contrasted with the modulated voice of the young orator; 'she knows the regular whine of the trade, just as you know the various intonations which belong to yours: and she is as persuasive as you.' But the explanation is not very satisfactory, and the line requires further illustration. [Comp. Petronius 6. 7, and his character of the old woman 'quae agreste holus vendebat.']

23–41. 'None of us knows himself—every one thinks only of his neighbour. Inquire about some rich man, and you will hear how he pinches himself; even on state occasions hardly bringing himself to open a bottle of wine, which has been kept till it has turned to vinegar, to drink with his onions. But you with your luxury and effeminacy are laying yourself open to remarks of the same kind on your personal habits.'

23. in sese descendere—'to explore the depths of his own bosom;' an extension of the metaphor which attributes depth to the secrets of the mind.

24. Jupiter, according to Phaedrus (4. 10), has furnished every man with two wallets, one containing his neighbour's faults, to hang round his neck, the other containing his own, to hang behind his back. So Catull. 22. 21 'Sed non videmus manticae quod in tergo est.' Hor. 2 S. 3. 299 'Respicere ignoto discet pendentia tergo.' Persius improves on the image by giving every one a single wallet to hang behind him, and making him look exclusively at that which hangs on the back of his neighbour who is walking before. [Seneca de Ira 2. 28.

8 'aliena vitia in oculis habemus, a tergo nostra sunt.']

25. It is not easy to account for the distribution of the dialogue that follows.

quaesieris apparently refers to the person who is addressed in the preceding lines, and again in the following. From vv. 42 foll. it would seem to be Persius' object to expose the inconsistency with which he ridicules his neighbour's avarice, being himself guilty of vices of another kind. Yet vv. 27–32, which contain the picture of the miser, are spoken not by him but by the person to whom he is talking, unless we follow the Scholia in dividing v. 27 'Hunc ais?' 'Hunc,' etc., contrary to the natural meaning of the line. We must then either understand 'quaesieris' loosely in the sense of 'quaesierit quispiam,' and reverse the order of the speakers, so as to leave vv. 27–32 for the representation of Alcibiades, or suppose that Persius means his hero not to ridicule the miser himself, but to listen while others do so, and flatter himself that nothing of the kind is said of *him*, not knowing that the scandals of his own life are dwelt upon with quite as much relish.

Vettidi is restored by Jahn for 'Vectidi' on the authority of numerous inscriptions. [L. Vetidius Rufus C. I. L. 10. 3663; a form 'Vettitia' occurs C. I. L. 12. 607 (Arles), *ib.* 4011 (Nîmes).]

cuius? comp. 2. 19 'Cuinam?' The person questioned does not know who is meant, till a description of the man is given.

26. aro, in the sense of possessing arable land. Hor. Epod. 4. 13, referred to by Jahn '*Arat* Falerni mille fundi iugera.'

Curibus, possibly mentioned, as

qui, quandoque iugum pertusa ad compita figit,
seriolae veterem metuens deradere limum
ingemit: *hoc bene sit!* tunicatum cum sale mordens   30
caepe et farratam pueris plaudentibus ollam
pannosam faecem morientis sorbet aceti?'
ac si unctus cesses et figas in cute solem,
est prope te ignotus, cubito qui tangat et acre
despuat 'hi mores! penemque arcanaque lumbi   35
runcantem populo marcentis pandere vulvas!
tu cum maxillis balanatum gausape pectas,

[29. *veteris* a.   30. *mordes* C.   31. *fariratam* a, *farrata* C. *olla* C.
33. *a si* a. *frigas* a, *figas* C.   34. *tangit* a.   37. *tunc cum* a C, *tu cum* ς.
pectes Priscian. 1 p. 333 K.]

Jahn thinks, to remind us of the old Sabines and their simple life, which the miserly owner of the 'latifundium' caricatures so grossly.

26. **quantum non miluus errat.** [Petronius 37 'ipse Trimalchio fundos habet *qua milui volant.*'] Imitated by Juv. 9. 54 foll. 'Cui tot montis, tot *praedia* servas Apula, tot *miluos intra tua pascua lassos.*' According to the Scholia 'quantum milui volant' was a proverbial expression for distance.

27. **dis iratis** for 'Deos iratos habentem.' '*Iratis* natus paries *Dis* atque poetis' Hor. 2 S. 3. 8. '*Dis inimice senex*' is Horace's address to a miser, v. 123 of the same Satire. There, as here, the expression seems to imply folly or madness, as in Ter. Andr. 663 'nescio, nisi mihi Deos satis fuisse iratos, qui auscultaverim,' which Jahn compares.

genio sinistro, as refusing the enjoyments which his nature claims, see note on 2. 3. The Scholia compare Ter. Phorm. 44 *Suum defrudans genium,* compersit miser:' the Delph. ed. compares Plaut. Truc. 184 'Isti qui cum geniis suis belligerant parcipromi,' which is the same as the prosaic 'ventri Indico bellum' of Hor. 1 S. 5. 7. The whole line is imitated by Juv. 10. 129 'Dis ille adversis genitus fatoque sinistro.'

28. Referring to the feast of 'Compitalia' (see Dict. Antiqq.), one of the rustic holidays, like the 'Paganalia' (Prol. 6) and the 'Palilia' (1. 72), celebrated with sacrifices and games. 'Ut quoque turba bono plaudat signata (?) magistro, Qui facit egregios ad pervia compita ludos' Calp. 4. 125 foll. To these Hor. refers 1 Ep. 1. 49 'Quis circum pagos et circum *compita* pugnax.' The yoke was hung up, with the other parts of the plough, as a symbol of the suspension of labour. ' Luce sacra requiescat humus, requiescat arator, Et grave, *suspenso vomere* cesset opus. Solvite vincla iugis' Tibull. 2. 1. 5 foll. ' Rusticus *emeritum palo suspendat aratrum*' Ov. F. 1. 665. 'Figere' is generally used where the implements are hung up permanently. ' Armis Herculis ad postem *fixis*' Hor. 1 Ep. 1. 5. 'Armaque *fixit* Troïa' Virg. Aen. 1. 248.

pertusa, 'Merito, quia per omnes quattuor partes pateant' Schol. ; equivalent to 'pervia' in Calp. l. c. 'Pertundere' is used for 'to make a passage through' Lucr. 4. 1286 foll. ' Guttas in saxa cadentes Umoris longo in spatio *pertundere* saxa,' and so 'pertusum vas' *ib.* 3. 1099, of the bottomless tub of the Danaides. The line then means 'at each return of the Compitalia.'

29. Cato R. R. 57, referred to by Jahn, bids the farmer give each slave at the 'Compitalia' a congius of wine over and above the usual allowance.

limus is explained by the Scholia and most of the commentators, of the pitch or other substance with which the jars were daubed ('linebantur' Hor. 1 Od. 20. 3): Jahn however understands it more simply of the dirt which would naturally adhere to it after so long keeping.

SAT. IV.

the aversion of the gods and the enemy of his genius, who, whenever he fastens up the yoke at the feast of crossroads and thoroughfares, in the extremity of his dread of scraping off the ancient incrustation from his dwarf wine jar, groans out, *May it be for the best!* as he munches onions, coats and all, with salt, and while his slaves are clapping their hands with ecstasy over the mess of meal, gulps down the mothery lees of expiring vinegar?'

30. **bene sit** was a common form of drinking healths. 'Bene vos, bene nos, bene te, bene me, bene nostram etiam Stephanium' Plaut. Stich. 708; also with the dative of the person, 'Bene mihi, bene vobis, bene amitae meae' *id.* Pers. 773; a wish for *future* blessings. 'Bene est' is a common phrase for the *present* pleasures of the table. 'Bene erat non piscibus urbe petitis, Sed pullo atque haedo' Hor. 2 S. 2. 120. Jahn. 'Bene erat iam glande reperta' Ov. F. 4. 399, Casaubon. Here it is a sort of grace, uttered with a groan by the miser, who fears he is doing wrong in drawing the wine, 'May it turn out well' or 'bring a blessing,' like Agamemnon's εὖ γὰρ εἴη, when he consents to his daughter's death (Aesch. Ag. 216).

'**tunica**' is used by Juv. 14. 153 'tunicam mihi malo lupini,' and elsewhere, of the pod or husk of a vegetable: but there is probably some humour intended in the use of the participle, which was an ordinary epithet of the common people (Hor. 1 Ep. 7. 65), perhaps like Horace's 'caepe trucidas' (1 Ep. 12. 21), a reference to the Pythagorean reverence for vegetable life. The onions of course are eaten with their skins as more filling, so that there may be no waste.

31. **farratam ... ollam**, a dish of 'puls,' a pottage made from spelt, the national dish of the Roman husbandmen. Comp. Juv. 14. 171 'Grandes fumabant pultibus ollae,' and Mayor's note. The 'puls' itself is called 'farrata' Juv. 11. 109. The plaudits of the slaves ('pueri') common on these occasions of licence, as an acknowledgment to the founder of the feast (see Calp. quoted on v. 28), are here bestowed on a meal which other labourers get every day. With 'plaudentibus ollam' Jahn compares Stat. Silv. 5. 3. 140 'Nec *fratrem* caestu virides *plausere* Therapnae.'

32. **pannosam**, 'mothery.' 'Arida ac *pannosa* macies' Sen. de Clem. 2. 6; comp. by Jahn.

morientis, 'unguenta moriuntur' Plin. 13. 20, lose their strength. Hor. 2 S. 3. 116 says of a miser 'acre potet acetum,' wine which has become mere vinegar: but Persius, as Casaubon remarks, strengthens every word — not 'acetum' merely, but 'pannosam faecem aceti morientis,' the very vinegar-flavour being about to disappear. [Comp. Plutarch περὶ εὐθυμίας 8; τοῦ Χίου .... ὃς πολὺν καὶ χρηστὸν οἶνον ἑτέροις πιπράσκων, ἑαυτῷ πρὸς τὸ ἄριστον ὀξίνην ἐζήτει διαγενόμενος.]

33. **unctus cesses.** '*Cessare*, et ludere, et *ungi*' Hor. 2 Ep. 2. 183. See note on v. 18.

figas in cute solem, a strong expression for 'apricari.' Expose yourself to the piercing rays ('tela') of the sun — what Juv. 11. 203 and Mart. 10. 12. 7 express more genially by 'bibere' or 'combibere solem.' [Seneca de Vita Beata 27. 3 'quaerite aliquem mollem cedentemque materiam *in qua* tela vestra *figatis*.']

34. 'You may be sure that some one is making reflections on you which you little dream of.'

cubito ... tangat. 'Nonne vides (aliquis *cubito* stantem *prope tangens* Inquiet) ut patiens, ut amicis aptus, ut acer' Hor. 2 S. 5. 42.

'He is as surely reflecting on you as if he were to jog you and make his remarks in your ear.'

acre despuere, like 'verum plorare' 1. 90.

35. **mores**, mode of life, 1. 26, 2. 62 note.

inguinibus quare detonsus gurgulio extat?
quinque palaestritae licet haec plantaria vellant
elixasque nates labefactent forcipe adunca,   40
non tamen ista filix ullo mansuescit aratro.'

" Caedimus, inque vicem praebemus crura sagittis.
vivitur hoc pacto ; sic novimus. ilia subter
caecum vulnus habes ; sed lato balteus auro
protegit. ut mavis, da verba et decipe nervos,   45
si potes. ' Egregium cum me vicinia dicat,
non credam?' Viso si palles, inprobe, nummo,
si facis in penem quidquid tibi venit amorum :
si puteal multa cautus vibice flagellas :
nequiquam populo bibulas donaveris aures.   50
respue, quod non es ; tollat sua munera Cerdo ;

[39. *palestra a. plantari a.*   40. *fluxasque* C.   *forfice a.*   41. *felix* C.
44. *alia eus* A, *altareus* B.   46. *potest a. dicta a.*   48. *amarum* codd.
amorum Iohannes Sarisberiensis.   51. *respuat a.   est a.*]

42-52. 'This is the way: we lash our neighbours and are lashed in turn. Avail yourself of your prestige if you like, but remember that what men say of you is worthless, if you are really a libertine or a usurer. Better be true to yourself and learn your own weakness.'

42. Casaubon seems right in supposing that Persius was thinking of Hor. 2 Ep. 2. 97 'Caedimur et totidem plagis consumimus hostem,' though the passage of arms is there a passage of compliments. 'We are like archers in a battle, who shoot many arrows, and are ourselves exposed to many shots,'—the image being chosen so as to express the suddenness of the wounds, which come from unknown quarters. The arrows of the tongue are a sufficiently common metaphor: τῶν γὰρ μεγάλων ψυχῶν ἰεὶς οὐκ ἂν ἁμάρτοις Soph. Aj. 154.

caedo seems to be used of wounding with a missile weapon—e.g. of battering doors with stones, Cic. Verr. 2. 1. 27.

43. vivitur hoc pacto. 'Isto non vivitur illic, Quo tu rere, modo' Hor. 1 S. 9. 48. Casaubon compares Hor. 2 S. 8. 65 'Haec est condicio vivendi.'

sic novimus seems to be equivalent to 'sic accepimus' or 'sic didicimus,' —'such is our experience.'

44. A continuation of the metaphor from battle. The archer receives a wound in the groin, and endeavours to conceal it with his belt, which is adorned with gold like that in Virg. Aen. 5. 312 ' *lato* quam circumplectitur *auro Balteus*.' In Virg. Aen. 12. 273 a man is pierced by a spear, 'ad medium, teritur qua sutilis alvo Balteus.' The belt was used to support the quiver, as in Aen. 5. l. c. 'You are touched, though you hide it, and fall back on your rank and popularity.' ['Caecum vulnus:' comp. Lucr. 4. 1120 ' Usque adeo incerti tabescunt *volnere caeco:*' Virg. Aen. 10. 733 uses the words of a wound in the back.]

45. ut mavis is from Hor. 1 S. 4. 21.
da verba. 3. 19.
decipe nervos, cheat your physical powers ('nervos' as in 2. 41) by fighting on, as if you were not wounded.

46. Imitated from several passages in Horace, as Casaubon remarks. The words are from 2 S. 5. 106 'Egregie factum laudet vicinia.' The matter from 1 Ep. 16. 19 foll. '.Sed vereor ne cui de te plus quam tibi credas . . . neu si te populus sanum recteque valentem Dictitet, occultam febrem sub tempus edendi Dissimules.' [Comp. also Sen. Ep. 59. 11 'Illud praecipue impedit,

"We keep inflicting wounds and exposing in our turn our own legs to shots. It is the understood rule of life, the lesson we have all of us learnt. You have a concealed wound in your groin, but the broad fold of your belt hides it. Well, just as you please, play the sophist and cheat your physical powers, if you can do so. 'Why, when I have the whole neighbourhood telling me of my excellence, am not I to believe them?' If the sight of money makes you change colour, disreputable as you are, if in your zeal for the main chance you flog the exchange with many a stripe, it will do you no good to have made your thirsty ears the receptacle of popular praise. No; reject what is not *you*; let Hob and Dick

quod cito nobis placemus: si invenimus qui nos bonos viros dicat, qui prudentes, qui sanctos, agnoscimus.']

47. Comp. 3. 109.

inprobe, placed as in Hor. 2 S. 2. 134, Lucr. 3. 1026. Jahn quotes Hor. 2 S. 3. ; 8 'argenti pallet amore :' but the paleness here is sudden, not chronic. [48. 'Amorum' Jahn (1868): Bücheler now keeps 'amarum,' but joins it with 'puteal.']

49. The traditional explanation of this line interprets it of exorbitant usury, as the mention of the puteal naturally suggests. Casaubon was apparently the first to reject it, as incompatible with his view that Nero is the object of the Satire, himself understanding it of the emperor's habit of going out at night in disguise and assaulting people in the streets, as recorded by Tac. A. 13. 25, Suet. Nero 26. Recent commentators, in exploding the notion of any reference to Nero, have returned to the old view, though Jahn so far modifies it as to suppose the allusion to be to the praetor's tribunal at the Puteal (Hor. 2 S. 6. 30), explaining 'flagellare puteal' of a litigious person who endeavours to gain his suit at any cost. The question is a difficult one: but if we make 'flagellare' metaphorical, there seems no reason why we should not understand it of usury. A usurer would naturally be called the 'scourge of the exchange,' as

Hor. 1 Ep. 15. 31 calls Maenius 'Pernicies et tempestas barathrumque macelli.'

multa... vibice is an ornamental extension of the metaphor after the manner of Persius. Whether we can assume a special technical sense of 'flagellare' on the strength of Pliny 33. 164, Mart. 2. 30. 4, as Jahn and Freund think, is very doubtful: in the former passage '*flagellat* annonam,' of forestallers and regraters, may be understood as here. 'makes himself the scourge of the market,' while in the other, 'laxas arca *flagellat* opes,' the word may refer to 'laxas,' and need only signify 'coercet;' 'prohibet ne latius evagentur.' [Friedländer on Martial l. c. quotes Seneca Ep. 101. 4 'ille qui et mari et terra pecuniam *agitabat*,' and explains 'flagellare' as = 'to keep the money going,' 'never let it rest.']

50. bibulas. From the common phrase 'aure bibere' or 'haurire,'

donaveris. A variety for 'aures dare,' 'praebere,' 'commodare' (see 2. 30), with an additional notion of absolute resignation.

51. tollat sua munera, probably referring to Hor. 1 Ep. 16. 33 foll. 'Qui dedit hoc' (a good name) 'hodie, cras, si volet, auferet: ut si Detulerit fasces indigno, detrahet idem: Pone, meum est, inquit: pono, tristisque recedo.'

tecum habita; noris, quam sit tibi curta supellex."

[52. *ut noris* a.]

51. **Cerdo**, Κέρδων, seems to have been a proper name, given to slaves and common people, so that it naturally stands for one of the rabble, the 'Hob and Dick' of Shakespeare's Coriolanus. Perhaps it had better be written with a capital, both here (compare 'Baucis,' v. 21) and in Juv. 4. 153 (opp. to 'Lamia,' v. 154), 8. 182 (opp. to 'Volesos Brutumque,' *ib.*). The notion that it means a cobbler seems to be founded on Martial, 3. 59. 1, 99. 1, where it is coupled with 'sutor,' as it is with 'faber,' in an inscription in Spon's

take their presents back again; live at home, and learn how slenderly furnished your apartments are."

Misc. p. 221, referred to by Jahn. [Petronius 60 'tres pueri' (slaves) ... 'quorum unum *Cerdonem*, alterum Felicionem, tertium Lucrionem (vocari aiebat.') In C. I. L. 5. 5300 'Cerdo' is the *cognomen* of a freedman; in 2. 4970. 130 we have 'Cerdo Titi,' i.e. slave of Titius.]

52. tecum habita. Compare Arist. Eth. N. 9. 4 συνδιάγειν ὁ τοιοῦτος ἑαυτῷ βούλεται. Hor. 2 S. 7. 112 'Non horam tecum esse potes.' '*Curtae* nescio quid semper abest rei' Hor. 3 Od. 14. 64. [For 'supellex' comp. Epictet. 1. 6. 15 ἡ ἑκάστου φύσις καὶ κατασκευή.]

SATURA V.

'VATIBUS hic mos est, centum sibi poscere voces,
centum ora et linguas optare in carmina centum,
fabula seu maesto ponatur hianda tragoedo,
vulnera seu Parthi ducentis ab inguine ferrum.'
'Quorsum haec? aut quantas robusti carminis offas   5
ingeris, ut par sit centeno gutture niti?

[*Ad magistrum equitum Cornutum* C.   4. *parchi* a.
5. *carminur offas* a.]

To Cornutus. The poet acknowledges his obligations to his old tutor, and descants on the Stoic doctrine of moral freedom, proving that all the world are slaves, as Stertinius in Hor. 2 S. 3 *proves to Damasippus that all the world are madmen. The subject is the same as that of Hor.* 2 S. 7, *the dialogue between Horace and Davus, and the treatment not unlike. Jahn has summed up the few particulars known about Cornutus, Prolegomena, pp.* 8-27. *L. Annaeus Cornutus was born at Lepta, flourished at Rome under Nero as a tragic poet, like Seneca, a grammarian (author of a commentary on Virgil, some fragments of which are preserved by Servius, and of a treatise,* De Figuris Sententiarum) *and a Stoic philosopher (author of a work against Athenodorus and Aristotle, and of another on the Theology of the Greeks, which still exists as a meagre epitome). The name* Annaeus *renders it probable that he was a freedman of that family, especially as Lucan is known to have been one of his pupils. He was banished by Nero, under the following circumstances. The* emperor *had a plan of writing the history of Rome, in verse, from Romulus downwards, and consulted Cornutus, among others, about the number of books of which the poem ought to consist. Some of his flatterers suggested* 400. *Cornutus replied that it would be too many for any one to read. It was retorted,* 'But your great philosopher, Chrysippus, wrote many more.' 'True,' said Cornutus, 'but they do some good to mankind.' *Nero, enraged, first thought of putting him to death, but eventually banished him to an island.*

1-4. Persius. 'Poets are allowed to wish for a hundred tongues when they have any great effort to make, either tragic or epic.'

1. 'Regibus hic mos est' Hor. 1 S. 2. 86.

centum, etc.; the fountain is Hom. Il. 2. 489 οὐδ' εἴ μοι δέκα μὲν γλῶσσαι, δέκα δὲ στόματ' εἶεν. Hostius [a poet who flourished at the beginning of the last century of the republic], author of a poem on the war with Istria, wished for 100, 'Non si mihi *linguae Centum* atque *ora* sient totidem *vocesque* liquatae' (Macrob.

SATIRE V.

Persius. 'It is a standing rule with poets to put in a requisition for a hundred voices, to bespeak a hundred mouths and a hundred tongues for the purposes of song, whether the work before them be a play to be mouthed by some dolorous tragedian, or the wounds of the Parthian dragging the dart from his groin.'

Cornutus. 'What do you want with things like this? What are these lumps of solid poetry that you have to cram, big enough to justify the strain of a hundred-throat power? Let those who mean

6. 3. 6), and so Virg. G. 2. 43, speaking of trees and their cultivation, Aen. 6. 625, of crimes and their punishment in Tartarus.

3. 'Whether the subject proposed be.'
ponatur, not as in 1. 70 (which Jahn compares), to set up a thing as complete, but to set before one as a thing to be done. See Freund s. v. and compare θεῖναι, θέσις.

hianda. Prop. 2. 31. 6 'Visus... tacita *carmen hiare* lyra.' Aesch. Ag. 920 χαμαιπετὲς βόαμα προσχάνῃς ἐμοί.

4. Imitated from Hor. 2 S. 1. 15 'Aut labentis equo describat *vulnera Parthi*,' which affords a presumption (not a certainty, as Persius sometimes takes Horace's words without his meaning) that **vulnera ... Parthi** is to be explained in the same manner here, of the wounds received by the Parthian.

ducentis, etc. will then be parallel to ' labentis equo,'—'drawing from his wounded groin (see 4. 44) the dart that has pierced him,'—a picture likely enough to appear in an epic poem (compare such passages as Virg. Aen. 10. 486), and sufficiently flattering to Roman vanity. This seems on the whole preferable to the interpretation mentioned by Ascens., and adopted by Nebriss., Casaubon, König, and Heinr., which makes 'vulnera Parthi' the wounds given by the Parthian, and ' ducentis,' etc. either ' drawing the bow from the groin,' instead of from the shoulder, or ' taking an arrow from the quiver,' which the Eastern nations carried near the groin.

5-18. Cornutus. 'What do *you* want with a hundred mouths? You are not going to write foolish tragedies, puffing like a pair of bellows, or croaking like a raven. Yours is the more prosaic walk of everyday satire.'

5. **Quorsum haec?** Hor. 2 S. 7. 21.

quantas, apparently = ' quas tantas,' constructed with ' ut.'

robusti, 'strong,' 'sturdy,' as if of food. Comp. 'grandi polenta' 3. 55 note.

offa, ' a lump,' whether of meal or of flesh. Freund s. v.

6. . **ingeris,** 'cram.' Saginandis anseribus polentae duas partes et furfuris quattuor... *ingerunt*' Pallad. 1, 30. 4.

grande locuturi nebulas Helicone legunto,
si quibus aut Prognes, aut si quibus olla Thyestae
fervebit, saepe insulso cenanda Glyconi ;
tu neque anhelanti, coquitur dum massa camino,   10
folle premis ventos, nec clauso murmure raucus
nescio quid tecum grave cornicaris inepte,
nec stloppo tumidas intendis rumpere buccas,
verba togae sequeris iunctura callidus acri,
ore teres modico, pallentis radere mores   15

[8. *procnes* a, *progenes* C.   9. *inviso* C.   *cycloni* C.   10. *camini* C.
11. *raucos* C.   12. *nescio qui* C.   13. *scloppo* a C, *stloppo* Schol. ς.
15. *terens* a.   *rodere* C.]

6. **centeno gutture**, for 'centum gutturibus,' [like 'centena arbore' Virg. Aen. 10. 207 for 'centum arboribus (remis).']
gutture niti, 'to press upon the throat,' as is done in a difficult swallow. The image is burlesqued by supposing the mouth to be wanted for eating, not for speaking, and thus we are prepared for the 'olla Thyestae' and the 'plebeia prandia.'
7. **grande**. 1. 14.
nebulas may be from Hor. A. P. 230 'Aut, dum vitat humum, nubes et inania captet,' as Jahn thinks, especially as both are speaking of tragic writing. Compare also the conception of Aristophanes' Clouds, which Persius is not likely to have forgotten. To 'collect mists' it would be necessary of course to ascend the mountain.
Helicone, as in Prol. 1 foll. 'Let those who set up to be great poets avail themselves of poetical privileges,' which are generally mere moonshine.
8. The stories of Tereus and Thyestes were common subjects of tragedy in Rome as well as at Athens. Attius wrote on both subjects. Varius was the author of a Thyestes, and Seneca, whose play is extant. See also Juv. 7. 12. 73, Mayor's notes. Thyestes was one of Nero's characters, Dio. 63. 9, etc. referred to by Mayor on Juv. 8. 228. The feast of Thyestes is mentioned twice by Horace as a stock tragic subject, A. P. 91, 186, and Progne's name occurs similarly, v. 187.

9. **fervebit . . . cenanda**, like 'discere . . . laudanda' 3. 46.
Glyco, as the Scholia inform us, was a slave, the joint property of Vergilius, also a tragic actor, and some other person—manumitted, on account of his great popularity, by Nero, who gave 300,000 sesterces to Vergilius for his share in him—tall and dark, with a hanging lower lip, and ill-looking when not dressed up—called 'insulsus' from his inability to understand a joke. Persius doubtless means to ridicule the people through their favourite actor, who was probably *too* tragic, and seemed as if he had really 'supped full of horrors,' in spite of the frequent repetition of the process.
10. Imitated, as the Scholia remark, from Hor. 1 S. 4. 19 foll. 'At tu conclusas hircinis follibus auras, Usque laborantes dum ferrum molliat ignis, Ut mavis, imitare.' Compare also Juv. 7. 111 (Jahn). [Plaut. Bacch. 22 'scio spiritum eius maiorem esse multum Quam *folles taurini halitant*.'] The meaning is the same as Horace expresses elsewhere, A. P. 97, by 'ampullas et sesquipedalia verba.'
anhelanti . . . dum, 'puffing while it is being done,' as 'laborantes dum' Hor. l. c. = 'labouring till it is done.'
massa. 2. 67 note.
12. No marked distinction seems intended between the three images of the bellows, the croaking, and the puffed cheeks.
clauso murmure answers to pre-

to talk grandiose go and catch vapours on Helicon, if there be any who are going to set Progne's or Thyestes' pot a-boiling, to be the standing supper of poor stupid Glycon. But you are not squeezing wind in a pair of panting bellows while the ore is smelting in the furnace, nor are you croaking mysterious nonsense to yourself in hoarse pent-up tones, nor straining and puffing your cheeks till they give way with a *plop*. No; your line is to follow the language of common life, with dexterous nicety in your combinations, and a moderate rounding of the cheek; your skill must be shown in rubbing against the bloated skin of morality, and pinning vice

mis ventos ('conclusas auras' Hor. l. c.) and to the process going on within the 'tumidae buccae.'

tecum ... cornicaris, an intensified variety of 'tecum loqueris,' the word [which, according to the Scholia, was invented by Persius,] being suggested by rauous.

grave is perhaps used here technically of a deep bass sound, opp. to 'acutus.'

inepte, perhaps from Hor. A. P. 140 'qui nil molitur *inepte*,' where the simple opening of the Odyssey is contrasted with the 'hiatus' of the cyclic poet,—'out of taste.' [Quint. 10. 3. 15 'si non ... cogitationem murmure agitantes expectaverimus.']

13. A graphic amplification, 'more Persii,' of Horace's 'tumido ore' A. P. 94.

stloppo, a word occurring nowhere else, perhaps coined by Persius, expressive of sound, like 'bombus' 1. 99 note. '*Stloppo* dixit μεταφορικῶς, a ludentibus pueris, qui buccas inflatas subito aperiunt, et totum simul flatum cum sonitu fundunt' Schol. The spelling 'stloppo' instead of 'scloppo,' which many MSS. give, is supported by Jahn from Priscian 1. p. 43 Keil.

intendis rumpere seems to be a mixture of 'intendis (temptas) rumpere' and 'intendis buccas dum rumpantur.' Compare 'buccae' Juv. 11. 34, for noisy talkers, whom Plautus (Bacch. 1088) calls 'buccones;' 'stloppo' with 'rumpere,' as the noise would be a concomitant of the bursting.

14. verba togae, like 'fabula togata' (Hor. A. P. 228), the talk of common life at Rome, opp. to the 'praetexta,' the symbol of tragedy, and the 'pallium,' which belonged to Greek subjects. We must bear in mind the relation of satire to the old comic drama, asserted by Persius himself, 1. 123. The whole line is imitated from Hor. A. P. 47 '*notum* si *callida verbum* Reddiderit *iunctura* novum' (compare also *ib.* 242 'Tantum *series* iuncturaque pollet, Tantum *de medio sumptis* accedit honoris'), so that 'notum' and 'de medio sumptis' answer to 'verba togae.'

iunctura (the same metaphor as in 1. 65, 92, though the application there is to the flow of the verse) refers here, as in Horace, to the combination of words in a happy phrase or expression.

acri is a well-chosen epithet, expressing the nicety of the material process, as we use 'sharp,' at the same time that it denotes keenness of mind.

15. ore teres modico. Jahn well compares 'ore rotundo' Hor. A. P. 323, which Persius doubtless was thinking of here and in v. 13. 'Os tumidum' is an exaggeration of 'os rotundum,' the fullness of the mouth in measured speech: but as Persius had gone beyond 'tumidum' he is here satisfied with something less than 'rotundum.'

modico qualifies teres, which itself denotes smoothness within compass. 'Oratio plena, sed tamen *teres*' Cic. de Or. 3. 52, 'with shapely mouth, moderately rounded.'

pallentis mores. 1. 26 'En *pallor* seniumque! O *mores!*' Here the paleness is doubtless that of dropsy and disease, as in 3. 94 foll. when any rough application to the skin would be acutely felt. Compare '*radere* teneras auriculas' 1. 107, '*radere* ulcus in tenero ore' 3. 114.

doctus et ingenuo culpam defigere ludo.
hinc trahe quae dicis, mensasque relinque Mycenis
cum capite et pedibus, plebeiaque prandia noris.'
  'Non equidem hoc studeo, bullatis ut mihi nugis
pagina turgescat, dare pondus idonea fumo.   20
secreti loquimur; tibi nunc hortante Camena
excutienda damus praecordia, quantaque nostrae
pars tua sit, Cornute, animae, tibi dulcis, amice,
ostendisse iuvat: pulsa, dinoscere cautus,
quid solidum crepet et pictae tectoria linguae.   25
hic ego centenas ausim deposcere voces,
ut, quantum mihi te sinuoso in pectore fixi,

[17. *dicas* ϛ.   18. *in margine* a.   *plebique* C.   19. *pullatis* a C.   '*pullatis*
... legitur et *bullatis*' Schol.   *bullatis* ϛ.   21. *secrete* a C, *secreti* ϛ.
22. *quandoque* C.   24. *pulsandi noscere* C.   26. *his* C.   *auxim* C.   *voces* a.
fauces C.]

16. ingenuo ... ludo answers to Aristotle's definition of εὐτραπελία (Rhet. 2.12) as πεπαιδευμένη ὕβρις. No precisely similar instance of this use of 'defigere' has been adduced, but it is apparently the same as that of 'figere' in such phrases as 'figere aliquem maledictis,' with the additional notion of driving *down*.

17. hinc, from common life, which is implied in the three preceding lines. König compares Hor. A. P. 317 foll. 'Respicere exemplar vitae morumque iubebo Doctum imitatorem, et vivas hinc ducere voces.'

Mycenis, a dative, like 'illis relinquo' Prol. 5, which Jahn compares.

18. cum capite et pedibus, which were put aside to show Thyestes what he had been eating: τὰ μὲν ποδήρη καὶ χερῶν ἄκρους κτένας 'Εθρυπτ' ἄνωθεν Aesch. Ag. 1594, 'Tantum ora servat et datas fidei manus' Sen. Thyest. 764, quoted by Casaubon.

plebeia prandia. The full opposition is between banquets of an unnatural sort in the heroic ages at Mycenae, known in these days only as stage-horrors, with no lesson for life, 'raw head and bloody bones,' as Dryden renders it, and everyday meals ('prandia,' not 'cenae') of the simplest kind, in common society at Rome, which show ordinary men as they are.

noris, the conj. used imperatively, as in 4. 52, because 'novi' has no imperative of its own.

19-29. P. 'No—I have no thoughts of swelling and vapouring. My song is meant to show my heart to you, that you may see how true it is, how devoted to you. If I want a hundred tongues, it is that I may tell you how dear you are to me.'

19. Heinr. and Jahn restore 'pullatis' from the larger number of MSS., including the oldest, and suppose [with the Scholia] the meaning to be 'sadcoloured,' i. e. tragic. It does not appear, however, that 'pullatus' is ever applied to tragedy, though commonly used of mourners: it answers more nearly to 'sordidatus,' and in fact is frequently applied to common people, 'Ne quis *pullatorum* media cavea sederet' Suet. Aug. 44; a most unfortunate association here, unless we can believe with Casaubon that 'nugae pullatae' mean trifles that please the vulgar. Unless then 'pullatis' be [as Jahn, too, thought] a mistake for 'ampullatis,' which may be worth considering, we must return to the common reading 'bullatis,' which has very respectable MS. support, and explain it by 'tur-

to the ground in sport which will do for gentlemen. Let this be your storehouse of materials; leave Mycenae its feasts with their baskets of extremities, and make yourself at home at the early dinners of common Roman folk.'

P. 'No, my aim is not to have my page distended with air-blown trifles, with a trick of making vapour look solid. My voice is for a private ear; it is to you, at the instance of the Muse within me, that I would offer my heart to be sifted thoroughly; my passion is to show you, Cornutus, how large a share of my inmost being is yours, my beloved friend; strike it, use every test to tell what rings sound and what is the mere plaster of a varnished tongue. An occasion indeed it is for which I may well venture to ask a hundred voices, that I may bring out in clear utterance how thoroughly I have lodged you in the very corners of my breast,

---

gescat.' 'Bullatus' ordinarily means 'furnished with bullae,' but it may mean 'formed like a bubble,' 'swelling,' just as 'falcatus' means both 'furnished with a scythe,' an epithet of 'currus,' and 'formed like a scythe,' 'crooked,' an epithet of 'ensis.' 'Air-blown trifles,' Gifford.

20. **pagina.** Virg. E. 6. 12.

dare pondus... fumo, from Hor. 1 Ep. 19. 42 'nugis addere pondus:' **dare... idonea**, from Hor. 1 Ep. 16. 12 'Fons... rivo dare nomen idoneus,' both quoted by Casaubon.

21. **secreti**, opp. to 'ad populum.'

hortante Camena seems to imply, 'I am inspired, as truly as any poet—as Homer himself when he sang of the ships and asked for a hundred tongues—and the spirit within me bids me to open my heart to you, and tell of our friendship.'

22. **excutienda.** 1. 49.

23. 'Te meae partem animae' Hor. 2 Od. 17. 5, 'animae dimidium meae' *id.* 1 Od. 3. 8.

dulcis, amice, Hor. 1 Ep. 7. 12. Jahn.

24. **iuvat**, of an occupation, Virg. Aen. 9. 613–615, where 'comportare *iuvat* praedas et vivere rapto' is opp. to '*iuvat* indulgere choreis.'

pulsa. 3. 21 note.

dinoscere cautus, like 'cautum adsumere' Hor. 1 S. 6. 51.

dinoscere... quid... crepet et... tectoria = 'dinoscere quid crepet a tectoriis.' 'Pauci dinoscere possunt Vera bona atque illis multum diversa' Juv. 10. 2 foll. 'Tectorium' or 'opus tectorium,' plaster or stucco for walls, so that the metaphor is from striking a wall to see whether it is solid stone or not.

25. **pictae tectoria linguae** is apparently to be resolved into 'quod tegit pictam linguam' as a thing covered with 'tectorium' might be called 'pictus,' though we should rather have expected the thing varnished to be the mind, and the tongue the varnisher. Casaubon quotes Auson. Id. 16. 12 'Sit solidum quodcunque subest, nec inania subter Indicet admotus digitis pallentibus ictus.' [So 'fucosus' is opposed to 'firmus' by Quintus Cicero de P et. Cons. 9. 35.]

26. **hic** is the reading of many MSS., including the oldest, and may very well be explained 'in hac re.' Compare Virg. G. 2. 45 foll. 'Non *hic* te carmine ficto Atque per ambages et longa exorsa tenebo.' 'His,' the other reading (Heinr., Jahn 1843), equivalent to 'ad haec,' seems scarcely so natural.

centenas, for 'centum,' like '*septenas* temperat unda vias' Prop. 3. 22. 16.

27. **sinuoso**; the breast is supposed to contain many 'sinus' or recesses. Jahn compares 'recessus mentis' 2. 73. [*Fauces* Bücheler.]

fixi expresses depth and permanence. We should have expected 'fixerim,' but the independent and dependent questions are confused, as in 3. 67 foll.

voce traham pura, totumque hoc verba resignent,
quod latet arcana non enarrabile fibra.
Cum primum pavido custos mihi purpura cessit   30
bullaque succinctis Laribus donata pependit;
cum blandi comites, totaque inpune Subura
permisit sparsisse oculos iam candidus umbo;
cumque iter ambiguum est et vitae nescius error
deducit trepidas ramosa in compita mentes,   35
me tibi supposui: teneros tu suscipis annos
Socratico, Cornute, sinu; tum fallere sollers

[28. *puta a. torum* C.   29. *quo* C. *arcanam* C.   30. *cui a.*   31. *succinctus a.*   35. *diducit* ς, *traducit* Servius Aen. 6. 136.   36. *seposui a, seposui* * C, *supposui* ς, Schol.   37. *tunc* C.]

28. **voce**, negligently repeated after 'voces.'
 traham; 'imoque *trahens* de pectore vocem' Virg. Aen. 1. 371.
 pura, opp. to 'pictae linguae' Lubin.
 resignent suggests a different metaphor, from the tablets of the mind.
29. **non enarrabile**, by a common human voice.
 fibra. 1. 47.
30–51. 'When first freed from boyish restraints, and exposed to the temptations of youth, I placed myself under your care. You became my guide, philosopher, and friend. Happily our days flowed on together—the morning spent in work, the evening in social pleasure. The same star must have presided over the birth of both: it were sin to doubt it.'
30. **pavido**, not 'timid on entering into life' (Lubin), nor 'fearful, and therefore requiring protection' (Casaubon, Jahn), but 'trembling under those who watched over me,' 'quod sub metu paedagogorum praetextati sunt,' as the Scholia say—whence the contrast of 'blandi comites' v. 32. Compare Ter. Andr. 55 'Dum *aetas, metus, magister,* prohibebant.'
 purpura, of the 'praetexta.' 'Per hoc inane *purpurae* decus precor' Hor. Epod. 5. 7, 'Quos ardens *purpura* vestit' Juv. 11. 155. Boys had regular 'custodes' (Hor. A. P. 161): but the praetexta' itself is called 'custos,' as the symbol of sanctity. Casaubon quotes Quint. Decl. 340 [p. 345 Ritter] 'Sacrum praetextarum, quo sacerdotes velantur, quo magistratus, quo infirmitatem pueritiae sacram facimus ac venerabilem:' the Delph. ed. refers to Pliny 9. 127 'Fasces huic securesque Romanae viam faciunt: idemque pro maiestate pueritiae est.' (Compare also for the general sentiment Juv. 14. 44 foll.) In the same way Propertius says to Cynthia 2. 17. 35 'Ipse tuus semper tibi sit *custodia* lectus,' with reference to the actual 'custodes' appointed for courtezans. For the custom of exchanging the 'praetexta' for the 'toga,' as well as for that of hanging up the 'bulla,' mentioned in the next line, see Dict. Antiqq. König refers to Catull. 68. 15 foll. 'Tempore quo primum vestis mihi tradita pura est, Iucundum cum aetas florida ver ageret, Multa satis lusi: non est Dea nescia nostri, Quae dulcem curis miscet amaritiem,' a graceful passage, which Persius may have had in his mind.
31. Compare 2. 70 note. König compares Prop. 3. 1. 131 foll. 'Mox ubi bulla rudi demissa est aurea collo, Matris et ante deos libera sumpta toga.'
 succinctis, 'quia Gabino habitu cincti di Penates formabantur, obvoluti toga supra umerum sinistrum, dextro nudo' Scholia. Jahn compares Ov. F. 2. 632 'Nutriat incinctos missa patella Lares.'
32. **blandi**, ('fuerunt').
 comites. 3. 1 note, here = 'aequales.'
 Subura, the focus of all business

and unfold in words all the unspeakable feelings which lie entwined deep down among my heart-strings.

When first the guardianship of the purple ceased to awe me, and the boss of boyhood was hung up as an offering to the quaint old household gods, when my companions made themselves pleasant, and the yet unsullied shield of my gown left me free to cast my eyes at will over the whole Subura—just when the way of life begins to be uncertain, and the bewildered mind finds that its ignorant ramblings have brought it to a point where roads branch off—then it was that I made myself your adopted child. You at once received the young foundling into the bosom of a second Socrates; and soon your rule, with artful surprise, straightens the

in Rome, Juv. 3. 5, where it is contrasted with a rocky island, 11. 51 'ferventi Subura,' and elsewhere.

33. permisit may be illustrated by the epithet 'libera' given to the 'toga.' Prop. cited on v. 31, Ov. F. 3. 771 foll. The Delph. ed. compares Ter. Andr. 52 'Nam is postquam excessit ex ephebis, Sosia, Liberius vivendi fuit potestas.'

sparsisse oculos. Jahn compares Val. Fl. 5. 247 'tua nunc terris, tua lumina tota Sparge mari.' 'To cast my glances everywhere.' Compare the passage from Catullus cited on v. 30.

iam candidus expresses the same as 'Cum primum' v. 30. The toga was yet new and clean, and the sense of freedom still fresh.

umbo, the gathering of the folds of the 'toga.' See Dict. Antiqq.

34. 3. 65 note. vitae nescius error answers to 'rerum inscitia' Hor. 1 Ep. 3. 33, 'ignorance of life or of the world.'

error is here the act of wandering. Compare Lucr. 2. 10 'Errare, atque viam palantes quaerere vitae' and Hor. 2 S. 3. 48 foll. 'Velut silvis, ubi passim Palantes *error* certo de tramite pellit, Ille sinistrorsum, hic dextrorsum abit : unus utrisque *Error*, sed variis illudit partibus.'

35. deducit, Jahn (1843) [and Bücheler] from the best MSS. for 'diducit,' which the other editors, and Jahn in his text of 1868, prefer. It seems doubtful whether any appropriate meaning could be extracted from 'diducit in compita,' as 'compita' signifies not the crossways, but the junction or point of crossing.

'Deducit' will have its ordinary sense of leading from one place to another, viz. from the straight path to the point where the roads begin to diverge, according to the image explained on 3. 56. Emphasis is thus thrown on 'vitae nescius error,' the guidance to which they have to trust is that of ignorance and inexperience, so that they do not know which way to turn.

36. supponere is used of supposititious children, and of eggs placed under a hen, the common notion being that of introducing a person or thing into a place ready for it, but not belonging to it. Such seems to be its force here, though it would perhaps be too much to suppose, with Jahn, that the metaphor is directly taken from children. It seems, however, to have suggested 'suscipis,' which is the technical term for taking up and rearing a child. 'Haec ad te die natali meo scripsi, quo utinam susceptus non essem' Cic. Att. 11. 9. 'Tollere,' which is a synonym of 'suscipere,' is used of supposititious children Quint. 3. 6. 97.

teneros ... annos is not equivalent to 'me tenera aetate,' as the words are not used literally of actual infancy, but metaphorically of the infancy of judgment which belongs to youth. [For 'teneros annos,' an expression which apparently is first found in the silver age, comp. Quint. 2. 2. 6 'ut et teneriores annos ab iniuria sanctitas docentis custodiat, et ferociores a licentia gravitas deterreat.']

37. Socratico involves the notion not only of wisdom, but, as Jahn remarks,

adposita intortos extendit regula mores,
et premitur ratione animus vincique laborat,
artificemque tuo ducit sub pollice vultum.   40
tecum etenim longos memini consumere soles,
et tecum primas epulis decerpere noctes:
unum opus et requiem pariter disponimus ambo,
atque verecunda laxamus seria mensa.
non equidem hoc dubites, amborum foedere certo   45
consentire dies et ab uno sidere duci.
nostra vel aequali suspendit tempora Libra
Parca tenax veri, seu nata fidelibus hora
dividit in Geminos concordia fata duorum,

[40. *araficemque* a.   41. *memini me* C.   45. *fodere* a.   47. *equalis* a.
suspendit a C, suspendi ς.   48. *perca* a.]

of the tender affection with which Socrates watched over youth.

37. **fallere sollers** is explained by Jahn, 'quae sollertiam adhibet, ubi de fallendo agitur—quae non fallit,' evidently an impossible rendering. The words can only mean 'skilful to deceive,' so that we must understand them either of the gradual art with which Cornutus led his pupil to virtue (Casaubon), or, as 'Socratico' would suggest, of the εἰρωνεία which surprises error into a confession that it is opposed to truth (compare 3. 52, 'curvos *deprendere* mores') by placing the two suddenly in juxtaposition —a view which would perhaps agree better with the language of the next line. There seems no affinity between the sense of 'fallere' here, and that of 'fallit regula' 4. 12, though the expressions are similar.

38. 3. 52, 4. 12, notes. **intortus**, apparently stronger than 'pravus.'

39. **premitur.** Jahn well compares Virg. Aen. 6. 80 'fingitque premendo,' so that the word prepares us for the image of moulding in the next line.

vinci laborat, like 'obliquo *laborat* Lympha fugax trepidare rivo' Hor. 2 Od. 3. 12, where a prose writer would have said 'vinci cogitur,' though 'laborat' is doubtless meant to show that the pupil's mind cooperated with the teacher.

40. A metaphor from wax or clay. **artificem**, passive. 'Quattuor *artifices* vivida signa, boves' Prop. 2. 31. 8, 'artificemque regat' Ov. A. A. 3. 556, of a horse broken in.

ducit ... vultum, like 'saxa ... *ducere* formam,' Ov. M. 1. 402, which Jahn compares, the clay or wax being said to spread the form, just as the workman is said to spread the clay, 'Ut teneros mores ceu pollice *ducat*, Ut si quis cera vultum facit' Juv. 7. 237, probably a copy from this passage. Compare also Virg. Aen. 6. 848 'vivos *ducent* de marmore vultus,' Hor. 2 Ep. 1. 240 '*duceret* aera Fortis Alexandri vultum simulantia,' where the notion is substantially the same. With the whole line Casaubon compares Stat. Achill. 1. 332 'Qualiter artificis victurae pollice cerae Accipiunt formas, ignemque manumque sequuntur.'

41. From Virg. E. 9. 51 'saepe ego *longos* Cantando puerum *memini* me condere *soles*,' as that is from Anth. Pal. 7. 80 ἥλιον λέσχῃ κατεδύσαμεν: 'consumere horas,' 'tempus,' etc. is sufficiently common. [Comp. the picture of the young Marcus Cicero and Cratippus given by the former ap. Cic. Fam. 16. 21.]

42. **epulis**, either the dat. or the instrumental abl. 'Prima nox,' the beginning of the night, with a reference to

moral twists that it detects, and my spirit becomes moulded by reason, and struggles to be subdued, and assumes plastic features under your hand. Aye, I mind well how I used to wear away long summer suns with you, and with you pluck the early bloom of the night for feasting. We twain have one work and one set time for rest, and the enjoyment of a moderate table unbends our gravity. No, I would not have you doubt that there is a fixed law that brings our lives into accord, and one star that guides them. Whether it be in the equal balance that truthful Destiny hangs our days, or whether the birth-hour sacred to faithful friends shares our united fates between the Heavenly Twins, and we break the

'decerpere primitias.' 'Dum primae decus affectat decerpere pugnae' Sil. 4. 138.

decerpere, 'to pluck off,' stronger than 'carpere,' like 'partem solido demere de die' Hor. 1 Od. 1. 20.

43. Casaubon compares Virg. G. 4. 184 'Omnibus una quies operum, labor omnibus unus.' Jahn supplies 'unam' for 'requiem,' from 'unum opus;' but perhaps it is better to make 'unum' a predicate, and explain the line 'disponimus opus, ita ut unum sit, et requiem ita ut pariter habeatur.' 'Disponere diem' is a phrase. Suet. Tib. 11, Tac. Germ. 30, and Pliny Ep. 4. 53 has 'disponere otium.'

44. verecunda = 'modica.'

laxamus seria, like 'laxabant curas' Virg. Aen. 9. 225, in which sense 'relaxare' is more common. 'Seria' Hor. 2 S. 2. 125 'Explicuit vino contractae *seria* frontis.'

mensa, probably instrum. abl., like 'somno' in Virg. l. c.

45. equidem. 1. 110 note.

non... dubites. 1. 5 note; 'foedere certo' Virg. Aen. 1. 62 = 'lege certa.' 'Has leges aeternaque foedera certis Imposuit Natura locis' Virg. G. 1. 60. Jahn compares Manil. 2. 475 (speaking of the stars), 'Iunxit amicitias horum sub *foedere certo*.'

46. consentire. 'Utrumque nostrum incredibili modo *Consentit* astrum' Hor. 2 Od. 17. 21, from whom Persius has imitated the whole passage.

ab uno sidere duci, apparently = 'cepisse originem ab uno sidere.' Both Horace and Persius are talking at random, as is evident from the fact that neither professes to know his own horoscope. Astrology, as Jahn remarks, was in great vogue in Persius' time, an impulse having been given to the study by Tiberius. Compare the well-known passage of Tacitus, H. 1. 22 'mathematicis... genus hominum potentibus infidum, sperantibus fallax, quod in civitate nostra et vetabitur semper et retinebitur.'

47. 'Seu *Libra* seu me Scorpios aspicit' Hor. 2 Od. 17. 17. ['Suspendi tempora' (see critical note) Bücheler. For the combination of 'vel' and 'seu' Bieger quotes Anth. Lat. 725. 10 (Riese) 'sive caprum mavis seu Fauni ponere munus': Pseudo-Virgil Catalepton 5. 10, 13 'seu furta dicantur tua... Vel acta puero cum viris convivia.']

48. 'Parca non mendax' Hor. 2 Od. 16. 39.

tenax veri, perhaps imitated from Virg. Aen. 4. 188 (of Fame) 'Tam *ficti pravique tenax* quam nuntia veri.' Fate is represented with scales in her hands (Mus. Capit. 4. t. 29), and also as marking the horoscope on the celestial globe (K. Rochette, Mon. inéd. t. 17, 2), Jahn. [See Jahn, Archäologische Beiträge, p. 170.] We must remember, too, the Stoic doctrine of fate and unchangeable laws.

nata fidelibus, 'ordained for faithful friends.' The hour of birth is said to be born itself, as in Aesch. Ag. 107 ξύμφυτος αἰών: Soph. Oed. R. 1082 συγγενεῖς μῆνες.

49. dividit in Geminos, like 'dividere nummos in viros.' Casaubon compares Manil. 2. 628 'Magnus erit *Geminis* amor et concordia duplex.'

Saturnumque gravem nostro Iove frangimus una : 50
nescio quod, certe est, quod me tibi temperat astrum.
  Mille hominum species et rerum discolor usus ;
velle suum cuique est, nec voto vivitur uno.
mercibus hic Italis mutat sub sole recenti
rugosum piper et pallentis grana cumini, 55
hic satur inriguo mavult turgescere somno,
hic campo indulget, hunc alea decoquit, ille
in Venerem putris; set cum lapidosa cheragra
fregerit articulos, veteris ramalia fagi,
tunc crassos transisse dies lucemque palustrem 60

[50. *iovem* a. *inam* a.   51. *quod* a C.   51. *certum* C.   54. *talis* a.
58. *putri set* C : *putrit set* c, agnoscunt Schol.: *putris set* a, Servius Georg. 4. 198.
59. *fecerit* a.   *faci* a.   'legitur et [fregerit], curvaverit' Schol.   60. *palustre* C.]

50. 'Te Iovis impio Tutela Saturno refulgens Eripuit' Hor. 2 Od. 17. 22 foll. The Delph. ed. compares Prop. 4. 1. 83 foll. 'Felicesque *Iovis* stellas, Martisque rapacis, Et *grave Saturni* sidus in omne caput.' [Saturn was supposed to be cold, Mars hot, Juppiter temperate : Cic. N. D. 2. 46 'ut cum summa Saturni refrigeret, media Martis incendat, his interiecta Iovis illustret et temperet ;' Vitruvius 6. 5. 11 'Iovis stella inter Martis ferventissimam et Saturni frigidissimam media currens temperatur.' See also Pliny 2. 8. '*Frigida* Saturni sese quo stella receptet' Virg. G. 1. 336.]
  nostro, including the notion of favourable.
  frangimus. Casaubon compares Stat. Silv. 1. 3. 7 '*frangunt* sic improba solem Frigora.'
  51. 'Nescio quid certe est' Virg. E. 8. 107. [But the best MSS. here read 'nescio quod.']
  temperat is from Hor. 2 Ep. 2. 187 'Scit Genius, natale comes qui *temperat astrum*,' though the sense here is changed, the star being said 'temperare,' not 'temperari.'
  me tibi temperat is a strange construction, illustrated by none of the commentators. 'Tempero' seems here to follow the analogy of 'misceo,' which is used with a dat. where the mingling of *persons* is spoken of. 'Miscere' and 'temperare,' as Freund shows, are sometimes used together, though they are contrasted Cic. Rep. 2. 23 'Haec ita *mixta* fuerunt, ut *temperata* nullo fuerint modo,' as 'temperare' means not only to mix, but to mix in due proportion, 'which blends me with thee.'
  52-61. The mention of their unanimity leads Persius to think of the variety of pursuits in the world. 'Men's pursuits are innumerable—each has his own—one is a merchant—one a bon-vivant—one an athlete—one a gambler—one a debauchee—but disease and decay bring remorse with them.'
  52. The Scholia compare Hor. 2 S. 1. 27 ' Quot capitum vivunt, totidem studiorum Milia.'
  rerum usus, 'the practice of life,' like 'usum vitae' v. 94.
  discolor may either be 'of many complexions,' or 'of a different complexion,' according as we take 'usus' to refer to the whole of mankind or to each man. If the latter, compare Hor. 1 Ep. 18. 3 'Ut matrona meretrici dispar erit atque *Discolor*.'
  53. velle suum. 1. 9.
  voto vivitur. 2. 7 ; 'trahit sua quemque voluptas' Virg. E. 65, Schol.
  54. Imitated from Hor. 1 S. 4. 29 ' Hic mutat merces surgente a sole ad eum quo Vespertina tepet regio,' Scholia.
  mercibus ... mutat ... piper, a

shock of Saturn together by the common shield of Jupiter, some star, I am assured, there is which fuses me with you.

Men are of a thousand kinds, and the practice of life wears the most different colours. Each has his own desire, and their daily prayers are not the same. One exchanges Italian wares under an Eastern sky for shrivelled pepper and seeds of cadaverous cumin; another prefers bloating himself with the balmy sleep that follows a full meal; one gives in to outdoor games; another lets gambling run through his means; but when the hailstones of gout have broken their finger-joints, like so many decayed boughs of an old beech, then they complain that their days have been passed in

variety for 'merces mutat pipere,' as in Hor. 2 S. 7. 109 'uvam Furtiva mutat strigili, and elsewhere.

sole recenti, of the East, like '*sole novo* terras inrorat Eous,' of the sunrise, Virg. G. 1. 288.

55. There is a force in **rugosum piper**, the shrivelling being the effect of the sun, which distinguishes it from the Italian pepper, as Jahn remarks. The Delph. ed. quotes Pliny 12. 26 'Hae, priusquam dehiscant decerptae tostaeque sole, faciunt quod vocatur piper longum: paullatim vero dehiscentes maturitate, ostendunt candidum piper, quod deinde tostum solibus colore rugisque mutatur.' Pepper, as a specimen of merchandize, is mentioned again v. 136, Juv. 14. 293.

pallentis ... cumini, an imitation of Horace's 'exsangue cuminum' (1 Ep. 19. 18), pale, because producing paleness, like 'pallidam Pirenen' Epil. 4. 'Cumin' was a favourite condiment, Pliny 19. 160 (Jahn) 'fastidiis cuminum amicissimum.' [Petronius 49 'putares, eum piper et cuminum non iniecisse.']

56. **satur** is emphatic, as both the pleasure and the fatness would arise as much from the full meal as from the 'siesta.'

inriguo, active, as in Virg. G. 4. 31, with reference to the poetical expressions, 'somnus per membra quietem *Inriget*' Lucr. 4. 907, 'fessos sopor *inrigat* artus' Virg. Aen. 3. 511; compare also Aen. 5. 854 foll.

57. For the sports of the 'campus' see Hor. 1 Od. 8. 4, 1 S. 6. 131, A. P. 162, 379 foll.

decoquere was used intransitively, by an obvious ellipse, of men running through their means. 'Tenesne memoria, praetextatum te decoxisse' Cic. 2 Phil. 18. Here the man is made the object, and the means of his ruin the subject of the verb. Hor. 1 Ep. 18. 21 joins 'damnosa Venus' with 'praeceps alea.' Juvenal dwells on the increase of gaming, 1. 88 foll.

58. **cheragra** is the spelling of the oldest MSS. and seems to be required by the metre: see Bentley and Orelli on Hor. 2 S. 7. 15. The epithet 'lapidosa,' combined with 'fregerit ... ramalia,' suggests that the metaphor may perhaps be from a hail-storm. Compare '*contudit* articulos' Hor. l. c., with 1 Ep. 8. 4 'quia grando *Contuderit* vites.'

59. **fregerit articulos**; 'postquam illi iusta cheragra *Contudit articulos*' Hor. 2 S. 7. 15 foll. of a man who went on gambling in spite of the gout.

veteris ramalia fagi is a picturesque paraphrase of Horace's epithet 'nodosus.' The expression is strengthened by the omission of the particle of comparison, changing it, in Aristotle's language (Rhet. 3. 4), from an εἰκών to a μεταφορά. '*Veteres*, iam *fracta* cacumina, *fagos*' Virg. E. 9. 9. Possibly, however, Heinr. may be right in connecting 'fregerit' closely with 'ramalia,' like the Greek διδάσκειν τινὰ σοφόν, 'has battered them into dead branches,' a usage which has some affinity to that of the cogn. acc.

60. Jahn compares Tibull. 1. 4. 33 'Vidi ego iam iuvenem, premeret cum serior aetas, Maerentem stultos praeteriisse dies.' König compares Cic. pro Sest. 9 'emersum subito e *diuturnis tenebris* lustrorum ac stuprorum ... qui non modo tempestatem impendentem intueri

et sibi iam seri vitam ingemuere relictam.
'At te nocturnis iuvat inpallescere chartis;
cultor enim iuvenum purgatas inseris aures
fruge Cleanthea. petite hinc puerique senesque
finem animo certum miserisque viatica cànis!'   65
'Cras hoc fiet.' 'Idem cras fiet.' 'Quid? quasi magnum
nempe diem donas?' Sed cum lux altera venit,
iam cras hesternum consumpsimus: ecce aliud cras
egerit hos annos et semper paulum erit ultra.

[62. *carthis* a C.   63. *enim est* C.   64. *cleteanthea* a, *cliantea* C.
65. *miserique* C.   66. *cras fiat* a.   67. *diest* a.   68. *externum* C.
69. *hos a* c, *hoc* C.]

temulentus, sed ne lucem quidem insolitam aspicere posset?' Not unlike is Virg. Aen. 6. 744 'Hinc metuunt cupiuntque, dolent gaudentque, neque auras Dispiciunt, clausae tenebris et carcere caeco.' The image of life in darkness is frequently found in Lucretius: 'Qualibus in tenebris vitae quantisque periclis Degitur hoc aevi, quodcunque est!' 2. 15: compare also 3. 77 ('Ipsi se in tenebris volvi caenoque queruntur,' which Persius may have imitated), 5. 11, 170. The conception here is of life passed in a Boeotian atmosphere, of thick fogs and pestilential vapours, which the sun never pierces—probably with especial reference to the pleasures of sense, of which Persius has just been speaking. So the 'vapour, heavy, hueless, formless, cold' in Tennyson's 'Vision of Sin.'

61. **sibi** with **ingemuere**.

vitam ... relictam means no more than their *past* life ('vitam anteactam' Casaubon). So 'iterare cursus Cogor *relictos*' Hor. 1 Od. 34. 4, 5, which has been similarly mistaken by the commentators. The acc. as in Virg. E. 5. 27 'ingemuisse leones Interitum.' [Or may 'vitam' be pressed? 'that their true life has been left behind in the race for enjoyment?' 'Multos transisse vitam, dum vitae instrumenta conquirunt' Seneca Ep. 45. 12.]

62-72. 'Your end is nobler: you give your nights to philosophy, that you may train youth. *That* is the true stay when old age comes. Yet men go on putting off the work of studying virtue to a morrow that never arrives.'

62. **nocturnis.** 1. 90.

iuvat, see the passage quoted on v. 24.

inpallescere. 1. 26.

63. **cultor** introduces the metaphor which is carried on in 'purgatas,' 'inseris,' and 'fruge.'

purgatas. 'cleared of weeds,' a common word 'in re rustica,' is from Hor. 1 Ep. 1. 5, where however the reference is to ordinary cleansing, as v. 86 'aurem lotus.' Compare Lucr. 5. 44 'At nisi purgatum est pectus, quae proelia nobis Atque pericula tum'st ingratis insinuandum!' where the metaphor is from clearing a country of wild beasts, κατά τε ὅρια πάντα καθαίρων Soph. Trach. 1011.

inserere aures fruge, a variety for 'inserere auribus fruges.' Jahn compares Cic. de Univ. 12 'Cum autem animis corpora cum necessitate insevisset.' For the general expression the Delph. ed. quotes Hor. 1 Ep. 1. 39 foll. 'Nemo adeo *ferus* est ut non *mitescere* possit, Si modo *culturae* patientem commodet aurem.'

64. **fruge,** generally of grain for eating—here of grain for seed. 'Nos *fruges* serimus, nos arbores' Cic. N. D. 2. 60. The metaphorical use of the word is not uncommon: 'Centuriae seniorum agitant expertia *frugis*' Hor. A. P. 341.

Cleanthes, Dict. Biog., used as a representative of the Stoics, as in Juv. 2. 7 'Aut iubet archetypos pluteum servare Cleanthas.' He was the preceptor of Chrysippus.

petite ... finem animo certum is from Hor. 1 Ep. 2. 56 'certum voto pete finem,' 'petere' signifying in both pas-

grossness and their sunshine choked by fogs, and heave a sigh too late over the life that is left behind them.

But your passion is to lose your colour in nightly study; you are the moral husbandman of the young, preparing the soil of their ears and sowing it with Cleanthes' corn. Yes! it is thence that all, young and old alike, should get a definite aim for their desires, and a provision for the sorrows of old age.' 'So I will, to-morrow.' 'To-morrow will tell the same tale as to-day.' 'What? do you mean to call a day a great present to make a man?' 'Aye, but when next day comes, we have spent what was to-morrow yesterday already; and there is always a fresh to-morrow baling out these years of ours and keeping a little in advance of us. Near

sages not 'to aim at' but 'to procure,' and 'animo' being dat. like 'voto,' with which it is here virtually synonymous, as in the expressions 'est animus,' 'fert animus.'

puerique senesque, probably a recollection of Hor. 1 Ep. 1. 26 'Aeque neglectum *pueris senibusque* nocebit,' which the Delph. ed. compares.

65. finem; compare 3. 60.

miseris, for which Heinr. substitutes Markland's conj. 'seris,' is sufficiently appropriate, as it is for the miseries of old age that the provision of philosophy is required, just as it is in decay that the evil of a bad life is felt, v. 58 foll.

viatica, alluding to a saying of Bias, ἐφόδιον ἀπὸ νεότητος εἰς γῆρας ἀναλάμβανε σοφίαν Diog. L. 1. 5. 88, attributed to Aristotle, *id.* 5. 11. 21, in another form, κάλλιστον ἐφόδιον τῷ γήρᾳ ἡ παιδεία. Casaubon and Jahn.

canis, frequently used substantively and coupled with an epithet, especially by Ovid. Freund s. v.

66. A reply from one of those addressed. 'I will do it to-morrow.' With 'hoc fiet' compare 'hoc age.' Persius answers, 'You will do to-morrow just what you do to-day.' Jahn quotes Ov. Rem. Am. 104 'cras quoque fiet idem,' said of a wound, 'It will be the same to-morrow,' where 'fiet' seems to be used for 'erit,' expressing perhaps that there will be a change which is no change. For the general sentiment the Delph. ed. compares Mart 5. 58 ['Cras te victurum, cras dicis, Postume, semper. Dic mihi, cras istud, Postume, quando venit? ... Cras vives? hodie iam vivere,

Postume, serum est: Ille sapit, quisquis, Postume, vixit heri!']

quasi magnum. Casaubon compares Hor. 1 S. 4. 9 foll. 'saepe ducentos, *Ut magnum,* versus dictabat.'

67. 'What? do you mean to say ('nempe') that you call a day a great present?' 'Nempe' implies 'Is this what you mean when you say *Idem cras fiet?*' 'Do you mean to higgle about a day?' This seems better than with Heinr. to punctuate 'quasi magnum nempe, diem donas?' or with Jahn to suppose 'Quid ... donas' to stand for two sentences. 'Quid, quasi magnum sit, mihi donas? nempe diem donas.'

cum ... venit expresses time coincident with, if not subsequent to, that of the principal clause—the sense being, 'The very coming of the to-morrow you speak of now, involves the loss of the to-morrow you spoke of yesterday, i. e. of to-day.'

68. hesternum, in reference to the present time of speaking, not to the time denoted by 'consumpsimus.'

aliud cras, 'a fresh to-morrow,' ever succeeding.

69. egerit is explained by Jahn 'impulerit,' as if from 'ago,' an error against which all the commentators, from the Scholia downward, have taken care to guard, some mentioning it expressly. '*Egero*' is used variously of emptying out earth, carrying out goods, baling out water, etc., from which it is easily transferred to the constant consumption of time, as in Val. Fl. 8. 453 'tota querellis *Egeritur* luctuque dies,' quoted by König, *ib.* 5. 299 'Nox Minyis *egesta* metu.'

nam quamvis prope te, quamvis temone sub uno 70
vertentem sese, frustra sectabere cantum,
cum rota posterior curras et in axe secundo.
  'Libertate opus est: non hac, ut quisque Velina
Publius emeruit, scabiosum tesserula far
possidet. heu steriles veri, quibus una Quiritem 75
vertigo facit! hic Dama est non tresis agaso,
vappa lippus, et in tenui farragine mendax:

[70. *quam prope se* a. *quamquam* ς.   71. *se* C.   76. *damasus non* a C.
       77. *tenuit ferragine* C.]

69. **hos annos,** which you have before you, and reckon on in advance.
   paulum erit ultra changes the metaphor.
70. A metaphor instead of a simile, as in v. 59.
   quamvis, etc., if you are behind it, it does not signify how near you may be—like our proverb, 'a miss is as good as a mile.'
71. **cantum,** the tire or rim of a wheel, instead of 'rotam,' as it would be the outside which a person behind would naturally hope to touch.
72. **cum,** instead of 'si,' as giving more rhetorical force, and more completely identifying the person with the thing to which he is compared.
   rota posterior curras, you run *in the character* of the hind wheel—your running is that of the hind wheel.
   in axe currere, like 'in cardine verti.'
73-90. 'Men want freedom — not civil freedom, a thing that in these blinded times is conferred on any one, no matter on whom. Take a miserable debased slave, enfranchise him, and he becomes a Roman at once, enjoys all the privileges, and is honoured with all the compliments. Well, he will reply, and am I not free—free to do as I please? No, you are not. How so? surely my enfranchisement gave *every* right that the law allows.'
73. **non hac** 'qua,' ut quisque, was the usual reading, but it appears to be supported by a single MS. only, five others having 'hac quam ut,' which comes to the same thing. [The readings are probably due to the Scholia, 'non illam libertatem dicit *qua* quis ... tribu Velina censetur': 'non illa *quam* Publius

emeruit.'] Heinr. adopts the reading of several copies, 'hac qua' or 'quam quisque,' understanding 'quisque' = 'quicunque.' The great majority of MSS. however read 'non hac ut quisque,' which Casaubon and Jahn follow, the one supposing that the relative can be omitted, and quoting Virg. Aen. 1. 530 'Est locus, Hesperiam Grai cognomine dicunt;' the latter giving as his explanation 'ut (*qua,* quasi dixerit *ita ut*) scabiosum tesserula far possidet, quisque (quicunque) Publius emeruit Velina,' where surely 'possideat' would be required. A far simpler way is to make 'non hac' the beginning of an independent sentence. 'It is not by *this* freedom that every fire-new citizen who gets his name enrolled in a tribe, is privileged to receive a pauper's allowance for his ticket.'
   ut quisque ... emeruit ... possidet, 'he receives it upon serving—as surely as he has served,' a common construction, for instances of which see Freund s. v. 'ut,' Madvig § 495. For the two ablatives, 'hac' and 'tesserula,' attached to the same predicate, see Madvig § 278 a. The former is to be compared with 'facere aliquid *lege,*' the latter with 'emere aliquid *pretio.*'
   Velina, probably chosen because instanced by Hor. 1 Ep. 6. 52 'hic multum in Fabia valet, ille Velina.'
74. **Publius,** 'Quinte, puta, aut *Publi* (gaudent praenomine molles Auriculae'), Hor. 2 S. 5. 32, of a similar case. The object of 'emeruit' is apparently involved in the sentence which follows: 'scabiosum tesserula far possidere,' after the analogy of 'merere stipendia,' so that we may render it 'has served.' 'Velina' defining the service, as if it were the legion in which

as the tire may be, revolving, in fact, under the same carriage-pole as you, you will never overtake it, for yours is the hind wheel, and your axle not the first but the second.

'The thing wanted is freedom—it is not *this* freedom which enables every new recruit for citizenship enlisting in the Veline tribe to get a quota of spoiled corn for his ticket. What an unproductive soil for truth, where a single twirl makes a citizen of Rome! Look at Dama here, a stable-slave for whom you would not give twopence, blear-eyed from low tippling, and ready to tell a lie about a slight feed of corn; suppose his master to give him a

the soldier had served. 'He has only to enter the service of the tribe in order to entitle himself to the allowance.'

scabiosum, like 'vilis tessera frumenti' Juv. 7. 174.

tesserula, a contemptuous diminutive of 'tessera,' the ticket which entitled the holder to a share in the 'frumentatio,' or monthly distribution of corn among the poorer citizens. See Dict. Ant., and Mayor's note on Juv. 7. 174. Julius Caesar limited the number of recipients (Suet. Iul. 41): Augustus complained of the demoralizing effect of the custom, which at one time he wished to abolish altogether (Aug. 42), and attempted to restrict the distribution to three times a year: but was deterred by the unpopularity of the step (*ib*. 40). On one occasion he resented this very practice of manumitting slaves, in order to entitle them to an extraordinary bounty ('congiarium'), by refusing to admit the new claimants, and giving the rest less per head than he had promised.

75. **heu steriles veri,** compare 2. 61, and the metaphor in v. 63 of this Satire.

sterilis, with gen. like 'virtutum sterile saeculum' Tac. H. 1. 3 (Jahn), also found in Pliny and Vell. Paterc.

Quiritem, 3. 106, rare in the sing., as the Scholia remark, 'found in poets and in some legal formulae;' Mayor on Juv. 8. 47.

76. **vertigo,** explained by 'verterit' v. 78. The reference is to the 'manumissio per vindictam,' which made a slave a full citizen, the lictor touching him with the 'vindicta,' the master turning him round and 'dismissing him from his hand,' with the words 'Hunc hominem liberum esse volo.'

facit. In prose we should have expected 'faciat,' as the sentence, though expressed in an independent form, is really meant to give the reason of the address 'Heu steriles veri.' Compare Virg. G. 2. 458 foll. 'O fortunatos nimium ... quibus ipsa ... *Fundit* humo facilem victum iustissima tellus.' ['Όταν οὖν στρέψῃ τις ἐπὶ στρατηγοῦ τὸν αὑτοῦ δοῦλον, οὐδὲν ἐποίησεν; Ἐποίησεν. Τί; Ἔστρεψε τὸν αὑτοῦ δοῦλον ἐπὶ στρατηγοῦ. Ἄλλο οὐδέν; Ναί· καὶ εἰκοστὴν αὐτοῦ δοῦναι ὀφείλει. Τί οὖν; ὁ ταῦτα παθὼν οὐ γέγονεν ἐλεύθερος; Οὐ μᾶλλον ἢ ἀτάραχος. Epictetus 2. 1. 26.]

hic Dama est, etc. It matters little whether we put a stop at 'est' or make 'agaso' the predicate.

Dama (Demetrius), used repeatedly by Horace as a slave's name, 1 S. 6. 38, 2 S. 5. 18, 101, 7. 54. [Dama occurs in several inscriptions as the name of a slave: C. I. L. 1. 602 (B.C. 49) 'Dama Vetti,' where it is coupled with 'Surns' as in Horace; *ib.* 14. 4134 'Ti. L. Dama;' *ib.* 2. 5406 'Dama L. Titi ser.']

non tresis, οὐκ ἄξιος τριωβόλου, Casaubon. Jahn compares Vatinius in Cic. Ep. Fam. 5. 10 'non semissis homo.'

agaso, 'a stable-boy.' 'Si patinam pede lapsus frangat *agaso*' Hor. 2 S. 8. 72, of the waiter at Nasidienus' table.

77. It is difficult to decide between 'vappa et lippus,' the common reading, supported by about half the MSS., and 'vappa lippus,' which Jahn prefers. 'Vappa' is twice coupled by Horace with 'nebulo,' 1 S. 1. 104, 2. 12, [comp. Catull. 28. 4 'cum isto Vappa,' Priap. 13. 6 'Nos *vappae* sumus et pusilla culti Ruris numina'], and 'lippus' may be explained as in 1. 79, 2. 72, as a

verterit hunc dominus, momento turbinis exit
Marcus Dama. papae! Marco spondente recusas
credere tu nummos? Marco sub iudice palles?   80
Marcus dixit: ita est; adsigna, Marce, tabellas.
haec mera libertas! hoc nobis pillea donant!
'An quisquam est alius liber, nisi ducere vitam
cui licet, ut voluit? Licet ut volo vivere: non sum
liberior Bruto?' 'Mendose colligis,' inquit   85
stoicus hic aurem mordaci lotus aceto.
'haec reliqua accipio; *licet* illud et *ut volo* tolle.'
'Vindicta postquam meus a praetore recessi,
cur mihi non liceat, iussit quodcumque voluntas,
excepto si quid Masuri rubrica vetavit?'   90

[78. *temporis a, turbinis* C.   82. *hec a.   donat* C.   84. *libuit a, voluit* C. *sim* C.
  87. *hoc reliqum* C.   *illud detuo* C.   90. *expecto* C.]

contemptuous term, probably implying
disease brought on by sensuality: on the
other hand, the stable-helper would be
naturally enough described as 'blear-
eyed from tippling swipes,' as in Hor. 1
S. 5. 16 'multa prolutus vappa nauta.'
'*Farrago* appellatur id quod ex pluribus
satis pabuli caussa datur iumentis'
Festus, p. 91; 'in the matter of a slight
feed of corn,' with reference to 'agaso.'
Freund unaccountably supposes 'farrago' here to have the sense of 'a
trifle.'
 78. verterit . . . exit, compare v.
189 'Dixeris . . . videt.'
 momento turbinis, like 'horae
momento' Hor. 1 S. 1. 7.
 exit, as in Hor. A. P. 22 'turbinis'
answering to 'rota.'
 79. Marcus, like 'Publius' v. 74.
 papae is understood by Jahn as an
expression of wonder that Dama continues the same as he was—no more
trusted as a citizen than he was as a
slave; but this would destroy the whole
spirit of the passage, which is clearly
ironical. Persius throws up his hands
with wonder at the transformation.
'After this can anybody think of his
antecedents — hesitate about lending
money on his security—feel qualms
when he is on the bench? Impossible—

he is a Roman—his word is good for
anything—so is his signature.' ['Familia vero, babae, babae!' Petronius
37.]
 80. palles, of fear, Hor. 1 Ep. 7. 7.
 81. dixit: ita est, a contrast to
'mendax.'
 adsigna, 'put your seal to,' 'as a
witness.' Compare Mart. 9. 88. 3 foll.
(König).
 82. 'Vult *libertas* dici *mera*' Hor. 1
Ep. 18. 8.
 pillea. note on 3. 106.
 83. The humour is increased by
making the man argue in a formal
syllogism, and advance as his major
premiss the definition of liberty given
by the Stoics themselves, [after the
popular opinion quoted by Aristotle,
Pol. 7 (6). 2 τὸ ζῆν ὡς βούλεταί τις·
τοῦτο γὰρ τῆς ἐλευθερίας ἔργον · εἶναί
φασιν.] Comp. Cic. de Off. 1 20, Par. 5,
1. 34. [Ἐλεύθερός ἐστιν ὁ ζῶν ὡς βούλεται ... Τίς οὖν θέλει ζῆν ἁμαρτάνων;
Οὐδείς ... Οὐδεὶς ἄρα τῶν φαύλων ζῇ
ὡς βούλεται· οὐ τοίνυν οὐδ' ἐλεύθερος Epictetus 4. 1. 1. Epictetus often addresses
his unenlightened hearer as ἀνδράποδον.
On the subject of the emancipation of
slaves under the empire, and on the
Stoical doctrine of freedom in general,
there are some interesting remarks in

turn,—presto, by the mere act of twirling he is turned out Marcus Dama. Prodigious! What, Marcus surety, and you refuse to lend money? Marcus judge, and you feel uneasy? Marcus has given his word, it is so. Pray, Marcus, witness this document. This is freedom pure and simple; this is what caps of liberty give us.' 'Why? can you define a free man otherwise than a man who has the power of living as he has chosen? I have the power of living as I choose; am I not more of a freeman than Brutus, the founder of freedom?' 'A false inference,' retorts our Stoic friend, whose ear has been well rinsed with good sharp vinegar. 'I admit the rest, only strike out the words *power* and *choose*.' 'Why, after the rod enabled me to leave the praetor's presence my own man, why should not I have power over whatever I have a mind for, except where the statutes of Masurius come in the way?'

Bernays' Heraklitische Briefe p. 98 foll.]

84. voluit, perf. because the will precedes the action.

85. liberior Bruto, 'more free than the hero of freedom himself.'

mendose colligis; 'colligere' is the technical term for logical inference, συλλογίζεσθαι.

86. stoicus hic seems to be Persius' way of describing himself, like the common expression 'hic homo,' ἀνὴρ ὅδε, Hor. 1 S. 9. 47.

aurem...lotus, v. 63 note.

mordaci. 1. 107.

aceto. König refers to Cels. 6. 7. 2. 3, to show that vinegar was used in cases of deafness. [Perhaps Persius thought of Horace's 'Italo perfusus aceto' 1 S. 7. 32.]

87. haec reliqua is the reading of the great majority of the MSS., opp. to 'licet *illud*.' Persius admits the major, but denies the minor.

accipio, like 'accipere condicionem,' 'legem.'

For licet illud et ut volo, some MSS. have 'licet ut volo vivere,' adopted by Orelli and Heinr., but it seems to be an interpolation from v. 84. Persius objects to 'licet' and 'volo' as the two obnoxious words, denying both that the man has a will and that he is free to follow it.

88. vindicta, instrum. abl. For the process see note on v. 76.

meus, 'my own master,' or rather 'my own property.' König compares Ter. Phorm. 587 'nam ego meorum solus sum meus.' [Plaut. Persa 472 'sua nunc est, mea ancilla quae fuit' ('her own mistress'). Seneca Ep. 20. 1 'si te dignum putas qui aliquando fias *tuus.*']

89. 'Iussit quod splendida bilis' Hor. 2 S. 3. 141.

90. The exception proves that the man has no notion of any but *civil* freedom, which is expressed as 'facultas eius quod cuique facere libet, nisi quod vi aut iure prohibetur' Inst. 1. 3. 1, Dig. 1. 5. 4, referred to by Jahn. [For Masurius Sabinus see Teuffel and Schwabe, History of Roman Literature 2. p. 25 (Warr's translation). He was a pupil of Ateius Capito, and gave his name to the school of jurists called *Sabiniani*. Among his voluminous writings the chief place must apparently be given to his three books *Iuris Civilis*. He was living as late as the time of Nero, and would thus be known to Persius as the greatest legal authority of the age. To which of his writings the word 'rubrica' applies is uncertain. Epictetus 4. 3 speaks of Μασουρίου νόμοι.] '*Rubricam* vocat minium, quo tituli legum annotabantur' Schol. Hence in Dig. 43. 1. 2 'sub rubrica' is used for 'sub titulo' Mayor on Juv. 14. 192.

vetavit for 'vetuit,' Servius on Virg. Aen. 201. Jahn. [Georges, Lexicon der Lateinischen Wortformen, s. v. *veto*, gives several instances of other first-conjugation forms, e. g. 'vetasti,' 'vetatus,' from late Latin. Heinrich would read 'vetabit.']

'Disce, sed ira cadat naso rugosaque sanna,
dum veteres avias tibi de pulmone revello.
non praetoris erat stultis dare tenuia rerum
officia atque usum rapidae permittere vitae:
sambucam citius caloni aptaveris alto.   95
stat contra ratio et secretam garrit in aurem,
ne liceat facere id quod quis vitiabit agendo.
publica lex hominum naturaque continet hoc fas,
ut teneat vetitos inscitia debilis actus.
diluis helleborum, certo conpescere puncto   100

[92. *veteres aulas* C: *veteres se abias* a: *veteres scabies* ς.   93. *erit* a.
95. *sambucem* B.   97. *id* om. a.   *vitiavit* a C.]

91–223. 'I will show you, if you will submit to be disabused patiently. The praetor cannot confer right of action on a fool. Reason, witnessed by nature and embodied in the unwritten law of humanity, treats ignorance as disability. It is so in all cases—a man who is ignorant of medicine may not practise— a man who knows nothing of naval matters may not command a ship. Can you distinguish truth from falsehood? right from wrong? are you contented and cheerful? sparing or generous, as occasion requires? free from covetousness? Satisfy me on these points, and I will call you free. Fail to substantiate your professions, and I retract the admission, and tell you that that you have no right of action whatever—no power to take a single step without a blunder.'

91. [The text of the following remarks may be given in the words of Epictetus 4. 1. 62-64 τί οὖν ἐστι τὸ ποιοῦν ἀκώλυτον τὸν ἄνθρωπον; ... ἐν τῷ βιοῦν, ἡ ἐπιστήμη τοῦ βιοῦν: though the germ of it all is to be found in Xenophon Mem. 1. 1. 16, 3. 9. 5.] The nose shows anger by snarling, 1. 109. Casaubon quotes Theocr. 1. 18 καί οἱ ἀεὶ δριμεῖα χολὰ ποτὶ ῥινὶ κάθηται. Lucil. Fr. 20 11 'Eduxique animam in primoribus naribus' ('primoribus partibus naris' L. Müller).

rugosa, as wrinkling up the nostrils. '*Corruget* nares' Hor. 1 Ep. 5. 23.

sanna. 1. 62.

92. **veteres avias**; as we should say, prejudices which you imbibed with your mother's milk. Compare 2. 31, where the grandmother is made to utter foolish wishes.

pulmone, mentioned as the seat of pride (3. 27), as Casaubon thinks, more probably than as the seat of wrath, which is Jahn's view.

93. ['*Tenui* ratione saporum' Hor. 2 S. 4. 35]. tenuia (trisyll. as in Virg. G. 1. 397, 2. 121, 4. 38) ... officia, not as distinguishing them from other broader duties, but expressing the nature of right doing, which is an art made up of innumerable details, and requiring exact study. ['Erat,' was not as you thought it was: the imperfect common in dialogue.]

rerum, equivalent to 'vitae.'

94. **usum ... permittere vitae** = 'permittere ut uterentur vita.'

rapidae appears to be a metaphor from a race-course, as in 3. 67, 8, the notion being that there is no power of stopping in the career of life, which consequently is no place for a man who cannot conduct himself.

95. **sambuca**; Dict. of Antiq.

citius = 'potius;' 'citius dixerim' Cic. 2 Phil. 11.

'*Calones* militum servi dicti, qui ligneas clavas gerebant, quae Graeci κᾶλα vocant' Festus p. 47: elsewhere of other slaves, Hor. 1 S. 6. 103, 1 Ep. 14. 42, here in its original sense, as Persius would naturally choose a *soldier's* slave as the lowest specimen of degraded humanity. See note on 3. 77.

alto points the same way; compare 'Pulfennius *ingens*' v. 190.

aptare sambucam ... caloni, like

'Attend, then, but drop that angry wrinkled snarl from your nostrils, while I pull your old grandmother out of the heart of you. It was not in the praetor's province to give fools command over the delicate proprieties of relative duty, or grant them the entry of the rapid race-course of life; you will get a hulking camp-follower to handle a dulcimer first. No, reason steps in your way and whispers privately in your ear that no one be allowed to do what he will spoil in the doing. It is a statute contained in the general code of humanity and nature, that ignorance and imbecility operate as an embargo on a forbidden action. What? compound hellebore, when you don't know the right point at which to steady the index of the steel-yard? The law of the healing art forbids you.

'aptantur enses dexteris' Hor. Epod. 7. 2, to make him use it gracefully, as if it were his natural instrument.

96. stat contra, 'confronts you,' 'stops your way.' '*Stat contra*, dicitque tibi tua pagina, Fur es' Mart. 1. 53 (54). 12, quoted by Jahn. 'Stat contra, starique iubet' Juv. 3. 290.

'*Ratio* tua coepit *vociferari*' Lucr. 3. 14.

[Garrio, to chatter,' whence 'garrulus.' 'Garrire ad aurem nunquam didici dominicam' Afranius ap. Non. p. 450: though the first reading of the Harleian MS. there is 'casaubon.' 'Gannire' is properly used of the whining of dogs, 'garrire' of human whispering. 'Garrire in aurem, auriculam' Mart. 1. 89. 1, 3. 28. 2, 5. 61. 3, 11. 24. 2. Lewis and Short quote 'gannire' in this sense from Apuleius M. 3. 20, but the first part of the word is erased in the MS.] With the general expression of the line, compare Hor. 1 Ep. 1. 7 'Est mihi purgatam crebro qui personet aurem,' of an inward monitor.

97. liceat, with reference to 'licet' v. 84.

98. publica lex hominum, opp. to 'Masuri rubrica' v. 90, as the Delph. ed. remarks.

natura seems to be mentioned as the source of the law, which is consequently accepted and acknowledged everywhere. [The doctrine of a supreme law of Nature, the actual source and ideal standard of all particular laws, was characteristic of the Stoics, and was the basis of the Roman juristical notion of a 'ratio naturalis' (Inst. 2. 1). 'Aliquod esse *commune ius* generis humani' Sen. Ep. 47. 3: 'lex naturae' *ib.* Vit. Beat. 15. 5; Ben. 3. 19. 2 'servum qui negat dare aliquando domino beneficium ignarus est *iuris humani*.' *Ib.* 4. 17. 3 'nec quisquam a *naturali lege* tantum descivit ut animi causa malus sit.' Quint. 12. 2. 3 'leges quae natura sunt omnibus datae, quaeque populis et gentibus constitutae.']

hoc fas; 'fas *omne*' is a common expression, Virg. Aen. 3. 55, etc.; and 'fas gentium,' 'patriae,' etc. occur in Tacitus (Ann. 1. 42, 2. 10).

99. teneat vetitos are connected by Casaubon, who explains them 'habeat pro vetitis.' Jahn says, 'Teneat, ita ut necessario eam sequantur.' Perhaps it would be more natural to explain it in the sense of restraining. 'That ignorance and incompetence should operate as a bar to forbidden actions,'—or, if we take inscitia debilis as equivalent to 'insciti et debiles,' 'should check them,' as if it were 'teneat se ab agendis vetitis.' So Ascens. 'Contineat in se nec emittat actus vetitos,' and Nebriss. 'Contineat se ab aliqua re agenda quam agere ratio, lex, et natura vetant.'

The use of actus in this sense seems chiefly to belong to later Latin. Freund thinks there is only one instance of it in Cicero (Leg. 1. 11) 'Non solum in rectis sed etiam in pravis *actibus*.' [But 'pravitatibus' seems there to be the right reading.]

100. This and the following example are from Hor. 2 Ep. 1. 114 foll. 'Navem agere ignarus navis timet: habrotonum aegro Non audet, nisi qui didicit, dare,' —speaking of those who rush into poetry without preparation.

nescius examen? vetat hoc natura medendi.
navem si poscat sibi peronatus arator,
luciferi rudis, exclamet Melicerta perisse
frontem de rebus. tibi recto vivere talo
ars dedit, et veri specimen dinoscere calles,   105
ne qua subaerato mendosum tinniat auro?
quaeque sequenda forent, quaeque evitanda vicissim,
illa prius creta, mox haec carbone notasti?
es modicus voti? presso lare? dulcis amicis?
iam nunc astringas, iam nunc granaria laxes,   110
inque luto fixum possis transcendere nummum,

[102. *perocinatus* a, *perornatus* C. 103. *exclamat* C. 104. *callo* A.
105. *specimen* a, *speciem* C, Priscian I. p. 433 K. 106. *oro* a. 108. *notasse* a.
109. *et* C. 111. *transcedere* a.]

100. **diluis helleborum.** Hellebore seems to have been sometimes taken pure, as in 4. 16 note, sometimes mixed.

certo, etc. The metaphor here is from a steelyard ('statera'), not as in 1. 6 foll., from a balance ('trutina').

conpescere, 'to check,' seems here to mean to bring to the perpendicular, so that the index ('examen') may show that there is an equipoise.

punctum is one of the points on the graduated arm, along which the weight is moved.

certo conpescere puncto, then, is to steady the index by bringing the weight to the point required. Thus the whole will mean, as Lubin explains it, 'Do you attempt to compound medicines who do not understand the use of the steelyard?'

101. **natura medendi,** 'the conditions of the healing art.'

102. **navem... poscat,** 'should ask for the command of a ship,' like 'vitem posce' Juv. 14. 193.

peronatus. The 'pero' was a thick boot of raw hide, 'crudus pero' Virg. Aen. 7. 690, 'alto... perone... qui summovet Euros Pellibus inversis' Juv. 14. 185, contrasted with the shoes which sailors wear on deck (Stocker).

103. **luciferi,** mentioned as the chief of the stars. Casaubon remarks that in that case the countryman would be ignorant even of his own trade, as he is bound to have some knowledge of the stars, Virg. G. 1. 204 foll.

exclamet, etc. From Hor. 2 Ep. 1. 80 'clamant perisse pudorem Cuncti paene patres.' Casaubon quotes Theognis 291 αἰδὼς μὲν γὰρ ὄλωλεν, ἀναιδείη δὲ καὶ ὕβρις Νικήσασα δίκην γῆν κατὰ πᾶσαν ἔχει.

Melicerta, as one of the patrons of sailors, Virg. G. 1. 437.

104. **frontem,** the seat of modesty, put for modesty itself, as in our word 'frontless.'

de rebus, 'from the world,' as in '*rerum* pulcherrima Roma,' etc.

'Cadat an *recto* stet fabula *talo*' Hor. 2 Ep. 1. 176; apparently from Pind. Isthm. 6. 12 ὀρθῷ ἔστασας ἐπὶ σφυρῷ. Jahn. Opp. to falling or stumbling. Not unlike is Juv. 10. 5 'dextro pede concipis.'

105. **ars.** So Cic. Tusc. 2. 4. says of the philosopher, 'In ratione vitae peccans... in officio cuius magister esse vult labitur, artemque vitae professus, delinquit in vita.' The word is emphatic here, as Persius means to deny that virtue comes except by training and study. [The Stoics were fond of drawing out the analogy between life and the arts so familiar to the readers of Plato: e. g. Epictetus 4. 1. 117 foll. οὕτως ἐφ' ἑκάστης ὕλης τὸν ἔμπειρον τοῦ ἀπείρου κρατεῖν πᾶσα ἀνάγκη. Ὅστις οὖν καθόλου τὴν περὶ βίον ἐπιστήμην κέκτηται, τί ἄλλο ἢ

So if a roughshod clodhopper, unacquainted with the pole-star, should ask for a ship, the gods of the sea would cry out that shamefacedness had vanished from nature. Tell me, has study given you the power of living correctly? are you well practised in testing the appearances of truth, and seeing that there is no false ring to show that the gold is coppered underneath? Have you discriminated what should be followed on the one hand and what avoided on the other, marking the former with chalk first, and then the latter with charcoal? Are your desires moderate, your house within compass, your temper to your friends pleasant? Can you shut up your granaries at one time, open them at another? and are you able to step across a coin fastened in the mud without

τοῦτον εἶναι δεῖ τὸν δεσπότην; Τίς γάρ ἐστιν ἐν νηῒ κύριος; Ὁ κυβερνήτης κ.τ.λ. Sen. Ep. 117. 12 'Sapientia... ars vitae est:' comp. Id. Vit. Beat. 8. 3.]

['Speciem' Jahn (1868) and Bücheler. See critical note]. Specimen has here its original sense of 'indicium,' as in Lucr. 4. 209 foll. 'Hoc etiam in primis *specimen* verum esse videtur, Quam celeri motu rerum simulacra ferantur.'

106. [Epictetus 1. 7. 6 has the simile of the true and the false coin: *ib.* 8 he says ἀνάγκη δοκιμαστικὸν γενέσθαι, καὶ διακριτικὸν τοῦ ἀληθοῦς καὶ τοῦ ψευδοῦς καὶ τοῦ ἀδήλου. Subaeratus (which should rather be 'subaereus') is, as Casaubon remarked, a translation of ὑπόχαλκος. Libanius, Μελέτη Κεφάλου: ὑμὸς βίος ἄνω καὶ κάτω στρεφόμενος μετὰ τῶν ψήφων ἀριθμουμένων (so Förster for ἀριθμούμενος) καθαρὸς ἠχεῖ πανταχοῦ, τὸν δὲ σὺν οὐδ' εἴ τις ὑπόχαλκος ἢ κίβδηλός ἐστιν οὐκ ἄν τις ἰσχυρίσαιτο.]

mendosum tinniat, like 'sonat vitium' 3. 21, 'solidum crepet' above, v. 25. The metaphor in this and the preceding line is not unlike Hor. 1 Ep. 7. 23 'Nec tamen ignorat quid distent aera lupinis.' The nom. to 'tinniat' would seem to be 'verum,' [unless we prefer to take the verb as impersonal.]

107. vicissim, 'on the other hand.'

108. prius... mox. Whether there is any point in making the knowledge of virtue precede that of vice is not clear. Hor. 1 Ep. 1. 41 gives the contrary process, 'Virtus est vitium fugere, et sapientia prima Stultitia caruisse.'

creta... carbone. 'Creta an carbone notandi' Hor. 2 S. 3. 246, of different classes of men. Compare note on 2. 1 and 4. 13 '*nigrum* vitio praefigere theta.'

109. modicus voti is found also in Sil. 5. 14. Jahn. Tacitus has 'modicum voluptatum' Ann. 2. 73, 'modicus pecuniae' *id.* 3. 72.

pressus, frequent as an epithet of style, opp. to 'diffusus' or 'abundans.' Here it seems to denote the avoiding of ostentatious or reckless expenditure, applied to lar probably because one mode of extravagance is over-building.

dulcis, like '*dulces* ignoscent... amici' Hor. 1 S. 3. 139 (referred to by Madan), 'indulgent,'—so that it answers to 'ignoscis amicis?' Hor. 2 Ep. 2. 210, in a similar list of questions for self-examination.

110. astringas, like 'astrictum limen' Ov. Am. 3. 1. 50, of a door shut.

granaria, 6. 25, implying large stores, as in Hor. 1 S. 1. 53 'Cur tua plus laudes cumeris *granaria* nostris?'

laxare, of opening. Virg. Aen. 2. 259 '*laxat* claustra Sinon.' Gr. χαλάω.

111. 'Avarus. In triviis *fixum* cum se demittit ob assem' Hor. 1 Ep. 16. 63 foll., a common joke in Rome being for boys to fasten a piece of money to a stone in the street, that they might laugh at any one who stooped to pick it up.

transcendere, 'to step across.' Persius seems here to contemplate a man knowing it would be no use to stoop, yet coveting the money. [Ἂν ἀργυρίδιον προβάλῃς, καταφρονήσει Epictetus 1. 18. 22, of the trained character. On the other hand Phileros in Petronius (43) says of a very ordinary person 'ab

nec glutto sorbere salivam Mercurialem?
"haec mea sunt, teneo" cum vere dixeris, esto
liberque ac sapiens praetoribus ac Iove dextro;
sin tu, cum fueris nostrae paulo ante farinae, 115
pelliculam veterem retines, et fronte politus
astutam vapido servas in pectore vulpem,
quae dederam supra relego, funemque reduco.
nil tibi concessit ratio; digitum exere, peccas,
et quid tam parvum est? sed nullo ture litabis, 120
haereat in stultis brevis ut semuncia recti.
haec miscere nefas; nec, cum sis cetera fossor,
tris tantum ad numeros satyrum moveare Bathylli.'

[112. *gluttu* C. 115. *nostro* a. 116. *politas* a. 117. *servans* C. sub *pectore* ς. 118. *repeto* ς. *finemque* a. 121. *et semuntiat* a. 123. *numero* C. *bathyllo* a, *beatilli* C.]

asse crevit, et paratus fuit *quadrantem de stercore mordicus tollere.*]
112. glutto, 'a glutton,' 1. 12 note. Freund refers to Fest. s. v. 'ingluvies,' p. 112, Müller; a predicate taken closely with sorbere. ['Glutto λιμβός' Gloss. Lat. Gr. p. 34. 34 G.]
saliva, 6. 24, of the watering of the mouth excited by dainties; here called Mercurialis, a name applied to traders (Hor. 2 S. 3. 25) as arising from avarice. See 2. 11 note.
113. haec mea sunt, the formula of asserting ownership. 'Hic meus est' Virg. Ecl. 9. 4.
teneo, as in Hor. 2 Od. 12. 21 '*quae tenuit* dives Achaemenes,' 3 Od. 17. 8 'tenuisse Lirim.'
esto again suggests a legal form.
114. dextro, like 'dextro Hercule' 2 11, 'by grace of the praetors and Jove.' [Λέγουσιν (οἱ φιλόσοφοι) μόνους τοὺς παιδευθέντας ἐλευθέρους εἶναι Epictet. 2. 1. 22. 'Ea libertas est, qui pectus purum et firmum gestitat' Ennius Trag. 340 (Vahlen).]
115. farinae, a metaphor from loaves, which might be of different qualities, 3. 112 note. ['Ac si diceret *nostrae vitae*,' Schol. The expression was probably colloquial.] König compares Suet. Aug. 4 'Cassius Parmensis ... ut pistoris ... nepotem sic taxat Augustum: Materna tibi *farina* ex crudissimo Ariciae pistrino.' The sense of the line seems to be 'after enrolling yourself just now among the philosophers,' as the Scholia explain it, though Casaubon supposes nostrae to be said modestly, and paraphrases the words 'Cum esses paullo ante vitiosissimus,' which is also the view of Brit., Plaut., König, Heinr.

116. pelliculam veterem retines seems to be suggested by Hor. 1 S. 6. 22 'quoniam in propria non pelle quiessem,' which is apparently an allusion to the fable of the ass in the lion's skin: with this he combines another image of the *fox* dressed up like a lion, Hor. 2 S. 3. 186 '*Astuta* ingenuum *vulpes* imitata leonem,' so as to confuse the details of the metaphor, 'keep your ass's skin, and in spite of your smooth looks are a fox at heart.'
fronte politus, instead of 'fronte polita,' like 'pede liber' 1. 13, 'cute perditus' 1. 23. This does not seem to belong to the metaphor.
117. Jahn refers to Archiloch. fr. 88 a 5 (Bergk.) κερδαλέη ἀλώπηξ. [Οἱ πλείους δ' ἡμῶν ἀλώπεκες, καὶ ὅσα ἐν ζώοις ἀτυχήματα. Τί γάρ ἐστιν ἄλλο λοίδορος καὶ κακοήθης ἄνθρωπος, ἢ ἀλώπηξ; Epictetus 1. 3. 7.]
vapido, of wine that has lost its spirit, opp. to 'incoctum *generoso pectus honesto*' 2. 74.
118. relego. Jahn, from the best MSS., the rest have 'repeto,' which is easier: but 'relego' may very well mean

greedily gulping down the water of treasure-trove in your mouth? When you can say with truth, "All this is mine, I have realized it," herewith be free and wise by favour of the praetors and Jupiter; but if, after being of our grain only a moment ago, you really keep your old skin, and though your brow is smooth enough, have a cunning fox still locked up in the musty cellar of your bosom, I beg leave to reconsider my concessions, and pull in the rope. No, reason has made no admission in your favour; move your finger, you make a wrong move; and where will you have a slighter thing than that? but no amount of incense will induce the gods to rule that one small grain of wisdom may get itself lodged in a fool's nature. It is sacrilege to attempt the union; if you are a clodhopper every other inch of you, you cannot dance even three steps of Bathyllus' satyr.'

'I revise,' 'reconsider.' Val. Fl. 6. 237 seems to use 'relego' in the sense of drawing back a spear.

funemque reduco, apparently of pulling in a beast who has had rope allowed him. 'Tortum digna sequi potius quam ducere funem' Hor. 1 Ep. 10. 48.

119. **nil ... concessit**, 'has given you power over nothing,' like 'ne liceat,' etc. v. 97.

digitum exere, a favourite expression with the Stoics. Epict. fr. 53 ἡ φιλοσοφία φησὶν ὅτι οὐδὲ τὸν δάκτυλον ἐκτείνειν εἰκῇ προσήκει, and so Plut. de Rep. Stoic. 13 has the expression ἀνδρείως τὸν δάκτυλον ἐκτεῖναι. [Δίχα αὐτοῦ (τοῦ κάνονος) μηδὲ τὸν δάκτυλον ἐκτείνοντες Epictetus 2. 11, 17.] Chrysippus is represented by Cic. Fin. 3. 17 to have said of reputation 'Detracta utilitate, ne digitum quidem eius caussa porrigendum esse.' These instances are quoted by Casaubon, who adds another Stoic dictum, ὁ μῶρος οὐδὲ φακῆν κακῶς (καλῶς) ἕψει. Something like our proverb, 'There is reason in the roasting of eggs.'

120. 'What smaller thing will you choose as a test?'

litabis, as in 2. 75 : taken in connexion with the next line it has virtually the force of 'impetrabis.'

121. The language, as Casaubon remarks, is more or less borrowed from Hor. 1 S. 3. 76 foll. 'Denique, quatenus excidi penitus vitium irae, Cetera item nequeant *stultis haerentia,* cur non *Ponderibus modulisque suis ratio utitur?*' who, curiously enough, is arguing against the Stoic dogma, that all faults are equal, a correlative of that here maintained by Persius.

brevis; as we talk of '*short* measure,' like 'curto centusse' v. 191. Jahn compares Hor. 2 S. 2. 37 'breve pondus,' where 'brevis'='exiguus.' ['Mit der Dummheit kämpfen die Götter selbst vergebens,' says Schiller.]

122. 'Folly and wisdom are incompatible.'

miscere, not unlike Aesch. Ag. 322 ὄξος τ' ἄλειφά τ' ἐγχέας ταὐτῷ κύτει, Διχοστατοῦντ' ἂν οὐ φίλως προσεννέποις.

122. **fossor**, doubtless with reference to Hor. 3 Od. 18. 15 foll. 'Gaudet invisam pepulisse *fossor Ter* pede terram.' fossor opp. to '*bellus* et urbanus' Catull. 22. 9 (Jahn).

123. [Ad numeros must not be confused with 'in numerum' Lucr. 2. 631. 'Numeri' are the parts of the dance, the various steps : so that the literal translation probably is 'You cannot dance the satyr of Bathyllus even as far as ('ad') three steps.' 'You cannot get even as far as three steps in dancing' etc. For the construction comp.] Hor. 2 Ep. 2. 125 'Nunc Satyrum, nunc agrestem Cyclopa movetur.' **Satyrum** (conjectured by Casaubon for the traditional 'satyri') is the reading of the oldest MS., and is rightly restored by Jahn in his edition of 1868.

Bathyllus, Dict. Biog., was a comic dancer in the time of Augustus, so that the mention of him here is another instance of Persius' habit of looking rather to books than to life.

'Liber ego.' 'Unde datum hoc sentis, tot subdite rebus?
an dominum ignoras, nisi quem vindicta relaxat?'   125
'I puer et strigiles Crispini ad balnea defer!'
si increpuit, 'cessas nugator?' servitium acre
te nihil inpellit, nec quicquam extrinsecus intrat,
quod nervos agitet; sed si intus et in iecore aegro
nascuntur domini, qui tu inpunitior exis   130
atque hic, quem ad strigiles scutica et metus egit erilis?

   Mane piger stertis. 'Surge!' inquit Avaritia 'heia
surge!' Negas; instat 'Surge!' inquit. 'Non queo.' 'Surge!'
'Et quid agam?' 'Rogitas? en saperdam advehe Ponto,
castoreum, stuppas, hebenum, tus, lubrica Coa;   135

[124. *sumis* C.   127. *nugutcor servivium* a.   128. *nequicquam* a.
129. *pectore* C.   130. *quid* a.   131. *scutita* a, *scytice* C.   134. *rogas en* a C.
rogitas ς. *seperdas* B, *saperdam* ς.   135. *rubrica* a.]

124–131. 'No matter, he replies, I *am free.* As if a man had no other masters than those from whom the praetor's enfranchisement delivers him! True, you can refuse to perform your old duties: but if you are under the command of your passions, you are as much a slave as ever.'

124. Persius meets this reassertion of freedom with a new answer. Before he had contended that fools had no *rights*: now he shows that they have no independent *power.*

Jahn restores *sentis* for 'sumis,' from the best MSS., so that the expression is borrowed from Hor. 2 S. 2. 31 'Unde datum sentis, lupus hic Tiberinus an alto Captus hiet?' and apparently equivalent to 'Quis tibi dedit hoc sentire?' 'Sumis' however has great probability on account of *datum*, both being regularly used as philosophical terms, the latter for *granting*, the former *taking for granted.*

subdite, voc., equivalent to 'cum subditus sis,' like 'Tune hinc, spoliis *indute* meorum, Eripiare mihi' Virg. Aen. 12. 947, for 'cum indutus sis.'

tot subdite rebus, imitated from Hor. 2 S. 7. 75 'Tune mihi dominus, rerum imperiis hominumque Tot tantisque minor?' as Jahn remarks.

125. Persius has again glanced at Hor. l. c. 'quem ter vindicta quaterque Imposita haud unquam misera formidine privet.'

relaxare dominum, a bold expression for 'relaxare imperium domini.' 'relaxat,' either general or for relaxavit,' like 'tollit' 4. 2.

126. A specimen of a command. 'I, puer, atque meo citus haec subscribe libello' Hor. 1 S. 10. 92.

The *strigiles* (Juv. 3. 263) would be carried to the bath, that the master might use them after bathing. König refers to Luc. Lexiph. 2. p. 320.

Crispinus, seemingly the name of the bathkeeper, may be taken from Horace, as Jahn thinks; but there is nothing to show it.

127. The man does not move, so the master addresses him sharply.

cessas; 'semel hic *cessavit*' of a slave, Hor. 2 Ep. 2. 14.

nugari, of wasting time, 1. 56, 70.

servitium acre, apparently a metaphor from a goad, which would agree with *inpellit.*

128. 'You are not a puppet, whose strings are pulled *externally*' Hor. 2 S. 7. 81 foll. 'Tu, mihi qui imperitas, aliis servis miser, atque Duceris, ut nervis alienis mobile lignum.' Casaubon shows that the image was a very common one, especially among the Stoics, occurring many times in Marcus Antoninus; e. g. 10. 38 μέμνησο ὅτι τὸ νευροσπαστοῦν ἐστιν ἐκεῖνο τὸ ἔνδον ἐγκεκρυμμένον, which shows the force of *extrinsecus* here. The original appears to be Plato, Laws, 1. p. 644 E τόδε δὲ

SAT. V.

'I'm free for all that.' 'Who gave you leave to think so, you, the slave of so many things? Have you no notion of any master but the one whom the wand frees you from?' 'Hallo, boy, carry Crispinus' flesh-brushes to the bath;' then suppose his tone grows sharper: 'What? dawdling and playing the fool?' the sting of bondage does not make you stir a step; nothing is communicated from without to jerk your wires; but if within, in that diseased heart of yours, masters keep growing up, how can you be said to come off unwhipped, any more than the slave whom the strap and the terror of his masters have sent running with the flesh-brushes?

You are snoring lazily in the morning. 'Get up,' says Avarice, 'come, get up.' *No*, say you. She keeps on, 'Get up.' 'I can't.' 'Get up.' 'And what am I to do?' 'You ask the question! Look here, fetch salt herrings from Pontus, castor, tow, ebony, frankin-

ἴσμεν, ὅτι ταῦτα τὰ πάθη ἐν ἡμῖν οἷον νεῦρα ἢ σμηρινθοί τινες ἐνοῦσαι σπῶσί τε ἡμᾶς καὶ ἀλλήλαις ἀνθέλκουσιν ἐναντίαι οὖσαι ἐπ' ἐναντίας πράξεις. These figures were called νευρόσπαστα or 'sigillaria.'

129. **iecore...nascuntur**, compare 1. 25 note.

130. 'Qui tu inpunitior' Hor. 2 S. 7. 105. Casaubon.

exis, 'come off,' 'escape.' 'Quia vivus *exierat*' Vell. 2. 82.

131. **ad strigiles**. Perhaps with reference to expressions like 'servi ad remum,' 'ad lecticam.'

scutica. 'Ne *scutica* dignum horribili sectere flagello' Hor. 1 S. 5. 119. Perhaps to be explained by '*metus* erilis.' [With the whole passage compare Epictetus 2. 1. 28 Ἐπεὶ σύ, ὁ ἄλλους στρέφειν δυνάμενος, οὐδένα ἔχεις κύριον; οὐκ ἀργύριον, οὐ καράσιον, οὐ παιδάριον, οὐ τύραννον; Ib. 4. 1. 57 Καὶ μή μοι πάππους αὐτοῦ καὶ προπάππους βλέπε, καὶ ὠνὴν ζήτει καὶ πρᾶσιν· ἀλλ', ἂν ἀκούσῃς λέγοντος ἔσωθεν καὶ ἐκ πάθους, Κύριε· κἂν δώδεκα ῥάβδοι προηγῶσι, λέγε δοῦλον ... Οὕτως οὖν πολλοὺς κυρίους ἔχομεν; Οὕτως. Ib. 86 Μή τι ἁπλῶς τὴν ἐν ἡμῖν ἀκρόπολιν καὶ τοὺς ἐν ἡμῖν τυράννους ἀποβεβλήκαμεν; οὓς ἐφ' ἑκάστοις καθ' ἡμέραν ἔχομεν, ποτὲ μὲν τοὺς αὑτούς, ποτὲ δ' ἄλλους. 'Servum tu quemquam vocas libidinis et gulae servus?' Sen. Ben. 3. 28. 4.]

132-160. 'One morning as you are sleeping you are roused by Avarice, who at last makes you get up and prepare for a voyage, where you are to traffic in all kinds of articles and struggle hard to make your fortune. Just as you are bustling away, Luxury takes you aside, rallies you on your mad hurry, reminds you of the discomforts you are about to undergo on shipboard, merely that you may swell your property a little, and ends by bidding you be wise and enjoy life while you can. Which of the two will you follow? you are pulled both ways, and a single act of resistance to either does not make you free. Even if you break your chain, you may still drag it along with you.'

132. The personifications remind us of those in the Choice of Hercules. Jahn.

133. **Negas** is said by the poet, like **instat**.

134. 'Well, and what am I to do?' [Bücheler reads 'rogăs, en, saperdas' from the best MSS. See critical note. He conjectures 'rogan.']

en ... advehe, like 'en accipe' Virg. Ecl. 6. 69, 'En age' G. 3. 42. '*Saperda* genus pessimi piscis' Fest. s.v. (p. 324 Müller), a fish for salting, seemingly of the herring sort. The best were found in the Palus Maeotis, Athen. 3. p. 119 b, 7 p. 308 e, Hesych. s. v., the Greek name being σαπέρδης or κορακῖνος. Jahn.

Ponto, ablative.

135. 'Virosaque *Pontus Castorea*' Virg. G. 1. 58.

stuppas, 'the coarse part of flax, tow, hards, oakum.' Fraund.

tolle recens primus piper ec sitiente camello;
verte aliquid; iura.' 'Sed Iuppiter audiet.' 'Eheu!
baro, regustatum digito terebrare salinum
contentus perages, si vivere cum Iove tendis!'
iam pueris pellem succinctus et oenophorum aptas: 140
'Ocius ad navem!' nihil obstat, quin trabe vasta
Aegaeum rapias, ni sollers Luxuria ante
seductum moneat 'Quo deinde, insane, ruis? quo?
quid tibi vis? calido sub pectore mascula bilis
intumuit, quod non extinxerit urna cicutae. 145
tu mare transilias? tibi torta cannabe fulto
cena sit in transtro, Veientanumque rubellum

[136. *et sitiente* a.   137. *audiat* C.   138. *varo* a.   141. *ocius* a. *qui in* a.   *trabea* C.   *vastra* a.   144. *callido* C.   145. *quam non* C. 146. *tun* ς. *tracilias* a.   147. *vellentanumque* C.]

135. **hebenum, tus.** 'Sola India nigrum Fert *hebenum*; solis est turea virga Sabaeis' Virg G. 2. 116 foll., so that the voyage is meant to extend over the East generally. Compare Hor. 1 Ep. 1. 45 foll. and note on v. 54 above.

lubrica Coa may either be 'oil-like Coan wine' Hor. 2 S. 4. 29, or 'gleaming Coan garments.' 'Coa decere puta' Ov. A. A. 2. 298, the former being the common interpretation, the latter Heinrich's.

136. 'Be the first to bargain for the pepper which the camel-driver has brought to Alexandria.'

recens, primus. Both point the same way; before others have time to bid. Comp. with Casaubon (if the reading 'primus' be certain) Lucil. Fr. 5. 19 'Sicut cum ficus *primus* propola *recentes* Protulit, et pretio ingenti dat *primitu*' paucos. [Ec' for 'ex' is indicated by 'et' of the best MSS.]

piper, from India, v. 54.

sitiente, thirsty from its journey over the desert, before the driver has had time to attend to its wants. The camel's powers of enduring thirst are well known. The whole line is parallel to Hor. 1 Ep. 6. 32 foll. which Plautius and others compare 'cave ne portus occupet alter, Ne Cibyratica, ne Bithyna negotia perdas.'

137. **verte aliquid,** i. e. 'Negotiare et speciem pro specie commuta' Schol. Jahn refers to Plaut. Curc. 484 ['vel qui ipsi vortant, vel qui aliis, ut vorsentur, praebeant'], but observes, with justice, that this would yield but a tame sense after the strong expressions preceding: he accordingly prefers to take 'vertere' as equivalent to 'versuram facere,' to borrow money in order to pay debts, applying iura to perjured denial of the debt thus contracted. iura however may refer to false swearing in general as a means of livelihood; compare Juv. 7. 13, where a poor poet is recommended to turn auctioneer rather than gain a living by perjury.

138. ['Baro' perhaps from 'barrus' an elephant, a great strong fellow, so a lubber, a lout. According to the Scholia here and Isid. Orig. 9. 4. 31, the word was used of a soldier's servant. Petronius uses it in the sense of a big man, 53, 63 'baro insulsissimus cum scalis constitit,' 'baro ille longus.' For the secondary sense comp. Cic. Fin. 2. 23 'nos barones stupemus;' Div. 2. 70 'baro' (you dolt!); Fam. 9. 26. 3 'ille baro te putabat quaesiturum;' Att. 5. 11. 6 'Bacelus, baro,' Gloss. Sang. p. 210. 10. 9. Diez, Etym. Wörterb. 1. p. 54 foll. 2nd ed. shows that 'baro' was used in mediaeval Latin as = *a man*: on the origin of the word he does not pronounce positively, but denies its Celtic descent, pointing out some pos-

SAT. V.

cense, glossy Coans; be the first to take the fresh-brought pepper from the camel's back before he has had his drink; borrow money for your debts and swear you never had it.' 'But Jupiter will hear.' 'Pah, you lout, you will go on to the end of the chapter satisfied with drilling a hole with your thumb in the salt-cellar that you have had so many a taste out of, if a life with Jupiter is what you aim at.' Now you are equipped and loading your slaves with packing-case and wine-holder. 'To the ship this moment.' There is nothing to prevent you from scouring the Aegean in a big vessel, unless it be that sly Luxury just takes you aside for a moment's lecture. 'Where are you off to now, you madman, where? What can you be wanting? there must be a great rising of bile in that caldron of a breast of yours, which a whole bout of hemlock would not extinguish. You skip across the sea? you eat your dinner off a bench with a coil of rope for a cushion? and a squab noggin ex-

sible Teutonic cognates. Gloss. Lat. Gr. p. 27. 54 G. '*baro ἀνήρ*.']
  terebrare salinum, ἁλίαν τρυπᾶν as in Apol. Tyan. Ep. 7, quoted by Casaubon, πάντα φασὶ δεῖν τὸν ἔμπορον κάλων σείειν· ἐμοὶ δ᾽ εἴη τὴν ἁλίαν τρυπᾶν ἐν Θέμιδος οἴκῳ, 'to scrape and scrape till you drill a hole in your salt-cellar.'
  salinum, the accompaniment of a frugal meal, as in 3. 25 note.
  139. contentus with terebrare.
  perages, 'aevum,' 'aetatem,' or 'vitam,' which is generally expressed. So διάγειν. [Vivere cum Iove, perhaps a playful allusion to the philosophical idea of a good life as a life with the gods: συζῆν θεοῖς M. Aurelius 5. 27. Seneca Ep. 31. 7 'hoc est summum bonum: quod si occupas, incipis deorum socius esse, non supplex': 73. 11 'hoc otium quod inter deos agitur, quod deos facit.' On this doctrine see Bernays, 'Theophrastos über Frömmigkeit' p. 139: 'Heraklitische Briefe' p. 100.]
  140. pellis seems to have been a sort of packing-cloth, as the 'sarcina' was carried in it. See Jahn.
  oenophorum, 'the wine-holder' or 'liquor-case,' was carried on journeys, Hor. 1 S. 6. 109. These the master, himself succinctus, equipped for travelling, thrusts on the slaves. Compare 'aptaveris' v. 95 note.
  141. 'Quick with these to the vessel;' the master's direction.
  vasta, apparently to give the notion of successfully contending with the ele-

ments. 'Vastis ictibus' Virg. Aen. 5. 198.
  142. rapias. Casaubon compares Stat. Theb. 5. 3 'rapere campum.' So 'corripere campum, spatia,' etc. Virg. Aen. 5. 144 foll., 316.
  sollers. Watching her opportunity and knowing your weak side.
  143. seductum. 2. 4, 6. 42.
  'Quo deinde ruis?' Virg. Aen. 5. 741. deinde seems to have the force of *now* or *next*—after this; like τὸ ἔπειτα, 'the next time coming,' 'for the present,' Soph. Ant. 611.
  144. 'Quid vis, insane, et quas res agis?' Hor. 2 S. 6. 29.
  mascula, of superior strength, perhaps like κτύπος ἄρσην Soph. Phil. 1455.
  bilis, of madness, Hor. 2 S. 3. 141, 2 Ep. 2. 137.
  145. intumuit. 2. 14, 3. 8.
  The urna contained half an amphora.
  cicutae, hemlock used as a cure on account of its coldness ('*calido* sub pectore'). Persius probably imitated Hor. 2 Ep. 2. 53, quoted by Casaubon, 'Quae poterant unquam satis expurgare cicutae?'
  146. 'Non tangenda rates *transiliunt* vada' Hor. 1 Od. 3. 24.
  cannabis is 'hemp,' so that 'torta cannabis' will be a rope.
  fulto is illustrated by Jahn from Juv. 3. 82 '*Fultus*que toro meliore recumbet,'—'with a hempen rope for your couch.' Comp. Prop. 3. 7. 47–50.
  147. He is apparently to lie on deck, and eat off a bench.

exalet vapida laesum pice sessilis obba?
quid petis? ut nummos, quos hic quincunce modesto
nutrieras, pergant avidos sudare deunces?   150
indulge genio, carpamus dulcia! nostrum est
quod vivis; cinis et manes et fabula fies.
vive memor leti! fugit hora; hoc quod loquor inde est.'
en quid agis? duplici in diversum scinderis hamo.
huncine, an hunc sequeris? subeas alternus oportet   155
ancipiti obsequio dominos, alternus oberres.
nec tu, cum obstiteris semel instantique negaris
parere imperio, 'rupi iam vincula' dicas;
nam et luctata canis nodum abripit; et tamen illi,
cum fugit, a collo trahitur pars longa catenae.   160
  'Dave, cito, hoc credas iubeo, finire dolores

[148. *vapidi a. picem* C. *cessilis a.* 149. *nummis* C. 150. *peragant* C, *pergant a. avido* ς. *sua dare* C. *sudore* c et fortasse Schol. '*cum periculo* deunces praestet.' 153. *locor a.* 157. *nec tuum a, instantibusque* C. 159. *arrumpit at tamen* C. *ast tamen* ς.]

147. **Veientanum.** [A poor kind of wine: see Marquardt, Röm. Alterthümer 7. p. 436, who quotes Martial 2. 53. 4, 3. 49. 1 'Veientana mihi misces, ubi Massica potas.' 'Pessimum vinum in Veienti nascitur,' says Porphyrion on Hor. 2 S. 3. 143.] 'Qui *Veientanum* festis potare diebus Campana solitus trulla, vappamque profestis' Hor. l. c. 'Et *Veientani* bibitur faex crassa *rubelli*' Mart. 1. 103 (104) 9.

  rubellum, a diminutive epithet, given to vines, Pliny 14. 23 'reddish.'

148. **exalet**, as the liquor would offend the smell before the taste.

  pice. Casks and jars were pitched in order to preserve the wine—so that Persius may mean either that the wine has been spoilt and made vapid by the action of the pitch, or by the failure of the pitch, the epithet **vapida**, in either case, signifying the effect of the pitch on the wine.

  sessilis is used more than once by Pliny of things with broad bottoms, e. g. of pears, N. H. 15. 56.

  obba, an old word for a drinking-cup, used by Varro in Non. 146. 8 foll., 545. 2 foll., and enumerated by Gell. 16. 7 among the obsolete vulgarisms employed by Laberius.

149. 'What is your object?, to get a greedy eleven per cent. profit on your money, after having realised a moderate five per cent. here?'

  quincunce. Dict. Ant. 'fenus.'

150. **nutrieras**, of increasing money by interest. 'Nummos alienos pascet' Hor. 1 Ep. 18. 35.

  pergant, 'proceed,' not in the sense of continuing, but of doing a thing as the next step. ['Peragant avido sudore' Jahn (1868); 'peragant avidos sudore deunces' Bücheler.]

  sudare, expressing the labour necessary to produce the increased profit.

  deunces, cogn. acc. like 'sudabunt roscida mella' Virg. E. 4. 30.

151. **genio.** 2. 3 note, 4. 27 note.

  nostrum est quod vivis = 'nostra est tua vita'—'your life belongs to me and you ('nostrum' answering to 'carpamus') (not to any one else, such as Avarice), and it is all we have.'

152. 'Fabula fias' Hor. 1 Ep. 13. 9, 'Iam te premet nox *fabulaeque manes*' 1 Od. 4. 18. 'You will exist only in men's talk about you' Juv. 1. 145. The Stoics thought that the dead had only a *temporary* existence as shades ('*diu* mansuros aiunt animos, *semper* negant' Cic. Tusc. 1. 31, quoted by Delph. ed.),

SAT. V.

haling the fumes of reddish Veientan all flat and spoilt by the pitch? And what is your aim? that your money which you had been nursing here at a modest five per cent. should grow till it sweats out an exorbitant eleven? No; give your genius play; let us take pleasure as it comes; life is ours and all we have; you will soon become a little dust, a ghost, a topic of the day. Live with death in your mind; time flies; this say of mine is so much taken from it.' La, what are you to do; you have two hooks pulling you different ways—are you for following this or that? You must needs obey your masters by turns and shirk them by turns, by a division of duty. Nay, if you have managed to stand out once and refuse obedience to an imperious command, don't say, 'I have broken my prison for good and all.' Why, a dog may snap its chain with an effort, but as it runs away, it has a good length of iron trailing from its neck.

'Davus, now mind, I am speaking seriously, I think of putting

so that three stages may be intended. 'You will become first ashes, then a shade, then a name.' But in 6. 41 the dead man is said to be 'cinere ulterior' at the time when his ashes are put into the urn.

153. vive memor leti, from Hor. 2 S. 6. 97 'Vive memor quam sis aevi brevis,' 2 Ep. 1. 144 'Genium memorem brevis aevi.'

hoc quod loquor inde est. This very speech I am making now is so much taken off from it. [Seneca Ep. 65. 18 '*hoc quod vivit*' (this very life) 'stipendium putat.'] 'Dum loquimur fugerit invida Aetas' Hor. 1 Od. 11. 7.

154. en quid agis. 3. 5.

scinderis. 'Scinditur incertum studia in contraria vulgus' Virg. Aen. 2. 39.

hamo, metaphor, as in Hor. 1 Ep. 7. 74 'Occultum visus decurrere piscis ad hamum.'

155. subeas, like 'dominum vehet' Hor. 1 Ep. 10. 40.

alternus for 'alternos.' 'You must submit to each of your masters in turn, and desert each in turn.' [See on v. 131.]

156. oberres has no grammatical connexion with dominos, though alternus refers to it in sense. 'Oberro,' as a fugitive slave.

157. The Delph. ed. compares Hor. 2 S. 7. 70 foll. 'O totiens servus! quae

belua ruptis, Cum semel effugit, reddit se prava catenis?' ['Instanti imperio' perhaps from Horace's 'vultus instantis tyranni.']

159. Madvig Opusc. p. 491 foll. contends that 'attamen' can only mean 'at least.' [Jahn accordingly reads (1868) 'et tamen' here on the authority of a few MSS. In his edition of 1843 he read 'ac tamen' here and in 2. 48.]

160. The dog is impeded by the chain which it drags along with it (Jahn), and can be recaptured with less difficulty (König). ['*Laxam catenam trahit* nondum liber,' of a man half-free, Sen. Vit. Beat. 16. 3.]

161–175. 'Take the case of the lover in the play: he talks about giving up his passion, as discreditable to a man with respectable connexions. The slave applauds his resolution, but finding him hark back immediately, tells him that all this is mere trifling, playing fast and loose, and that nothing will do but a determination not to re-enter the place which one has once left heart-whole. Here we have real freedom at last, far better than what the praetor confers.'

161. An imitation of the opening scene in the *Eunuch* of Menander, which Terence has translated, substituting the names Phaedria and Parmeno for Chaerestratus and Davus. Supposing Terence's to be a close translation, Persius' imitation is sufficiently

praeteritos meditor:' crudum Chaerestratus unguem
abrodens ait haec. 'An siccis dedecus obstem
cognatis? an rem patriam rumore sinistro
limen ad obscenum frangam, dum Chrysidis udas   165
ebrius ante fores exstincta cum face canto?'
'Euge, puer, sapias, dis depellentibus agnam
percute.' 'Sed censen plorabit, Dave, relicta?'
'Nugaris; solea, puer, obiurgabere rubra.
ne trepidare velis atque artos rodere casses!   170
nunc ferus et violens; at si vocet, haud mora, dicas,
*Quidnam igitur faciam? nec nunc, cum accersor et ultro
supplicet, accedam?* Si totus et integer illinc

[163. *atrodens* a.   167. *dispellentibus* a.   168. *censem* a.   170. *radere*
        cassas c.   171. *voce et* C.   172. *accessor* a, *arcessat* C.]

free. Horace, on the other hand (2 S. 3. 259 foll.), follows Terence exactly, though omitting several lines. [Similarly Epictetus 4. 1. 19 quotes from Menander the case of Thrasonides: παιδισκάριόν με, φησί, καταδεδούλωκεν Εὐτελίς, ὃν οὐδεὶς τῶν πολεμίων πώποτε.]

161. **finire dolores praeteritos meditor** is from Hor. l. c. 'an potius mediter finire labores?'

162. **crudum** properly means 'bleeding' ('cruor,' 'cruidus'). Freund. Here then it is to be connected with 'abrodens.'

163. **abrodens**, 'gnawing away.'
siccis, opp. to 'ebriis.' '*Siccis* omnia nam dura Deus proposuit' Hor. 1 Od. 18. 3. 'Forum puteaique Libonis Mandabo *siccis*' 1 Ep. 19. 8, 9.
obstem seems to be used in its primary sense of standing before.

164. **rumore sinistro**, like 'sinistri sermones' Tac. Ann. 1. 74, 'sinistra fama' *ib.* 6. 32, etc.

165. **limen**, because the lover was shut out. Hor. 1 Od. 25, etc. Persius may have been thinking of Hor. Epod. 11. 22 '*Limina* dura quibus Lumbos et *infregi* latus'.
rem ... frangam. Hor. 2 S. 3. 18 'omnis *res mea* ... fracta est.' 'Rem patris oblimare' 1 S. 2. 62. The language is taken, not from Terence, but from other writers, if not from common life.

Chrysis is the Thais of Terence.
udas, variously explained wet with ointment ('postes superbos Unguit amaracino' Lucr. 4. 1179), with wine ('uda ... Lyaeo tempora' Hor. 1 Od. 7. 22), or with tears ('Uda sit ut lacrimis ianua facta meis' Ov. 1 Am. 6. 18, 'Limina ... lacrimis umida supplicibus' Prop. 1. 16. 4): it might also mean wet with rain ('Non hoc semper erit liminis aut *aquae Caelestis* patiens latus' Hor. 3 Od. 10. 19).

166. Hor. 1 S. 4. 51 '*Ebrius*, et, magnum quod dedecus, ambulet ante Noctem *cum facibus*.'
exstincta, probably from his drunken carelessness, if not from the rain.
canto, referring to the παρακλαυσίθυρον or serenade, such as we have in Hor. 1 Od. 25. 7.

167. Davus encourages his master—hence **puer** instead of Terence and Horace's 'ere.'
sapias; 'sapias, vina liques' Hor. 1 Od. 11. 6, quoted by Jahn.
depellentibus. So 'depulsor' is found in inscriptions as an epithet of Jupiter. Grut. 30. 3 (Jahn). [Compare no. 2414 in vol. ii. of the Berlin Corpus Inscriptionum.] The more common word is 'averruncus.' In Greek ἀποτρόπαιος, ἀπωσίκακος, or ἀλεξίκακος.

168. **percutere**, like 'ferire,' a sacrificial term. '*Percussi* viscera

an end to this trouble that has been weighing on me:' so says Chaerestratus as he bites his nail to the quick. 'Monstrous, that I should be an open scandal to my sober relatives, and bring my patrimony to a smash, while I sing drunken songs at Chrysis' dripping door with my light out.' 'Bravo, young gentleman, show your sense; kill a lamb to the powers that preserve us.' 'But do you think she'll cry, Davus, when I've left her?' 'Now you're trifling. She'll be boxing your ears with her red slipper, my boy. No, no; don't go and be restiff at one moment and gnawing at the net that keeps you tight, all fury and violence; and then, if she gives you a call, say at once, *What am I to do? not to go to her even when I am sent for and she goes out of her way to beg me!* If you have got away whole, and left nothing behind you,

tauri' Ov. F. 1. 347. So 'percutere foedus' occurs as well as 'icere' or 'ferire foedus.'

169. **nugaris**, dallying where action is required, like 'cessas *nugator*' above, v. 127.

solea, referring to the story of Hercules and Omphale, also alluded to Ter. Eun. 1027. The Greeks have a verb for the process, βλαυτόω.

obiurgare, a word used for correction. 'Obiurgare verberibus' Sen. De Ira 3. 12; ['colaphis' Petronius 34: 'femur et latus interdum obiurgare' Quint. 10. 3. 21.] 'flagris obiurgaretur' Suet. Oth. 2. In Ter. Eun. 67 foll. Parmeno says, 'Haec verba una [*illa una* Wagner] me hercle falsa lacrimula ... Restinguet, et te ultro accusabis, et ei dabis Ultro supplicium.'

170. **trepidare**, of beasts who will not submit. Casaubon. Compare Prop. 2. 4. 5 'Primo iuvenes *trepidant* in amore feroces, Dehinc domiti post haec aequa et iniqua ferunt.' So πείθεσθαι seems to be used of a beast in a net, Aesch. Ag. 1049, though it would more naturally apply to one submitting to the yoke.

rodere casses. Compare the fable of the Lion and the Mouse. The line must be taken in close connexion with the next, as Davus does not tell his master not to struggle, but not to struggle at one time and give way at another.

171. Jahn makes Davus' speech end with **dicas**, so that Chaerestratus is supposed to say **haud mora**, 'anon,' or 'coming directly;' but 'cum accersor' evidently refers to **si vocet**. In Terence, the lover has received a summons before the scene begins, and he deliberates whether to obey it. In Persius he is trying to resolve under the pressure of disappointment, and even then cannot make up his mind; so that his servant tells him that if he *should* be summoned back, he is pretty sure to entertain the question seriously. Thus 'igitur' has the same force as in the corresponding line in Terence: 'Quid igitur faciam? non eam ne nunc quidem, Cum arcessor ultro?' whereas, according to Jahn's punctuation, it would have none.

haud mora then means, you would instantly say, 'What am I to do *now?*'

172. **nec nunc**, apparently for 'ne nunc quidem,' as in Hor. 2 S. 3. 259 foll., and twice in Petronius—perhaps, as Jahn thinks, a colloquialism.

Jahn reads **arcessat** ['accersat' Bücheler] to agree with 'supplicet.' He appears right in his reasoning that either the ind. or subj. would be admissible in this construction, the one actually occurring in the parallel passage from Terence, the other in that from Horace. [MS. authority is divided between 'accessor' and 'arcersat.' For the difference between 'accerso' and 'arcesso' see H. Nettleship, Contributions to Latin Lexicography, s. v. 'Arcesso.']

173. **totus**, without leaving any part of you behind.

integer has the same sense. So Hor. 2 Od. 17. 5 'A te meae si partem

exieras, ne nunc.' hic hic, quod quaerimus, hic est,
non in festuca, lictor quam iactat ineptus.   175
'Ius habet ille sui palpo, quem ducit hiantem
cretata Ambitio? vigila, et cicer ingere large
rixanti populo, nostra ut Floralia possint
aprici meminisse senes. quid pulchrius? at cum
Herodis venere dies, unctaque fenestra   180
dispositae pinguem nebulam vomuere lucernae

[174. *nunc nunc* a, *ne nunc* C.   *quem* ς.   175. *quem* a.   176. *que* a.
ducit a, *tollit* C.   178. *ponsint* a.   179. *tum* a.]

animae rapit Maturior vis, quid moror altera, Nec carus aeque, nec superstes *Integer?*'
174. **hic** is an adverb, not a pronoun, as 'in festuca' shows. 'Quod petis, hic est' Hor. 1 Ep. 11. 29, 'Hic est aut nusquam, quod quaerimus' *ib.* 17. 39.
175. **festuca**, generally explained as a synonym for 'vindicta' here and in Plaut. Mil. 961 (quoted by Delph. ed.) 'quid? ean ingenua an festuca iacta serva a libera est?' The Scholia have 'non *in ea virga* qua a lictore percutitur.' Jahn refers to [Gloss. Lat. Gr. 71. 45 G] '*Festuca, κάρφος, ῥάβδος.*' On the other hand, Plutarch, De S. N. Vind. p. 550, says that one of the lictors threw *stubble* on the manumitted slave, which would accord sufficiently well with the ordinary use of 'festuca,' as in Varro L. L. 5. 31. 38 'qui homo in pratis per faenisecta *festucas* corradit.' 'Vis festucaria' occurs in Gel. 20. 10. 10. At any rate the word appears to be technical, not used rhetorically in a contemptuous sense. Casaubon says that 'exfestucare' occurs in the laws of the Alemanni and Saxons, and elsewhere in mediaeval Latinity.
'No symbol was of such universal application among ancient nations as the "stipula," the "festuca," the "culm," the "hawm." Thrice was the hawm to be cast when the Teuton bequeathed his land to the stranger in blood. Thrice was the hawm to be flung down before the sovereign when the lieges refused their assent to the doom; and once was the hawm to be cast up in the air before that Senior whom his lieges rejected and spurned away. To this usage, therefore, the sternly indignant Frankish Proceres resorted, proclaiming that they cast off their faith, and with one act in the open field—the field of council—did they cast the hawm—they no longer Charles's lieges—Charles no longer their Senior or King.' (Palgrave, Hist. of Normandy and England, vol. 2.)
ineptus, because the ceremony does not convey real freedom.
176-188. 'Is freedom compatible with the vanity of the political aspirant, who courts the mob and desires to be remembered for the splendour of his official shows? Or take the superstitious man, who observes Jewish ceremonies and seeks to propitiate the wrath of Isis—*his* bondage speaks for itself.' The instances are rather awkwardly introduced, as we might have expected that Persius, having at last found real freedom, would dwell upon it, rather than speak of other kinds of slavery. But there is spirit in the abruptness, which, at any rate, avoids the faults of formality and sameness.
176. **palpo**, 1. 112, equivalent to 'ambitor.'
ducit hiantem, imitated from Hor. 1 S. 2. 88 'emptorem inducat hiantem,' and perhaps from Virg. G. 2. 508 foll. 'hunc plausus hiantem . . . Corripuit,' where 'hiantem' = 'avidum.' The man follows with his mouth open, expecting to receive something. The sense of the passage appears to be, 'Is the political aspirant free? if so, take all the necessary steps to gratify your ambition—these being described in such a manner as to show that they are really the badges of servitude. Persius is probably imitating the way in which Horace (1 Ep. 6) puts the question round about the true end of life (e.g.

SAT. V.

not even then.' Here, here is the man we're looking for. No connexion with the straw which the stupid lictor tosses about.

'But perhaps the maker of smooth speeches, whom the whitewashed goddess of canvassing carries along with his mouth always open, is master of himself? Oh, then, be astir early and late; overwhelm the squabbling populace with showers of vetches, that the old gentlemen of the next generation, as they prose in the sun, may have stories to tell of our feast of Flowers. Can anything be finer? But when Herod's day is come, and the lamps arranged in the greasy windows with violets to support send up their unctuous

vv. 31 foll.) 'Virtutem verba putas, ut Lucum ligna: cave ne portus occupet alter:' compare also vv. 56 foll.

177. **cretata** = 'candidata:' the gown being rubbed with chalk to make it whiter. See Isidore Or. 19. 24. 6.

Ambitio, 'the goddess of canvassing,' not to be rendered *ambition*, though elsewhere the Latin word is nearly equivalent to the English.

vigila seems to be like 'lucet, eamus' Hor. 1 Ep. 6. 56. 'Be on the move early and late,' the requirements of a canvass being apparently as exacting as those of dependence on the great and wealthy. Juv. 3. 127 foll., 5. 19 foll.

cicer. 'In cicere atque faba bona tu perdasque lupinis' Hor. 2 S. 3. 182. A plebeian article of food. Hor. A. P. 249 'fricti ciceris... et nucis emptor.' Tickets for shows, money, etc. used to be scrambled for. Mart. 8. 78, Suet. Dom. 4.

178. **rixanti**,'squabbling for a thing,' 'multo cum sanguine saepe *Rixantes*' Lucr. 6. 1286, of those who struggled for funeral piles during the plague.

nostra, like 'eamus' Hor. 1 Ep. 6. 56, the poet identifying himself with the person addressed 'celebrated in our aedileship.'

Floralia [see Marquardt, Röm. Alterthümer 6. p. 481. The festival of Flora was kept from April 28 to May 3. The immoralities of the Floralia are the subject of complaint on the part of philosophers and Christians; see Lactant. Inst. 1. 20. 10, and Seneca Ep. 97. 7, quoted by Marquardt *ib.* p. 364 note.]

179. **aprici** = 'apricantes,' like 'apricis mergis' Virg. Aen. 5. 128. The old men delight in basking, like the old women, 4. 18, 19.

at. Jahn supposes the meaning to be that the successful political aspirant, apparently free, is really a slave to superstition; but it is evident that Persius means to mark two kinds of slavery, not one only. Whether he intends that the same person is a slave in several respects is not clear: the second person is used here, as in various other places in the Satire, but we need only suppose that he means to touch his auditor's conscience in one part, if he fails to do so in others. So the end of Satires 3 and 4. At the same time there is nothing incongruous in representing men of worldly eminence as slaves to superstition. Horace, in his various mentions of Judaism, evidently implies that it was spreading, talked of among the higher orders, if not favoured by them. The account in the latter part of Juv. Sat. 6 looks the same way. [Comp. an often-quoted fragment of Seneca ap. Augustin. Civ. D. 6. 11 'Cum interim usque eo sceleratissimae gentis' (Indaeorum) 'consuetudo convaluit, ut per omnes iam terra recepta sit: victi victoribus leges dederunt.' A case of the conversion of a noble Roman lady to Judaism in the reign of Tiberius is mentioned by Josephus Ant. 18. 3 (4).]

180. **Herodis... dies** seems to be Herod's birthday, which would naturally be celebrated by the Herodians.

fenestra. Lights were set up on doors and windows at festivals. Juv. 12. 91 foll., and Mayor's note. Jahn refers to Jos. Ant. 12. 11, Sen. Ep. 95, compared by Casaubon, to show that it was a Jewish custom. Comp. Tertull. Apol. 35 'cur die laeto non... lucernis diem infringimus?'

181. **pinguem nebulam vomuere**

portantes violas, rubrumque amplexa catinum
cauda natat thynni, tumet alba. fidelia vino:
labra moves tacitus recutitaque sabbata palles
tum nigri lemures ovoque pericula rupto,   185
tum grandes galli et cum sistro lusca sacerdos
incussere deos inflantis corpora, si non
praedictum ter mane caput gustaveris alli.'
    Dixeris haec inter varicosos centuriones,
continuo crassum ridet Pulfennius ingens,   190
et centum Graecos curto centusse licetur.

[183. *nat a.* *tymni* C. 184. *recutit atque* C. 185. *periculo a.* 186. *hinc grandes* C. *luscra* a. 188. *alit* C. 190. *fulfenius* a, *pulfenius* C. 191. *cureo a. ligetur a.*]

is illustrated by Tertull. l. c. ' clarissimis lucernis vestibula *nebulabant*' (where however another reading is 'enubilabant,' which would agree better with 'clarissimis'), Sen. l. c. 'nec lumine di egent et ne homines quidem delectantur *fuligine*.'

  182. violas, another mark of rejoicing. Juv. 12. 90 ' omnes violae iactabo colores.'

  amplexa catinum, 'coiled round the dish,' indicating the size of the tunny's tail. ' Angustoque vagos pisces urgere catino' Hor. 2 S. 4. 77.

  183. The tunny was frequently used in sacrifices, being eaten at the temple, according to the Scholia, which however may only be reasoning from the present passage. The tail of the tunny is large. Persius probably refers to the whole fish, not to the tail merely.

  natat seems to be like 'vagos' in Hor. l. c., referring to the nature of the fish in its native element, so that there is a contrast between 'amplexa' and 'natat,' as between 'vagos' and 'angusto urgere.' Compare Ov. A. A. 1. 516 ' Nec *vagus* in laxa pes tibi pelle *natet*.'

  tumet, probably referring to the bulging shape of the jar, which seemed to expand with the wine. The expressions in this and the preceding lines appear to be intentionally contemptuous; but Persius is apt to paint rather coarsely, even where he does not mean to ridicule.

  184. ' Labra movet, metuens audiri ' Hor. 1 Ep. 16. 60, of muttered prayer.

  sabbata palles. ' Metuentem sabbata patrem' Juv. 14. 96, and Mayor's note. Persius seems to mix up feasts and fasts rather strangely, apparently with the notion that all the Jewish observances were gloomy.

  palles, as in Hor. 3 Od. 27. 28.

  185. Having begun to speak of superstition, Persius proceeds to enumerate other kinds.

  tum, 'next,' as if the same person indulged each kind in order. Note on v. 179.

  nigri, not strictly equivalent to ' nocturni,' though the association of night with images of terror doubtless gives occasion to the conception.

  lemures. Hor. 2 Ep. 2. 208 ' Somnia, terrores magicos, miracula, sagas, *Nocturnos lemures*, portentaque Thessala rides ?'

  lemures and pericula are apparently constructed with ' incussere,' though in that case we must suppose a zeugma.

  ovo pericula rupto. The Scholia say priests used to put eggs on the fire and observe whether the moisture came out from the side or the top, the bursting of the egg being considered a very dangerous sign. This observation was called ὠοσκοπική. Jahn.

  186. Two kinds of superstition—the old one of Cybele and the latter one of Isis imported from Egypt.

  grandes galli, like Juvenal's ' in-

SAT. V.

clouds, and a tunny's tail expatiates in a curled state round a red dish, and the white jar is bulging with wine, you move your lips in silence and turn pale at the circumcised sabbath. Then there are black hobgoblins and the perils of the broken eggshell; there are the big orders of Cybele, and the one-eyed priestess with her timbrel, hammering into you gods who make your body swell all over, unless you have taken the prescribed morning dose, three mouthfuls of a head of garlic.'

Talk in this way among the military gentlemen with the large calves, that great overgrown Pulfennius breaks into a horse-laugh in your face, and offers a clipped hundred-as piece for a lot of a hundred Greeks.

gens Semivir' (6. 512). Compare also the following lines, where he speaks of the worshippers of Isis.

sistro. 'Isis et irato feriat mea lumina sistro' Juv. 13. 93, Mayor's note, where Ov. ex Ponto 1. 1. 51 foll. is quoted to show that blindness was a special visitation from Isis. Hence the priestess is supposed to be called lusca, as having herself felt the wrath of the goddess. Visconti (Mus. Pio. Cl. 5. p. 60 foll.) ap. Jahn speaks of two seals which represent Egyptian priests as one-eyed.

187. 'Incutere metum, terrorem, formidinem, religionem,' are all found. See Freund. Persius, as is his wont, strengthens the expression. Compare Virg. Aen. 5. 679 'excussaque pectore Iuno est;' *ib.* 6. 78 'magnum si pectore possit Excussisse deum.'

inflantis, seemingly of the swelling of the whole body by disease, as in 2. 14, 3. 95, rather than of ulcers. The present participle seems to express the habit, so that 'inflantis si non gustaveris' = 'qui inflabunt si non gustaveris.'

188. praedictum, 'prescribed.' 'Praedictaque dona ferebat' Stat. Achill. 2. 145.

caput ... alli. Col. 6. 34. 1. So 'caput porri, ulpici.' The custom appears to be mentioned nowhere else.

189-191. 'Talk in this way to the soldiers, and they will set you down as a fool.' So much is clear, that Persius wishes to give a parting kick to his old enemies the soldiers; but whether he speaks indignantly, 'And yet all this precious truth is laughed down,' or defiantly, 'All this is true, though, or even because the soldiers laugh at it,' is not easy to see.

189. See 3. 77 note.

varicosos. 'Varicosus fiet haruspex' Juv. 6. 397, from being always on his legs. So here the soldiers, from being always on the move. 'Grandes magna ad subsellia surae' Juv. 16. 14, of the military. Compare *id.* 24, 3. 248. [Fronto ad Verum 1 'scilicet hoc te a centurionibus vel primipilaribus, elegantissimis altercatoribus, didicisse !']

190. crassum ridet, like 'subrisit molle' 3. 110. Horace's 'dulce ridere,' 'ridere decorum.'

ridet, as in 3. 89.

[Pulfennius, not 'Fulfennius' (see critical note) is the right form. C. I. L. 5. 7814. 'L. Polfennius Cerdo;' 'Pulfennius' C. I. L. 10. 4864, 4873, 4985 ; 9. 3354. A name 'Pulfatius' is found in an inscription at Ostia, C. I. L. 14. 1519.]

ingens, like 'torosa iuventus' 3. 89, 'caloni alto' v. 95.

191. Compare 3. 79.

Graecos, like 'doctores Graios' 6. 38, contemptuously, philosophy being hated not only for its own sake but as a foreign importation.

curto, he will not even bid a whole centussis, but only a clipped coin. [' Tanquam nonaginta novem,' Schol.] The abl. of price. Compare Plaut. Capt. 274 'Eugepae ! Thalem talento non emam Milesium.' [Varro περὶ ἐδεσμάτων ap. Gell. 15. 19. 2 'nunc illum (panem) qui norunt volunt emere milibus centum, te qui novit nemo centussis.']

SATURA VI.

ADMOVIT iam bruma foco te, Basse, Sabino?
iamne lyra et tetrico vivunt tibi pectine chordae?
mire opifex numeris veterum primordia vocum
atque marem strepitum fidis intendisse Latinae,
mox iuvenes agitare iocos et pollice honesto 5
egregius lusisse senex. mihi nunc Ligus ora
intepet hibernatque meum mare, qua latus ingens

[2. *neclyra* a. *tricae* C.   5. *tum iuvenes* Servius Aen. 1. 306.   6. *iussisse* a. *senes* ς. *ligusyora* a.   7. *hibetnatque* a, *hiberna que* C.]

A vindication of his right to spend his income in moderate enjoyment. To Caesius Bassus, mentioned in Persius' life as one of his intimate friends, deputed (by Cornutus) to edit his Satires after his death—classed with Horace as a lyric poet by Quintilian (10. 1. 96), who however thinks him inferior to some of his contemporaries; killed, according to the Scholia, in the famous eruption of Vesuvius—probably the same with the author of a treatise on Metres, which is referred to by Maximus Victorinus, Terentianus Maurus, Diomedes, and Rufinus, and still exists in an interpolated epitome—but different from Gavius Bassus, who wrote works on the origin and signification of words, and on the gods. Jahn.

[The text of this Satire might be taken from the words of Seneca, Ep. 5. 3, 4: 'hoc primum philosophia promittit, sensum communem, humanitatem et congregationem': 'frugalitatem exigit philosophia, non poenam.']

1–11. 'Are you wintering in your Sabine retreat and writing verses there? I am living in my retirement on the Ligurian coast, at Ennius' favourite port of Luna.'

1. Compare Hor. 1 Ep. 7. 10 'Quod si bruma nives Albanis illinet agris, Ad mare descendet vates tuus,' etc., also 2 S. 3. 5 foll.

bruma = 'the depth of winter.'

foco... Sabino, as Jahn thinks, suggests the notion of primitive life (Virg. G. 2. 532, etc.) which would be in keeping with what follows about Bassus' tastes.

2. tetrico. 'Tetrica ac tristis disciplina Sabinorum' Livy 1. 18.

vivunt here = 'vigent,' with which it is sometimes coupled.

3. mire, adv. or adj., if the latter, compare Hor. 2 S. 4. 7 'Sive est naturae hoc sive artis, *mirus* utroque.'

opifex... intendisse, Epil. 11.

primordia vocum, from Lucr. 4. 531, where it signifies the beginnings of articulate sound. Here it is apparently to be explained by 'tetrico pectine' and 'marem strepitum,' of the simple and manly versification of antiquity, which Bassus doubtless affected. Persius probably thought of Virg. Aen. 6. 646 'Obloquitur *numeris* septem discrimina *vocum.*'

numeris... intendisse. With reference to the stringing of the lyre, Virg. Aen. 9. 776, speaks of stringing the numbers on the chords; and Persius

SATIRE VI.

Has winter made you move yet to your Sabine fireside, dear Bassus? are your lyre and its strings and the austere quill that runs over them yet in force? Marvellous artist as you are at setting to music the primitive antiquities of our language, the manly utterance of the Latian harp, and then showing yourself excellent in your old age at wakening young loves and frolicking over the chords with a virtuous touch. As for me, the Ligurian coast is giving me the benefit of its warmth, and the sea is wintering just

goes further, and talks of stringing sounds on the numbers.

vocum [, which properly means 'notes,'] may denote archaism of language as well as of metre; but there appears not the slightest reason to suppose with Jahn that Bassus actually wrote a poem on the subject of language.

4. **marem strepitum**: like 'mares animos' Hor. A. P. 402.

fidis ... Latinae, like Horace's boast, 4 Od. 3. 23, 1 Ep. 19. 33; compare also 1 Ep. 3. 12. 'Our national lyre,' except that Persius probably lays a further stress on 'Latinae,' and means that Bassus kept up the ancient national character of Roman poetry, as opposed to later refinements.

5. **iuvenes ... iocos**, like 'marem strepitum.'

agitare iocos, in Ov. M. 3. 319 = 'iocari.' Here it seems to mean rather more—'to busy one's self with young love,' as a writer, not as an actor. 'Agitare' follows the sense of 'agere.'

iocus in the favourite Horatian sense of love, so that 'iuvenes agitare iocos' is nearly = 'iuvenum curas referre' Hor. A. P. 82, a natural subject of lyric poetry.

honesto seems rightly explained by Jahn as emphatic, the tones of Bassus' love-lyrics suiting not only the lightness of youth but the gravity of old age.

6. **egregius** is the reading of a few of the best MSS., approved by Bentley on Hor. 1 Od. 1. 5.

lusisse, like 'iocos,' with a reference to love (Hor. 2 Ep. 2. 214), as well as to composition (Virg. E. 1. 10). A poet is said to do the deed he writes about, Virg. E. 9. 19: [comp. Thuc. 1. 5 οἱ παλαιοὶ τῶν ποιητῶν τὰς πύστεις τῶν καταπλεόντων ... ἐρωτῶντες.]

mihi. The Scholia say that Persius' mother married a second time in Liguria, so he would naturally reside there. [Ernst Curtius, 'De Auli Persii Flacci Patria,' one of the papers in the 'Satura Philologica' published in honour of H. Sauppe, thinks it probable that the whole district between the promontory of Volaterrae or Populonia and the harbour of Luna was subject to Volaterrae; and that Persius was therefore still within the precincts of his native town.]

Ligus ora, like 'femina Ligus' Tac. Hist. 2. 13.

7. 'Et lacus aestivis *intepet* Umber aquis' Prop. 4. 1. 124. 'Est ubi plus *tepeant hiemes*' Hor. 1 Ep. 10. 15. 'Tepidas brumas' 2 Od. 6. 17.

hibernat, like Horace's 'hiemat' (2 S. 2. 17), where however *sharp* wintry weather is meant. [The expression 'aquis hiemantibus' is remarked upon by Sen. Ep. 114. 19 as used by Sallust.]

meum, not merely 'my residence,' but 'suiting me,' 'kind to me.'

dant scopuli et multa litus se valle receptat.
'Lunai portum, est operae, cognoscite, cives!'
cor iubet hoc Enni, postquam destertuit esse   10
Maeonides Quintus pavone ex Pythagoreo.

Hic ego securus vulgi et quid praeparet auster
infelix pecori, securus et angulus ille
vicini nostro quia pinguior, etsi adeo omnes
ditescant orti peioribus, usque recusem   15
curvus ob id minui senio aut cenare sine uncto,
et signum in vapida naso tetigisse lagoena.
discrepet his alius! geminos, horoscope, varo
producis genio. solis natalibus est qui

[9. *luni* a. *praetum* C. *cognoscere* C.   11. *pavonem* a C.   *quinto pavone ex Pythagoreo* Charis. p. 98 Keil.   15. *horti* a C.   16. *obit* a C.   *unto* a.   18. *varro* a.   19. *ingenio* C.   *es qui* C.]

8. dant...latus, as in Virg. Aen. 1. 105 = 'obiciunt latus,' the sea being sheltered by the rocks forming the port.
valle for 'sinu,' as if the scene were inland. Abl. of manner.
se...receptat, as in Virg. G. 1. 336, the freq. here perhaps marking the numerous bends. Jahn.
9. A line from Ennius, Ann. 16. (Vahlen.)
est operae, parenthetical, like 'fas est' v. 25, 'venit Hesperus' Virg. E. 10. 77.
opera, for opportunity or working time, especially in the gen., which seems to be partitive. 'Operae mi ubi erit, ad te venero' Plaut. Truc. 883.
cognoscite, not 'cognoscere,' is the reading of the best MSS. 'Cognoscere,' of listening to a narrative, as [often in Cicero, and] in Juv. 3. 288.
cives (as Jahn says) is a mark of the simple gravity of the old man. So his epitaph, 'Adspicite, O cives, senis Enni imaginis formam.'
10. cor. Ennius used to say that he had *three hearts*, because he understood Greek, Latin, and Oscan. Gell. 17. 17. 1, referred to by Plautius. The heart was often spoken of as the seat of the understanding: comp. Cic. Tusc. 1. 9, where Ennius is quoted as using 'cordatus' for *wise*. 'Curis acuens mortalia corda' Virg. G. 1. 123.

cor...Enni, periph., like 'virtus Scipiadae' Hor. 2 S. 1. 72.
destertuit, found elsewhere? For Ennius' dreams, compare on Epil. 2 foll.
11. From Cic. Ac. pr. 2. 16 and Lucr. 1. 120 foll., it would appear that Ennius did not pretend to have been changed into Homer, but only to have seen him in a vision. Britannicus however, on Epil. 3 and here, refers to Porphyrio for the statement that Ennius said at the beginning of his Annals that Homer's spirit had passed into him in sleep. Homer's revelations however turned on the doctrine of metempsychosis, he having been a peacock in one stage of the process (note on Epil. 2), and so Persius represents Ennius as having been himself Homer and peacock, just as in Epil. 3 he uses the word 'memini,' as if it were Ennius' word about his own recollection, when it was really used of Homer's. Thus in Hor. 2 S. 5. 41 Furius is confounded with his own Jupiter.
Quintus is explained by the Scholia as if it were a numeral—the stages being a peacock, Euphorbus, Homer, Pythagoras, Ennius. Persius might very well have intended a pun; but then we should rather have had 'a' than 'ex,' as in 'alter ab illo,' 'a Iove tertius Aiax,' even if this gradation of transformations

SAT. VI.

as I like it to do, where the sides of the cliffs present a vast barrier, and the shore retires into a deep bay. 'Acquaint yourselves with the haven of Luna, now's your time, good people all!' so says Ennius' brain, when he had been roused from dreaming himself Maeonides Quintus developed out of Pythagoras' peacock.

While I live here, without a care for the vulgar or for what mischief the south wind may be brewing for the cattle, without a care either because that nook of my neighbour's is better land than mine, even if all my inferiors in birth should grow rich over my head, I would stick to my resolution, seeing no reason why *I* should lose my height and my bulk with premature old age, or dine without something savoury, or poke my nose into the seal of a bottle of flat wine. Another man may take a different view; aye, good horoscope, you sometimes give birth to twins whose star is strangely different. You will find a man who on his birthday, of all days in

were established. Should Quintus be taken with Maeonides, as if it were a double name, Ennius and Homer in one, Homer with a Roman praenomen? The names were sometimes reversed in poetry, and Homer's would naturally take the precedence. 'Quintus fiam e Sosia' Plaut. Amph. 305.

12-24. 'Here I live, undisturbed by thoughts of public opinion, a bad season, or the success of my neighbours. Let who will grow rich, why should I stint myself? Men have different passions, one for spending, one for sparing: I will enjoy myself without running into either extreme.'

12. **securus**, with gen., Virg. Aen. 1. 350.

quid, etc. 'Quid cogitet umidus Auster' Virg. G. 1. 462. For the double construction, see 3. 51.

13. 'Arboribusque satisque Notus pecorique sinister' Virg. G. 1. 444; 'nocentem Corporibus . . . Austrum' Hor. 2 Od. 14. 15, 'plumbeus Auster' 2 S. 6. 18.

infelix, with dat., Virg. G. 2. 239.

securus put before et for the sake of emphasis. 'Aeneas ignarus abest . . . *ignarus et* absit' Virg. Aen. 10. 85.

angulus. 'O si *angulus ille* Proximus accedat' Hor. 2 S. 6. 8. '*ille* terrarum mihi praeter omnes *Angulus* ridet' 2 Od. 6. 13.

14. **adeo**, emphatic. 'Though not only one man of inferior extraction but *all* should grow rich.

15. Hor. l. c.

16. **minui**, 'to shrink or lose flesh.'

senio. 1. 26. 'Amore *senescit* habendi' Hor. 1 Ep. 7. 85.

unctum, 'a dainty,' as in Hor. 1 Ep. 17. 12, A. P. 422 (compare 1 Ep. 15. 44 'ubi quid melius contingit et *unctius* ').

17. 'Signo laeso non insanire lagoenae' Hor. 2 Ep. 2. 134.

naso tetigisse. Scrutinizing the state of the seal so closely that he can touch it with his nose, and so learn by the smell that it is good for nothing. A condensed picture, 'more Persii.'

18. 'Another man may differ from these tastes of mine if he likes—indeed twin brothers do not always think alike.'

geminos; sentiment from Hor. 2 Ep. 2. 183 foll.

horoscope, Manil. 3. 190, 200.

varo ... genio may either be a genius with two aspects, the same genius presiding over both, or a genius differing from the genius of the other, just as 'varus' in its literal sense is an epithet both of a bowlegged man and of the legs themselves.

19. **producis**, of birth. 'Ego is sum qui te produxi pater' Plaut. Rud. 1173; 'cum *geminos produceret* Arria natos' Prop. 4. 1. 89. Elsewhere of education,

tinguat holus siccum muria vafer in calice empta, 20
ipse sacrum inrorans patinae piper; hic bona dente
grandia magnanimus peragit puer. utar ego, utar,
nec rhombos ideo libertis ponere lautus,
nec tenuis sollers turdarum nosse salivas.
Messe tenus propria vive et granaria, fas est, 25
emole; quid metuis? occa, et seges altera in herba est.
'Ast vocat officium: trabe rupta Bruttia saxa
prendit amicus inops, remque omnem surdaque vota
condidit Ionio; iacet ipse in litore et una
ingentes de puppe dei, iamque obvia mergis 30
costa ratis lacerae.' nunc et de caespite vivo

[23. *scombros* a. *lautis* a.   24. *turdorum* a, *turdarum* C, testantur Pompeius Commentum p. 161 Keil, Sergius in Donatum p. 494 Keil.   26. *emule* a. *metuis* a, *metuas* C.   27. *avocat* vel *advocat officium* C, correxit idem.   29. *iovio* a.   30. *deliamque* C. *mergit* A.]

'Et laevo monitu pueros producit avaros' Juv. 14. 228.
19. **natalibus**, 1. 16 note, 2. 1 foll. Hor. 2 S. 2. 60, which Persius has in view.
solis, unlike Horace's Avidienus, he keeps no other feast.
20. **tinguat**, not expressive of meanness, but simply opp. to **siccum**, which is itself opp. to 'unctum' v. 16.
muria was an ingredient in sauce ('ius') along with oil (Hor. 2 S. 4. 65), so that the miser may have used it as a substitute for oil, which was the ordinary accompaniment; v. 68, Hor. 2 S. 2. 58, 3. 125.
vafer, of the low cunning of parsimony.
empta, with 'muria.' It was bought in a cup for the occasion, not kept in a jar in the storeroom.
21. **ipse**, emphatic, as in Hor. 2. S. 2. 61.
sacrum. Hor. 1 S. 1. 71, 2 S. 3. 110; perhaps referring, as Jahn thinks, to such expressions as Homer's ἇλς θεῖος: the language of early religion.
inrorans, like 'instillat' Hor. 2 S. 2. 62.
22. Imitated from Hor. 1 Ep. 15. 27 'rebus maternis atque paternis *Fortiter absumptis*.' Compare also Ov. M. 8.

847 'demisso in viscera censu,' which Juv. 11. 40 has copied.
magnanimus, like 'fortiter,' as if the undertaking were a great one, referring also to the spirit of generosity or μεγαλοψυχία, on which the spendthrift would pride himself.
peragit answers to our 'gets through.'
puer, 'while yet a youth.' Gifford notices the rapidity of the metre: contrast it with the slowness of v. 20.
utar. Hor. 2 Ep. 2. 190 '*Utar*, et ex modico, quantum res poscet, acervo Tollam, nec metuam quid de me indicet heres, Quod non plura datis invenerit.'
23. **rhombos**. Hor. 2 S. 2. 47, Epod. 2. 50, Juv. 4 passim.
ponere. 1. 63.
lautus ponere. Epil. 11.
24. **tenuis**; 'exacta *tenui* ratione *saporum*' Hor. 2 S. 4. 36. Jahn.
sollers. 5. 37.
turdarum, fem. for the sake of variety, or perhaps, as the Scholia say, because epicures could distinguish the gender of thrushes as well as their breeding by the taste. Thrushes were great delicacies, Hor. 2 S. 5. 10, 1 Ep. 15. 41.
saliva, for 'sapor,' effect for cause.

the year, sprinkles his dry vegetables with brine, like a knowing dog as he is, bought in a cup and shakes the precious pepper over his plate with his own hand, while here you have a fine spirited young fellow gobbling through an immense estate. Enjoyment, enjoyment for me, not that I go to the expense of serving up turbots for my freedmen or am a connoisseur in the delicate juices of hen thrushes.

Live up to the produce of your own estate each year. Grind out your granaries: you may, without fear, you have only to harrow, and a new crop is already in the blade. 'Aye, but there are claims on me, a shipwrecked friend is clinging forlornly to the Bruttian cliffs; all his means and his prayers are drowned in the deep Ionian waters; he is now lying on the beach, and with him the huge gods from his vessel's stern, and the ribs of the wreck which are beginning to invite the cormorants.' Now, then, break a bit of turf from your landed capital, and be generous to the poor man, that he may not have to go about with his picture on a board of

'Sua cuique vino saliva innocentissima est' Plin. 23. 40.

25–40. 'Live up to your means. You want to be able to help your friends? Very well, then sell something—the emergency will justify you. Your heir will resent this, and visit it on you by giving you a mean funeral, and morose censors will say it all comes of foreign philosophy. Will this trouble you in your grave?'

25. **messe**, 'the year's harvest.' Jahn's construction making **tenus** adv. is very harsh.

propria, opp. to 'aliena.' 'Live up to your income, but not beyond.'

vive, of supporting life. Hor. 1 Ep. 12. 8, 2 Ep. 1. 123.

granaria. 5. 110.

26. **emolere granaria**, a strong expression. 'Grind out your granaries' = have all your store ground up for use.

in herba est, 'is already in the blade.' 'Luxuriem segetum tenera depascit in herba' Virg. G. 1. 112, 'adhuc tua messis in herba est' Ov. Her. 17. 263.

27. A supposed objection — 'if I spend my income, how shall I be able to serve a friend in an emergency?'

vocat officium. Juv. 3. 239. Here 'officium' is relative duty, as in Cicero's treatise.

trabe rupta. 1. 89 note. 'Fractis trabibus' Juv. 14. 296.

28. **prendit.** 'Prensantemque uncis manibus capita aspera montis' Virg. Aen. 6. 360. Casaubon.

surda, 'unheard.' 'Istius tibi sit *surda* sine arte lyra' Prop. 3. 5. 58, '*surdo* verbere caedit' Juv. 13. 194.

vota condidit, as vows are said 'cadere.'

30. *Paintings*, not images, of the gods. 'Aurato fulgebat Apolline puppis' Virg. Aen. 10. 171.

dei shows that there were sometimes more than one, and so Hor. 1 Od. 14. 10 'Non *di* (integri) quos iterum pressa voces malo.' The mention of the gods seems merely ornamental, not indicative, as Turnebus ap. Stocker thinks, of the shipwrecked man's piety.

mergis. Jahn compares Hor. Epod. 10. 21 'Opima quod si praeda curvo litore Porrecta *mergos* iuveris.

31. **costa**, of a ship. Plin. 13. 63, also Virg. Aen. 2. 16, where the language is from shipbuilding.

lacerae. 'At *laceras* etiam *puppes* furiosa refeci' Ov. Her. 2. 45.

caespite vivo, of turf growing. Hor. 1 Od. 13. 19, Ov. M. 4. 300. Here for the mass of landed property, from which something is to be sacrificed, with reference to the phrase 'de vivo detra-

frange aliquid, largire inopi, ne pictus oberret
caerulea in tabula. sed cenam funeris heres
negleget, iratus quod rem curtaveris; urnae
ossa inodora dabit, seu spirent cinnama surdum,   35
seu ceraso peccent casiae, nescire paratus.
tune bona incolumis minuas? et Bestius urguet
doctores Graios, 'Ita fit, postquam sapere urbi
cum pipere et palmis venit nostrum hoc maris expers;
fenisecae crasso vitiarunt unguine pultes.'   40
haec cinere ulterior metuas? At tu, meus heres
quisquis eris, paulum a turba seductior audi.
o bone, num ignoras? missa est a Caesare laurus
insignem ob cladem Germanae pubis, et aris

[34. *neglegat* B.   *rem* om. α.   35. *hossa* α.   *inhonora* α, *inodora* C : 'inodora ... aut inhonora' Schol.   36. *picent* α.   *castae* C.   37. *et* α, *sed* C.
39. *piper* α C.   40. *crassa* α.   41. *hic meride ulterior* α.   43. *obenum
ignoras* α.]

here' or 'resecare,' to deduct from the capital. 'Dat de lucro: nihil detrahit *de vivo*' Cic. Fl. 37.

32. **pictus.** 1. 89 note.

33. **caerulea**, as it would be a seapiece, doubtless with a daub of green all over.

in tabula with 'pictus.'

cenam funeris, 'the funeral banquet,' given to the friends of the deceased, and sometimes to the public (Suet. Caes. 26): distinguished from the scanty meal left on the tomb for the dead, 'feralis cena' Juv. 5. 85, or 'novendialis.' Jahn. The sentiment from Hor. 2 Ep. 2. 191, quoted on v. 22.

34. **iratus** with quod.

curtaveris. 'Quantulum enim summae *curtabit* quisque dierum' Hor. 2 S. 3. 124, 'Curtae nescio quid semper abest rei' 3 Od. 24. 64.

35. ['Inhonora' Bücheler. See critical note.] Spices were thrown into the funeral fire. 'Congesta cremantur *Turea dona*' Virg. Aen. 6. 224. 'Cur *nardo* flammae non oluere meae?' Prop. 4. 7. 32.

surdum, of smell, like 'exsurdare' Hor. 2 S. 8. 38, of taste.

36. **ceraso.** Adulteration with cherry bark, mentioned nowhere else, though Pliny (12. 98) speaks of adulteration with storax and laurel twigs.

'Dum myrrham et *casiam* flebilis uxor emit' Mart. 10. 97. 2. Jahn.

spirent . . . peccent mark that the clauses are dependent on *nescire*. He knows not which of the two be the cause—rhetorically equivalent to saying he knows nothing of either.

paratus. 1. 132. Here expressing deliberation.

37. The heir's reply to the complaint. **Incolumis** = 'inpune,' perhaps with an antithetical reference to *minuas*, 'Are you to impair your property and lose nothing in your own person?' [Jahn in his text of 1868, following the suggestion of Sinner, transposes 'tune bona incolumis minuas' to v. 41, and 'haec cinere ulterior metuas' in v. 41 to this line: Bücheler returns to the old order.]

Bestius. Hor. 1 Ep. 15. 37. Introduced here 'more Persii' (2. 14 note), and awkwardly enough, as the charge against philosophy has no relation to the context.

38. **Ita fit.** Cic. N. D. 3. 37 'Ita fit: illi enim nusquam picti sunt qui naufragia fecerunt in marique perierunt.' ' This is the history of it.' Bestius seems

sea-green. But your heir will neglect your funeral feast in revenge for your clipping your property: he will put your ashes into the urn in an unfragrant state, resolved to ask no questions, whether it be that the cinnamon has lost its sense of smell, or that the casia has become involved with cherry bark. As if you were going to impair your property and lose nothing in your own person! And Bestius is severe on the Greek teachers, 'That's how it is, ever since this unpickled philosophy of ours came to town with pepper and dates, our haymakers have spoilt their porridge with those nasty thick oils.' Do you mean to say that you would be afraid of this on the other side of the grave? However, *my* heir, whoever he may be, will perhaps step aside from the crowd and let me say a word to him. My good sir, haven't you heard the news? bays have arrived from the emperor in honour of a signal victory over the Germans; the cold ashes are being shovelled away to censure everybody: the rich man for spending money and also for wanting an expensive funeral, and the heir for grumbling at having no more to spend. **sapere.** 1. 9.

39. Everything is jumbled in the condemnation: foreign pepper (5. 55, 136), foreign palms, and foreign notions.

palmis, 'dates.' 'Quid vult palma sibi rugosaque carica (dixi)' Ov. F. 1. 185, Freund; or perhaps oil, Cato R. R. 113, Jahn.

nostrum, of the age. 1. 9, 2. 62.

maris expers, from Hor. 2 S. 8. 15 'Chium maris expers,' not mixed with salt water, which was supposed to make the wine more wholesome (Athen. 1. p. 32 D, repeated by Jahn), and so Jahn understands it here. The metaphor from wine would agree with 5. 117, and with the classification with pepper and palms. 'Maris expers' = 'insulsum' (Heinrich), so that 'sapere maris expers' would be an oxymoron. Casaubon takes 'maris' from 'mas,' in which case Persius must have intended a pun, as he evidently took the words from Horace.

40. **faenisex** is the commoner form.

crasso... unguine, an epithet of *bad* ointment, Hor. A. P. 375, here applied contemptuously to all condiments.

vitiarunt; 2. 65, spoilt their good honest meal by mixing it.

pultes. 4. 31 note.

41. 'Would you be afraid of this when you are yourself removed beyond those ashes which are to suffer by the supposed neglect?' 5. 152 'cinis et manes et fabula fies,' note.

41–60. 'I would address *my* heir in this way—Here is an occasion of national rejoicing—I mean to celebrate it by an act of patriotic bounty. Do you mean to question my right? I am not obliged to leave you what I have? If you despise it, I can easily get another heir—some beggar, who is what my own ancestors were, and therefore my kinsman even in law.'

42. **quisquis eris** indicates Persius' own indifference.

seductior; 2. 4, 'paulum' with 'seductior' or with 'audi?'

43. For Caligula's German expedition, see Suet. Cal. 43 foll. He ordered a triumph which was to be unprecedentedly splendid, and cheap in proportion, as he had a right to the property of his subjects—changed his mind, forbade any proposal on the subject under capital penalties, abused the senate for doing nothing, and finally entered the city in ovation, on his birthday. This happened, as Gifford observes, when Persius was seven years old, so that he may have been struck with it. Perhaps he intended a suppressed sneer at Caligula to glance off on Nero.

num ignoras. Surely you have heard the news, and will not wonder at my enthusiasm.

laurus, for the 'laureatae litterae,'

frigidus excutitur cinis, ac iam postibus arma, 45
iam chlamydes regum, iam lutea gausapa captis
essedaque ingentesque locat Caesonia Rhenos.
dis igitur genioque ducis centum. paria ob res
egregie gestas induco; quis vetat? aude.
vae, nisi conives! oleum artocreasque popello 50
largior; an prohibes? dic clare! 'Non adeo,' inquis?
exossatus ager iuxta est. Age, si mihi nulla

[46. *victis* a, *captis* C, Priscian. 1. pp. 333, 350 K. 47. *que* om. a. *rhenus* a.
48. *patria* a. 49. *egregia* a. 50. *conlues* a. *arcocreasque* a. 51. *largiar* a. *audeo* C.]

or 'laureatae' simply, the letter bound with bay, in which the general announced his victory to the senate.
45. Compare Virg. Aen. 11. 211 'cinerem et confusa ruebant Ossa focis.'
frigidus, perhaps alluding to the rarity of such rejoicings. Lubin.
postibus, *for* the temple gates; 'in postibus arma' Virg. Aen. 7. 183. So Aen. 3. 287, Aesch. Ag. 579.
46. Caligula chose captives who were to appear in procession, Suet. Cal. 47.
['**gausapa** genus est pillei, quo captivorum capita induebantur' Schol. '*Gausapum*' was a general word for cloth stuff with wool on one side, and is thus distinguished from 'amphimallum' by Pliny 8. 193. Lucilius 20. 1 and Hor. 2 S. 8. 11 use it for a napkin. The material seems first to have been used for clothing in the early Augustan age (Pliny l. c.). The forms of the word are 'gausapus' (Gloss. Lat. Gr. p. 32 G. '*gausarus*' ἐνδρομίς); 'gausapa' fem. (Messalla ap. Charis. p. 104 Keil, Pliny l. c., Petronius 28. 4); 'gausapum' (Mart. 11. 152 lemma, Gloss. Sang. p. 211 G.); 'gausapo' abl. sing. and 'gausapa' nom. acc. pl. (Cassius Severus ap. Charis. p. 104, Ov. A. A. 2. 300); 'gausape' acc. sing. (Persius 4. 37), 'gausape' abl. sing. Lucilius and Horace ll. cc., Augustus ap. Charis. p. 104, who says 'tunica gausapa' was the choicer expression. The Greek form was γαυσάπης (Charis. l. c.); γαύσαπαι Strabo p. 218 Casaubon. See also Priscian 1. p. 333, 350 Keil. Martial has 'gausapina paenula,' and 'gausapinae' alone,

14. 145, 147; 6. 59, 2, 8.] From Suet. l. c., it appears that Caligula 'captivos ... coegit rutilare et submittere comam,' and the provision of false hair would be quite in keeping with the whole of the sham as Persius represents it. Casaubon however refers to Varro, as showing that the Gauls, who were dressed like the Germans, and actually selected to figure in this triumph (Suet. l. c.), wore 'gausapa,' and the dress was not uncommon at Rome.
47. '**esseda** Britanna' Prop. 2. 1. 76, 'Belgica' Virg. G. 3. 204, common, or considered so be so, to the various barbarians of the west of Europe. ['In Britannia ne ab essedariis decipiaris, caveto,' Cicero to Trebatius then in Britain, Div. 7. 6; 'essedum aliquod suadeo capias' *ib.* 7.]
locat may point to the intended cheapness of the display, as of course it does to the fraud, as if the materials were always kept on hand.
Caesonia was first Caligula's mistress, afterwards, on the birth of a daughter, his wife, Suet. Cal. 25.
Rhenos, explained by almost all the commentators as 'Rhenanos:' but pictures or images of different parts of the conquered territory were borne in triumph. Jahn refers to Ov. A. A. 1. 223 foll. 'Quae loca, qui montes, quaeve ferantur aquae ... Hic est Euphrates, praecinctus harundine frontem : Cui coma dependet caerula, Tigris erit.' So the Nile in the triumphal representation, Virg. G. 3. 28. Thus the pl. is sarcastic.

from the altars; the empress has begun to contract for arms for the temple-gates, and royal mantles, and yellow woollen for the prisoners, and chariots, and Rhines as large as life. Well, I am coming forward with a hundred pair in acknowledgment to the gods and our general's destiny for this brilliant advantage. Who's to say me nay? Just try. Woe to you if you don't wink at it! I am to treat the mob with oil and bread and meat. Do you mean to hinder me? Speak out. You won't accept the inheritance, you say? Here is a field, now, cleared for ploughing. Suppose none

48. Caligula punished those who did not swear by his genius, Suet. Cal. 27. 'Mille Lares *Geniumque ducis* qui tradidit illos Urbs habet' Ov. F. 5. 145 of Augustus; König. Juv. 4. 145, 7. 21, calls Domitian 'dux,' with like sarcasm—perhaps referring to a similar exploit of his, a sham triumph with manufactured captives, Tac. Agr. 39.

centum paria, from Hor. 2 S. 3. 85 'Ni sic fecissent, gladiatorum dare centum Damnati populi paria atque epulum,' where it is part of the provision of a will. These displays were not confined to the Emperor, but were sometimes given by private persons, Suet. Claud. 34 'gladiatorio munere vel suo vel alieno,' Juv. 3. 34 Mayor's note, though of course on a scale like this they required princely means.

paria, alone, as in Sen. Ep. 7. 4 'ordinariis paribus.'

49. induco. 'A me autem gladiatorum par nobilissimum *inducitur*' Cic. Opt. Gen. Orat. 6. 17.

aude, as we should say, 'I dare you.'

50. coniveo, nearly = 'concedo,' in connection with which it is used, Cic. Ph. 1. 7, opp. to 'ferendum non puto.' Persius threatens to go further, if his heir blames him.

oleum; Caesar gave the people 2lbs. of oil per man, on the occasion of his triumphs, after all his wars were over, Suet. Caes. 38. Nero gave oil to the senate and equites when he dedicated warm baths and gymnasia, Suet. Nero 12, Tac. Ann. 14. 47, König.

artocreas, = 'visceratio,' according to [Gloss. Lat. Gr. p. 209. 48 G.] quoted by Casaubon and Jahn, so that we must suppose bread and meat to have been distributed separately, though most commentators explain the word as a kind of meat-pie. It occurs in an inscription (Orell. 7. 4937)... ORNETVR DEDICATIONE ARTOCREA | POPVLO CVPRENSI DEDIT, which however throws no light on its exact meaning.

popello, semi-contemptuous, as in 4. 15.

51. 'Don't mutter, but speak out.'

adeo seems to be a verb, 'adire hereditatem' is a common phrase, 'to enter on or accept an inheritance,' and 'adire nomen' is used for 'to assume a name by will,' Freund s. v., and the sense agrees with what follows—whereas no parallel instance of the adverb 'adeo' is produced. Perhaps there should be a question at 'inquis;' 'Do you say, I won't accept?'

52. exossatus ager iuxta est. The early commentators explain 'exossatus' 'cleared of stones,' after the Scholia, who singularly render it 'lapidibus plenus,' referring to Ov. M. 1. 393 'lapides in corpore terrae *Ossa* reor dici:' γῆ ὀστώδης is used by Menander, the rhetorician, (ap. Casaubon) for stony ground. Casaubon and later editors interpret it *exhausted*, boneless, and hence without strength. Might it be literally 'cleared of bones,' like the field in Hor. 1 S. 7, having been once used as a burying-ground, and now prepared for cultivation? In that case Persius will say, 'Here is a good piece of property just by—I can easily find an heir for it.' If we take it *exhausted*, it will be open to us either to make Persius speak, 'Suppose all I have is a field, and that nearly worn out, I can still,' etc., or to make the heir say, 'That is as good as ('iuxta') spoiling your property for good and all.' [Jahn in his

iam reliqua ex amitis, patruelis nulla, proneptis
nulla manet patrui, sterilis matertera vixit,
deque avia nihilum superest, accedo Bovillas 55
clivumque ad Virbi, praesto est mihi Manius heres.
'Progenies terrae?' Quaere ex me, quis mihi quartus
sit pater : haut prompte, dicam tamen; adde etiam unum,
unum etiam : terrae est iam filius, et mihi ritu
Manius hic generis prope maior, avunculus exit. 60
  Qui prior es, cur me in decursu lampada poscis?
sum tibi Mercurius; venio deus huc ego ut ille
pingitur; an renuis? vin tu gaudere relictis?

[54. *patruis* C.   55. *accede* a.   56. *verbi* C, cf. *Verbius* in R. Aen. 7. 762. *mannius* a et in ras. C : ita v. 60.   57. *que ex* a.   58. *haut* C.   *tamen* om. a.   59. *si terrae* C.   *ritum* C, *tecum* a.   60. *Manius;* vid. ad v. 56.   61. *est* a. *decursum* C.   *poscas* C.   62. *hunc* a.   *illi* a.   63. *vis* C.   *relictus* a.]

text of 1868, and Bücheler read 'Non adeo' inquis 'Exossatus ager iuxta est,' making 'adeo' an adverb.]
  52. Age, si; Hor. 2 S. 3. 117.
  53. amita is the 'aunt' by the father's side, 'matertera' by the mother's. Observe that all the supposed relatives named here are *females*. He actually left his property to his mother and sisters, as appears from his life, which also speaks of a paternal aunt.
  54. sterilis ... vixit, had died without issue.
  55. Bovillae, between Rome and Aricia (Hor. 1 S. 5. 1), the first stage on the Appian road, called 'suburbanae,' Prop. 4. 1. 33, Ov. F. 3. 667.
  56. clivum ... Virbi, mentioned more than once by Martial (2. 19. 3, etc.), as 'clivus Aricinus;' Virbius, the Italian Hippolytus, being the hero of Aricia, Virg. Aen. 7. 761 foll. It was a great resort for beggars, Mart. l. c., Juv. 4. 117, Mayor's note, and Persius says that one of these is ready to be his heir. 'Multi Mani Ariciae,' was an old proverb, Fest. s. v. 'Manius,' (p. 145 Müller) who appears to understand it of the town in the days of its prosperity, when many great men were there—from this it may easily have passed into a sneer in the altered days of the place, so that 'one of the aristocracy of Aricia' would be synonymous with a beggar. But the name is given to a slave by Cato, R. R. 141. [Petronius 45 'iam *Manios aliquot* habet et mulierem essedariam et dispensatorem Glyconem.']
  57. Progenies terrae, is the heir's comment. 'You step at once from your relatives to the son of nobody knows who.' 'Terrae filius' occurs in Cic. Att. 1. 13 'terrae filio nescio cui.' [Petronius 43 'et ille stips, dum fratri suo irascitur, nescio cui terrae filio patrimonium elegavit.']
  58. patres is used generally of ancestry, so Persius calls the great-great-grandfather ('abavus') 'quartus pater.' ['Pilumnusque illi quartus pater' Virg. Aen. 10. 619.]
  haud prompte, dicam tamen, μόλις μέν, ἐξερῶ δ' ὅμως, or something like it, would be the Greek equivalent. Jahn compares Lucan 1. 378 'invita peragam tamen omnia dextra.'
  adde etiam unum. 'Demo unum, demo etiam' (if this and not 'et item' be the true reading) 'unum,' Hor. 2 Ep. 1. 46.
  59. 'At last he is a son of earth.'
  ritu, with 'generis,' though Jahn separates them, 'by regular descent.'
  60. maior avunculus was the great-grandmother's brother, 'magnus' being the grandmother's, and 'maximus' the great-great-grandmother's. Freund referring to Paulus and Gaius, Isid. Orig. 9. 6. 17, gives 'proavunculus.' Persius does not pretend strict accuracy (prope

of my paternal aunts survive me, none of my female cousins on the father's side; suppose I have no female first cousin twice removed in existence, my maternal aunt dies without issue, and there is no representative of my grandmother living, why, I go to Bovillae, to Virbius' hill, and there is Manius, an heir ready to my hands. 'What, a groundling?' Ask me who is my great-great-grandfather. Give me time and I can tell you. Go back one step more, and one more. I come to a groundling at last; and so in strict legal descent Manius here turns out to be something like my great-great-uncle.

Why should you, who are before me in the race, ask for my torch before I have done running? You should regard me as Mercury. I present myself to you as a god, just as he does in his picture. Will you take what I leave and be thankful? There is something

or he would not only have had to push the relationship several degrees back, but he would have said 'patruus,' not 'avunculus.' 'Avunculus maior' is sometimes used for 'avunculus magnus,' and 'avunculus' simply for 'avunculus maior;' see Freund.

exit, like 'evadit,' 'turns out to be,' 1. 45 note, though here there seems no definite metaphor. Persius' argument is like Juv. 8. 272, tracing the noble to Romulus' gang. Compare also Juv. 4. 98, where the 'terrae filii' are ennobled as little brothers of the earth-born giants.

61-74. Persius continues to his heir, 'Why wish to succeed before your time? Inheritance is *fortune*—take it for what it is worth. *All* I leave will be yours, but mark—it is what I *leave*, not what I *have* or *have had*. Your selfishness only makes me resolved on being selfish too. You would have me save—not only for you, but for your descendants, who are as likely as not to be spendthrifts and profligates.'

61. For the λαμπαδηφορία see Dict. Ant. [Cornificius ad Herennium 4. 46 'in palaestra, qui taedas candentes accipit, celerior est in cursu continuo quam ille qui tradit ... defatigatus cursor integro facem ... tradit.' The runner is represented by Persius as being asked to give up his torch before he has run his allotted space, before he is tired out.]

prior, 'you who are before me, and whose turn is not yet come.' Jahn seems right in laying a stress on in decursu 'while I am running,' 'before I have done running.' ['Nunc cursu lampada tibi trado' Varro R. R. 3. 16. 9.] 'Decursus,' as he remarks, is the word for a Roman custom of running in armour at funeral games, Virg. Aen. 11. 189. Cicero has 'decursus mei temporis' Fam. 3. 2, and 'decursus honorum' de Or. 1. 1.

poscis, 'without waiting till I give it up.' The well-known passage, Lucr. 2. 79, is not quite parallel, as the succession there is of life, here of inheritance.

62. **Mercurius.** 2. 11 note.

63. **pingitur**, i. e. 'with a money bag.' [Preller, Römische Mythologie p. 599, mentions 'viele kleine Bronzestatuen, welche ihn (Mercurius) gewöhnlich mit den beiden herkömmlichen Attributen des Schlangenstabes und des Beutels darstellen.'] Jahn refers to Mus. Borb. 6. 2, 8. 38, Müller Mon. Art. Ant. 2. t. 29 foll. The Delph. ed. compares Hor. 2 S. 3. 67 'an magis excors Reiecta praeda, quam praesens Mercurius fert?'

renuis. v. 51.

vin. Bentley, on Hor. 2 S. 6. 92, distinguishes between 'vin tu' and 'vis tu,' supposing the one to be a simple question, the other a virtual command. Jahn however quotes Sulpicius in Cic. Fam. 4. 5 'visne tu te, Servi, cohibere?' Here the answer expected seems to be affirmative, whether we suppose a command or a mere question to be intended.

gaudere, as we should say, 'to take and be thankful.'

relictis, of 'leaving by will.'

dest aliquid summae. Minui mihi; sed tibi totum est,
quidquid id est. ubi sit, fuge quaerere, quod mihi quondam 65
legarat Tadius, neu dicta repone paterna.
'fenoris accedat merces; hinc exime sumptus,
quid reliquum est?' Reliquum? nunc, nunc inpensius ungue,
ungue, puer, caules! mihi festa luce coquetur
urtica et fissa fumosum sinciput aure, 70
ut tuus iste nepos olim satur anseris extis,
cum morosa vago singultiet inguine vena,
patriciae inmeiat vulvae? mihi trama figurae
sit reliqua, ast illi tremat omento popa venter?

Vende animam lucro, mercare atque excute sollers 75
omne latus mundi, nec sit praestantior alter
Cappadocas rigida pinguis plausisse catasta:

[64. *des* B. 66. *cadius* a. *pone* a C, *oppone* aut *repone* ς. 68. *inperisius* a. *angue* a, *surge* C. 69. *coquatur* C, *coquetur* a. 71. *tuus hic* a, *tusista* C. 73. *inmelat* C. *matronae immeiere vulvae* Probus Cathol. p. 36 Keil. 74. *omento paventur* a. 76. *ne sit* C. 77. *pavisse* a. *catastas* C.]

64. **summae.** Hor. 2 S. 3. 124, quoted on v. 34, *id.* 1 S. 4. 32.
mihi, emphatic, 3. 78, οὐχ ἵνα τι μὴ ἐκείνῳ, ἀλλ' ἵνα αὐτῷ.
65. **quidquid id est**; Virg. Aen. 2. 49.
fuge quaerere; Hor. 1 Od. 9. 13.
66. [The names **Tadius** and 'Tadia' are common in inscriptions.]
neu dicta repone paterna, = 'neu sis pater mihi,' compare 3. 96, 'do not give me my father's language over again.' So '*reponis* Achillem,' 'bring again on the stage,' Hor. A. P. 120. ['Oppone' Jahn (1868) from one of his Paris MSS. 'Neu dicta, Pone paterna,' etc. Bücheler.]
67. This line has hitherto been taken by itself, 'hinc' being referred to 'merces.' 'Get interest, and live on *it*, not on your principal.' 'Accedat,' 'exime,' and 'reliquum,' however, are clearly correlatives, so that we must suppose the whole 'Fenoris ... reliquum est,' to be uttered by Persius as a specimen of the paternal tone which the heir adopts. 'Carry your interest to your account—then subtract your expenses—and see what is over,' i.e. see whether you have managed to live on the interest of your money or not. 'Hinc' then had better be referred to the whole sum after the addition of the interest, though the other view is possible. Compare Hor. A. P. 327 foll. 'si de quincunce remota est Uncia, quid superat? ... Redit uncia: quid fit?' The father by using technical terms implies that he wishes his son to be familiar with accounts.
merces, as in Hor. 1 S. 2. 14, 3. 88; here it is rendered definite by 'fenoris,' as there by the context.
68. Persius repeats **reliquum** indignantly, like 'cuinam' 2. 19.
inpensius, opp. to 'instillat,' Hor. 2 S. 2. 62.
ungue ... caules, Hor. 2 S. 3. 125.
69. **puer**, 'his slave,' as in 5. 126.
festa luce, v. 19, 4. 28, Hor. 2 S. 2. 61, 3. 143.
70. **urtica**, Hor. 1 Ep. 12. 7 'herbis vivis et *urtica*,' where some interpret it a fish. Persius however plainly means a vegetable, imitating Horace, 2 S. 2. 116 foll. 'Non ego ... temere edi luce

short of the whole sum. Yes, I have robbed myself for myself; but for you it is all, whatever it may be. Don't trouble yourself to ask what has become of what Tadius left me years ago, and don't remind me of my father. 'Add the interest to your receipts. Now, then, deduct your outgoings, and there remains what?' Remains what, indeed? Souse the cabbages, boy, souse them with oil, and don't mind the expense. Am I to have nettles boiled for me on holidays, and smoked pig's cheek split through the ear, that your young scape-grace may gorge himself on goose's inwards? are my remains to be a bag of bones, while he has a priestly belly wagging about with fat?

Sell your life for gain; do business; turn every stone in every corner of the world, like a keen hand; let no one beat you at slapping fat Cappadocians on the upright platform; double your

profesta Quidquam praeter *holus fumosae* cum pede pernae,' while he as plainly took the word from the passage in the Epistles.

siuciput, 'pig's cheek,' Plaut. Men. 211 ['sincipitamenta.'] Petron. 135 'faba ad usum reposita et sincipitis vetustissimi particula.' Smoked pork was a common rustic dish. Hor. l. c., Juv. 11. 82, Pseudo-Virg. Moret. 57.

71. nepos, in the double sense. The folly of saving is more apparent, the more distant the descendant who will squander the money.

exta, like σπλάγχνα, of the larger organs of the body. '*Exta* homini ab inferiore viscerum parte separantur membrana' Plin. 11. 197: here of the liver, a well-known dainty, Hor. 2 S. 8. 88, Juv. 5. 114, Mayor's note. With the sentiment compare Hor. 2 S. 3. 112 'Filius, aut etiam haec libertus ut ebibat heres ... custodis?' also 1 Ep. 5. 12.

73. trama, as explained by Sen. Ep. 90. 20, seems to be the thread of the warp ('stamen'), not of the woof ('subtegmen'), as Serv. says on Virg. Aen. 3. 483, quoting this passage, and Jahn after him. And so the image seems to require, which is from a cloak, where the nap is worn away and only the threads remain. Casaubon quotes Eur. Aut. Fr. 12 (Nauck) τρίβωνες ἐκβαλόντες οἴχονται κρόκας.

figurae, 'the shape.' 'Formai figura' Lucr. 4. 69. Gen. or dat.? if the former, 'the mere thread of my shape,' the skeleton. 'Is my shape to dwindle to a thread?'

74. reliqua, possibly with a sneering reference to 'reliquum' v. 68.

tremat, 'wag before him.'

omento, 'the adipose membrane,' 2. 47.

popa, subst. used adjectively, from the fatness of the priests' assistants ('popae'). 'Inflavit cum *pinguis* ebur Tyrrhenus *ad aras*' Virg. G. 2. 193.

75–80. 'Well—go on heaping up more wealth—more, more, more. Are you never to stop? *Never.*' Persius still speaks to his heir, who is assumed to value wealth for its own sake (v. 71), and condemns him as it were to the fate of constantly seeking and never being satisfied—not unlike the punishment of the Danaides, as explained by Lucr. 3. 1009 foll.

75. Vende animam lucro. Casaubon quotes a Greek proverb, θανάτου ὤνιον τὸ κέρδος, and Longin. Subl. 44. 9 τὸ ἐκ τοῦ παντὸς κερδαίνειν ὠνούμεθα τῆς ψυχῆς: 'the life.'

excute, metaphorical, as in 1. 49, 5. 22.

76. latus mundi, Hor. 1 Od. 22. 19.

ne sit praestantior alter. 'Dum ne sit te ditior alter' Hor. 1 S. 1. 40, which leads us to take 'ne' here 'lest.' Compare Hor. 1 Ep. 6. 20 foll.; 'praestantior alter' Virg. Aen. 6. 164.

77. For Cappadocian slaves, see Hor. 1 Ep. 6. 39 '*Mancipiis* locuples eget aeris *Cappadocum* rex,' Mart. 10. 76. 3 'Nec de *Cappadocis* eques *catastis*.'

rem duplica. 'Feci; iam triplex, iam mihi quarto,
iam deciens redit in rugam: depunge, ubi sistam.'
Inventus, Chrysippe, tui finitor acervi. 80

[79. *depinge* ς. 80. *iuventus* a C, corr. c.]

77. **rigida,** 'fixed upright.' 'Rigidae columnae' Ov. F. 3. 529. Jahn.

plausisse; '*plausae* sonitum cervicis amare' Virg. G. 3. 186, 'pectora *plausa*' Aen. 12. 86. The buyer claps the slaves to test their condition, hence 'pingues.'

catasta, Mart. l.c., Dict.Ant.'Let no one beat you as a judge of slave-flesh.'

78. Imitated from Hor. 1 Ep. 6. 34 oll. 'Mille talenta rotundentur, totidem altera—porro Tertia succedant, et quae pars quadret acervum,' and imitated in turn by Juv. 14. 323 foll.

quarto, as if 'ter' had preceded.

79. **redit,** of revenue; 'reditus,' and so doubtless in Hor. A. P. 329.

rugam, 'the fold of the garment,' Plin. 35. 57, as 'sinus' is used of a purse: 'rugam trahit' in the imitation by Juv. 14. 325 looks as if he had misunderstood the meaning here to be capital. 'There it is—three, four, ten times over it comes into my purse: prick a hole where I am to stop.' Chrysippus, the man to limit your heap is found at last.

'makes you frown dissatisfaction.' Casaubon however explains 'rugam' there of the 'sinus.' Is there any allusion to 'duplica,' as if there were a fold for each sum?

depunge, better than 'depinge' (though 'depinge' is adopted by Jahn), like 'fige modum.' The man himself wishes to be checked.

80. 'Why then Chrysippus' problem has been solved,'—implying that the man expects an impossibility.

acervi [the heap spoken of in the fallacious argument 'sorites']. 'Ratione ruentis acervi' Hor. 2 Ep. 1. 47. Casaubon compares Cic. Acad. 2. 29, where the words 'nullam nobis dedit cognitionem *finium*, ut in ulla re statuere possimus *quatenus*,' will explain 'finitor.' Chrysippus' own solution was to halt arbitrarily at a certain point (*quiescere*, ἡσυχάζειν, ἐπέχειν), and decline answering.

CHOLIAMBI.

Nec fonte labra prolui caballino,
nec in bicipiti somniasse Parnaso
memini, ut repente sic poeta prodirem.
Heliconidasque pallidamque Pirenen

[3. *memini me ut a* C. *prodierim* C.   4. *aeliconiadas a. pallidam pyrenen* C. *sirenen a.*]

[Choliambos in fine *a*, ante I saturam habet C.]

'My antecedents, I believe, were not poetical: if I appear at the feast of the poets, it is only on sufferance. After all, one can sing without inspiration: at least parrots and magpies do.'

[These lines, which have no real connection with anything in the Satires, appear in the best MSS. at the end of the book, but the Scholia support the inferior MSS. in regarding them as a prologue. On this supposition Conington wrote as follows:] The Prologue may be regarded in two aspects, both historical. It may be intended as a remnant of the old practice of writing the *Satura* in a variety of metres. There is some reason to think that it is actually an imitation of Lucilius, as one of the speakers in Petronius' Satirae, c. 4, says, apropos of the education of youth, 'Sed ne me putes improbasse schedium Lucilianae humilitatis, quod sentio et ipse carmine effingam,' and then gives twenty-two verses, the first eight scazons, the rest hexameters. On the other hand, the introduction of a Prologue marks a late stage of poetical composition. To prologuize implies consciousness—the poet reflecting on his work—so early poets do not prologuize at all—as Homer: afterwards the exordium becomes personal, and contains a prologue, as would be the case in the Aeneid, if the lines *Ille ego* were genuine: then the prologue is a separate poem, as here. Lastly, we have a prose introduction, as in Statius' Silvae, Ausonius, and modern writers—a more natural method, and in some respects more graceful, as separating off matter which may be extraneous to the poem itself, but leading, on the other hand, to interminable and indeterminate writing, to the substitution of criticism for poetry, precept for practice. Of modern English writers, Wordsworth is in one extreme, Tennyson in the other.

Here the Prologue is, of course, to *all* the Satires—not, as some have thought, to the first only. He disclaims the honours of poetry, not without sarcasm, and insinuates that much which professes to come from inspiration really has a more prosaic source—want of bread or love of money. There seems no notion of satire as a prosaic kind of writing, so that Casaubon and Jahn's references to Horace (1 S. 4. 39; 2. 6. 17) are scarcely apposite, except as showing something of the same sort of modesty on the part of both.

1. **fons caballinus**, a translation of Hippocrene. *caballinus* sarcastic, like *Gorgonei caballi*, also of Pegasus (Juv. 3. 118), the term being contemptuous, though its derivatives in modern languages have, as is well known, lost that shade of meaning. ['Vectum Pegaseo volucri pendente caballo' Anth. Lat. 388 (Reise).]

EPILOGUE IN SCAZON IAMBICS.

I NEVER got my lips well drenched in the hack's spring—nor do I recollect having had a dream on the two-forked Parnassus, so as to burst upon the world at once as a full-blown poet. The daughters of Helicon and that cadaverous Pirene I leave to the

labra prolui. Virg. Aen. 1. 739, of Bitias, 'pleno se proluit auro.' Hor. 1 S. 5. 16 'prolutus vappa.' The action implies a deep draught, here taken by stooping down to the spring. (Contrast the opposite expression, 'primoribus labris attingere.') 'I never drank those long draughts of Hippocrene, of which others boast.' Here, as in the next verse, the image is doubtless borrowed from the Exordium of Ennius' Annals, as we may infer from Prop. 3. 3. 6 'Parvaque tam magnis admoram fontibus ora Unde pater sitiens Ennius ante bibit.' Persius may have had his eye on two other passages of the same elegy. See v. 2 'Bellerophontei qua fluit umor equi,' and v. 52 'Ora Philetea nostra rigavit aqua,' and perhaps also on Hor. 1 Ep. 3. 10 'Pindarici fontis qui non expalluit haustus, Fastidire lacus et rivos ausus apertos.' ['Iuvat integros accedere fontes, Atque haurire' Lucr. 4. 2.]

2. biceps, δίλοφος, a perpetual epithet of Parnassus. The mountain has not really two tops, but as the Castalian spring rises from between two ridges, it is said to have them (Urlichs and Millingen, referred to by Jahn). Propertius, l. c., represents himself as lying down to sleep under the shadow of Helicon. The source of both passages is again Ennius' account of himself, preserved to us by Cic. Acad. pr. 2. 16. 51, to the effect that he had gone to sleep on Parnassus, seen Homer in a dream, and heard that it was Homer's spirit which was then animating himself. Compare S. 6. 10, where Ennius' 'somnia Pythagorea' are again ridiculed.

2. nec ... memini is a sneer at Ennius' own words (Ann. 15, Vahlen), 'memini me fiere pavum,' said of Homer (Tert. de An. 33 foll., note on 6. 10). So Ov. M. 15. 160 'Ipse ego (nam memini) ... Euphorbus eram.'

3. memini, humorous; 'never that I can remember;' implying that Ennius must have had a good memory.

ut repente, 'so as to come before the world all at once as a poet.'

prodirem, 'to come forth *from* this preparatory process,' which is also expressed by 'sic,' 'on the strength of this' (not like 'sic temere,' as Casaubon and Jahn). 'A ready made poet by the immediate agency of the gods.' Possibly Persius was thinking of Hor. 1 Ep. 19. 7 'Ennius ipse pater nunquam nisi *potus* ad arma *Prosiluit* dicenda,' which might also warrant a conjecture that Ennius himself used some similar phrase.

poeta prodirem, 'prodis e iudice turpis Dama' Hor. 2 S. 7. 54.

[Heliconidas, which Jahn (1868) and Bücheler adopt, is probably right, in spite of the authority of a, which has aeliconiadas.] The form 'Heliconis' is found in Stat. Silv. 4. 4. 90; Lucr. 3. 1037 has 'Heliconiadum.' The reference is perhaps to the opening of Hesiod's Theogony (Μουσάων Ἑλικωνιάδων ἀρχώμεθ' ἀείδειν), where Hesiod relates how the Muses made him a poet.

4. pallidam, as causing studious paleness: 'pallentis grana cumini' 5. 55; perhaps with some reference to Horace's 'expalluit haustus,' quoted on v. 1.

Pirene, mentioned from its connection with Pegasus, who was said to

140 PERSII

illis remitto, quorum imagines lambunt 5
hederae sequaces: ipse semipaganus
ad sacra vatum carmen adfero nostrum.
quis expedivit psittaco suum chaere
picamque docuit nostra verba conari?
magister artis ingenique largitor 10
venter, negatas artifex sequi voces;
quod si dolosi spes refulgeat nummi,
corvos poetas et poetridas picas
cantare credas Pegaseium nectar.

[5. *ambiunt* a. 8. *expediit* a. *cere supine* a (i. e. χαῖρε συ, πῖνε, Jahn). 9. *picasque* a C. *verba nostra* C. 12. *refulserit* C: '*refulserit* et *refulgeat*,' Schol. 14. '*Pegaseium melos* ... in aliis *nectar*,' Schol. *nectar* a, *melos* C.]

have been broken in there. Statius (Theb. 4. 60) follows or coins a story that it was produced, like Hippocrene, by a stroke of Pegasus' hoof.

5. 'To the poets, whose ivy-crowned busts adorn our public libraries.' Hor. 1 S. 4. 21. For the ivy, see Hor. 1 Od. 1. 29. Juvenal apparently imitates this passage (7. 29) 'ut dignus venias hederis et imagine macra.'

No sneer seems to be intended in lambunt or sequaces, which are simply poetical. ['Relinquo' Jahn (1843): but remitto, which he has since adopted, has better authority.]

6. semipaganus is rightly explained by Jahn after Rigalt with reference to the *Paganalia*, a festival celebrated by members of the same *pagus*. Dion. Hal. 4. 15; Sicul. Flacc. de Cond. Agr. pp. 164, 165 Lachmann. [See Preller, Römische Mythologie p. 404.] This has more spirit than the interpretation of the Scholia, 'half a rustic,' and agrees with the image in the next line. Compounds with *semi* generally mean '*only* half,' not '*at least* half.'

8. Persius does not *say* that he writes for bread, which would have been too obviously untrue, as he was a wealthy man, but hints it in order to ridicule his contemporaries by affecting to classify himself with them.

expedivit, 'made easy.' Comp. our use of *impediment*.

suum not *foreign* (Jahn), as the parrot did not come from Greece, but simply 'its own'—'that cry which it is now so ready with.' So there is no opposition between χαῖρε and '*nostra verba*,' as if the magpie were intended to talk *Latin* as distinguished from Greek. The parrot talks Greek as the fashionable language for small talk, as now a days he might talk French, while 'nostra verba' means human speech. The antithesis is merely one of those which a man might use almost without intending it, between language viewed as belonging to its original owner and as afterwards appropriated—just as the parrot speaks 'expedite,' while the magpie 'conatur,' though it is not meant that the former succeeds more perfectly than the latter. For the practice of keeping parrots and magpies in great houses, see Martial, referred to below. After v. 8 the inferior MSS. have a line, 'Corvos quis olim concavum salutare?' where 'concavum' would doubtless refer to the sound, though one MS. gives 'Caesarem,' as in the first passage of Martial.

chaere (χαῖρε). Mart. 14. 73. 2 'Caesar ave;' hence the pie is said 'salutare,' *ib.* 76. 1.

10. Jahn refers to Theocr. 21. 1 ἁ πενία, Διόφαντε, μόνα τὰς τέχνας ἐγείρει, Plaut. Stich. 178 'paupertas omnes artes perdocet.' Comp. also Hor. 1 Ep. 5. 18 of wine, 'addocet artes;' Virg. G. 1. 145 'Tum variae venere artes: labor omnia vicit Improbus, et duris urgens in rebus egestas' (quoted by Plautius).

ingeni largitor. Plautius and

gentlemen whose busts are caressed by the climbing ivy—as for me, it is but as a poor half-brother of the guild that I bring my verses to the festival of the worshipful poets' company. Who was it made the parrot so glib with its 'Good morning,' and taught magpies to attempt the feat of talking like men? That great teacher of art and bestower of mother-wit the stomach, which has a knack of getting at speech when nature refuses it. Only let a bright glimpse of flattering money dawn on their horizon, and you would fancy jackdaw poets and poetess pies to be singing pure Pierian sweetness.

Casaubon quote Manil. 1. 78 'Et labor ingenium miseris dedit.' Jahn refers to Cicero's account of 'ingenium,' Fin. 5. 13 'Prioris generis (virtutum quae ingenerantur suapte natura) est docilitas, memoria, quae fere omnia appellantur uno ingeni nomine.' 'Ingeni largitor,' then, is a kind of oxymoron. [Prop. 2. 1. 4 'ingenium nobis ipsa puella facit.']

11. **venter** as in Hom. Od. 17. 286 foll. γαστέρα δ' οὔπως ἔστιν ἀποκρύψαι μεμανῖαν.

negatas ... voces. Casaubon quotes Manil. 5. 378 'Quin etiam linguas hominum sensusque docebit Aërias volucres ... Verbaque praecipiet naturae lege *negata*.'

artifex sequi, like 'ponere lucum Artifices' 1. 70, 'skilled to attain,' not, as Casaubon explains, 'making them follow.'

sequi, then, is rhetorically put for 'assequi' or 'consequi,' perhaps to express difficulty.

voces, 'words.'

12. **dolosi**, a general epithet of money though with a special application here—'beguiling them to the effort.' It might be almost said to refer to 'spes' as well as to 'nummi.'

refulgeat, 'flash on the sight.' Virg. Aen. 1. 402, 588; 6. 204. 'Refulsit certa spes liberorum parentibus' Vell. 2. 103 (Freund), 'non tibi divitiae velut maximum generis humani bonum refulserunt' Sen. Cons. ad Helv. 16. (Jahn.) [**Nummi**, money in general, as in Juv. 14. 139 'crescit amor nummi quantum ipsa pecunia crevit.' Professor Gildersleeve and Mr. Morgan ('Classical Review,' 1889, p. 10 foll.) prefer to take it of a single coin.]

13. 'Raven poets and poetess pies,' the substantive standing for an epithet, like 'popa venter' 6. 74. Possibly Persius meant to reverse the order to show how completely he identified the birds with the human singers.

poetridas has more MS. authority than 'poetrias.' Both ποιητρίς and ποιητρία are formed according to analogy, though only the latter is found.

14. Jahn quotes Pind. Ol. 7. 7 καὶ ἐγὼ νέκταρ χυτόν, Μοισᾶν δόσιν, ἀθλοφόροις ἀνδράσιν πέμπων. Theoc. 7. 82 οὕνεκα οἱ γλυκὺ Μοῖσα κατὰ στόματος χέε νέκταρ. Heinr. thinks Persius had in view Hor. 1 Ep. 19. 44 'Fidis enim manare poetica mella Te solum,' and suggests that 'cantare' should be 'manare.' Comp. also Lucr. 1. 947 'Et quasi Musaeo dulci contingere melle.' The epithet 'Pegaseius' makes the image still more forced, unless we suppose the 'nectar' to be the waters of Hippocrene, which is supported by a poem [Onestes 3. 4 in Jacobs' Anthologia Graeca] Πηγασίδος κρήνης νεκταρέων λιβάδων, quoted by König.

INDEX

TO THE INTRODUCTORY LECTURE AND THE NOTES.

Abacus, 1. 131.
Accerso and *arcesso*, 2. 45., 5. 172.
Accusative, of object, 3. 43., 5. 184: cognate, 1. 11; after *moveri* 5. 123; *pallere* 1. 124; *sudare* 5. 150; *trepidare* 3. 88; *vivere* 3. 67.
Acervus, 6. 80.
Acetum, 4. 32., 5. 86.
Actus, 5. 99.
Adeo, 6. 14.
Adferre, 1. 69.
Adire hereditatem, 6. 51.
Adjectives not agreeing with their own word, 1. 13, 23., 5. 116.
Admovere, 2. 75.
Adnuere, 2. 43.
Aerumna, 1. 78.
Agaso, 5. 76.
Albae aures, of an ass, 1. 59.
Albus = albatus, 1. 16.
Alcibiades, 4. 1.
Alea, 5. 57.
Allium, 5. 188.
Ambages, 3. 20.
Amita, 6. 53.
Amomum, 3. 104.
Angues, as genii of a place, 1. 113.
Angulus, 6. 13.
Anseris exta, 6. 71.
Anticyra, 4. 16.
Antiope, 1. 78.
Antitheta, 1. 86.
Apricus, 5. 179.
Aqualiculus, 1. 57.
Arcadia, asses of, 3. 9.
Arcesilas, 3. 79.
Aristae, 3. 115.
Aristophanes, 1. 124.
Arma virum, 1. 96.
Articuli, 5. 59.
Artifex, 5. 40.
Artocreas, 6. 50.
Asper nummus, 3. 69.
Astringere, 5. 110.
Astrology, 5. 46.
Attis, 1. 93.
Attius Labeo, 1. 76.
Auster, 6. 12.

Austerity, affected, of Romans, 1. 9.
Avia, 2. 31., 5. 92.

Baca, 2. 66.
Baro, 5. 138.
Bassaris, 1. 101.
Bassus, Caesius, p. xviii, xx., 6. 1.
Bathing, Roman habits with regard to, 3. 93.
Bathyllus, 5. 123.
Baucis, 4. 21.
Beatulus, 3. 103.
Belle, 1. 49.
Bene sit, 4. 30.
Bestius, 6. 37.
Beta, 3. 114.
Biceps Parnasus, Chol. 2.
Bicolor membrana, 3. 10.
Bidental, 2. 27.
Bilis, 2. 13., 3. 8., 5. 144.
Blandus, 4. 15.
Bombus, 1. 99.
Bovillae, 6. 55.
Bracatus, 3. 53.
Brisaeus, 1. 76.
Bruttia saxa, 6. 27.
Brutus, 5. 85.
Bulla, 5. 31.
Bullatus, 5. 19.
Bullire, 3. 34.

Caballinus fons, Chol. 1.
Cachinno, 1. 12.
Caecum occiput, 1. 62.
Caecum vulnus, 1. 134.
Caedere, 4. 42.
Caeruleus, 6. 33.
Caesonia, 6. 47.
Calabrian wool, 1. 65.
Caligula, 6. 43.
Calliroë, 1. 134.
Callis, 3. 57.
Calo, 5. 95.
Camellus, 5. 136.
Campus, 5. 57.
Candidus, 4. 20.
Candidus lapis, 2. 1.
Cani, 5. 65.

INDEX.

Canicula, 3. 5, 49.
Canina littera, 1. 110.
Cannabis, 5. 146.
Cantus, 5. 71.
Cappadocian slaves, 6. 77.
Caprificus, 1. 25.
Carbo, 5. 108.
Casia, 6. 36.
Castigare, 1. 7.
Catasta, 6. 77.
Catinum, 5. 182.
Cato, 3. 45.
Caudam iactare, 4. 15.
Caulis, 6. 69.
Causae rerum, 3. 66.
Cedrus, 1. 42.
Cena funeris, 6. 33.
Centenus, 5. 6.
Centussis, 5. 191.
Cerasus, 6. 36.
Cerdo, 4. 51.
Cevere, 1. 87.
Chaerestratus, 5. 162.
Cheragra, 5. 58.
Chrysippus, 6. 80.
Chrysis, 5. 165.
Cicer, 5. 177.
Ciconia, 1. 58.
Cicuta, 5. 145.
Cinnama, 6. 35.
Cippus, 1. 37.
Cirrati, 1. 29.
Citrea lecta, 1. 53.
Cleanthes, 5. 64.
Coa, 5. 135.
Coin, true and false, simile from, 5. 106.
Colligere, 5. 85.
Columbus, 3. 16.
Comes, 3. 1.
Compitalia, 4. 28.
Conivere, 6. 50.
Conpages, 3. 58.
Conpescere, 5. 100.
Corbis, 1. 71.
Corneus, 1. 47.
Cornicari, 5. 12.
Cornutus, p. xviii, xix., 5. 37.
Cortex, metaphorical, 1. 96.
Costa, 6. 31.
Crassus, 2. 36.
Craterus, 3. 65.
Cratinus, 1. 123.
Creta, 5. 108.
Cretatus, 5. 177.
Creterra, 2. 52.
Crispare, 3. 87.
Crispinus, 5. 126.
Crudus, 1. 51, 92., 2. 67., 5. 162.
Cubito tangere, 4. 33.
Cuminum, 5. 55.

Cures, 4. 26.
Curtare, 6. 34.
Curtus, 5. 191.
Curvi mores, 3. 52.
Custos, 5. 30.
Cute perditus, 1. 23.
Cuticula, 4. 18.

Dama, 5. 76.
Damocles, 3. 40.
Dare, 6. 8.
Darkness, metaphor from, 5. 60.
Dative after *pellere*, 1. 83 ; *ingemere*, 5. 61; *relinquere*, 5. 17; Chol. 5; *ridere*, 3. 86.
Davus, 5. 161.
Decerpere, 5. 42.
Decoctus, 1. 125.
Decoquo, 5. 57.
Decursus, 6. 61.
Defendere aliquid alicui, 1. 83.
Deinde, 5. 143.
Delumbis, 1. 104.
Depellentes di, 5. 167.
Despumare, 3. 3.
Deunx, 5. 150.
Dictation in schools, 1. 29.
Digitum exerere, 5. 119.
Diminutives in colloquial Latin, 1. 33.
Dinomache, 4. 20.
Discinctus, 3. 31.
Discolor, 5. 52.
Disponere, 5. 43.
Dius, 1. 31.
Domitian, assassination of, p. xxii.
Dropsy, 1. 55., 3. 63.
Ducere, 2. 63., 5. 40.

Ebullire, 2. 10.
Ec for *ex*, 5. 136.
Ecfluere (eff-), 3. 20.
Ecfundere (eff-), 1. 65.
Edictum, 1. 134.
Education, Roman, in time of Persius, 3. 45.
Egerere, 5. 69.
Elegidium, 1. 51.
Elevare, 1. 6.
Eliquare, 1. 35.
Emolere, 6. 26.
Enim, 1. 63.
Ennius, p. xxvii., 6. 10 ; Chol. 2.
Epictetus, p. xxii.
Equidem, 1. 110.
Ergenna, 2. 26.
Error, 5. 34.
Essedum, 6. 47.
Euphrates of Tyre, p. xxi.
Eupolis, 1. 124.
Evil eye, the, 2. 54.

INDEX.

Ex tempore, 3. 62.
Examen, 1. 6., 5. 101.
Excutere, 1. 49; *excusso naso*, 1. 118.
Exire, 1. 45.
Exossatus, 6. 52.
Exsuperare, 3. 89.

Fables, popular, perhaps alluded to by Persius, 2. 37.
Fabula, 5. 152.
Facere silentium, 4. 7.
Falernum indomitum, 3. 3.
Fallere, 4. 12., 5. 37.
Far, 2. 75.
Farina, 3. 112., 5. 115.
Farratus, 4. 31.
Fas, 5. 98.
Fate, representations of, in art, 5. 46.
Fax, 3. 116.
Feniseca, 6. 40.
Fertum, 2. 48.
Festa lux, 6. 69.
Festuca, 5. 175.
Fever, treatment of, 3. 90.
Fibra, 1. 47., 2. 26.
Fidelia, 3. 73., 5. 183.
Figura, 1. 86., 5. 73.
Finis extremumque, 1. 48.
Fistula, 3. 14.
Flagellare, 4. 49.
Floralia, 5. 188.
Fortunare, 2. 45.
Fossor, 5. 122.
Foxes, simile from, 5. 117.
Fractus, 1. 18.
Frangere, 5. 50, 165.
Fratres aëni, 2. 56.
Fulta cor aerumnis, 1. 78.
Funem reducere, 5. 118.

Galli, 5. 186.
Games of schoolboys, 3. 48.
Garrire, 5. 96.
Gausapa, 6. 46.
Gemini, 5. 49.
Genitive after *inanis*, 2. 61; *modicus*, 5. 109; *sterilis*, 5. 75.
Genius, 2. 3., 4. 27., 6. 18, 48.
Germana pubes, 6. 44.
Glutto, 5. 112.
Glycon, 5. 9.
Gods, in stern of ship, 6. 30.
Gold in temples, 2. 55 foll.
Graeci, 5. 191.
Grai doctores, 6. 38.
Granaria, 5. 110., 6. 25.
Grandis, 1. 14., 3. 55.

Hebenum, 5. 135.
Helicon, 5. 7.
Heliconis, Chol. 4.

Helvidius Priscus, p. xxi.
Hercules, 2. 12.
Herodis dies, 5. 180.
Hiare, 5. 3, 176.
Hibernare, 6. 7.
Hic = hereupon, 1. 32.
Hircosus, 3. 77.
Honestum, 2. 74.
Horace, influence of, upon Persius, pp. xxiii, xxix, xxx foll., 1. 116.
Hostius, 5. 1.
Hucine, 3. 15.

In with accus. after *dividere*, 5. 49; with abl. where accus. would be expected, 2. 61; 4. 33.
Inane, 1. 1.
Incurvare, 1. 91.
Incusa auro dona, 2. 52.
Incutere, 5. 187.
Inducere, 6. 49.
Infamis digitus, 2. 33.
Infelix, 6. 13.
Infinitive, perfect of, 1. 42.
Infinitive, use of, as a substantive, 1. 9; after *artifex*, 1. 70, Chol. 11; *callidus*, 1. 118; *cautus*, 5. 24; *lautus*, 6. 23; *melior*, 4. 16; *mobilis*, 1. 60; *opifex*, 6. 3; *praetrepidus*, 2. 54; *intendere*, 5. 13; *laborare*, 5. 39; *laudare*, as cogn. accus., 1. 86.
Infundere monitus, 1. 79.
Ingenium, Chol. 10.
Ingenuus ludus, 5. 15.
Ingerere, 5. 6.
Inpellere, 2. 13.
Inpensius, 6. 68.
Inriguus, 5. 56.
Inrorare, 6. 21.
Inserere aliquid aliqua re, 5. 63.
Inspicere, 3. 88.
Integer, 5. 173.
Intendere, 6. 4.
Intepere, 6. 7.
Inter pocula, 1. 30.
Intus pallere, 3. 42.
In voto esse, 3. 49.
Ita fit, 6. 48.
Italus, 1. 129.
Iocus, 6. 5.
Judaism, conversions to, 5. 179.
Iunctura, 1. 65., 5. 14.
Iunix, 2. 47.
Jupiter, star of, 5. 50.
Iuvat, 5. 24.

Labeo, 1. 5.
Lacer, 6. 31.
Laena, 1. 32.
Lagoena, 6. 17.

L

Lallare, 3. 18.
Lapillus melior, 2. 1.
Lares, 5. 31.
Latina fides, 6. 4.
Latus mundi, 6. 76.
Laureatae litterae, 6. 43.
Laxa cervix, 1. 98.
Laxare, 5. 44, 110.
Lemures, 5. 185.
Liber = a play, 1. 76.
Licinus, 2. 36.
Lightning, persons struck by, buried, not burnt, 2. 26.
Ligus ora, 6. 6.
Linea, 3. 4.
Litare, 2. 75., 5. 120.
Lucan, p. xvi.
Lucilius, pp. xxvii, xxix foll., 1. 114.
Lucilius, his dislike of the old Roman tragedians, 1. 76; imitated by Persius, Chol. 1., S. 1. 1, 27, 35., 3. 69., 4. 1., 5. 136.
Luctificabilis, 1. 78.
Lucus, a common-place in poetry, 1. 70.
Ludere in aliquid, 1. 127.
Luna, 6. 9.
Lupus, 1. 125.

Maeonides Quintus, 6. 11.
Maior avunculus, 6. 60.
Maior domus, 3. 92.
Mamma, 3. 18.
Mane, 3. 1.
Manes, 1. 38.
Manius, 6. 56.
Mantica, 4. 24.
Marcus, 5. 79.
Marcus Aurelius, p. xxii.
Margites, p. xxvii.
Maris expers, 6. 39.
Mas, 6. 4.
Masculus, 5. 144.
Masurius Sabinus, 5. 90.
Matertera, 2. 31.
Mefitis, 3. 99.
Melicerta, 5. 103.
Mena, 3. 76.
Menander imitated by Persius, 5. 161.
Mens Bona, 2. 8.
Meracus, 4. 16.
Mercurialis, 5. 110.
Mercurius, 6. 62.
Mergus, 6. 30.
Messalla, 2. 72.
Meta, 1. 131., 3. 68.
Metuere deos, 2. 31.
Meus, 5. 88., 6. 7.
Miluus, 4. 26.
Mimallonis, 1. 99.
Minui, 6. 16.

Mollis flexus, 3. 68.
Montis promittere, 3. 65.
Mores, 2. 62.
Moriens acetum, 4. 32.
Mucius, 1. 115.
Multum with adjective, 3. 86.
Muria, 6. 20.
Musonius Rufus, p. xxii.
Mutare, 5. 54.
Muttire, 1. 119.

Natalia, 6. 19.
Natta, 3. 31.
Nec nunc, 5. 172.
Nerius, 2. 14.
Nero, verses attributed to, 1. 99; supposed allusions to, p. xxiv.
Nervi, 2. 41.
Nihil de nihilo gignitur, 3. 84.
Non with present subj., 1. 5.
Nonaria, 1. 133.
Nuces, 1. 10.
Numae vasa, 2. 59.
Numerus, 5. 123.
Nummus, 3. 70; Chol. 12.

Obba, 5. 148.
Oberrare, 5. 156.
Obiurgare, 5. 169.
Obstipus, 3. 80.
Occare, 6. 26.
Ocimum, 4. 22.
Oenophorus, 5. 140.
Officia, 5. 93.
Oleum, 6. 50.
Omentum, 2. 47.
Orca, 3. 50.
Ordo, 3. 67.
Orestes, 3. 118.
Os: in ore esse &c., 1. 42.
Oscitare, 3. 59.
Ovum ruptum, 5. 185.

Pacuvius, p. xxvii., 1. 77.
Palilia, 1. 72.
Pallentes mores, 5. 15.
Pallor, 1. 26.
Palma, 6. 39.
Palpo, 5. 176.
Panaetius, p. xx.
Pannosus, 4. 32.
Pannucius, 4. 21.
Papae, 5. 79.
Pappare, 3. 17.
Paria, 6. 48.
Parthus, 5. 4.
Participle present, expressing habit, 5. 187; in *-rus*, 1. 100.
Patella, 3. 26.
Patrare, 1. 18.
Patruus, 1. 11.

INDEX.

Pede liber, 1. 13.
Pedius, 1. 85.
Pellis, 3. 95., 5. 140.
Penus, 3. 73.
Peragere, 5. 139.
Perducere, 2. 56.
Per leve, 1. 64.
Perna, 3. 75.
Pero, 5. 102.
Persius, memoir of, by Probus, p. xvi foll.; country of, 6. 6; life of, p. xvi-xx; his want of political feeling, p. xxiii; his hatred of the military, p. xviii., 3. 77; literary merits of, p. xxxiii; awkwardness in his composition, 2. 14., 6. 37; looked to books rather than life, 5. 123; confused by the grammarians with Horace, p. xxxi note.
Pertundere, 4. 28.
Pes, 4. 12.
Pexus, 1. 15.
Phalaris, 3. 39.
Phalerae, 3. 30.
Philosophers banished from Italy, p. xxi.
Philosophy, position of, in Rome, p. xxiii foll.
Pica, Chol. 13.
Picta lingua, 5. 25.
Pingue, 3. 33.
Pinsere, 1. 58.
Piper, 5. 55.
Pituita, 2. 57.
Pix, 5. 148.
Plasma, 1. 17.
Plebecula, 4. 5.
Plotius Macrinus, 2. 1.
Plural used contemptuously, 3. 79.
Pluteus, 1. 106.
Poetris, Chol. 13.
Polenta, 3. 55.
Ponere, 1. 53, 70., 3. 111., 5. 3.
Popa, 6. 74.
Popellus, 4. 15.
Porticus sapiens, 3. 53.
Posticus, 1. 62.
Pote, 1. 56.
Praedictus, 5. 188.
Praelargus, 1. 14.
Praetego, 4. 45.
Praetor, 5. 88.
Prandium, 3. 85.
Prayer, usually secret, 2. 5; proper objects of, 2 *passim*.
Premere, 5. 39.
Prendere, 6. 28.
Present where past would be expected, 3. 2.
Pressus, 5. 109.
Primordia vocum, 6. 3.

Progenies terrae, 6. 57.
Progne, 5. 8.
Prologue or Epilogue to the Satires, pp. vi, 138.
Proluere labra, Chol. 1.
Properare, transitive, 3. 23.
Prose, development of, from poetry, p. xxviii.
Protensus, 1. 57.
Publius, 5. 74.
Puella, 3. 110.
Pulfennius, 5. 190.
Pulmentaria, 3. 102.
Pulmo, 1. 14., 3. 27.
Pulpa, 2. 63.
Puls, 4. 31.
Punctum, 5. 100.
Puppets, metaphor from, 5. 128.
Purgatae aures, 5. 63.
Puta, 4. 9.
Puteal, 4. 49.

Quando, 1. 46.
Quartus pater, 6. 57.
Questions, direct and indirect, confused, 3. 67., 5. 27.
Quincunx, 5. 149.
Quinta hora, 3. 4.
Quirites, 3. 106., 5. 75.

Radere, 3. 114.
Ramale, 5. 59.
Rapere Aegaeum, 5. 142.
Rara avis, 1. 46.
Ratio, 5. 96.
Recessus mentis, 2. 73.
Recitations, 1. 15.
Recutitus, 5. 184.
Redire of revenue, 6. 79.
Refulgere, Chol. 12.
Regustatus, 5. 138.
Relaxare, 5. 125.
Relegere, 5. 118.
Reparabilis, 1. 102.
Reponere, 6. 66.
Res mirae, 1. 111; *res populi*, 4. 1.
Rheni, 6. 47.
Rhombus, 6. 23.
Rings, 1. 16.
Rivers, pictures or images of, borne in triumphal processions, 6. 47.
Rixari, 5. 178.
Rubellum, 5. 147.
Rubrica, 1. 66., 5. 90.
Rudere, 3. 9.
Ruga, 6. 79.

Sabbata, 5. 184.
Salinum, 3. 25.
Saliva, 1. 104., 2. 33., 5. 110., 6. 24.

Sambuca, 5. 95.
Sanna, 1. 62.
Saperda, 5. 134.
Sardonyx, 1. 16.
Sartago, 1. 80.
Σίρξ, 2. 63.
Satire, history of in Rome, p. xxvi; relation of to the comic drama, 5. 14.
Saturn, star of, 5. 50.
Scomber, 1. 43.
Scutica, 5. 131.
Secare, 1. 114.
Securus, 6. 12.
Semipaganus, Chol. 6.
Seneca, pp. xix, xxi, xxv.
Senio, 3. 48.
Sensus, 1. 69.
Sepia, 3. 13.
Sessilis, 5. 148.
Shipwrecked sailors, 1. 88., 6. 33.
Siccus, 5. 163.
Sinciput, 6. 70.
Sinister, 5. 164.
Sinuosus, 5. 27.
Sistrum, 5. 186.
Sitire, 1. 60.
Sive = *vel si*, 1. 67.
Slaves, emancipation of, by the Romans, 5. 75.
Socrates, 4. 1.
Solon, 3. 79.
Sonare, with accus., 3. 21.
Specimen, 5. 105.
Splen, 1. 12.
Spondaic verse, 1. 95.
Staius, 2. 19.
Stemma, 3. 28.
Stloppus, 5. 13.
Stoic habit of cutting the hair, 3. 54; doctrine of *fame*, 1. 47; *prayer*, 2 passim; *an all-seeing Deity*, 2. 17–30; *the aim of life*, 3. 60; *ethics as depending on metaphysics*, 3. 66; *the universe as a* πόλις, 3. 72; *freedom*, 5. 73 foll.; *law of Nature*, 5. 98; *life as an art*, 5. 105 ; *life with the gods*, 5. 139.
Stoicism, its contact with Rome, p. xx; change of, from a philosophy into a religion, p. xxii; religious development of, not anticipated by Persius, p. xxv.
Strigil, 5. 126.
Stringere, 2. 66.
Studere, 3. 19.
Stuppa, 5. 135.
Subaeratus, 5. 106.
Subducere costam Appennino, 1. 95.
Subeo, 2. 55; 3. 106.
Subplantare, 1. 35.

Subura, 5. 32.
Succinere, 3. 20.
Sufflare, 4. 20.
Sumen, 1. 53.
Summa boni, 4. 17.
Summa saliva, labra, 1. 104.
Supellex, 4. 52.
Supponere, 5. 36.
Surdus, 6. 35.
Surrentinum vinum, 3. 93.
Suscipere, 5. 36.

Tadius, 6. 66.
Talo recto, 5. 104.
Tectoria, 5. 25.
Temperare, 5. 51.
Tendere versum, 1. 65.
Teneri anni, 5. 36.
Tepidus, 1. 84.
Terebrare, 5. 138.
Teres, 5. 15.
Text of Persius, pp. xxxvii–viii.
Theocritus, *Charites* of, p. xxvii.
Theta, 4. 13.
Thrasea, p. xxi.
Thyestes, 5. 8.
Tiberius, letter of, to Senate, 3. 42.
Tinnire, 5. 106.
Titi, of Romans, 1. 20.
Togae verba, 5. 14.
Torch-race, 6. 61.
Totus, 5. 173.
Trabeatus, 3. 29.
Trabs, 1. 89., 6. 27.
Trama, 6. 73.
Transcendere, 5. 111.
Transilire, 5. 146.
Transtrum, 5. 147.
Transvectio equitum, 3. 29.
Trepidare, 5. 170.
Tresis, 5. 76.
Trisns, 3. 100.
Troiades, of the Romans, 1. 4.
Trossulus, 1. 82.
Trumpets at funerals, 3. 103.
Trutina, 1. 7.
Tuccetum, 2. 42.
Tunicatus, 4. 30.
Turda, 6. 24.
Tuscum fictile, 2. 60.

Udus; *in udo*, 1. 105.
Ultra, with comparative force, 3. 15.
Umbo, 5. 33.
Uncae nares, 1. 40.
Unctum, 6. 16.
Unguis ecfundere, 1. 65.
Urna, 5. 145.
Urtica, 6. 70.
Usus, 5. 52, 94.

INDEX.

Vapidus, 5. 117.
Vappa, 5. 77.
Varicosus, 5. 189.
Varus, 4. 12., 6. 18.
Vastus, 5. 141.
Vegrandis, 1. 97.
Veientanum, 5. 147.
Velina, 5. 73.
Venas tangere, 3. 107.
Vendere, 1. 122.
Venosus, 1. 76.
Venus, offerings to, 2. 70.
Veratrum, 1. 51.
Verba dare, 3. 19.
Verginius Flavus, p. xvii.
Verrucosus, 1. 77.
Vertere, 5. 137.
Vertigo, 5. 76.
Vessels, metaphor from, 3. 23.
Vetavit, 5. 90.

Vettidius, 4. 25.
Viatica, 5. 65.
Vibix, 4. 49.
Vide sis, 1. 108.
Vindicta, 5. 88.
Vin tu, 6. 63.
Violae, 5. 182.
Violaris dies, 1. 40.
Virbius, 6. 56.
Viridis limus, 3. 22.
Virtue as a mean, doctrine of, 4. 11.
Vivere, 6. 2, 25.
Vocative for nominative, 1. 123., 3. 28., 5. 124.
Vulpes, 5. 117.

Washing in the Tiber, habit of, 2. 15.

Y, letter, symbol of the two ways, 3. 56.

THE END.

WORKS

BY

HENRY NETTLESHIP, M.A.,
CORPUS PROFESSOR OF LATIN LITERATURE.

8vo, Twenty-one Shillings.
CONTRIBUTIONS TO LATIN LEXICOGRAPHY.

Crown 8vo, Seven Shillings and Sixpence.
LECTURES AND ESSAYS ON SUBJECTS
CONNECTED WITH LATIN LITERATURE AND SCHOLARSHIP.

8vo, sewed, One Shilling.
THE ROMAN SATURA.

8vo, sewed, Two Shillings.
ANCIENT LIVES OF VERGIL.

---

2 vols. 8vo, Twenty-four Shillings.
ESSAYS BY THE LATE MARK PATTISON, sometime Rector of Lincoln College. Collected and arranged by HENRY NETTLESHIP, M.A.

Second Edition. 8vo, Sixteen Shillings.
LIFE OF ISAAC CASAUBON (1559–1614). By MARK PATTISON, B.D. With a Portrait.

Oxford
AT THE CLARENDON PRESS
LONDON: HENRY FROWDE
OXFORD UNIVERSITY PRESS WAREHOUSE, AMEN CORNER, E.C.

[P. T. O.

Crown 8vo, Seven Shillings and Sixpence.

LECTURES AND ESSAYS ON SUBJECTS
CONNECTED WITH LATIN LITERATURE AND SCHOLARSHIP.

By HENRY NETTLESHIP, M.A., Corpus Professor of Latin Literature in the University of Oxford.

CONTENTS.

I. Moritz Haupt.
II. Early Italian Civilization: considered with especial reference to the evidence afforded on the subject by the Latin Language.
III. The Earliest Italian Literature.
IV. The Pro Cluentio of Cicero.
V. Catullus.
VI. Suggestions Introductory to a Study of the Aeneid.
VII. Horace:
    (1) Life and Poems.
    (2) The De Arte Poetica.
    (3) The Text.
    Note on Mr. Verrall's Studies in Horace.
VIII. Verrius Flaccus.
    Note on the Glosses of Placidus.
IX. The Noctes Atticae of Aulus Gellius.
X. Nonius Marcellus.
XI. Thilo's Servius.
XII. Critical Miscellanies.

Oxford
AT THE CLARENDON PRESS
LONDON: HENRY FROWDE
OXFORD UNIVERSITY PRESS WAREHOUSE, AMEN CORNER, E.C.

CLARENDON PRESS BOOKS
LATIN AND GREEK
Grammars and Exercise Books
Extra fcap 8vo

Mr. J. B. ALLEN's Elementary Series

Rudimenta Latina. Comprising accidence and exercises of a very elementary character for the use of beginners. 2s.

An Elementary Latin Grammar. 266th thousand. 2s. 6d.

A First Latin Exercise Book. Eighth edition. 2s. 6d.

A Second Latin Exercise Book. Second edition. 3s. 6d.

Key (see note p. 35) to both Exercise Books. 5s. net.

An Elementary Greek Grammar. Containing accidence and elementary syntax. 3s.

Mr. J. B. ALLEN's Latin Readers

With notes, maps, vocabularies and English exercises; stiff covers, 1s. 6d. each. These books are of the same and not of graduated difficulty.

Lives from Cornelius Nepos.

Tales of Early Rome.

Tales of the Roman Republic, Part I. } Adapted from the Text of Livy.

Tales of the Roman Republic, Part II.

Other Latin Readers, etc

Tales of the Civil War, edited by W. D. LOWE. 1s. 6d.

Scenes from the Life of Hannibal. Selected from Livy. Edited by W. D. LOWE. 1s. 6d.

Caesar in Britain; Selections from the Gallic War. Edited by W. D. LOWE. Illustrated. 1s.

Extracts from Cicero, with notes, by HENRY WALFORD. In three Parts. Third edition. Part I. Anecdotes from Grecian and Roman History. 1s. 6d. Part II. Omens and Dreams: Beauties of Nature. 1s. 6d. Part III. Rome's Rule of her Provinces. 1s. 6d. Parts I-III, 4s. 6d.

Extracts from Livy, with notes and maps, by H. LEE-WARNER. New edition. Part I. The Caudine Disaster. Part II. Hannibal's Campaign in Italy. Part III, by H. LEE-WARNER and T. W. GOULD. The Macedonian War. 1s. 6d. each.

A First Latin Reader, by T. J. NUNNS. Third edition. 2s.

An Introduction to Latin Syntax, by W. S. GIBSON. 2s.

Mr. C. S. JERRAM's Series

Reddenda Minora; or easy passages, Latin and Greek, for unseen translation. For the use of lower forms. Sixth edition, revised and enlarged. 1s. 6d.

Anglice Reddenda; or extracts, Latin and Greek, for unseen translation. First Series. Fifth edition. 2s. 6d. Also Latin extracts (First and Second Series), 2s. 6d.; Greek extracts, 3s. Vol. I, Latin, 2s. 6d.; Vol. II, Greek, 3s. Second Series. New edition. 3s. Third Series. 3s.

Greek Readers and Primers

Greek Reader. Selected and adapted with English notes from Professor von Wilamowitz-Moellendorff's *Griechisches Lesebuch*, by E. C. MARCHANT. Crown 8vo. 2 vols., each (with or without Vocabulary), 2s.

Selections from Plutarch's Caesar. Crown 8vo, large type. Edited by R. L. A. DU PONTET. 2s. (With or without Vocabulary.)

Greek Readers; Easy, by EVELYN ABBOTT. In stiff covers. 2s. **First Reader,** by W. G. RUSHBROOKE. Third edition. 2s. 6d. **Second Reader,** by A. M. BELL. Second edition. 3s. **Specimens of Greek Dialects;** being a Fourth Greek Reader. With introductions, etc, by W. W. MERRY. 4s. 6d. **Selections from Homer and the Greek Dramatists;** being a Fifth Greek Reader. With explanatory notes and introductions to the study of Greek Epic and Dramatic Poetry, by EVELYN ABBOTT. 4s. 6d.

A Greek Testament Primer. For the use of students beginning Greek, by E. MILLER. Second edition. Paper covers, 2s.; cloth, 3s. 6d.

Xenophon (see p. 43)

Easy Selections, with a vocabulary, notes, illustrations carefully chosen from coins, casts and ancient statues, and map, by J. S. PHILLPOTTS and C. S. JERRAM. Third edition. 3s. 6d.

Selections, with notes, illustrations, and maps, by J. S. PHILLPOTTS. Fifth ed. 3s. 6d. Key (see p. 35) to §§ 1-3, 2s. 6d. net.

A Greek Primer, for the use of beginners in that language. By the Right Rev. CHARLES WORDSWORTH. Eighty-sixth thousand. 1s. 6d. Graecae Grammaticae Rudimenta. Nineteenth edition. 4s.

An Introduction to the Comparative Grammar of Greek and Latin. By J. E. KING and C. COOKSON. Extra fcap 8vo. 5s. 6d.

Latin Dictionaries

A Latin Dictionary. Founded on Andrews's edition of Freund's Latin Dictionary. Revised, enlarged, and in great part rewritten, by CHARLTON T. LEWIS and CHARLES SHORT. 4to. 25s.

A School Latin Dictionary. By C. T. LEWIS. 4to. 12s. 6d.

Elementary Latin Dictionary. By C. T. LEWIS. Square 8vo. 7s. 6d.

Greek Dictionaries

A Greek-English Lexicon. By H. G. LIDDELL and ROBERT SCOTT. Eighth edition, revised. 4to. 36s.

An Intermediate Greek Lexicon. By the same. 12s. 6d.

An Abridged Greek Lexicon. By the same. 7s. 6d.

Latin and Greek Prose Composition

Mr. J. Y. SARGENT's Course. Extra fcap 8vo

Primer of Latin Prose Composition. 2s. 6d.

Passages for Translation into Latin Prose. Eighth edition. 2s. 6d. Key (see note below) to the eighth edition, 5s. net.

Primer of Greek Prose. [Out of print.] Key (see note below), 5s. net.

Passages for Translation into Greek Prose. 3s.

Exemplaria Graeca. Select Greek versions of the above. 3s.

Other Prose Composition Books. Extra fcap 8vo

Ramsay's Latin Prose Composition. Fourth edition.
Vol. I: Syntax and Exercises. 4s. 6d. Or Part 1, First Year's Course, 1s. 6d.; Part 2, Second Year's Course, 1s. 6d.; Part 3, Syntax and Appendix, 2s. 6d. Key (see note below) to the volume, 5s. net.
Vol. II: Passages for Translation. 4s. 6d.

Jerram's Graece Reddenda. Being exercises for Greek Prose. 2s. 6d.

Unseen Translation

Jerram's Reddenda Minora and Anglice Reddenda. See p. 33.

Fox and Bromley's Models and Exercises in Unseen Translation. Revised edition. Extra fcap 8vo. 5s. 6d. A Key (see note below) giving references for the passages contained in the above, 6d. net.

Latin and Greek Verse

Lee-Warner's Helps and Exercises for Latin Elegiacs. 3s. 6d. Key (see note below) 4s. 6d. net.

Rouse's Demonstrations in Latin Elegiac Verse. Crown 8vo. 4s. 6d. (Exercises and versions.)

Laurence's Helps and Exercises for Greek Iambic Verse. 3s. 6d. Key (see note below) 5s. net.

Sargent's Models and Materials for Greek Iambic Verse. 4s. 6d. Key (see note below) 5s. net.

Nova Anthologia Oxoniensis. Edited by ROBINSON ELLIS and A. D. GODLEY. Crown 8vo buckram extra, 6s. net; on India paper, 7s. 6d. net.

Musa Clauda. Being translations into Latin Elegiac Verse, by S. G. OWEN and J. S. PHILLIMORE. Crown 8vo, boards, 3s. 6d.

Latin Prose Versions. Contributed by various Scholars, edited by G. G. RAMSAY. Extra fcap 8vo, 5s.

KEYS

Application for all Keys to be made direct to the Secretary, Clarendon Press, Oxford, and accompanied by a remittance. Keys can be obtained by teachers or bona fide private students.

Annotated editions of Latin Authors

For Oxford Classical Texts see p. 41; for Oxford Translations, p. 21.

Aetna. A critical recension of the Text, with prolegomena, translation, commentary, and index verborum. By ROBINSON ELLIS. Crown 8vo. 7s. 6d. net.

Avianus, The Fables. With prolegomena, critical apparatus, commentary, etc. By ROBINSON ELLIS. 8vo. 8s. 6d.

Caesar, De Bello Gallico, I-VII. In two crown 8vo volumes. By ST. G. STOCK. Vol. I, Introduction, 5s.; Vol. II, Text and Notes, 6s.

The Gallic War. By C. E. MOBERLY. Second edition. With maps. Books I-III, 2s.; III-V, 2s. 6d.; VI-VIII, 3s. 6d.

The Civil War. New edition. By the same editor. 3s. 6d.

Catulli Veronensis Liber rec. ROBINSON ELLIS. Second edition, with notes and appendices. 8vo. 21s. net.

Commentary. By the same. Second edition. 8vo. 18s. net.

Carmina Selecta. Text only, for Schools. 3s. 6d.

Cicero, de Amicitia. By ST. GEORGE STOCK. 3s.

de Senectute. By L. HUXLEY. 2s.

in Catilinam. By E. A. UPCOTT. Third edition. 2s. 6d.

in Q. Caecilium Divinatio and **in C. Verrem Actio Prima.** By J. R. KING. Limp, 1s. 6d.

pro Cluentio. By G. G. RAMSAY. Second ed. 3s. 6d.

pro Marcello, pro Ligario, pro Rege Deiotaro. By W. Y. FAUSSET. Second edition. 2s. 6d.

pro Milone. By A. C. CLARK. 8vo. 8s. 6d. By A. B. POYNTON. Second edition. Crown 8vo. 2s. 6d.

Philippics, I, II, III, V, VII. By J. R. KING. Revised by A. C. CLARK. 3s. 6d.

pro Roscio. By ST. GEORGE STOCK. 3s. 6d.

Select Orations, viz. in Verrem Actio Prima, de Imperio Gn. Pompeii, pro Archia, Philippica IX. By J. R. KING. Second edition. 2s. 6d.

Select Letters. With introductions, notes, and appendices. By A. WATSON. Fourth edition. 8vo. 18s. Text only of the large edition. By the same. Third edition. Extra fcap 8vo. 4s.

Selected Letters. By C. E. PRICHARD and E. R. BERNARD. Second edition. 3s.

De Oratore Libri Tres. With introduction and notes. By A. S. WILKINS. 8vo. 18s. Or separately, Book I. Third edition. 7s. 6d. Book II. Second edition. 5s. Book III. 6s.

Horace, Odes, Carmen Saeculare, and Epodes. By E. C. WICKHAM. 8vo. Third edition. 12s. Crown 8vo. Second edition. 6s.

Selected Odes. By the same. 2nd ed. 2s. Odes, Book I. 2s.

Satires, Epistles, De Arte Poetica. By the same. Cr. 8vo. 6s.

Text only: miniature Oxford edition. On writing-paper for MS notes, 3s. net; on Oxford India paper, roan, 4s. 6d. net.

Iuvenalis ad satiram sextam additi versus xxxvi exscr. E. O. WINSTEDT. With a facsimile. In wrapper, 2s. 6d. net.

Thirteen Satires. By C. H. PEARSON and H. A. STRONG. Cr. 8vo. 9s.

Livy, Book I. By Sir J. R. SEELEY. Third edition. 8vo. 6s.

Books V-VII. By A. R. CLUER. Revised by P. E. MATHESON. 5s. Separately: Book V, 2s. 6d.; Book VI, 2s.; Book VII, 2s.

Book IX. By T. NICKLIN. Crown 8vo, 2s. 6d.; with vocabulary, 3s.

Books XXI-XXIII. By M. T. TATHAM. Second edition, enlarged. 5s. Separately: Book XXI, 2s. 6d.; Book XXII, 2s. 6d.

Lucretius, Book V. Edited by W. D. LOWE. Crown 8vo. 1-782, 2s.; 783-1457, 2s.; together, 3s. 6d.

Noctes Manilianae. By ROBINSON ELLIS. Crown 8vo. 6s.

Martialis Epigrammata Selecta (W. M. LINDSAY's Text and critical notes). Crown 8vo. 3s. 6d. On India paper. 5s.

Books I-VI, VII-XII. Edited by R. T. BRIDGE and E. D. C. LAKE, each 3s. 6d. Notes only, each 2s.

Nepos. By OSCAR BROWNING. Third edition, revised by W. R. INGE. 3s.

Nonius Marcellus, de compendiosa doctrina I-III. Edited, with introduction and critical apparatus, by J. H. ONIONS. 8vo. 10s. 6d.

Ovid, Heroides, with the Greek translations of Planudes. Edited by ARTHUR PALMER. 8vo. With a facsimile. 21s.

Ibis. With scholia and commentary. By ROBINSON ELLIS. 8vo. 10s. 6d.

Metamorphoses, Book III. Edited by M. CARTWRIGHT. Crown 8vo. 2s. With or without vocabulary. **Book XI.** Edited by G. A. T. DAVIES. Crown 8vo. 2s. With or without vocabulary.

Stories from the Metamorphoses, Edited by D. A. SLATER. Crown 8vo, illustrated. 2s. 6d. With or without vocabulary.

Tristia. Edited by S. G. OWEN. 8vo. 16s. Extra fcap 8vo. Third edition. Book I, 3s. 6d. Book III, 2s.

Selections. By G. G. RAMSAY. Third edition. 5s. 6d.

Persius, The Satires. With a translation and commentary, by JOHN CONINGTON. Edited by HENRY NETTLESHIP. Third edition. 8vo. 8s. 6d.

Plautus, Captivi. By WALLACE M. LINDSAY. Second edition. 2s. 6d.

Mostellaria. By E. A. SONNENSCHEIN. Second edition. Fcap 8vo. Text interleaved. 4s. 6d.

Rudens. By the same. 8vo. 8s. 6d. **Editio minor**, Text and Appendix on Metre interleaved. Second edition. 4s. 6d.

Trinummus. By C. E. FREEMAN and A. SLOMAN. Third edition. 3s.

Plauti Codex Turnebi. By W. M. LINDSAY. 8vo. 21s. net.

Pliny, Selected Letters. By C. E. PRICHARD and E. R. BERNARD. Third edition. 3s.

Propertius. Index Verborum. By J. S. PHILLIMORE. Crown 8vo. 4s. 6d. net. Translation by the same. Extra fcap 8vo. 3s. 6d. net.

Selections. See Tibullus.

Quintilian, Institutionis Oratoriae Lib. x. By W. PETERSON. 8vo. 12s. 6d. School edition. By the same. Extra fcap 8vo. Second edition. 3s. 6d.

Sallust. By W. W. CAPES. Second edition. 4s. 6d.

Scriptores Latini Rei Metricae. Edited by T. GAISFORD. 8vo. 5s.

Selections from the less known Latin Poets. By NORTH PINDER. 7s. 6d.

Tacitus. Edited, with introductions and notes, by H. FURNEAUX. 8vo.
    Annals. Books I-VI. Second ed. 18s. Books XI-XVI. Second edition, revised by H. F. PELHAM and C. D. FISHER. 21s.
    Annals. (Text only.) Crown 8vo. 6s.
    Annals, Books I-IV. 5s. Book I. Limp, 2s. Books XIII-XVI (abridged from Furneaux's 8vo edition). By H. PITMAN. 4s. 6d.
    De Germania. Vita Agricolae. 6s. 6d. each.
    Dialogus de Oratoribus. Edited, with introduction and notes, by W. PETERSON. 8vo. 10s. 6d. net.

Terence, Adelphi. By A. SLOMAN. Second edition. 3s.
    Andria. By C. E. FREEMAN and A. SLOMAN. Second edition. 3s.
    Phormio. By A. SLOMAN. Second edition. 3s.
    'Famulus.' By J. SARGEAUNT and A. G. S. RAYNOR. 2s.

Tibullus and Propertius, Selections. By G. G. RAMSAY. Third edition. 6s.

Velleius Paterculus. By ROBINSON ELLIS. Crown 8vo. 6s.

Virgil. By T. L. PAPILLON and A. E. HAIGH. Two volumes. Crown 8vo. Cloth, 6s. each; or stiff covers, 3s. 6d. each.
    Text only (including the minor works emended by R. ELLIS). Miniature Oxford edition. By the same editors. 32mo. On writing-paper, 3s. net; on Oxford India paper, roan, 4s. 6d. net.
    Aeneid, Books I-III, IV-VI, VII-IX, X-XII. By the same editors. 2s. each part. Book IX, by A. E. HAIGH, 1s. 6d.; in two parts, 2s.
    Bucolics and Georgics. By the same editors. 2s. 6d.
    Bucolics. 2s. 6d. Georgics, Books I, II, 2s. 6d. Books III, IV, 2s. 6d. Aeneid, Book I. Limp cloth, 1s. 6d. All by C. S. JERRAM.

Literature of the Early Empire: selections edited by A. C. B. BROWN. Crown 8vo, in two parts, each 2s. 6d.; together 4s. 6d.

Latin Works of Reference

Lewis and Short's Latin Dictionaries. See p. 34.

The Latin Language, being an historical account of Latin Sounds, Stems, and Flexions. By W. M. LINDSAY. 8vo. 21s.

Selected Fragments of Roman Poetry. Edited, with introduction and notes, by W. W. MERRY. Second edition. Crown 8vo. 6s. 6d.

Fragments and Specimens of Early Latin. With introductions and notes. By J. WORDSWORTH. 8vo. 18s.

Selections from the less known Latin Poets. By NORTH PINDER. 8vo. 7s. 6d.

Latin Historical Inscriptions, illustrating the history of the Early Empire. By G. McN. RUSHFORTH. 8vo. 10s. net.

Scheller's Latin Dictionary. Revised and translated into English by J. E. RIDDLE. Folio. 21s. net.

Professor Nettleship's Books

Contributions to Latin Lexicography. 8vo. 21s.

Lectures and Essays. Second Series. Edited by F. HAVERFIELD. With portrait and memoir. Crown 8vo. 7s. 6d. (The first series is out of print.)

The Roman Satura. 8vo. Sewed. 1s.

Professor Sellar's Books

Roman Poets of the Republic. Third edition. Crown 8vo. 10s.

Roman Poets of the Augustan Age. Crown 8vo. viz.: **Virgil.** Third edition. 9s., and **Horace and the Elegiac Poets,** with a memoir of the Author, by ANDREW LANG. Second edition. 7s. 6d.

(A limited number of copies of the first edition of *Horace*, containing a portrait of the Author, can still be obtained in Demy 8vo, price 14s.)

Post-Augustan Poetry from Seneca to Juvenal. By H. E. BUTLER. 8vo. 8s. 6d. net.

The Principles of Sound and Inflexion, as illustrated in the Greek and Latin Languages. By J. E. KING and C. COOKSON. 8vo. 18s.

Comparative Philology. By T. L. PAPILLON. Ed. 3. Crown 8vo. 6s.

Fontes Prosae Numerosae collegit A. C. CLARK. 8vo. 4s. 6d. net.

The Cursus in Mediaeval and Vulgar Latin. By the same Author. 8vo. 2s. net. The two bound together, 4s. 6d. net.

Professor Ellis's Lectures

8vo, each 1s. net. Published by Mr. Frowde.

Juvenal, The New Fragments.—Phaedrus, The Fables.—The Correspondence of Fronto and M. Aurelius.—Catullus in the Fourteenth Century.—A Bodleian MS of Copa, Moretum, and other Poems of the Appendix Vergiliana. (Cr. 8vo.)—The Elegiae in Maecenatem.—The Annalist Licinianus, with an Appendix of Emendations of the Text.—Prof. Birt's Edition of the Vergilian Catalepton.

OXFORD CLASSICAL TEXTS

The prices given of copies on ordinary paper are for copies bound in limp cloth; uncut copies may be had in paper covers at 6d. less per volume (1s. less for those priced from 6s. in cloth). All volumes are also on sale interleaved with writing-paper and bound in stout cloth; prices in square brackets.

Greek

Aeschylus. A. SIDGWICK. 3s. 6d. [7s. 6d.] (India paper, 4s. 6d.)

Antoninus. J. H. LEOPOLD. 3s. [5s. 6d.] (India paper, 4s.)

Apollonius Rhodius. R. C. SEATON. 3s. [5s. 6d.] (India paper, 4s.)

Aristophanes. F. W. HALL, W. M. GELDART. (India paper, 8s. 6d.)
    I. Ach., Eq., Nub., Vesp., Pax, Aves. 3s. 6d. [7s. 6d.] (India paper, 4s. 6d.)
    II. Lys., Thesm., Ran., Eccl., Plut., fr. 3s. 6d. [7s. 6d.] (India paper, 4s. 6d.)

Bucolici Graeci. U. VON WILAMOWITZ-MOELLENDORFF. 3s. [7s.] (India paper, 4s.)

Demosthenes. S. H. BUTCHER. (India paper, 12s. 6d.)
    I. Orationes I–XIX. 4s. 6d. [8s. 6d.] II. i. Orationes XX–XXVI. 3s. 6d. [7s. 6d.]

Euripides. G. G. A. MURRAY. (India paper, Vols. I–III, 12s. 6d.; Vols. I–II, 9s.; Vol. III, 4s. 6d.)
    I. Cyc., Alc., Med., Heracl., Hip., Andr., Hec. 3s. 6d. [7s. 6d.]
    II. Suppl., Herc., Ion, Tro., El., I. T. 3s. 6d. [7s. 6d.]
    III. Hel., Phoen., Or., Bacch., Iph. Aul., Rh. 3s. 6d. [7s. 6d.]

Hellenica Oxyrhynchia cum Theopompi et Cratippi fragmentis. B. P. GRENFELL, A. S. HUNT. 4s. 6d.

Herodotus. K. HUDE. (India paper, 12s. 6d.)
    Vol. I (Books I–IV). 4s. 6d. [10s.] Vol. II (Books V–IX). 4s. 6d. [10s.]

Homer, 3s. per volume. [5s. 6d. per volume.]
    Iliad. (Vols. I and II.) D. B. MONRO, T. W. ALLEN. (India paper, 7s.)
    Odyssey. (Vols. III and IV.) T. W. ALLEN. (India paper, 6s.)

Hyperides. F. G. KENYON. 3s. 6d.

Longinus. A. O. PRICKARD. 2s. 6d.

Plato. J. BURNET. Vols. I–III, 6s. each [12s. each] (India paper, 7s. each). Vol. IV. 7s. [14s.] (India paper, 8s. 6d.) Vol. V. 8s. [16s.] (India paper, 10s. 6d.)
    I. Euth., Apol., Crit., Ph.; Crat., Tht., Soph., Polit.
    II. Par., Phil., Symp., Phdr.; Alc. I, II, Hipp., Am.
    III. Thg., Chrm., Lch., Lys.; Euthd., Prot., Gorg., Men.; Hp., Io, Mnx.
    IV. Clit., Rep., Tim., Critias. Also Republic, separately, 6s. [12s.]; on quarto writing-paper, 10s. 6d.
    V. Part I, Minos, Leges, I–VIII; Part II, Leges IX–XII, Epinomis, Epistulae, Definitiones, Spuria.
    First and fifth tetralogies separately, paper covers, 2s. each.
    Apology and Meno separately, paper covers, 2s.

Theophrasti Characteres. H. DIELS. 3s. 6d.

Thucydides. H. STUART JONES. (India paper, 8s. 6d.)
    I. Books 1–4. II. Books 5–8. 3s. 6d. each. [7s. 6d. each.]

Xenophon. E. C. MARCHANT. (Vols. I–III, India Paper, 12s. 6d.)
    I. Historia Graeca. 3s. [7s.]   III. Anabasis. 3s. [7s.]
    II. Libri Socratici. 3s. 6d. [7s. 6d.]   IV. Institutio Cyri. 3s. 6d. [7s. 6d.]

Aristotle. I. BYWATER.
    Ethica Nicomachea. 4s. [8s.]; on quarto writing-paper, 10s. 6d.
    De Arte Poetica. 2s. [4s. 6d.]

Latin

Asconius. A. C. Clark. 3s. 6d. [6s.]

Caesar, Commentarii. R. L. A. Du Pontet. (India paper, 7s.)
Bellum Gallicum. 2s. 6d. [6s.] Bellum Civile. 3s. [7s.]

Catullus. R. Ellis. 2s. 6d. [5s.] (With Tibullus and Propertius, on India paper, 8s. 6d.)

Cicero, Epistulae. L. C. Purser. (India paper, 21s.)
    I. Epp. ad Fam. 6s. [12s.]; II. ad Att., Pars i (1–8), Pars ii (9–16), 4s. 6d. each [8s. 6d. each]; III. ad Q. F., ad M. Brut., Fragm. 3s. [5s. 6d.]
    Orationes. (Rosc. Am. etc, Mil. etc, Verrinae, India paper, 18s. 6d.)
        Rosc. Am., I. Pomp., Clu., Cat., Mur., Cael. A. C. Clark. 3s. [7s.]
        Pro Milone, Caesarianae, Philippicae. A. C. Clark. 3s. [7s.]
        Verrinae. W. Peterson. 4s. [8s.]
        Quinct., Rosc. Com., Caec., Leg. Agr., Rab. Perduell., Flacc., Pis., Rab. Post. A. C. Clark. 3s. [7s.]
        Post Reditum, De Domo, Har. Resp., Sest., Vat., Prov. Cons., Balb. W. Peterson. [In the press.]
        Tull., Font., Sull., Arch., Planc., Scaur. A. C. Clark. [In the press.]
    Rhetorica. A. S. Wilkins. (India paper, 7s. 6d.)
        I. De Oratore. 3s. [7s.] II. Brutus, etc. 3s. 6d. [7s. 6d.]

Horace. E. C. Wickham. 3s. [5s. 6d.] (India paper, 4s. 6d.)

Lucretius. C. Bailey. 3s. [5s. 6d.] (India paper, 4s.)

Martial. W. M. Lindsay. 6s. [12s.] (India paper, 7s. 6d.)

Nepos. E. O. Winstedt. 2s. [4s. 6d.]

Persius and Juvenal. S. G. Owen. 3s. [5s. 6d.] (India paper, 4s.)

Plautus. W. M. Lindsay. (India paper, 16s.)
    I. Amph.—Merc. II. Miles—fragm. 6s. each. [13s. 6d. each.]

Propertius. J. S. Phillimore. 3s. [5s. 6d.] (India paper, see Catullus.)

Statius. (Complete on India paper. 10s. 6d.)
    Silvae. J. S. Phillimore. 3s. 6d. [6s.]
    Thebais and Achilleis. H. W. Garrod. 6s. [12s.]

Tacitus, Opera Minora. H. Furneaux. 2s. [4s. 6d.]
    Annales. C. D. Fisher. 6s. [12s.] (India paper, 7s.)
    Historiae. C. D. Fisher. 4s. [7s. 6d.]

Terence. R. Y. Tyrrell. 3s. 6d. [7s. 6d.] (India paper, 5s.)

Tibullus. J. P. Postgate. 2s. [4s. 6d.] (India paper, see Catullus.)

Vergil. F. A. Hirtzel. 3s. 6d. [8s. 6d.] (India paper, 4s. 6d.)

Appendix Vergiliana. R. Ellis. 4s.

Annotated Greek Classics

For Oxford Classical Texts, see p. 40; for Oxford Translations, p. 21.

Extra fcap 8vo

Aeschylus. By ARTHUR SIDGWICK. New editions with the text of the *Oxford Classical Texts*.

- **Agamemnon.** Sixth edition revised. 3s.   **Choephoroi.** New edition revised. 3s.   **Eumenides.** Third edition. 3s.   **Persae.** 3s.   **Septem contra Thebas.** 3s.
- **Prometheus Vinctus.** By A. O. PRICKARD. Fourth edition. 2s.

Aristophanes. By W. W. MERRY.

- **Acharnians.** Fifth edition. 3s.   **Birds.** Fourth edition. 3s. 6d.
- **Clouds.** Second edition. 3s.   **Frogs.** Fifth edition. 3s.
- **Knights.** Second edition. 3s.   **Peace.** 3s. 6d.
- **Wasps.** Second edition. 3s. 6d.

Cebes, Tabula. By C. S. JERRAM. Stiff covers, 1s. 6d.; cloth, 2s. 6d.

Demosthenes. By EVELYN ABBOTT and P. E. MATHESON.

- **Against Philip.** Vol. I: Philippic I, Olynthiacs I–III. Fourth edition. 3s. Vol. II: De Pace, Philippic II, de Chersoneso, Philippic III. 4s. 6d. Philippics I–III (reprinted from above). 2s. 6d.
- **On the Crown.** 3s. 6d.
- **Against Meidias.** By J. R. KING. Crown 8vo. 3s. 6d.

Euripides.

- **Alcestis.** By C. S. JERRAM. Fifth edition. 2s. 6d.   **Bacchae.** By A. H. CRUICKSHANK. 3s. 6d.   **Cyclops.** By W. E. LONG. 2s. 6d.   **Hecuba.** By C. B. HEBERDEN. 2s. 6d.   **Helena.** By C. S. JERRAM. Second edition. 3s.   **Heracleidae.** By C. S. JERRAM. 3s.   **Ion.** By C. S. JERRAM. 3s.   **Iphigenia in Tauris.** By C. S. JERRAM. New edition revised. 3s.   **Medea.** By C. B. HEBERDEN. Third edition. 2s.

Herodotus, Book IX. By EVELYN ABBOTT. 3s.

- **Selections.** With a map. By W. W. MERRY. 2s. 6d.

Homer, Iliad. By D. B. MONRO. I–XII. With a brief Homeric Grammar. Fifth edition. 6s. Book I, with the Homeric Grammar, separately. Third edition. 1s. 6d. XIII–XXIV. Fourth edition. 6s.
Book III (for beginners), by M. T. TATHAM. 1s. 6d. Book XXI. By HERBERT HAILSTONE. 1s. 6d.

Homer, Odyssey. By W. W. MERRY.
I–XII. Sixty-sixth thousand. 5s. Books I and II, separately, each 1s. 6d. Books VI and VII. 1s. 6d. Books VII–XII. 3s.
XIII–XXIV. Sixteenth thousand. 5s. Books XIII–XVIII. 3s. Books XIX–XXIV. 3s.

Lucian, Vera Historia. By C. S. Jerram. Second edition. 1s. 6d.

Dialogues prepared for Schools. By W. H. D. Rouse. Text 2s., Notes in Greek 2s.

Lysias, Epitaphios. By F. J. Snell. 2s.

Plato. By St. George Stock. Euthyphro. 2s. 6d. Apology. Ed. 3. 2s. 6d. Crito. 2s. Meno. Ed. 3. 2s. 6d. Ion. 2s. 6d.

Euthydemus. With revised text, introduction, notes, and indices, by E. H. Gifford. Crown 8vo. 3s. 6d.

Menexenus. By J. A. Shawyer. Crown 8vo. 2s.

Selections. By J. Purves with preface by B. Jowett. 2nd ed. 5s.

Plutarch, Lives of the Gracchi. By G. E. Underhill. Crown 8vo. 4s. 6d.

Coriolanus (for Junior Students). With introduction and notes. 2s.

Sophocles. By Lewis Campbell and Evelyn Abbott. New and revised edition. Two volumes: Vol. I text 4s. 6d.; Vol. II notes 6s.
Or singly 2s. each (text and notes), Ajax, Antigone, Electra, Oedipus Coloneus, Oedipus Tyrannus, Philoctetes, Trachiniae.

Scenes from Sophocles, edited by C. E. Laurence. With illustrations. 1s. 6d. each. (1) Ajax. (2) Antigone.

Select Fragments of the Greek Comic Poets. By A. W. Pickard-Cambridge. Crown 8vo. 5s.

Golden Treasury of Ancient Greek Poetry. By Sir R. S. Wright. Second edition. Revised by E. Abbott. Extra fcap 8vo. 10s. 6d.

Golden Treasury of Greek Prose. By Sir R. S. Wright and J. E. L. Shadwell. Extra fcap 8vo. 4s. 6d.

Theocritus. By H. Kynaston. Fifth edition. 4s. 6d.

Thucydides. Book III. By H. F. Fox. Crown 8vo. 3s. 6d. Book IV. By T. R. Mills. With an introductory essay by H. S. Jones. Crown 8vo. 3s. 6d. Notes only, 2s. 6d.

Xenophon. (See also p. 34.)

Anabasis. Each of the first four Books is now issued in uniform cloth binding at 1s. 6d. Each volume contains introduction, text, notes, and a full vocabulary to the Anabasis. Book I. By J. Marshall. Book II. By C. S. Jerram. Books III and IV. By J. Marshall. Books III, IV, 3s. *Vocabulary to the Anabasis*, by J. Marshall. 1s.

Cyropaedia, Book I. 2s. Books IV and V. 2s. 6d. By C. Bigg.

Hellenica, Books I, II. By G. E. Underhill. 3s.

Memorabilia. By J. Marshall. 4s. 6d.

Editions etc of Greek Authors mostly with English notes

Appian, Book I. Edited with map and appendix on Pompey's passage of the Alps, by J. L. STRACHAN-DAVIDSON. Crown 8vo. 3s. 6d.

Aristophanes, A Concordance to. By H. DUNBAR. 4to. £1 1s. net.

Aristotle.

   The Poetics. A revised Greek text, with critical introduction, English translation and commentary, by I. BYWATER. 8vo. 16s. net.

   De Arte Poetica Liber recognovit I. BYWATER. See p. 40.

   Ethica Nicomachea recognovit I. BYWATER. See p. 40.

   Contributions to the Textual Criticism of Aristotle's Nicomachean Ethics. By I. BYWATER. Stiff cover. 2s. 6d.

   Notes on the Nicomachean Ethics. By J. A. STEWART. 2 vols. Post 8vo. £1 12s.

   The English Manuscripts of the Nicomachean Ethics. By J. A. STEWART. Crown 4to. 3s. 6d. net.

   Selecta ex Organo Capitula: in usum Scholarum Academicarum. Crown 8vo, stiff covers. 3s. 6d.

   The Politics, with introduction, notes, etc, by W. L. NEWMAN. 4 vols. Medium 8vo. 14s. net per volume.

   The Politics, translated into English, with introduction, notes, and indices, by B. JOWETT. Medium 8vo. Vol. I, 10s. net; Vol. II, 8s. 6d. net.

   Aristotelian Studies. On the Structure of the Seventh Book of the Nicomachean Ethics. By J. COOK WILSON. 8vo. 5s.

   On the History of the Aristotelian Writings. By R. SHUTE. 8vo. 7s. 6d.

   Physics, Book VII. With introduction by R. SHUTE. 2s. net.

   The Works of Aristotle. Translated into English under the Editorship of J. A. SMITH and W. D. ROSS. 8vo.

      Parva Naturalia. By J. I. BEARE and G. R. T. ROSS. 3s. 6d. net.

      De Lineis Insecabilibus. By H. H. JOACHIM. 2s. 6d. net.

      Metaphysica. (Vol. VIII.) By W. D. ROSS. 7s. 6d. net.

      De Mirabilibus Auscultationibus. By L. D. DOWDALL. 2s. net.

      Historia Animalium. (Vol. IV.) By D'ARCY W. THOMPSON. 10s. 6d. net.

      De Generatione Animalium. By A. PLATT. 7s. 6d. net.

      De Partibus Animalium. By W. OGLE. 5s. net.

Aristoxenus. Edited, with introduction, music, translation, and notes, by H. S. MACRAN. Crown 8vo. 10s. 6d. net.

Demosthenes and Aeschines on the Crown. With introductory essays and notes, by G. A. SIMCOX and W. H. SIMCOX. 8vo. 12s.

Heracliti Ephesii Reliquiae. Edited by I. BYWATER, with Diogenes Laertius' Life of Heraclitus, etc. 8vo. 6s.

Herodas. Edited, with full introduction and notes, by J. ARBUTHNOT NAIRN. With facsimiles of the fragments and other illustrations. 8vo. 12s. 6d. net.

Herodotus, Books V and VI. Terpsichore and Erato. Edited, with notes and appendices, by E. ABBOTT. With two maps. Post 8vo. 6s.

Homer, A Concordance to the Odyssey and Hymns; and to the Parallel Passages in the Iliad, Odyssey, and Hymns. By H. DUNBAR. 4to. £1 1s. net.

    Odyssey. Books I-XII. Edited, with English notes, appendices, etc, by W. W. MERRY and J. RIDDELL. Second edition. 8vo. 16s.

    Books XIII-XXIV. Edited, with English notes, appendices, and illustrations, by D. B. MONRO. 8vo. 16s.

    Hymni Homerici codicibus denuo collatis recensuit A. GOODWIN. Small folio. With four plates. £1 1s. net.

    Scholia Graeca in Iliadem. Edited by W. DINDORF, after a new collation of the Venetian MSS by D. B. MONRO. 4 vols. 8vo. £2 10s. net. See also p. 47.

    Opera et Reliquiae, recensuit D. B. MONRO. Crown 8vo, on India paper. 10s. 6d. net. 'The Oxford Homer.'

    Homerica. Emendations and Elucidations of the Odyssey. By T. L. AGAR. 8vo. 14s. net.

Index Andocideus, Lycurgeus, Dinarcheus, confectus ab L. L. FORMAN. 8vo. 7s. 6d. net.

Menander's Γεωργός, the Geneva Fragment, with text, translation, and notes, by B. P. GRENFELL and A. S. HUNT. 8vo, stiff covers. 1s. 6d.

Νόμος Ῥοδίων Ναυτικός. The Rhodian Sea-Law. Edited, with introduction, translation, and commentary, by W. ASHBURNER. 8vo. 18s. net.

Plato, Philebus. Edited by E. POSTE. 8vo. 7s. 6d.

    Republic. Edited, with notes and essays, by B. JOWETT and L. CAMPBELL. In three volumes. Medium 8vo, cloth. £2 2s.

    Sophistes and Politicus. Edited by L. CAMPBELL. 8vo. 10s. 6d. net.

    Theaetetus. Edited by L. CAMPBELL. 2nd ed. 8vo. 10s. 6d. net.

    The Dialogues, translated into English, with analyses and introductions, by B. JOWETT. Third edition. Five volumes, medium 8vo. £4 4s. In half-morocco, £5. *The Subject-Index to the second edition of the Dialogues,* by E. ABBOTT, separately. 8vo, cloth. 2s. 6d.

    The Republic, translated into English, by B. JOWETT. Third edition. Medium 8vo. 12s. 6d. Half-roan, 14s.

    Selections from JOWETT's translation, with introductions by M. J. KNIGHT. Two volumes. Crown 8vo. 12s.

Polybius, Selections. Edited by J. L. STRACHAN-DAVIDSON. With maps. Medium 8vo, buckram. 21s.

Sophocles, The Plays and Fragments. Edited by L. CAMPBELL.
Vol. I: Oedipus Tyrannus. Oedipus Coloneus. Antigone. 8vo. 16s.
Vol. II: Ajax. Electra. Trachiniae. Philoctetes. Fragments. 8vo. 16s.

Strabo, Selections. With an introduction on Strabo's Life and Works.
By H. F. TOZER. With maps and plans. Post 8vo, cloth. 12s.

Thucydides. Translated into English by B. JOWETT. Second edition, revised. 2 vols. 8vo. 15s.
Vol. I: Essay on Inscriptions, and Books I-III.
Vol. II: Books IV-VIII, and Historical Index.

Xenophon, Hellenica. Edited, with introduction and appendices, by G. E. UNDERHILL. Crown 8vo. 7s. 6d. Also with the Oxford Text by E. C. MARCHANT, one volume. 7s. 6d. net.

Older Clarendon Press Editions of Greek Authors

The Greek texts in fine and generally large type; the Scholia (and some of the texts) have not appeared in any later editions. The annotations are in Latin.

Aeschinem et Isocratem, Scholia Graeca in, edidit G. DINDORFIUS. 8vo. 4s.

Aeschylus ex rec. G. DINDORFII. Tragoediae et Fragmenta. Second edition. 8vo. 5s. 6d. Annotationes. Partes II. 8vo. 10s.
Quae supersunt in codice Laurentiano typis descripta edidit R. MERKEL. Small folio. £1 1s. net.

Apsinis et Longini Rhetorica recensuit JOH. BAKIUS. 8vo. 3s.

Aristophanes ex rec. G. DINDORFII. Comoediae et Fragmenta. Tomi II. 8vo. 11s. Annotationes. Partes II. 8vo. 11s. Scholia Graeca. Partes III. 8vo. £1. J. Caravellae Index. 8vo. 3s.

Aristoteles ex recensione IMMANUELIS BEKKERI. Accedunt Indices Sylburgiani. Tomi I-XI. 8vo.
The nine volumes in print (I (Organon) and IX (Ethica) are out of print) may be had separately, price 5s. 6d. each.

Choerobosci Dictata in Theodosii Canones, necnon Epimerismi in Psalmos edidit THOMAS GAISFORD. Tomi III. 8vo. 15s. net.

Demosthenes ex recensione G. DINDORFII. Tomi IX. 8vo. £2 6s.
Separately: Textus, £1 1s. Annotationes, 15s. Scholia, 10s.

Etymologicon Magnum. Edited by T. GAISFORD. Folio. (Out of print.)

Euripides ex rec. G. DINDORFII. Tragoediae et Fragmenta. Tomi II. 8vo. 10s. Annotationes. Partes II. 8vo. 10s. Scholia Graeca. Tomi IV. 8vo. £1 16s. Alcestis. 8vo. 2s. 6d.

Harpocrationis Lexicon ex recensione G. Dindorfii. Tomi II. 8vo. 21s. net.

Hephaestionis Enchiridion, Terentianus Maurus, Proclus, etc. edidit T. Gaisford. Tomi II. 12s. 6d. net.

Homerus
    Ilias, cum brevi annotatione C. G. Heynii. Accedunt Scholia minora. Tomi II. 8vo. 15s.
    Ilias. Ex rec. G. Dindorfii. 8vo. 5s. 6d.
    Scholia Graeca in Iliadem. See p. 45.
    Scholia Graeca in Iliadem Townleyana recensuit Ernestus Maass. 2 vols. 8vo. £1 16s. net.
    Odyssea. Ex rec. G. Dindorfii. 8vo. 5s. 6d.
    Scholia Graeca in Odysseam ed. G. Dindorfius. Tomi II. 8vo. 18s. net.
    Seberi Index in Homerum. 8vo. 6s. 6d.

Oratores Attici ex recensione Bekkeri: Vol. III. Isaeus, Æschines, Lycurgus, etc. 8vo. 7s. 6d. net. Vols. I and II are out of print.

Paroemiographi Graeci edidit T. Gaisford. Out of print.

Index Graecitatis Platonicae confecit T. Mitchell. 1832. 2 vols. 8vo. 5s.

Plotinus edidit F. Creuzer. Tomi III. 4to. 42s. net.

Plutarchi Moralia edidit D. Wyttenbach. Accedit Index Graecitatis, Tomi VIII. Partes XV. 8vo, cloth. £3 10s. net.

Sophoclis Tragoediae et Fragmenta. Ex recensione et cum commentariis G. Dindorfii. Third edition. 2 vols. Fcap 8vo. £1 1s.
    Each Play separately, limp, 1s.; text only, 6d.; text on writing-paper, 8s.
              Tragoediae et Fragmenta cum annotationibus G. Dindorfii. Tomi II. 8vo. 10s.
    The text, Vol. I, 5s. 6d. The notes, Vol. II, 4s. 6d.

Stobaei Florilegium ad MSS fidem emendavit et supplevit T. Gaisford. Tomi IV. 8vo. £3 3s. net.
        Eclogarum Physicarum et Ethicarum libri duo: accedit Hieroclis Commentarius in aurea carmina Pythagoreorum. Recensuit T. Gaisford. Tomi II. 8vo. 12s. 6d. net.

Suidae Lexicon. Edited by T. Gaisford. Three vols. Folio. Large paper copies, £6 6s. net. (A few copies remain.)

Xenophon. Ex rec. et cum annotatt. L. Dindorfii.
    Historia Graeca. Second edition. 8vo. 10s. 6d.
    Expeditio Cyri. Second edition. 8vo. 10s. 6d.
    Institutio Cyri. 8vo. 10s. 6d.
    Memorabilia Socratis. 8vo. 7s. 6d.
    Opuscula Politica Equestria et Venatica cum Arriani Libello de Venatione. 8vo. 10s. 6d.

Greek Literature

The Attic Theatre. By A. E. HAIGH. Third edition, revised and in part rewritten by A. W. PICKARD-CAMBRIDGE. Illustrated. 8vo. 10s. 6d. net.
A few copies of the second edition can still be obtained.

The Tragic Drama of the Greeks. By A. E. HAIGH. With illustrations. 8vo. 10s. 6d. net.

Ancient Classical Drama. By R. G. MOULTON. Ed. 2. Cr. 8vo. 8s. 6d.

The Rise of the Greek Epic. By GILBERT MURRAY. 8vo. 7s. 6d. net.

The Interpretation of Greek Literature. An Inaugural Lecture by GILBERT MURRAY. 8vo. 1s. net.

Greek Historical Writing and Apollo. Two Lectures by U. VON WILAMOWITZ-MOELLENDORFF. Translation by GILBERT MURRAY. 8vo. 2s. net.

The Erasmian Pronunciation of Greek. A Lecture by I. BYWATER. 8vo. 1s. net (published by Mr. Frowde).

The Value of Byzantine and Modern Greek. A Lecture by S. MENARDOS. 8vo. 1s. net.

Ionia and the East. By D. G. HOGARTH. 8vo. With a map. 3s. 6d. net.

Coins and Inscriptions

Historia Numorum. A Manual of Greek Numismatics. By BARCLAY V. HEAD. [Second edition in the press.]

A Manual of Greek Historical Inscriptions. By E. L. HICKS. New edition, revised by G. F. HILL. 8vo. 10s. 6d. net.

The Inscriptions of Cos. By W. R. PATON & E. L. HICKS. Ry. 8vo. £1 8s.

A Grammar of the Homeric Dialect. By D. B. MONRO. 8vo. Ed. 2, 14s.

The Sounds and Inflections of Greek Dialects (Ionic). By H. W. SMYTH. 8vo. £1 4s.

A Glossary of Greek Birds. By D'ARCY W. THOMPSON, C.B. 8vo. 10s. n.

Practical Introduction to Greek Accentuation. By H. W. CHANDLER. 8vo. 2nd ed. 10s. 6d. Also an abridgement. Ext. fcap 8vo. 2s. 6d.

Palaeography: Papyri

Catalogus Codicum Graecorum Sinaiticorum. Scripsit V. GARDTHAUSEN. With facsimiles. 8vo, linen. £1 5s. net.

On abbreviations in Greek MSS. By T. W. ALLEN. Royal 8vo. 5s.

An Alexandrian erotic fragment and other Greek papyri, chiefly Ptolemaic. Edited by B. P. GRENFELL. Small 4to. 8s. 6d. net.

New classical fragments and other papyri. Edited by B. P. GRENFELL and A. S. HUNT. 12s. 6d. net.

Revenue laws of Ptolemy Philadelphus. Edited by B. P. GRENFELL and J. P. MAHAFFY. £1 11s. 6d. net.

Palaeography of Greek papyri, by F. G. KENYON. 8vo. 10s. 6d.

www.ingramcontent.com/pod-product-compliance
Lightning Source LLC
Chambersburg PA
CBHW020905230426
43666CB00008B/1324